Republicanism in Reconstruction Texas

Republicanism in Reconstruction Texas

by Carl H. Moneyhon

University of Texas Press
Austin and London

Library of Congress Cataloging in Publication Data

Moneyhon, Carl H   1944–
    Republicanism in Reconstruction Texas.

    Bibliography: p.
    Includes index.
    1. Republican Party. Texas. 2. Texas—Politics
and government—1865–1950. I. Title.

JK2358.T4   1979   329.6'009764   79-14283
ISBN 0-292-77553-9

FOR MY MOTHER AND FATHER

AND FOR PATRICIA

Contents

Acknowledgments   xi

Introduction   xiii

1. Texas in 1865   3
2. The Unionist Origins of Texas Republicanism   21
3. From Unionism to Republicanism   42
4. Organizing the Republican Party   61
5. Radicals and Conservatives: Factionalism and the Split of Texas Republicanism   82
6. Texas Republicans in the State Election of 1869   104
7. The Price of the Republican Coalition: The Radicals and the Twelfth Legislature   129
8. Tyranny, Taxes, and Corruption: Crisis of the Radical Coalition   152
9. "We Have Met the Enemy and We Are Theirs": The 1872 General Election   168
10. The Last Fight   183

Appendices

1. Returns on Selected Elections, 1859–1873   197
2. Correlations of Political and Ecological Data   224
3. Delegates to the Constitutional Convention of 1866   226
4. Delegates to the Constitutional Convention of 1868–1869   236
5. Cluster Analysis of the Constitutional Convention of 1868–1869   248

Notes   253

Bibliographical Essay   289

Index   301

Maps

1. Centers of Ethnic Population, 1865   11

2. Texas in 1865   13

3. Pease Vote Compared to Antisecession Vote   48

4. Vote for Davis, 1869   125

5. White Vote for Davis, 1869   127

6. Republicans in the Twelfth Legislature, 1870   132

7. Vote for Davis, 1873   190

Photographs

following page 128
Andrew Jackson Hamilton
Elisha M. Pease
Edmund J. Davis
James Winwright Flanagan
Morgan C. Hamilton
William T. Clark
Edward Degener
George W. Whitmore

Tables

1. Election Returns for Governor, 1859 — 197
2. Vote on Secession, 1861 — 202
3. Election Returns for Governor, 1869 — 207
4. Election Returns for Congress, First District, 1871 — 212
5. Election Returns for Congress, Third District, 1871 — 213
6. Election Returns for President, 1872 — 214
7. Election Returns for Governor, 1873 — 219
8. Pearson's *r* for Unionist and Select Data — 224
9. Pearson's *r* for Republican and Select Political and Ecological Data — 225
10. Pearson's *r* for Unionist and Republican Data — 225
11. Biographical Data on the Convention of 1866 — 226
12. Biographical Data on the Convention of 1868–1869 — 236
13. Agreement Matrix for Administration and East Texas Blocs — 250
14. Agreement Matrix for West Texas and Black Blocs — 251
15. Agreement Matrix for Democratic Bloc — 252

Acknowledgments

Many people have assisted and encouraged me as I researched and wrote this book. I owe much to Professor John Hope Franklin of the University of Chicago, with whom this study originally began as a dissertation, for his gentle criticism and helpful suggestions. He was always on the mark. Professors Arthur Mann and John Coatsworth, also from the University of Chicago, read the manuscript in its early stages and it has benefited from their thoughts.

I want to thank specially Professors Llerena Friend and Robert Cotner, now retired, and Barnes F. Lathrop and Lewis L. Gould of the University of Texas at Austin. They provided me with my early interest in history and showed me that Texas was a worthy field of study. All have continued to encourage me with their ideas and help.

Professor Michael Perman at the Chicago Circle campus of the University of Illinois read this manuscript and provided detailed criticisms of its organization and content. It is different as a result.

Without the staffs at the Austin Public Library, the San Antonio Public Library, the Texas State Archives, the Manuscripts Division of the Library of Congresss, the National Archives, and the University of Texas Archives whose aid paved the way through their resources, this project would have been impossible. Mary Beth Fleischer at the Barker Texas History Center at the University of Texas was particularly helpful.

Rhonda Reagan and Cheryl Patterson helped type this manuscript and I am indebted to them for relieving part of that onerous burden.

Introduction

A group of self-styled "Conservatives" met at Austin, Texas, on July 21, 1870, to discuss the political situation in the state. The result of their meeting was an address that condemned the Republican administration of Governor Edmund J. Davis. In almost hysterical tones they attacked Davis for assuming despotic powers. In every action of his newly installed administration they saw limitations placed on their civil rights by the government. The Conservatives viewed the state police force and the militia as organizations through which the governor would wrest away their constitutional liberties. They regarded legislation that broadened the appointive powers of the chief executive and provided close supervision of elections as a similar intervention by the government. Efforts to create a public school system and to support the construction of railroads raised fears among the Conservatives that the Republicans would saddle the state with an "enormous" debt. They found proof that Davis intended to rule Texas permanently, by whatever means he had at hand, in his reliance upon secret political societies like the Union League. The men who met at Austin believed that they were in the middle of a revolution against traditional political society. They called upon all citizens to help them stop the activities of the Republicans.[1]

For white people in Texas and elsewhere in the South, the actions of their state government were further indications that the world had turned upside down. The "bottom rail" was on the top, and evidence of a new order existed at every turn. Former slaves lined up alongside their old masters at the polls. Black children swarmed town streets and country roads on the way to public schools in a region where their learning to read would have been a crime only a decade before. An occasional black person who could afford the fare even asserted the right to ride in a first class coach "on the cars." In a political society that had always possessed limited government, state legislatures actively intervened to provide a variety of new social services and to help finance transportation and industrial development. Along with these changes had come added requirements for tax revenues. The state also assumed greater police powers. Southerners blamed state Republican parties and their leaders, a varied assortment of local whites or "scalawags," immigrants from the North or "carpetbaggers," and blacks, for the upheaval. They saw their world in turmoil and viewed the Republicans as radicals who had betrayed their community and the white race.

The object of so much feeling in its time, Southern Republicanism has intrigued historians of the American political process in the period since its appearance. A popularly-based party appeared that threatened a fundamental change in the character of Southern society. Its policies embraced different views of black people and the role of government than those that had long prevailed in the local community. To understand the dynamics of the Republican movement is to better grasp the nature and possibility of social change. The attention that Southern Republicanism has attracted, therefore, is hardly surprising.

Study of the Republican parties in the South has focused on two major questions. What caused their development and the formation of basic policies in the first place? What prevented their ultimate success? Historians have used two different models to provide answers.

The oldest of these explained Southern Republicanism as the creation of outsiders who did not share the political traditions and the social ideology of the South. This model is associated principally with the work of William A. Dunning and his students at Columbia University. They believed that a coalition of "ambitious northern whites," a few "inexperienced" southern whites, and "unintelligent" blacks started the party in response to national policy. Without a base in the community, ignorant and out of touch with the "intelligent and substantial classes," they could not put together a program that met local needs. An internal crisis occurred when blacks began to seek greater concessions on civil rights from the party. Northerners were willing to grant them, but Southerners were not, and as a result Southerners abandoned the party to the hands of "carpetbaggers" and "barbarous" freedmen who pursued even more radical programs. The flight of whites into Conservative and Democratic parties, coupled with the national government's withdrawal of force from the South, ended the radical regime. The white majority reasserted itself, and what the Dunningites considered the legitimate leadership of the Southern states returned to power. Without a substantial base in society, Republicanism could not succeed without outside intervention.[2]

Since the 1930s the Dunning model has come under attack from "revisionist" historians who have emphasized the local origins of portions of the movement and found that the "scalawags" were not as unrepresentative as the Dunningites had suggested. David Donald is typical of this group. His innovative work on local white Republicans in Mississippi showed that a large number of antebellum politicians, especially Whigs, worked to create the postwar Union party in that state. The founders of this political base for Republicanism were neither inexperienced nor ignorant. The party and its program, at least for a time, tried to obtain the same goals pursued by prewar Whigs. Why did they fail to produce a viable party? Donald concluded that in Mississippi the moderate course of these men led to collapse when they confronted the opposition of extremists in their own party, carpetbaggers and blacks, and the Democrats. Most of the Whigs left the party, putting it into the hands of radicals who embarked on a program of extensive change. The moderates could not accept such a course and fused with the Democrats to overthrow the Republican governments. Moderation failed when confronted with fanaticism.[3]

Another group of revisionists has suggested the class origins of Southern Republicanism. Typified by scholars such as Allen W. Trelease, they have suggested that Republicanism represented the implementation of policies that had been popular among poor white farmers before the war and that the freedmen believed were necessary afterward. The rise of the new parties represented the removal of the old planter class from power, but not by an illegitimate or unrepresentative group of adventurers. These scholars have seen the development of the Republican party as reflecting class interests, poor whites and blacks against planters. Why did they not succeed? Trelease suggested that the old Democratic leadership, given the disposition of a ruling class to maintain power, resorted to violence against Republican voters to convince blacks to stay away from the polls, and whites to cast their votes for a different party. Because they lacked economic power, a coalition of the poor could not stand up against the force of those who had such power and were willing to use it to uphold their position.[4]

What caused Southern radicalism? Was it outside influence, the abandonment of parties by moderates, or class conflict? This study originated in an effort to test the basic models and revise understanding in the light of insights gained from modern scholarship for the Republican party in Texas. The two major studies dealing with the local party there are in the Dunning tradition, but recent work has demonstrated its basic inadequacies.[5] In preparing this study the inapplicability of the Dunning interpretation was quickly apparent, but the Texas experience also did not fit closely the alternate models. Prewar political elites reappeared in the Republican party after the war and tried to accomplish the same things they had attempted before, but they did not drop out before a challenge from "radical" carpetbaggers and blacks or from a coalition of representatives of lower-class interests. Instead the old leaders continued to control politics and work for their goals, simply using whatever tools were available to obtain the greatest number of votes. In a sense existing interests used democratic politics—in fact became representatives of other groups with sometimes contradictory interests—in order to obtain their own ends. Radicalism and Republicanism were part of a continued and traditional search for power.

This study is an examination of that search and its failure. It focuses on Republican leaders, constituents, ideology, policies, and relations with the national party, in an attempt to uncover the bases of the local movement. In exploring these elements it also attempts to demonstrate the weaknesses and problems that led to collapse.

Republicanism in Reconstruction Texas

CHAPTER 1

Texas in 1865

On June 17, 1865, President Andrew Johnson initiated the reconstruction of Texas when he appointed a provisional governor and provided him with the authority to take steps to restore civil government in the state. Johnson outlined a simple process, empowering his appointee to call together the loyal people of the state in a convention to alter and amend the state's constitution in such a manner as to allow the resumption of constitutional relations between Texas and the federal government. Johnson's proclamation defined loyalty in a way that allowed all persons who could subscribe to the oath of amnesty issued on May 29 to participate in the process. With the exception of individuals who had served the Confederacy in positions of considerable authority or whose wealth had lent prestige to the Southern cause, most Texans were able to participate in the process of restoration. Even in the case of individuals specifically excluded, the president provided a means for them to play a role in politics by the liberal extension of clemency if they would make special application to him for pardon.[1]

The president's plan for reunion represented an extraordinary concession by a conqueror to a conquered people, for it placed restoration of the Southern states in the hands of their own people. It probably could not have been any other way, since Americans both North and South held a strong commitment to constitutional federalism. As Phillip S. Paludan points out, federalism made possible local control over daily life and "provided Americans with the cherished experience of controlling their destiny." They would not give up the freedom acquired under such a system readily, even if it meant foregoing goals that could be accomplished with greater centralization. Few men held more firmly to the federalist ideal than President Johnson. He maintained that despite the war the right of the

Southern states to control their own internal matters had never ceased to exist, and he approached reconstruction from that point of view.[2]

Theoretically the president had told Southerners to reestablish civil authority and go about their business. In fact, however, the South did not have complete freedom in its domestic affairs. In Congress many Republicans believed that a permanent restoration of the Union required the guarantee of security to Southern loyalists and of justice to the freed slaves. In addition they had come to believe in a greater national authority that permitted intervention against the states in order to protect the rights of individual citizens. The motives behind these principles varied among individuals and were often, as Michael L. Benedict suggests, related to Northern party politics, but in 1865 a Southern politician had to take them into account, or risk the intervention of the federal government.[3]

Could Southern politicians change in a manner that would meet the needs of Republican leaders in the North? President Johnson had made such change more difficult with his policies, since the restoration of local government forced politicians to be responsive to local constituencies also. White Texans' continued access to political processes placed limits on the actions of their leaders. For a Texas politician in 1865 there were two groups whose needs had to be met—Northerners who wanted reconstruction accomplished on a basis acceptable to them and the local constituency with its own demands.

The local interests that needed to be served were those of a predominantly rural and agrarian population. At the end of the war the land bound together the vast majority of Texans. The 1860 census showed that almost 95 percent of the state's population lived either on farms or in small villages. These people, for the most part, worked directly in agriculture, cultivating cotton, wheat, corn, and similar marketable crops, or raising livestock. The state contained some urban centers, San Antonio, Houston, Galveston, and Austin being the largest, but the cities were arms of the agrarian economy, providing services and goods to the countryside. Some manufacturing had developed in these communities in the antebellum period—by 1860 the state possessed 983 establishments that employed a total 3,449 workers—but the majority of them processed the raw materials produced by the rural population. Like the cities, manufacturing depended on the farm rather than having an independent existence. No statistic better illustrates agriculture's domination of the local economy than the value of capital used in farming as compared to manufacturing. In 1860 farming consumed almost forty times more capital, exclusive of labor: $130,926,767 compared to $3,272,450. Texas had a varied economy, but agriculture dominated it and helped produce a homogeneity of interests that influenced the postwar political scene.[4]

If the farm dominated the economic life of the state, cotton culture set the pattern of farm life. Despite the variety of agricultural goods produced in the local economy, cotton was the chief commercial crop and the principal source of antebellum wealth. In the early stages of economic growth cotton had competed with various grain crops, chiefly wheat and corn, but after statehood the staple had begun to replace the grains. During the 1850s a boom in cotton production had taken place and farmers had rushed to expand their fields. Production increased from 58,161 to 431,463 bales in the last decade before the war. Its prominence as an export product indicated the importance of cotton to the state's economy. In 1865 Galveston merchants shipped $9,691,751 worth of goods from their port; cotton accounted for $9,669,515 of the total. But cotton was also supreme in the minds of Texans, and dominated the hopes and aspirations of most farmers. Even if they did not grow it, they wanted to and saw it as the quickest way to wealth and position. In the 1850s the editors of the *Texas State Gazette* spoke for all these people when they proclaimed that Texas had unlimited possibilities for cotton production, and predicted the state would become the national center of its cultivation. Texas remained a land of opportunity, and cotton presented the best chance.[5]

The needs of the cotton cultivator made unique demands on political society. As Charles Sydnor has indicated, cotton was simple to grow. Any small landowner could produce it given several acres, seeds, and a few simple tools. Wealth from the crop, however, demanded a larger scale of operation. Planters faced a host of problems that had to be solved in order to survive. They had to have land and a lot of it, not just for production but for future use after the repeated planting of the cash crop had destroyed the fertility of the soil. In their search for wealth farmers tended to plant the same crop in their fields, year after year, until they exhausted them. Farming experiences in the older cotton states and even in some areas of eastern Texas provided reminders to planters of the disaster that accompanied inadequate productive land. On his trip through the bottom lands of the Neches and Trinity rivers in 1853 Frederick Law Olmsted noted a landscape of abandoned homes and deserted plantations, symbols of the cost of prevailing agricultural practices.[6]

In addition to enough land, planters needed a labor force adequate to farm it. Obtaining enough workers was never a simple problem, since cotton culture presented distinctive organizational requirements. Planters needed a large number of people in the fields, frequently more than they had available, when they planted and harvested their crops. At those times house servants, women, and children worked alongside field hands. It was not uncommon for planters to draw upon the laborers on neighboring plantations if they could be acquired. To clean the fields planters pushed their normal work days into round-the-clock labor. At other times, however, fewer people were needed. Robert W. Fogel and Stanley L. Engerman have estimated that only 34 percent of the workers' time went into the production of the staple crop during the year. The successful growth of cotton demanded a labor force that met the needs of planting and harvest but did not drain the planter's resources when diverted from work on the cash crop. While a variety of systems potentially met such needs, antebellum Texans had used Negro slavery to serve theirs. The Civil War ended that form of organization. It did not, however, change the needs of the local plantation owner.[7]

Another recurring need of planters and farmers engaged in the growth of cotton was for a sufficient supply of liquid capital to carry on year-to-year operations. An inadequate supply of money had been a problem in Texas during the Republic, and a shortage of banks and a tendency to invest annual profits in land and slaves had done little to change that situation after it became a state. Texans managed, in part, to avoid the restrictions placed on them by such a situation through the extensive use of merchant credit. D. E. E. Braman informed prospective immigrants to the state in 1854: "Credit in Texas is the universal rule, and prompt payment, the exception; the system runs through all business, from the smallest account to the most important contract." The use of credit, however, sharply cut profits since merchants usually charged from 10 to 12.5 percent per annum for its extension. In order to remain solvent, planters had to avoid debt as much as possible and cut the drain on capital represented by credit. Olmsted noted that Texans minimized expenses by purchasing only items essential for operations—slaves, corn, bacon, salt, sugar, molasses, tobacco, clothing, medicine, hoes, and plow-iron. The land- and slave-poor element of the cotton planters' economic life influenced their political perspective.[8]

A final concern among planters was the need to develop a cheap and efficient transportation system. In the antebellum years, wagons drawn by oxen provided the chief means for carrying farm products to market. The system was fairly reliable, but it was also expensive. The average fees varied from twenty to twenty-three cents to ship a ton of goods each mile. The cost added to the farmers' operating expenses by increasing the prices of goods purchased and the cost of marketing their own. When cotton prices were down, the fixed expense of shipping could devastate planter's profits. Through the 1850s Texans looked for ways to cut the amount of money that had to be spent for transportation. Railroad construction appeared to serve that need and captured the broadest local support. The idea of providing low-cost service to the cotton-producing counties along the Brazos and Colorado rivers inspired General Sidney Sherman's Buffalo Bayou, Brazos, and Colorado road, the first constructed in the state. The BBB&C showed that railroads could cut costs and deserved support by reducing shipping fees along the thirty-two mile route from $1.50 per bale to about .75. The saving that could be achieved with railroads was apparent, but the capital to finance construction was not available among personal investors. Olmsted noted that the people with money in Texas seldom invested in such improvements, but usually put their profits back into fieldhands and land. Texans searched for alternate ways to build railroads, but the need for better transportation remained a pressing matter in the mid-nineteenth century.[9]

Through the antebellum era government provided the legal framework within which Texans solved their problems of land, labor, credit, and transportation. In the case of land, tax policies made it easy to amass large quantities of property for actual and speculative use. The maintenance of low property tax rates (twelve and one-half cents on the hundred dollars valuation through the prewar years) made possible land ownership without a heavy loss of working capital to the government. The practice of allowing landowners to assess their own property in the county of their residence rather than in the county where the land was located also worked to the benefit of large land-holders, since this policy made underassessment and nonassessment of property easier. The election of county assessors was another aspect of government that worked in favor of the planter since few elected officials would challenge the valuation placed upon the land by a prominent citizen of the county, especially if that citizen had helped the assessor gain his office in the first place. The law also helped the planter maintain a labor force through the institution of slavery. The state provided not only the necessary statutes but the police force necessary to insure that institution. In the 1850s the state also used its funds to underwrite the bonds of private railroad companies, thus directly supporting the transportation interests of the cotton farmers. Using $2,000,000 in United States bonds acquired in the Compromise of 1850 that had been placed in the school fund, the state initiated construction of a railroad system prior to the war, with loans to favored companies of $6,000 per mile at 6 percent. After depleting the school fund, the state legislature began giving away the public lands with pledges of sixteen sections per mile of track laid. As a whole, prewar state government attempted to provide for the interests of local businessmen and farmers with minimal claims on their individual financial resources. The result was a tradition of limited public services in areas such as education or charity. While Texans supported the idea of general public education, the cost of such a system prevented its implementation. Public officials shunted money appropriated for schools into areas they considered more important, like transportation. In its reluctance to tax private capital and divert money from individual use, the state government even hesitated to provide protection to the frontier against Indian attack and tried to shift the burden to the federal government. Government did not intervene in society in a positive way, but it did provide the laws and ordinances that allowed the cotton farmer to thrive.[10]

Considering the importance of government in establishing the rules within which the state economy operated, it is not surprising that politics attracted the state's elites. The agricultural elite of planters and slaveowners, or their representatives among the state's lawyers, controlled public offices and subsequent legislation and executive decisions. The slaveholding farmers, although only one-third of the agricultural population, owned or controlled 60 to 70 percent of the state's improved acreage, its livestock and corn. They produced about 90 percent of the annual cotton yield. Their interests were substantial, and they could not afford to have government in the hands of individuals who might act contrary to their needs. Their actual service at all levels of government demonstrated their control. The complex structure of laws that served them also indicated their association with local politics.[11]

Throughout the antebellum period the agricultural elite's power in government was not challenged. As a result politics was usually a struggle among sectional elites over the allocation of resources, rather than a conflict of differing classes or of differing types of economic interests. A feeling of commonality among all classes of white farmers worked to continue this system. Visitors noted that Texans believed strongly in equality among themselves and suggested such feelings grew from the opportunities that existed in the state to gain wealth and acquire social status. Immigrant guides fostered the idea and encouraged farmers to come to Texas where great wealth could be acquired with investment of only a little capital and much hard work. The idea of shared opportunity held together the white population, and the availability of vast unoccupied lands reinforced their hopes for a good future. In the 1850s farmers wildly pushed the agricultural frontier westward and increased the acres in production from 643,476 to 2,650,781. Available land made every white person a potential planter. If anyone might rise to power, it followed that it was not in anyone's interest to challenge policies designed to further the interests of the cotton economy. No challenge was offered.[12]

The idea of race also helped unite white yeomen and planters into a community and helped preclude threats to elite control of government. For Texans the presence of over 180,000 black slaves, 30 percent of the population, was a disquieting reality. Whites shared common stereotypes of blacks that promoted fear, perceptions of the slaves as "licentious" and with "animal propensities," a people who lacked self-discipline. Occasional slave uprisings and even the rumor of violence helped give credence to these fears. Olmsted captured a typical white view of slavery and the slaves when he discussed abolition with a Texan on his trip through the state. The woman told him,

"Northern folks talk about abolishing slavery, but there wouldn't be any use in that; that would be ridiculous, unless you could some way get rid of the niggers. Why, they'd murder us all in our beds—that's what they'd do." The plantation and legal slavery provided a means to control the black population. Few whites could imagine a world without such order. Their fear helped keep all in line and reluctant to bring about upheaval with a challenge to planter domination of government.[13]

A possibility for politics based upon ethnic groups existed in Texas before the war, but it did not develop. The state contained sizeable minorities of Mexicans and Germans who, if they operated together, might challenge the power of planters, at least in county government. Some twenty thousand Germans lived in counties along the state's western frontier, bound together as a homogeneous community by life-style and national origin. They remained isolated during the prewar years and generally desired to be left alone. Both factors weakened them as a political force, although some individuals had hoped to organize the Germans for political action. Olmsted admired what these communities had accomplished on the frontier and believed that they would ultimately work to create a free state in western Texas, but he concluded they had yet to "occupy the position [to] which their force and character should entitle them."[14]

The Germans stayed out of local politics by choice but the twelve thousand Mexicans stayed out because the "American" community kept them out, sometimes with the use of force. Bitterly hated by the Anglos, perhaps because of feelings originating in the Texas Revolution, the Mexicans could vote, but they seldom had an opportunity to play active roles in politics. Olmsted believed that they had potential for political power, especially in some of the southwestern counties or in San Antonio, but he also understood that they did not have the power to respond to violence directed at them by the Anglos. Prior to the Civil War the American community had frequently resorted to force when Mexicans asserted rights to land or to political power. Whole communities of Mexicans had been driven from their homes. Olmsted noted that while they had the numbers to take over government in San Antonio, such a step would result in a "summary revolution." Neither the Germans nor the Mexicans were in a position to challenge the status quo in prewar Texas.[15]

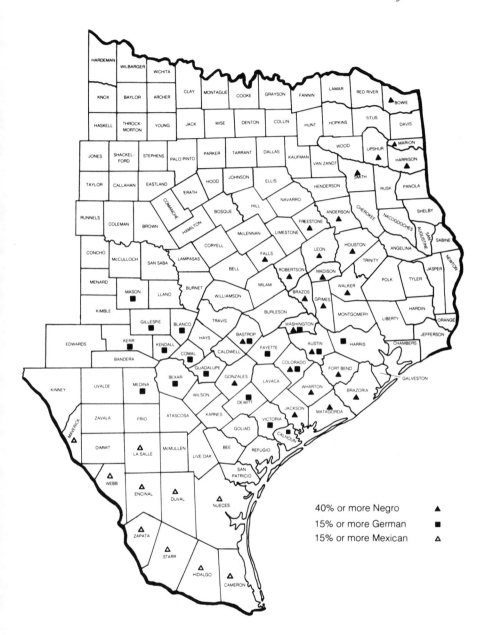

MAP 1. Centers of Ethnic Population, 1865

Free of challenges from other classes or groups, the agrarian elite devoted itself to settling disputes among its members. Local politics usually centered on questions of how resources would be distributed among themselves rather than on basic policies. Few of them, for example, disagreed over the desirability of building railroads, but they could fight over where the roads would be built and who should supply money for their support. The divisions among elites tended to follow sectional lines with politicians representing the special interests of their particular region. During the prewar years and through much of the reconstruction, four distinct sectional interests appeared to influence local politics. The four reflected economic and cultural subdivisions that approximated the areas encompassed by the congressional districts. In this study they will be referred to as Central Texas, roughly the same as the Third Congressional District; East Texas, the First; West Texas, the Fourth; and Northeast Texas, the Second. The competition of these sections would remain an important element in postwar political problems.[16]

The most powerful of the four was the central district between the Trinity River on the east and the Colorado River on the west. The rich lands of Central Texas made it the center of plantation agriculture and of wealth. Although it was the home of only 20 percent of the state's free inhabitants, it was the location of 35 percent of the slave population. Its people produced 43 percent of the state's cotton crop and possessed some 34 percent of the real and personal property. By 1860 its chief cities, Galveston and Houston, were the most rapidly growing urban centers in the state and vied with each other to tie the hinterlands into their market structure with financial services and transportation. State government responded readily to the interests of this section in the antebellum years. If this area did not control the state government completely, it certainly dominated its operations. One aspect of the district's power was demonstrated by state railroad policies that provided most public aid to roads designed to connect Galveston and Houston to the surrounding agricultural areas, rather than help rival enterprises. By the end of 1860 the legislature had loaned money to six companies for the construction of 392 miles of track, and all but the 15 miles of the Indianola road radiated out of the Houston-Galveston commercial center. The construction of these roads not only aided the development of

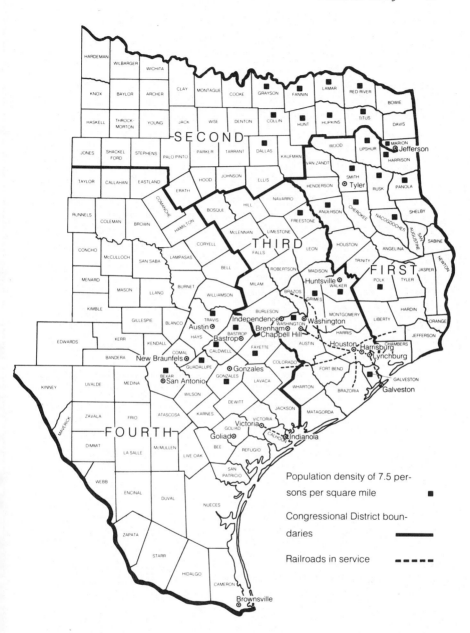

MAP 2. Texas in 1865

these urban areas but also made easier marketing the crops of Central Texas, thus increasing the profits and the power of local farmers. The section had used government to its advantage in the prewar years; it could be expected to continue to do so afterwards.

Between the Trinity and Sabine rivers lay East Texas and the First Congressional District. This region was one of the oldest areas of settlement in the state, originating in 1779 when Gil Ibarbo formed the community of Nacogdoches. While older than its western neighbor, it had not by 1860 experienced the same prosperity. The lands along the coast and upon its rivers appeared more easily exhausted, and visitors to the state noted the large numbers of abandoned farms within it. Some growth took place in the counties along its northern boundary prior to the war, especially in Upshur, Harrison, Smith, Rusk, and Panola, but while farms expanded and the number of slaves increased, persistent transportation problems slowed its development. The lack of easily navigable rivers meant that the lands of East Texas were denied ready access to markets, and consequently were less profitable. For the landowners, development of transportation was a primary concern. Most looked to the Mississippi River valley as their closest market and worked to obtain river improvements and the construction of railroads that would provide a link. Since these improvements threatened to divert commerce from Houston and Galveston to Shreveport and New Orleans, however, they received little support from a state government dominated by Central Texas. The state's reluctance to back a Pacific railroad through East Texas provided a persistent source of irritation prior to the war and promoted sentiment there for dividing the state. In the gubernatorial campaign of 1853 Lemmuel D. Evans expressed the feeling of many when he ran for office calling for separation of Texas into smaller states. "Eastern Texas has interests distinct and separate from the West," he argued. "She has supported the Government and paid all the taxes, while the West has received all the money and land, and has had all the offices." For the people of East Texas, politics had been a futile struggle for power and a share of the state's wealth, a struggle not to be abandoned with the collapse of the old government. In fact, the collapse opened the possibility of securing the section's goals.[17]

To the west of the Colorado River was the Fourth Congressional District, West Texas. It was a region with a much greater variety of land and climate than the other two sections and, therefore, different economic possibilities. Before the war settlement was limited, for the most part, to a strip of land between the Colorado and Nueces rivers. Some cotton plantations could be found along the coast, even some sugar production, but cattle and sheep ranching characterized the interior. As in East Texas, a major problem that blocked economic development was the lack of transportation. Trade generally flowed to the Gulf through the port of Indianola, but shipments from there to the interior had to be made by ox cart or mule train, slow and expensive means of transportation. Merchants in the region preferred Indianola as a port because they believed that commissions, wharfage, and other services at Galveston were too costly, but the expansion of a transportation system that would allow shipment through Galveston and Houston to be avoided was frustrated by the state legislature. The government would not provide the necessary support for railroads in West Texas. The west also had other demands that ran counter to the interests of those who controlled state government. It required protection from raiding Indians as much as it needed transportation. However, that protection required money, and the funds to provide a sufficient force to stop these raids came from the legislature very slowly. Both issues sparked resentment among Westerners toward Central Texas and contributed to the same desire to divide the state that was apparent in East Texas.

The final district was the state's youngest, the land bounded by the Red River to the north and the headwaters of the coastal rivers in the south. Northeast Texas, or the Second District, had the greatest agricultural potential in the state in the 1850s; however, it had not been achieved because of inadequate transportation. The inability of farmers in the region to get their goods to distant markets promoted the production of crops such as food grains that could be sold locally rather than the staples that were the basis of great wealth. The latter could not be shipped conveniently. As a result wheat was a more important crop than cotton, and small farms were more common than plantations. That did not mean, however, that local farmers were not interested in growing cotton. The ambition of the farmers of Northeast Texas could be seen by 1860 when the opening of the Red River to steamboat traffic and the establishment of better marketing ties with Shreveport had been accomplished. Eastern counties in the region began to shift from grains to cotton, and the number of slaves at work on the farms climbed sharply. The interests of farmers in Northeast Texas were similar to those of farmers elsewhere. As with East and West Texas, however, they found their ambitions thwarted by government policies that denied them transportation and a solution to the Indian problem. They represented another group opposed to Central Texas's domination of state government.

The only chance that existed to counter the power of Central Texas in politics was the use of coalitions among outside groups. The most successful manipulator against the plantation leadership that controlled the government in the antebellum period was Sam Houston. In 1859 he forged a successful alliance that appealed to discontented Texans in his bid for the governorship. His campaign emphasized the theme that the Democratic party represented only the planting interests of the state and was no longer egalitarian. Houston asked the voters where was the frontier protection needed to open up the western lands. Where were the public schools that would allow individuals to acquire the knowledge necessary for growth and prosperity? He answered that each had been lost in a legislature dominated by planters. The party formed by Houston took the name Unionist, in part because of the founder's pro-Union sympathies, but also because the candidate used the Democratic party's secessionist agitation as proof that the old leaders were cutting off opportunities for common people. Texas Unionists were not men devoted to the federal government. They were simply using Unionism as a symbol to unify people opposed to the existing distribution of political power in the state.[18]

The secession crisis demonstrated the local nature of the Texas brand of Unionism. Houston opposed secession, but except for the frontier areas where the removal of federal military protection meant disaster, he could not resurrect the coalition that had put him in power in 1859. In the gubernatorial race, Unionism had reflected local issues; in 1861 Unionists faced the alternative of supporting the South and its institutions or the national government. Although many remained loyal to the Union, the majority, sometimes reluctantly, went with their section. In the gubernatorial election Houston had won with 30 percent of the eligible voters, but only 11 percent of the eligible voters voted to oppose secession two years later. While Houston had managed to attract votes from throughout the state, frontier states provided most of the support for the Union in 1861. Oran M. Roberts, a prominent secessionist and Democratic politician, provided a good analysis of the dilemma faced by Unionists when he suggested that in the secession crisis the people of the state saw Lincoln's election as a threat to their social and economic institutions. The threat was perceived as strong enough to unite previously hostile slaveholders and nonslaveholders. It also combined most white Texans in favor of secession.[19]

Four years of war made sectional pressures for economic development even stronger than they had been, but the resources available for development were fewer. After the Civil War, the possibility existed for the reestablishment of the old Union coalition of 1859 and another assault on the power of Central Texas. The war, however, had caused changes that made a return to prewar politics difficult. It destroyed the homogeneity that had characterized the antebellum community and added new problems to the political arena. Economic restoration, violence, and the place of the freed slaves in society demanded attention, in addition to the regional interests of the prewar years.

On the surface the economy of Texas appeared to have benefited from the war. It had been relatively safe from federal forces, and as a result planters from Arkansas and Louisiana had moved into the state to protect their slaves from confiscation or from escaping behind Yankee lines. The expansion of the local work force quickly led to an enlargement of the acres of cotton under cultivation and growth of production beyond prewar averages. The economy made further gains because of the state's nearness to Mexico. Many of the goods of the Confederacy that were destined for international trade moved through Texas to the Mexican port of Matamoros from which they could be shipped without fear of seizure by Yankee blockaders. Since the international trade required specie, the result of the movement of these goods was the continued circulation of gold coins to a far greater extent than elsewhere in the South. The use of gold rather than Confederate paper apparently softened the impact of the Southern cause's collapse for at least some of the state's businessmen.[20]

For most Texans, however, the war was damaging. It diminished the money available in a society that had never had much liquid capital. The greatest source of investment capital in the prewar era, the school fund, had been plundered when the legislature allowed local railroads to pay back loans to the fund in Confederate and state paper at face value. As a result the school fund was practically bankrupt at a time when the state needed money to accomplish reconstruction. The financial collapse of the state government was completed when soldiers in General J. O. Shelby's division camped near Austin raided the treasury after the breakup and carried off the few negotiable funds that remained. For most individuals the situation was not much better. Major William "Buck" Walton, later to head the state Democratic committee, returned from the war to his farm near Austin with only a pair of pants, two shirts, and no money. "I had nothing," he later wrote, "but a wife and four children and a house with something like about $2200 due on it. My Negroes had all been freed, & they were poorer than I was." This shortage of money only complicated the traditional political struggles of deciding how state tax revenues would be spent. Money, or the lack of it, would be a major problem.[21]

Another new dimension to postwar political life would be the personal hostilities created by the war; these would hinder Texans' abilities to cooperate with one another. For the Texans who had decided not to support the Confederacy and their state, the war had been a hell that they would not forget. These individuals brought into the postwar era a strong sense that they had been wronged and that those wrongs should be redressed. Thousands of Texans had refused to fight for the South and had run away from their homes to hide in the hills or to enter federal lines. During the war, home defense forces busily worked to prevent them from escaping, and the results were often bloody. Along the western border McDuff's Texas Rangers carried on a reign of terror against Union sympathizers, including a massacre along the Nueces River of one group of German Unionists who had been fleeing toward Mexico. Along the Red River frontier Confederate officials uncovered a Unionist conspiracy to support any federal army that began operations in the area. Provost Marshall James G. Bourland arrested and tried sixty-eight men at Gainesville. The court martial found thirty-nine of them guilty and executed them. In addition Confederate tax agents pursued Union supporters who had not paid their taxes and confiscated the lands of many. Massacres and persecution created extremely bitter feelings among those Texans who had remained loyal to the Union. Benjamin Truman, sent to Texas to observe the constitutional convention in 1866, reported to President Johnson that they were more hostile to the Confederates than men anywhere else in the South. These experiences worked against any cooperation with individuals responsible for secession or the activities of the state government during the war.[22]

At the same time, those who supported the Confederate cause came to see their opponents as guilty of treason. The trial of the Unionists at Gainesville suggests more about their accusers than the accused, since it showed the fear of many Texans that their opponents intended to interfere with slave property and arm the slaves against their masters. They appeared to be promoting a race war. Their opposition was not just political dissent but a threat to the viability and stability of society and could not be countenanced. This attitude toward political opponents continued in the postwar era, accompanied by violence directed at former Unionists, freed slaves, and even the federal occupation army. Soldiers of the First Texas Cavalry Union Volunteers, a unit recruited among Texans, faced such hostility that their commander requested that they not be disbanded until the "poisoned hatred" directed against them died down. Neither those who had opposed the war nor those who had supported it would be able to work with the others easily. The war had created a major psychological barrier to political restoration.[23]

Different economic needs and political hatred were new ingredients in postwar politics; the freed slaves were a third. The war had created a new citizen whose very freedom challenged the existing social order of Texans. After a lifetime of slavery, the freed slaves wanted to move, and although many stayed where they had lived all their lives, enough left that they created, in the words of one scholar, "a social and agricultural problem." John Bates, a slave of Harry Hogan in Limestone County, remembered being told that he was free and the desire to start a new life that it created. His master had been reluctant to tell his slaves what had happened. When he did and offered them permission to stay on the plantation Bates said, "We all sho' feels sorry for him, the way he acts and hates to leave him, but we wants to go." Another slave left the plantation unsure of his future and stopped to think: "I's not realize what I's in for till after I's started, but I wouldn't turn back." For these slaves there could be no return to the old days.[24]

The freed slaves wanted to exercise their freedom. That would be hard for white Texans to accept. They also wanted education and the means to better their lives. In some respects that would be even harder for whites to agree to, since it gave blacks not only the status but the substance of liberty. In the autumn following the breakup, the Bureau of Refugees, Freedmen, and Abandoned Lands started operations in the state and set up the first schools. Former slaves saw these schools as an opportunity and filled them. The editors of *Flake's Bulletin* attended one school in Galveston and wrote of their tour: "We saw fathers and mothers together with their grown up children, all anxiously engaged in the pursuit of knowledge. . . . We are informed that their progress is rapid, and from what we saw, the pupils are deeply interested in learning to read." The pressure for education among the freed slaves would be an important part of postwar politics, for it demanded of the state services that had never been provided before and of landowners taxes that had never been paid.[25]

Some whites welcomed the educational desires of the former slaves and encouraged planters to provide books and schools for their laborers. The editor of the *Galveston News* said of one such planter: "This is the right spirit. We are glad to see it prevailing in one manifestation or another to a very large extent. Nothing should be done to alienate our former slaves, but everything to conciliate and elevate them." But for most the schools represented the horror of a new age and a waste of time. Dr. J. M. Baker from Grimes County summed up the view of many when he wrote: "The destiny of the negro race. This may be told in one sentence—subordination to the white race." The *Houston Telegraph* noted schools for freed slaves in that city. "We do not know who supports them," the editors wrote, "but suppose the government has to foot the bills. We believe such schools are not entitled to any of the school fund belonging to the State, as the pupils are not descendents of those gallant men who won Texas Independence from Mexico." The desire for education among blacks represented both a social and financial challenge to whites that would provoke a common response and make possible even greater racial unity among the latter than had existed before the war.[26]

New dimensions had been added to the old agricultural society of Texas. Combined, they would make up the context within which Texans would attempt to restore their state to the Union. Sectional jealousies, economic crisis, war-produced violence and hatred, black aspirations, and white racism complicated all efforts at restoration and limited the ability of the state's leaders to respond to the new situation. The state had to be brought into the Union, but Andrew Johnson tied that process to the complex issues that had emerged in Texas before reconstruction ever began.

CHAPTER 2

The Unionist Origins of Texas Republicanism

President Johnson's selection of Andrew Jackson Hamilton as provisional governor for Texas placed the initiative of solving the problems of reconstruction into the hands of the leaders of the antebellum Unionist movement. Hamilton's appointment did not threaten the white-dominated, agrarian social order of the state, since Unionists shared its values and goals, but the appointment did challenge the near-monopoly on political power that had been exercised by the dominant central district. Hamilton represented the return to power of the individuals and sections whose interests had not held a major voice in prewar state government. Given the advantages of presidential support and strong leadership by a Unionist governor, the movement had potential for establishing long-term control over the state government, the more so since the varying needs that had originally spawned Unionism remained. However, restoring the old coalition presented a difficult problem since, unlike the opposition Democratic party, its supporters had been unable to agree on a single course of action with regard to secession. While most Democrats had gone with the South, some Unionists had supported their state in secession, others had retired from public life or refused to take an active stand on the issue, and others had left Texas to support the national cause. If prewar Unionism could be recreated in the postwar era, a prerequisite would be the development of a plan upon which renewed cooperation could be based, of a program upon which Unionists, no matter what their course during the war, could agree. If Unionism was to succeed, it would be with cautious and diplomatic activity by its leaders, avoiding those problems that separated its members.

Given the circumstances, Hamilton was not a particularly fortuitous choice. He was an individual whose career had won him either devoted friends or determined enemies; few people were ambivalent toward him. While Hamilton was the available man, some observers did not think he was the best choice to carry out the president's policies. "Colossal Jack" had a reputation for bluster and blunder rather than statesmanship; Gideon Welles considered him a profuse talker but questioned his profundity, capability, and sincerity. The provisional governor's intense personal style of politics won him as many enemies as friends and caused some to wonder at the president's wisdom in appointing him. He did not appear to be the man for the sensitive job that lay ahead.[1]

Hamilton had been born in Alabama but moved to Texas in 1846. He was a politically ambitious lawyer and was actively engaged in the state's antebellum political struggles. He held his first public office as state attorney general from January to August 1850, then went to the state legislature as a representative from Travis County. His political career was flamboyant, characterized by general opposition to the state's regular Democratic leadership, and he earned the nickname "Colossal Jack." In pursuit of office he first affiliated with the Democratic Party, then associated briefly with the Know-Nothings, then with Sam Houston's Union movement after 1859. When Houston was elected governor in 1859 Hamilton went to Washington as a congressman and served there until he returned to the state after its secession. Back in Texas in 1861 he continued active opposition to the Democratic leadership, served in the legislature, then fled the state when his antagonism to the Confederate cause led to his threatened arrest.

In the North Hamilton actively engaged in national politics and especially lobbied for an invasion of Texas. He also schemed to bring cotton through the federal blockade, and in pursuing that end had dealings with President Abraham Lincoln. Perhaps this contact led Lincoln, who hoped to encourage Union sympathy in the South, to appoint Hamilton a general in the United States Army in 1862, although he never actively commanded a military force. Instead, he used his position to serve as a spokesman for Southern Unionism. In 1862 the president appointed him military governor of Texas and he accompanied General Nathaniel P. Banks in an invasion of the Rio Grande region. For a short time in 1864 Hamilton actually exercised the duties of governor in the area along the Texas-Mexican border after federal troops occupied Brazos Santiago.

After Lincoln's assassination, Hamilton returned to Washington where he sought reappointment under Johnson as provisional governor of the state. He was successful, apparently because of the president's haste to restore civil government in the South and also due to the lack of another acceptable candidate. Shortly after the issuance of the June 17 proclamation, Hamilton left for Texas.[2]

On July 22, the provisional governor arrived at Galveston where the town's citizens provided him a cordial reception. The local Union Association requested him to speak on the state's political situation, and Hamilton took this opportunity to explain the task that he saw before Texans. Before an assembly of the city's prominent leaders the governor made his remarks the following day from the steps of the county courthouse. His address centered upon the evils that had been visited on the state by secession, condemning those who had led in that folly. The failure of secession meant that a new order had arrived, and he represented himself as its instrument. Hamilton did not, however, elaborate on his meaning, simply advising his audience to accept the situation. The speech was a strong one, but it also contained words of reassurance. He insisted that he would not carry out his duties as governor with any personal desires for vengeance against those who had driven him from the state, and he promised fairness. From his courthouse address it was apparent that Johnson's man in Texas still lacked precise ideas of the way reconstruction should be carried out. His program remained to be developed.[3]

On July 25, the governor started the process of reunion in a "Proclamation to the People of Texas," in which he stated his intention to adhere to the provisions for reorganizing the state set forth by the president. Despite Hamilton's acceptance of the liberal formula designed by Johnson for reconstituting the electorate, and the promise to call an early convention to revise the constitution, the proclamation also indicated that after only three days at home he had become concerned with the plan's definition of loyalty. Hamilton warned Texans not to take the amnesty oath in bad faith, as doing so would only delay reunification. Individuals who swore to uphold all the laws and proclamations of the United States passed during the rebellion, but who retained some hope for gradual and compensated emancipation, particularly concerned him.[4]

What had prompted Hamilton's interest in the operation

of the president's program of amnesty? The governor's belief that the antebellum Union movement should serve as the basis for a restored, loyal government accounts for part of it. When he arrived at Galveston, Hamilton had initiated meetings with local members of the Unionist faction and had written to President Johnson that they, including those who had fought with the Confederacy, either welcomed the federal victory or accepted the situation. As the amnesty operated, however, it readmitted too many opponents. Hamilton received warnings that a too-hasty effort to convene a constitutional convention would prevent the Unionists from maintaining control. The governor realized, therefore, that Johnson's policy could prevent him from securing his own political goals. As he expressed concern with the loyalty of applicants for amnesty, he delayed to allow his own party time to organize. Significantly, at the same time that he warned against abuse of the president's amnesty, he called upon loyal men throughout the state to meet with him at Austin for consultation and organization. Although the end was not apparent in 1865, Hamilton's efforts to restore the Unionist movement would be the first step toward the development of the state's Republican party.[5]

The appointments that he made to public offices demonstrated the governor's attempt to use the Union movement to form the nucleus of a loyal government. To the most important post in his government, secretary of state, Hamilton named James H. Bell, an old Texan who had been a close associate of former governors Elisha M. Pease and Sam Houston. He had been a strong Unionist during the prewar crisis, but had served as an associate justice on the state supreme court during the war. Bell's appointment was an important concession to those Unionists who had remained in the state through the war and had, for whatever reason, not actively opposed the Confederate state government. As comptroller, the governor selected Albert H. Latimer, a well-to-do farmer from northeastern Texas. Latimer was a Unionist whose career added prestige to the administration, for he had been a signer of the Texas Declaration of Independence and a prominent politician in the Republic. When Latimer resigned to accept a federal appointment, Hamilton allowed the Northeast to retain control of the comptroller's office by replacing him with Robert H. Taylor of Fannin County. Like Bell, Taylor had been prominent in the prewar movement but had felt the need to go with the state in the crisis and had served in the Confederate army. William Alexander, a refugee because of his Unionism, received the attorney general's office. The appointments of Bell, Latimer, Taylor, and Alexander indicated that the governor was not as concerned with an individual's course during the war as with his politics before it. Filling county offices created problems, however, for the governor relied upon the recommendations of local politicians and accepted their word for the loyalty of the candidates. In some cases this led to appointments that raised fears among local Unionists that traitors were being put back into office, although Hamilton worked to remove such officials when mistakes were brought to his attention. While individual appointments were based upon a variety of determinants, it was clear, on the whole, that the governor intended to use public office in a way that would allow Unionism to be rewarded.[6]

His inability to find out exactly who could be considered loyal presented a major problem for Hamilton in his appointments. His recognition of the problem was apparent in his announcement of the process for voter registration issued on August 25. It marked a shift away from President Johnson's policies. The proclamation established enrolling boards in each county to be headed by the chief justice, assisted by district and county clerks, which were to administer the amnesty oath and register loyal citizens entitled to vote. The president's policy had implied that all citizens who subscribed to the oath, other than those excluded from the general amnesty, would be allowed to vote; but the governor moved to make the two independent. No one who had not taken the oath of amnesty could be a voter, but not all persons who took the oath would be entered on the voting lists. Registration officers kept two books, one listing individuals who had taken the oath, the other those who had taken the oath and were entitled to vote. Further, the proclamation empowered the chief justice on the board to interrogate applicants and make the final decisions as to the loyalty of the applicant and his right to vote. While this system added to Hamilton's ability to prevent his political opposition from organizing, its administration varied enough at the local level to keep it from serving its purpose as well as it might have.[7]

But if the governor was to restore the Union coalition he would have to do more than hold back his opponents. He also needed to provide the old party with new reasons for unity. That unity would be elusive, for the war had introduced new problems that many of the old Unionists could not agree upon. It had brought experiences that provided them with different perspectives on these problems. Of the issues that faced Unionist politicians, none created more internal disagreement than the definition of status for freedmen. Three major factions within the party were apparent early, factions that correlated with the particular wartime experiences of their adherents. Refugees, especially those who had contact with Republican politicians in the North, held a view on granting civil and political rights to the freedmen that approximated those of the people they had associated with. This did not mean they had become "abolitionized." They had come to believe that if the Southern states were to be rapidly restored, concessions on these issues would have to be made to the North. Having been in the North, they could not delude themselves that they would ever be allowed to maintain slavery; therefore they had been forced to develop alternative definitions of the status of blacks in postwar society. For the Texas Unionist who had remained at home and perhaps fought for the Confederacy, understanding what the North expected would be more difficult, especially when the local newspapers suggested that more viable alternatives existed than those indicated by the returning refugees. Disagreement over what should be done concerning the freedmen would be a major impediment to the unity of Unionism.

When the refugees returned home they brought with them views on the question of blacks that would have horrified most antebellum white Texans and did frighten those who had stayed in the state during the war. A few Unionist refugees had adopted the belief that the situation demanded a "radical" redefinition of the status of blacks in society. Attorney General William Alexander was one such individual. Alexander had been a lawyer in Galveston prior to the war but had found himself unwelcome in the state because of his Unionist politics. He left the state and went to New York where he associated with another old Texan, Lorenzo Sherwood. The latter had been a prominent railroad promoter in antebellum Texas who had been a strong opponent of slavery. He had served in the state legislature where his attacks upon the "peculiar institution" won him many enemies, and several years before secession he moved from the state. Sherwood had become a friend of abolitionists and congressmen who were hostile to slavery and introduced Alexander to such men. His experience convinced the attorney general that the federal government wanted the states to integrate blacks into the local political system by the extension of the suffrage. Alexander did not believe in unrestricted voting rights, but he did think that the North would not allow race to serve as a qualification. If there were to be restrictions, they would have to be applicable to both whites and blacks. In a letter to the *Galveston News* in September 1865, the attorney general explained his belief and argued that for the state to take the step of giving equal civil and political rights to the freedmen would make the process of reconstruction easier. He indicated that Southerners were mistaken to believe that the policies of President Johnson represented the will of most Northerners. Unless each state insured a republican form of government, ruled by a majority of all its people, Alexander suggested, Congress would be forced to intervene. He saw no course open to Texans other than concession to the will of the victor.[8]

Most local Unionists, however, did not see the situation in the same way as Alexander, and subsequently they sought far less for the freedmen. Most Unionists accepted the position of Governor Hamilton. His view indicated the complexity of the problem for a Southerner who needed to develop a policy agreeable to the North and yet harmonizing with his prejudices and preconceptions about blacks. For the governor there was no question concerning the capabilities of blacks; they were inferior. But like Alexander, he understood that the North would not allow the old system of control and utilization to exist. Hamilton's solution was for whites to labor at elevating the freedmen, show them how to make their own labor arrangements, and protect them by extending basic civil rights, especially the right to testify equally with whites in the state courts. He did not favor universal suffrage, but he thought the state should not place impediments in the way of the attainment by freedmen of the right to vote at some future date. His view was adopted by his close associates, particularly Secretary of State Bell and former governor Elisha M. Pease, who publicly espoused it. Bell advocated "justice" for blacks, but balked at granting them the right to vote. Pease, who was working with the administration in assessing the state's fiscal situation, adopted a view similar to Bell's and argued that Texans had to accept the fact of emancipation and extend a measure of civil rights to Negroes, but he too hesitated on the question of suffrage.

Pease indicated precisely the basis for his stand; it was a course expected by the North. "If we concede these things by our own constitution and laws," he wrote a friend, "we place ourselves in the same situation in regard to the negro, as all the great states of the northwest, and indeed the great portion of the free states occupy, and we shall receive their sympathy and cooperation in restoring us to an equal position in the Union." Further, Pease suggested that extension of civil rights such as the rights to serve on juries or testify in trials would be the best way to avoid the issue of black suffrage. "No considerable number can be arrayed against us in this question," he wrote, "when it is seen that we concede to the negro all the rights that are given him by the great mass of the civilized world."[9]

For some Unionists, however, the stands of Hamilton, Alexander, Bell, and Pease were unacceptable and represented a threat to the social and economic bases of Texas society. James W. Throckmorton had been an ardent Unionist prior to the war and in the Secession Convention of 1861 he had been one of eight individuals who had refused to vote for secession. He had remained in Texas during the war and, despite his opposition to secession, had entered into the Confederate service. He typified those Unionists who viewed any action other than the simple recognition of the fact of emancipation as unnecessary and dangerous. It is difficult to determine why Throckmorton was so hostile, but his correspondence suggests that he saw the efforts of the administration at Austin as detrimental in the extreme to the ability of farmers to obtain labor. He apparently went to the capital after Hamilton's arrival in an effort to secure qualified or compensated abolition, a logical course for a man who was a slaveholder, but he found the people at Austin unreceptive to his ideas. He returned to McKinney deeply incensed at what he considered to be widespread abolitionist and "radical" sentiments among the governor's supporters. Throckmorton saw allowing blacks to serve on juries as a first step toward full citizenship and, consequently, a step toward depriving agriculture of its necessary labor force. Unable to secure concessions from Hamilton, Throckmorton set about developing a new system that would provide coerced labor.[10]

The inability of men such as Throckmorton to see the need for concessions on the status of the freedmen presented a significant threat to the governor's plans, for their leadership was an important component in reestablishing the Union party, especially in northeastern Texas. But Throckmorton had placed himself in a position that did not allow compromise with the administration, which he considered to be moving too far. Even though he cooperated with Hamilton, he early sought other political allies. After his journey to Austin, Throckmorton wrote to his friend, Benjamin Epperson, "I take it that it is our policy to look out for ourselves—certain it is I do not intend to be abolitionized, nor to be the aides or abettors in the further humiliation & degradation of our people."[11]

Dissent among Unionists over the status of the freedmen created an opportunity for the Democratic leadership to retain some of their power. Through the summer of 1865 the Democrats had moved cautiously, unsure of what actions they would be allowed to take by the North, many of them restrained by law from holding office. The situation that summer, however, opened avenues of operation for the Democrats, and they looked for continued political power by cultivating alliances with those Unionists who felt unable to support Hamilton.

Throckmorton was a candidate for Democratic overtures, and so was Judge John Hancock, a prominent planter from Travis County. Hancock had played an active role in opposition politics in antebellum Texas, running for Congress as a Know-Nothing in 1855, and serving in the state legislature as a Unionist in 1860. In 1861 he had resigned his seat in the legislature rather than take the oath of allegiance to the Confederacy, although he remained in Austin where he practiced law in the state courts. For unknown reasons, in 1865 Hancock left Texas for the North where he supported General George McClellan for president and lobbied to prevent a military invasion of Texas. He apparently hoped up to the end of the war that Texas might be readmitted to the Union without a military government and without the consequent dislocation of labor. His interests appeared to be similar to those of Throckmorton, and his work placed him in direct opposition to the activities of Governor Hamilton. Unable to accept the change in the status of black labor implicit in emancipation, both Throckmorton and Hancock provided useful friends for the Democratic party.[12]

Through the summer overtures were made, first to Hancock. At a meeting held in Houston on June 13, 1865, even before the federal troops had occupied the state, the Democratic leaders openly proposed a combination with Hancock. Prominent leaders urged that he become a candidate for governor in the regular elections the following August if the military allowed them to take place. Hancock's ambition was to secure a place for himself in the United States Senate, and the support of the regular Democratic leadership would be difficult to turn down. While Hancock did not run for governor since the army refused to allow an election, the contact had been made and the pattern of cooperation established.[13]

Unionist reaction to the Democrats' moves was prompt. The Houston meeting prompted the editor of the *Bulletin* at Galveston, Ferdinand Flake, to warn the Democrats to keep out of state politics until after the reconstruction had been accomplished; the time was not right for them to attempt to reassert their power. Flake realized that political leaders wanted to hold on to power so long as even the smallest chance existed, but there was no chance. Union men would control the destiny of the country. "We desire to see Unionist and Secessionist cooperate in the good work of restoring Texas to civil law and prosperity," he wrote, "but we want Union men to take the lead for the reason that they *only* will have the confidence of the administration and of the people." The distress created among Unionists by Democratic activity was evidenced further by members of the administration who warned President Johnson that the old Secessionists had refused to accept emancipation and were biding their time until they could restore the plantation system. Hamilton informed Johnson that these men had joined together throughout the state and formed the nucleus of a determined and powerful opposition to an acceptable reorganization of the state government. Hamilton believed that wealthy planters were behind this opposition and he appealed, without success, to the president to exclude from the amnesty all rebels who possessed over $20, 000 in property. Bell and Pease joined with United States District Judge Thomas Duval to inform Johnson that the slaveholders had joined with the Secessionists in a plot to restore the old order at the first opportunity.[14]

More dangerous for the Unionists than this chipping away at the coalition, however, was the move Secessionists made to link themselves with President Johnson on the national scene, a move which forced Hamilton to call a constitutional convention before he was ready. The Secessionists had recognized as early as the summer of 1865 that differences existed between the president and various members of Congress over reconstruction. They saw Johnson's policies of rapid restoration and continued devotion to states' rights as more favorable to their interests than those of his opponents and moved to establish themselves as his supporters. Doctor J. M. Baker identified the president as an opponent of the centralization represented by the Republican party and urged every friend of human liberty to back the president in the coming struggle. Baker believed that a new struggle was imminent, one that would see the South fight by Johnson's side to restore constitutional liberty. An old Democratic leader, Ashbel Smith, wrote the president and informed him of the support growing in the South for his course. Secretary Gideon Welles noted in his diary that the support of men such as Smith greatly pleased him. Through the summer of 1865 Secessionist leaders and the Democratic press of the state encouraged friendliness toward the executive's program of rapid restoration and urged its general support. With strong and positive assertions of loyalty coming from among the Secessionists, President Johnson must have wondered at Hamilton's warnings of disloyalty and his delay at convening a constitutional convention in the state.[15]

By September 1865, Governor Hamilton's program was in trouble. Unionists such as John Hancock and James W. Throckmorton were covertly establishing other political arrangements that threatened efforts to restore the old party coalition. The Secessionists were active, strengthening their position by encouraging dissidents within the Unionist party and by undermining the relationship between the president and his provisional governor. The president, who desired a rapid restoration of the Southern states to their normal constitutional relationship, was pressuring Hamilton to move more rapidly in administering amnesty oaths and registering voters so that a convention might be held. Given the internal problems in his party and the agitation of the Secessionists, haste was not a policy that the governor found desirable. He delayed organization in an effort to secure local political stability and responded to presidential pressure with complaints that inadequate mail facilities, lack of presses, and the difficulty of finding officers qualified to administer the amnesty oath made an early constitutional convention impossible. Postponement of the convention, however, only worsened the relationship between the two, and the governor had to send a personal messenger to Washington to explain the situation in Texas.[16]

A month later, the president's pressure forced Hamilton to take the step he had not wanted to take. On November 17 the governor provided for the election of delegates to a constitutional convention to meet at Austin. The proclamation evidenced foot-dragging on the part of Hamilton for, while he had acted, he delayed the canvass until January 8, 1866. It was clear the governor's action was not a course he considered best for the state, but it fit the needs of the president. "If the question affected only Texas, I would delay action still longer," he wrote to Johnson. "But I regard the question as one of National proportions which will not justify me in limiting my views alone to the interests of Texas." National problems, therefore, had forced Unionists to move before they were ready.[17]

In the canvass for seats in the convention, Unionists found themselves opposed not only by Secessionists but also by Unionists. Hamilton's supporters campaigned in January with a program that reflected the governor's ideas on reconstruction. The thrust of their appeal centered on the belief that the state must meet the demands of the people of the North or face a delayed reunion, an approach that reflected both their desire for early restoration and their perception of the state's situation relative to the North. While suggesting several specific concessions, the most common among the administration's followers were repudiation of the military debt, acceptance of emancipation, and the protection of the freedmen in their liberty. In order to shield the freedmen from efforts to reenslave them, they advocated an extension of rights to judicial process, but none argued for Negro suffrage. Beyond the issues of reconstruction the Unionists demonstrated little common purpose, a state of affairs which indicated the old coalition had not yet developed comprehensive or clearly defined political goals.[18]

The administration's opposition had found, however, an issue that could be used to unite a variety of potentially hostile interests without the need to put forward a generally acceptable program. That issue was race. Unionists who opposed Hamilton used it as readily as any Democrat. In the 56th District where W. C. Dalrymple ran against Secretary Bell, the former refused to address himself to any issues other than that of the status of the freedmen. Where Bell supported giving them some basic civil rights, Dalrymple conceded them nothing but a position at the bottom of society as the "hewers of wood and drawers of water." Dalrymple accepted emancipation but was unwilling to secure blacks in their freedom by providing equality in the courts or access to the suffrage. He asked his district to support him to perpetuate a white man's government. "The patriot must strike now," he appealed, "for our cherished institutions and the ascendency of the white race." In the 55th District E. M. Pease encountered John Hancock who accused the former governor of "radical" views on the race issue, while he would favor extending the suffrage to blacks when he favored giving it to mules. Both Bell and Pease denied that they wanted anything like Negro suffrage, but their denials availed nothing. Dalrymple and Hancock went to the convention as Unionist delegates.[19]

In their racial appeal these anti-Hamilton Unionists did not differ markedly from their Secessionist opponents who also showed total opposition to efforts to integrate blacks into the local political system. James Armstrong, of Austin, informed voters in his district, "to add the Negro element to that now governing, would soon work the death of the body politic." He appealed to the complex of ideas developed by the white community toward slaves in the antebellum period, concluding that such a move was beyond the bounds of natural law and reason. A strong belief that the North would not push the state to accept such measures also pervaded the Secessionist appeal to the electorate. Other areas of cooperation had not been clearly marked out between these two traditional opponents, but hostility to Hamilton's efforts for reconstruction helped pave the way for a political alliance.[20]

When the delegates assembled at Austin on February 7, 1866, the relative strengths of the three major factions contending for power was not clear. President Johnson had sent an observer to the convention, Benjamin C. Truman, who believed that of the seventy members present on the first day about twenty-four fell into the category of "radical" Union men, as he characterized the Hamilton Unionists. The remaining delegates were either "conservative" Unionists or Secessionists, although he could not analyze their respective strengths. Truman informed the president that the structure of the convention insured that the "conservative" Unionists would control it and that the course taken would probably be satisfactory to Johnson. Subsequent events in the convention would prove Truman's assessment to be accurate as to the composition of the delegation. In actions to revise the state constitution and take steps to make Texas acceptable for restoration, the "conservatives" were dominant, and the course they took would force Hamilton's supporters into a redrafting of their program.[21]

Together, the two Unionist groups commanded an overwhelming majority at Austin, but their split was apparent immediately on the first day when the delegates elected a chairman. The Hamilton group nominated one of their most prestigious members, Albert Latimer, while the "conservatives" selected James Throckmorton. The Secessionists were also split, one faction supporting former governor Hardin R. Runnels of Davis County who had been a strong proponent of secession, the other backing William M. Taylor of Houston County, a state legislator before the war and a general in the Confederate Army. The following vote probably represented the strengths of the various factions: Latimer received twenty-four votes, Throckmorton polled twenty-two, and the two Secessionists split the remaining twenty-two votes. The vote for chairman indicated that no party would dominate the convention on its own, that whatever was accomplished would be done through compromise. Aware that they could not elect a candidate of their own, after the initial test of numbers both Runnels and Taylor withdrew and the Secessionists threw their support to the Unionist candidate most amenable to their interests. On the second ballot Latimer again received twenty-four votes, but Throckmorton polled the remaining forty-four and became chairman. The ballot showed that the "conservatives" could command a majority of the voters in the convention, but it also indicated that the Secessionists would have a decided influence as they could shift their votes in such a way as to prevent cooperation between the two Unionist factions. For the Secessionists a policy was necessary to secure their goals, but to avoid forcing the Unionists into a position where they could see that they had more in common with each other than with their old antagonists.[22]

The delegates renewed their sparring two days later when I. A. Paschal, a Hamilton Unionist from Bexar, introduced a resolution to inform the provisional governor of the convention's organization and of its readiness to take the "constitutional oath." Paschal's move aimed directly at the problem of loyalty and reflected the governor's belief that many people had been elected to the convention who had been and remained disloyal. The insistence on the oath was intended to keep such individuals from sitting in the convention, and subsequently drew fire from the Secessionists. O. M. Roberts proposed a substitute that would have informed the governor of the convention's organization but omitted all reference to an oath, then withdrew the substitute when John Hancock offered an amendment to Paschal's motion that struck out "constitutional oath" and replaced it with a provision that those people in the convention who had not taken the president's amnesty oath take it. Paschal quickly moved to amend Hancock's amendment so that all members of the convention would swear to the president's oath. A move to table failed, then the delegates voted thirty-nine to forty-one against Paschal's amendment and went on to accept Hancock's amendment and the resolution as amended.[23]

The struggle over the oath indicated that while Unionists were split over leadership, on some issues, such as loyalty, the Throckmorton "conservatives" could not prevent a split in which some adherents to the faction would line up with the Hamilton men. That evening the "conservative" leadership decided to reconsider their action, although the cause for their decision is not clear. They may have come to see their course as *Flake's Bulletin* did, as creating too much suspicion of disloyalty, or they may have seen the potential split in the "conservative" faction. For whatever reason, Hancock moved a reconsideration of the vote adopting his amendment when the convention reassembled the next morning, and the delegates, except for eleven Secessionists, voted overwhelmingly to do so. Paschal then introduced a new motion that each member be given "the oath to support the Constitution of the United States," and the convention adopted it by a voice vote.

Finally organized, the convention proceeded to its business and asked Governor Hamilton to provide it with whatever instructions he believed proper, to which he replied with a message that carefully put forward his administration's program. It reflected the governor's efforts both to address local problems and to be responsive to national demands, although in the latter case he was hindered by neglect in Washington. Despite the fact that he had pressed Johnson for guidelines to present to the delegates after he called the convention, Hamilton had received no reply from the president and was left to guess at what specifically was expected.

The action that he called for addressed three major points that he considered necessary to meet Northern demands and to resolve local problems created by the war. The first of these was that the convention make a clear and explicit denial of Texas's right to secession. The denial, he believed, was necessary to convince the North that the state had recanted of its political heresy; it was "evidence" of acquiescence in the results of the war. The second action was related to the first, for if secession had no basis in law the debt created to support the secessionist cause was illegal, and Hamilton called for its repudiation. Repudiation was a symbol for the North, but at home it had very practical meaning for it threw into doubt many private transactions during the war. Hamilton explicitly suggested that the purchase of state land script with Confederate money or state treasury warrants, and the payment for university lands with the same medium, should be considered aid to the Confederate cause, and, as such, illegal. While not mentioned by the governor, his policy also threw into doubt the payments made by various state railroads to the school fund. All of these transactions had practically bankrupted the state for they had resulted in filling the state treasury with worthless paper. For interests with a stake in Texas's future development, recovery of these funds was important. If railroads were to be built or state facilities to be expanded into the new sections of Texas, it would require the return of monies to the treasury. Hamilton had touched upon an issue of vital importance both to those who had unloaded worthless Confederate paper on the state and to those who wanted the state's money. It would be an issue to fight over.[24]

The third action called for by the governor was acquiescence in the emancipation of the slaves and provision for their freedom by the granting of basic civil rights. Texans did not have to approve of the end of slavery, but they had to "cheerfully acquiesce," and that meant providing legal protection to the freedmen. Hamilton argued that they must have an equality with the white population in this area. Specifically they must have the right to sue in the courts, the right to testify under rules applicable to whites, the right to equal punishment, and the right to acquire and hold property. The governor was unwilling even to exclude them from political participation if it was to be solely on the basis of race. The new situation demanded that nothing be done to keep the black population in a condition of dependence. While once again Hamilton had called for "symbolic" action to appease the North, he also had advocated a policy with very specific local implications. By creating a free black population, the delegates would potentially threaten the power of established planters in the state. The labor of blacks was a critical requisite for agricultural wealth, and a free and mobile labor force was not completely dependable. As Texas grew, the less well developed portions of the state might enter into competition for the labor of this population and attract it, through higher wages or other incentives, to relocate. Hamilton's policy was one that could work to the advantage of newer sections of the state, but was a clear threat to the old, and as such would create considerable political turmoil.[25]

On February 13 Unionists responded to Albert Latimer's introduction of an ordinance that declared secession and all acts subsequent to it null and void and denied the right to secede, with action that indicated Hamilton's program had struck some note of response. The passage of Latimer's proposal would have thrown into doubt the validity of all actions of the state government during the war. The Secessionists made a motion to table the proposed ordinance, but were unable to find the necessary number of votes. Further action was delayed, however, when the ordinance and other proposals which touched upon the issue of the legality of secession were sent to the Committee on the Condition of the State. While the Unionists had not been able to force immediate action on the question, they were able to prevent their opponents from removing it from consideration.[26]

Before the delegates would return to the problem of secession, however, they turned to an issue that would tie up the proceedings for almost a month, the status of the freedmen. In the convention Hamilton Unionists, "conservative" Unionists, and a faction of "conservative" Secessionists would be responsible for putting together constitutional provisions concerning blacks that Benjamin Truman would characterize as the most liberal obtained in the Southern states. The struggle that developed centered on Article III that defined the franchise, Article VIII that detailed the rights of the freedmen, and Article X that provided for public education. The Hamilton Unionists pushed to secure as equitable a treatment for blacks as possible, but found themselves forced to compromise time after time. On the franchise little was possible, although Hamilton had hoped to prevent the exclusion of blacks solely upon the basis of color, and the delegates voted specifically to that end. In Article VIII administration supporters attempted to secure the freedmen's right to act as witnesses in any civil or criminal case, but in a vote on February 24 that probably demonstrated the full strength of the governor's party in the convention, they failed by a vote of twenty-two to fifty-one. Unable to gain full rights they went on to support the resolution introduced by the "conservative" Secessionist, O. M. Roberts, that allowed blacks to act as witnesses in all cases involving their rights or injuries to them. In the ensuing vote the Hamilton men, the "conservative" Unionists, and the supporters of Roberts passed the compromise measure over the opposition of the die-hard Secessionists, sixty-four to seventeen. In one other effort, a small group of Unionists attempted to provide for freed slaves' education by devoting a portion of the common school fund to them, but only six members voted even to consider the proposal. As a result of their efforts the delegates changed the state constitution to declare that slavery should no longer exist; that blacks were to be protected in their rights of property and person; that they were to have the rights to sue and be sued, to contract and be contracted with, to acquire and transmit property; and that they were allowed to testify in cases involving others of their race. Texans had made their first step in adjusting to the new situation created by the war; their solution had not been one thought wise by Governor Hamilton, but it was probably as much as was possible from the men at Austin in 1866.[27]

With the issue of the freedmen resolved, the delegates returned to the other issues that Hamilton had considered necessary to be acted upon. On March 9 the Committee on the Condition of the State introduced majority and minority reports on the legality of secession. The first declared the ordinance null and void and of no further effect; the second attacked the majority report as a virtual assertion of the legality of the secession ordinance and subsequent legislative acts and proposed a declaration that it was null and void from the beginning, *ab initio*. When a delegate moved the substitution of the minority report, the Secessionists responded with an emotional appeal that accused the Unionists of trying to "invalidate all the marriages" and "bastardize all the children of the country." They suggested that supporting the minority report would annul every debt and every contract made in the state after its secession. Whether emotions or fear that an *ab initio* declaration would create disorder swayed the delegates was not clear, but a sizeable portion of the "conservative" Unionists shifted from their position of February 13 and defeated the effort to substitute the minority report thirty-four to forty-four. Three days later they adopted the majority report by a vote of forty-six to thirty-six.[28]

On the question of the state debt, however, the "conservatives" joined together with administration supporters in repudiation. It was a strong stand that denied the state's obligation to pay some $3,000,000 owed for the purchase of supplies, transportation, and soldiers' pay, $1,888,397 circulating in treasury warrants, and $998,440 of 8 percent state bonds in private hands. Repudiation even prevented the state from repaying $1,137,406 that it had borrowed from the school fund. While the majority justified its action upon the argument that the debt had fallen into the hands of speculators, it is possible that the delegates also considered the practical results of their action, clearing the way for future economic development by preventing the cost of the war from falling upon postbellum society. These results had a decided appeal to the underdeveloped sections of the state. Such areas required transportation facilities to grow, transportation needed the backing of the state government and its treasury, and that backing could not be given if the state burdened itself with the debt of a dead cause. Further, since the newer portions of the state probably were less heavily involved in financing the war, repudiation would represent a smaller loss and less of a burden to their inhabitants. While a variety of motives surely influenced the individual delegate in the convention, the sectional appeal of repudiation was apparent, and the coalition of the developing districts of the state against the developed that had been the base of prewar Unionism reasserted itself. The convention's action on the debt indicated that the sectional interests that had inspired Unionism continued to be a potentially powerful force, even overriding the antagonisms that had grown among the party's adherents.[29]

Cooperation also appeared when the delegates turned to the development of railroad policies. Both Hamilton and "conservative" Unionists joined together to support constitutional provisions that encouraged railroad construction, by granting state bonds to companies that actually constructed track. The policy was another sectional one, since the bonds had to be backed with tax monies, and taxes would have hit hardest the long-settled and developed regions of the state. Most Texans favored railroads; the problem always was who would bear the burden of financing them. The policies of the convention threw that load upon those farmers and planters who possessed the rich lands of central Texas, although only over their objections. However, while the constitution provided for the future development of transportation in the state, it also created problems for it placed the decision on what roads would be financed in the hands of the legislature. Control of that body would be critical, for its actions would determine the direction of the state's economic growth.[30]

But while sectional interests at times drew together the old Unionists, the experiences of the war remained to plague efforts at making a stable coalition. Differing experiences during the war separated old party members who could no longer see problems from the same perspective. That was particularly true of the issues involving freed slaves. The variety of stands taken by Unionists also meant that when each attempted to justify and validate his actions, there was always potential conflict with a person whose actions had been different. That conflict appeared on the issue of the validity of secession; it also surfaced when the convention sought to protect Confederate and state officers from legal actions against them for carrying out their duties during the war. For the "conservative" Unionists such a move was fully warranted. Men live in a community whose rules they must obey and, consequently, they should not be punished for upholding the order of the community. To the Hamilton Unionists, who had chosen to oppose the local community, the results of the war had proven that they were right. For them, efforts to protect in the law those individuals who had punished Unionists for their stand against secession could be seen as nothing but wrong. The "conservative" position dominated the convention, but only at the expense of convincing those who opposed it that the state was falling back under the control of the people who had led it into the disaster of secession. When the convention exempted Confederate officials from legal responsibility for their acts, Governor Hamilton came to the hall and condemned the delegates for their treason. With great passion he warned them: "You have an account to settle before the people yet. You have not done with this. You shall confront them, and shall answer to them, and if God spares my life I pledge myself to go before the people of the State and draw these men up and make them answer."[31]

The constitutional convention showed that Hamilton's efforts to restore the old Unionist coalition could not be implemented. Too much had intervened between 1861 and 1866; while the old interests remained, the war provided too many different experiences to separate members of the party. Time might have helped to bring the Unionist factions back together, but the pressure for speedy action placed upon Texans by President Johnson meant it would not be available. A single Northern policy on reconstruction might have made possible renewed Unionist cooperation along the lines of the prewar party, but the split between the president and Congress only facilitated the development of differences among Texans. For the Hamilton Unionists the adjournment of the convention marked the beginning of a reassessment of political strategies and the search for some means to stall the Secessionist return to power that they feared had been provided for by the delegates. While his supporters at home prepared for the June 25 election called for by the convention, Governor Hamilton travelled to Washington where he hoped to encourage the president to change his policies. However it was Congress that Unionists began to see as their only salvation. William Alexander expressed the growth of this feeling in Texas when he wrote a friend in the North: "Our only hope is that Congress will stand firm and do its duty until the President finds out that he has been misinformed, and does his also. If his policy prevails, Heaven help the South." Texans had seen differences between the president and Congress and had begun to exploit them before they had been fully developed or even recognized by Northerners.[32]

CHAPTER 3

From Unionism to Republicanism

Events during Governor Hamilton's administration presented a dilemma to his supporters. They had attempted to implement a program of reconstruction that they believed met the minimum requirements of the North and recognized the results of the war, but had found their program pushed aside in the constitutional convention. From this point of view the actions at Austin represented both a suicidal course destined to prevent the early readmission of Texas to the Union and a flagrant repudiation of their own Unionist stand during the war. They believed that the situation had to be changed, but they faced the problem of how to effect the change in such a way as to insure that their program of reconstruction would be secured. This was even more difficult since the convention's actions probably represented the will of a majority of the existing electorate. That electorate could be changed, however, by disfranchising the men who had led the state in secession, or by admitting to the franchise the freedmen. Most Unionists could accept neither of these steps. Such actions represented a major departure from the set of ideas about government and race within which they had operated. The summer of 1866, however, would be a period of challenge to Unionists that would force a reorganization of values and witness the emergence of Republicanism among the supporters of A. J. Hamilton.

In the constitutional convention Governor Hamilton's chief supporters formed the Union Caucus to further his programs; after adjournment these individuals organized the campaign to support a proadministration slate for public office in the state election. Calling themselves the Union party, they proposed a platform that reflected their concern with the course taken by their opponents in the convention. They did not call for a radical restructuring of Texas society; in fact they argued for rapid restoration with minimal upheaval and the state's "industry undisturbed." But they reasserted their belief that the actions taken by their opposition were leading to the very ends they hoped to avoid and suggested that citizens had to abandon any course designed to justify what had happened in the past. The Union party and its program offered the best way to end the uncertainty of the situation and bring peace, for it was devoted to republican forms of government, recognized the supremacy of the national Constitution, believed secession null and void from the beginning, and supported the national government. It alone had acquiesced in abolition and had attempted to ameliorate the condition of the freed people by offering them just treatment. Above all, the supporters of the Union party claimed they alone possessed the confidence of president and Congress and could speed the process of reconstruction. The *Southern Intelligencer* encouraged support of the party on the grounds that its candidates and programs represented "neither more nor less than the Sam Houston platform—the Constitution and the Union." [1]

The candidates of the Union party reflected the continued effort to restore the old coalition, for the individuals nominated represented the interests of its chief sectional components. The choice for governor was Elisha M. Pease, a longtime participant in state politics. Pease had come to Texas from Connecticut in 1836 and settled in the central district, but through his service in the Republic he had acquired lands in the western counties which brought him into association with the frontier interests of the state. He actively supported policies designed to hasten the development of the frontier sections during his tenure in the state legislature and also as governor. His advocacy of these interests was particularly demonstrated in his backing of legislation to provide state aid for the development of railroads and to facilitate the rapid removal of the Indians. The other nominees further reflected old Unionism—C. C. Binkley for attorney general, James H. Shaw for comptroller; Sam Harris, treasurer; Francis M. White, land office; and, particularly, Ben H. Epperson for lieutenant governor. The selection of Epperson, a close friend of the administration's chief opponent in the convention, Throckmorton, represented a concerted effort by Hamilton's supporters to attract voters from the Unionists who might be swayed by the stand of the "conservatives." Epperson's course during the war had been similar to that of his friend; his views on reconstruction were also like Throckmorton's. His appearance on the Union party ticket could be of great potential value.[2]

However, the Union party faced strong opposition in their search for office since after the convention's adjournment the "conservative" Unionists and the Secessionists managed to combine on a slate of officers to enter the election. The Secessionists, led by Oran M. Roberts, apparently broached the topic of a coalition by offering James W. Throckmorton the nomination on a ticket comprised of both "conservative" Unionists and members of the antebellum Democratic party. When first contacted Throckmorton hesitated, but after discussion and the introduction of more Unionists to the slate, he agreed to run. For the Secessionists Throckmorton's agreement to run offered a means of continuing their control over the state, for while he was a Unionist (and consequently an acceptable candidate for national political purposes), he also held views that approximated their own on the status of the freed slaves and the policies that needed to be implemented to end reconstruction.[3]

The question of what brought Throckmorton and his supporters into the coalition is more complex. If the gubernatorial candidate's thoughts typified those of his followers, probably the agreement developed out of their perception of the requirements of the national government. Unlike Hamilton, Throckmorton believed there were alternatives and saw disagreement over policy between President Johnson and the Congress. For Throckmorton the state had options, the right to decide for itself on the conditions of reconstruction. From this view the position of Hamilton and his backers was not understandable. If a choice existed, what white Southerner could advocate the civil rights program indicated by the governor? Throckmorton concluded that they had been radicalized, motivated by a bloodthirsty and proscriptive feeling toward those who had remained and supported the state during the war. There was no longer a basis for political cooperation between the "conservatives" and the administration. As a result the former turned for allies to those whose views on what needed to be done were similar to their own.[4]

In the campaign the "radicalism" of the Union party ticket was the issue, and the Conservative Unionists repeatedly directed the attention of the electorate to the implications of "radicalism" as they saw it. Their provision of a definition for "radical" began in the public letter to Throckmorton that offered him a nomination because he opposed the party that sought to secure black suffrage in the convention and to place whites on the level of their former slaves. Conservative Unionist candidates declared their own opposition to any efforts to create political equality for blacks and argued the superiority of the white race.[5]

Because the "radicals" supported "social and political equality for the negro," the Conservative Unionists also concluded that the Union party was in alliance with the likes of Thaddeus Stevens and Charles Sumner in the Congress. That meant they supported a consolidated and centralized government that would destroy the power of the states and leave the citizenry without power to prevent encroachments and tyranny by the central government. "Radicalism" threatened constitutional government in the United States; therefore it had to be defeated. If not, radicals would be able to accomplish all of their goals—impose Negro rights upon Southern society, disfranchise and punish those in the South who had supported the Confederacy, and permanently exclude the South from the Union.[6]

If their opponents conspired with Stevens and Sumner, the Conservative Union party represented the only true support for the president's plan of reconstruction in the state, according to its campaign rhetoric. Part of the campaign aimed at demonstrating that the party adhered to an acceptable program of reunion, that of the president. John Hancock used a trip to Washington, on which he delivered the ordinances of the constitutional convention, to talk with Johnson and express praise and backing for the president's program. The local press argued that only the Conservative Unionists stood with the president in his opposition to Negro suffrage, centralization, and the other goals of his antagonists in Congress, and that it was the duty of Texans to give him their support. Linking the party to a Northern program was important for local success, since not doing so would suggest that a vote for Conservative Unionism would be a fruitless exercise. Whether or not the party actually reflected the desires of the president was immaterial; they believed that they did and appropriated his name to help them insure victory in the state canvass. Equally successful was their effort to connect the Unionists with the radicals in Congress. One correspondent wrote to the *Galveston News* that if Pease and his fellows were not themselves radicals they were certainly in the fellowship with men who were and were, therefore, guilty by association.[7]

The Union party attempted with little success to combat the accusations of the Conservatives. Pease denied that he favored Negro suffrage, although he admitted his willingness to grant qualified suffrage if reunion depended upon it. Denials, however, would not put down the clamor. One correspondent demanded clarification on the party's stand from Hamilton. He wrote: "We believe you have been misrepresented to affect the approaching election, and wish you to place the facts properly before the people." The editor of the major Union party newspaper, *Flake's Bulletin*, in a fancied encounter with a supporter of the Conservative party illustrated the problem of countering the Conservative charges:

"I am not a Radical," says the Union man.

"Yes, you are," replies his opponent; "Here it is in black and white, printed in the *Telegraph, News*, and a half dozen other papers. They all say so."

"Well, but we are none of us Radicals. Gov. Pease denies negro suffrage; and Judge Bell also denies it; we are all of us opposed to it."

"That has got nothing at all to do with it. Don't you see it here? Read it for yourself. You are a Radical; you believe in negro suffrage. The *News* says so."

"Don't you think I know what I believe in, and in what all the rest of us believe?"

"Don't care anything about it. You are a Radical and in favor of nigger suffrage, and if you wasn't a fool, you would know it— and Gov. Pease and Judge Bell would know it too. They believe in nigger suffrage, and are therefore Radicals. They are Radicals, and therefore believe in negro suffrage."

That is the logic.[8]

Finding the charges of radicalism impossible to refute, Pease emphasized the issue of Unionism in his own canvass, focusing upon the emotional appeal of the issue much as Houston had done in 1859. He charged that Throckmorton and his party represented the disunionists of the prewar years who hoped to perpetuate themselves in power. Pease charged them with abusing their offices throughout the war and bankrupting the state in support of treason, hardly actions that made them deserving of power. Pease found this approach unfruitful, however, and Conservative Unionists responded by accusing him of trying to resurrect dead issues. Since the war had settled the question of union and loyalty, how could these issues remain proper ones for political consideration?[9]

On the defensive before the public, Unionists attempted to

increase their chances for election through organization. Although little information exists on the Union League movement in Texas, in part because of its secret nature, its introduction as an aid to the Union cause appears to have taken place in April 1866. Rumor indicated that Major A. H. Longley, editor of the administration's *Southern Intelligencer* at Austin, was its leader, but exactly how it was organized is not known. It may have been based upon local Union Associations such as the one formed at Galveston the previous summer, which pledged to support no man for public office who had ever freely and voluntarily tried to overthrow the United States government. Throckmorton reported that Pease claimed the support of at least fifteen thousand men organized in the League shortly after the canvass began, but in most of the state the organization does not appear to have passed beyond the planning stage. In a letter to the Union party's gubernatorial candidate, General Edmund J. Davis who had been a member of the administration faction in the constitutional convention, complained that the "home-guard" of Unionists proposed at Austin had not materialized and that local organization of all sorts was lacking.[10]

The Pease candidacy received a fatal blow on April 26 when Ben Epperson, his slate's candidate for lieutenant governor, withdrew from the ticket. Epperson had never been comfortable on the Union party ticket because of its stand on reconstruction, and soon after his nomination he had written Throckmorton to urge the Conservative Union candidate to withdraw and let him come out against Pease. Throckmorton refused, and, in turn, asked his friend Epperson to abandon the Union ticket. Throckmorton believed such a move would destroy the Pease faction, and he promised Epperson support for the United States Senate if he dropped out of the race for lieutenant governor. Epperson agreed to his friend's request in a letter to J. W. Thomas of the *Paris Press*, stating that he could stand with no party that made a man's position on secession the basis for political participation. The time was not one for renewed party battles, he believed, and he condemned the one raging in the state. Epperson's defection was serious because it left the northern counties unrepresented on the Union ticket. The party's leaders decided to replace him with Livingston Lindsay of Fayette County and to continue what now appeared to be a hopeless campaign. Unionists around the state despaired of Pease's election.[11]

The election was a disaster for the Union party. Pease re-

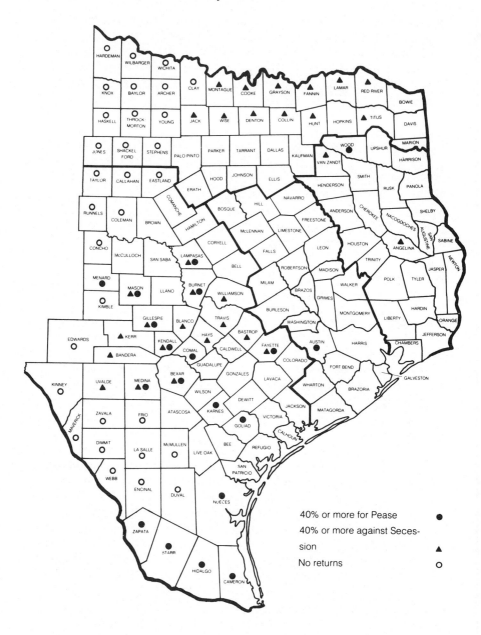

MAP 3. Pease Vote Compared to Antisecession Vote

ceived only 12,694 votes to Throckmorton's 49,314. In the Second District, the home of the Conservative Unionist candidate, Pease received only 18 percent of the 13,346 votes cast, a poor showing since that section had delivered strong support to Houston in 1859 and against secession in 1861. Pease did better in the First and Third Districts, but he still polled only 30 and 26 percent of the votes. He received a majority in only one section, the southwestern counties that constituted the Fourth District. The failure to restore the old Unionist coalition was complete and Throckmorton's candidacy helped make it impossible. With the latter on the Conservative Union ticket, Texans did not face the problem of deciding between a Unionist and Secessionist. Rather they had to choose between the views on reconstruction held by two well-known Unionists. It is hardly surprising that Texans chose the candidate whose program provided the least threat to existing society. It did not matter that the Unionist candidates were not radical, that they went only so far as they believed the situation required. Local voters understood that their program implied the greatest change to the community, given the choice they opted not to change.[12]

For Unionists the triumph of the Throckmorton slate created concern and fear since it appeared to them a rejection of the only program of reconstruction that would secure the state's readmission to the Union. Their loss presented itself clearly: their old opponents had returned to power, even if led by one of their former allies. The subsequent actions of the state government only served to confirm them in their views.

The immediate problem proved not to be the governor, but the legislature that had been elected along with him. In fact Unionists received encouragement from the sentiments expressed by Throckmorton in his inaugural address, when he indicated his intention to guarantee equal justice under the law to all classes of men, regardless of race and color. He further pledged his administration to a policy of enlarged and liberal charity toward those whose political opinions differed from those of his own party. But the encouragement that came from the governor rapidly dissipated when the Eleventh Legislature met and began to carry on in a manner that convinced Unionists disaster was at hand. Its members manifested little tendency toward the justice and charity called for by Throckmorton. Instead they proceeded to reward the old Democratic and Secessionist leaders of the state. When they chose new United States

Senators they selected for one position Oran M. Roberts, who had worked for compromise in the convention of 1866 but had been one of the state's most prominent Secessionists. Unionists also noted legislative action that proscribed Union men, that gave state funds to the projects of former Confederates, and regulated the lives of the freed slaves. These actions by the legislators quickly drew the fire of Unionists who accused them of a total lack of concern for the well-being of the state and a desire to reinstitute slavery. In short, the Unionists asserted, the legislature was still disloyal.[13]

The election of O. M. Roberts, the man who had presided over the Secession Convention, forced most Unionists to conclude that the Conservatives had not accepted the results of the war. Why otherwise would they elect a man who had led the state into war? Ferdinand Flake accused the legislators of sending Roberts to Washington for the specific purpose of precipitating a fight over the test oath demanded by Congress. If admission meant sending loyal men to Washington, he believed, the Conservatives would just as soon not be represented. During the election they had been willing enough to work with men such as John Hancock, but now they refused to honor their pledges and support such a questionable Conservative as Hancock for the Senate. The evidence indicates that the former Secessionists decided to support Roberts and oppose Hancock almost solely because of their stands during the war. Representative R. K. Gaston of Tyler wrote to Roberts that when he considered the alternatives in the election he had decided "never to vote for a man for that high position who acted the part (Hancock) did in our late struggles."[14]

Of more immediate importance to the Unionists than the election of Roberts was what appeared to be a concerted effort on the part of the Conservatives to eliminate them from any participation in the political process. On September 8 the legislature reapportioned the state and tied many counties with Unionist strength to strongly anti-Unionist black belt counties. The men who had followed Hamilton and Pease believed that the act represented a purposeful effort by the legislature to make sure that they could not obtain even the smallest number of political offices. The Judiciary Act of October 11 that redistricted the state courts eliminated the districts of two of the three judges affiliated with the Union party. This caused even more objections. Unionists complained that Conservatives had turned the courts into instruments of political persecution. Men indicted during the period of the Hamilton government now received acquittals in the Conservative courts. They charged that blacks and Union men fared poorly before Confederate judges. John L. Haynes, a former member of the First Texas Cavalry, wrote Pease that loyal men had no chance of justice in the courts when a case involved "rebel" interests. Haynes called the state courts "organized rebel vigilance committees . . . , even worse, for they act under the semblance of law." [15]

Of course the legislature was not the only branch of government that the Unionists believed the Conservatives used against them. In spite of Throckmorton's promise to pursue a policy of liberality toward his political opponents, they suspected him of systematically removing from state offices all clerks who adhered to the Union party. Through the governor's influence the federal government withdrew its printing contract from the Union party's *Southern Intelligencer*. The *Texas State Gazette*, the administration's organ at Austin, became the official printer of federal statutes and the proceedings of Congress for Texas. It particularly galled Unionists to see the government at Washington used against their interests. [16]

The legislature's enactments concerning the freed slaves also upset the Union men. A steady stream of bills crossed the governor's desk, each in some way limiting the rights of former slaves. One law restricted the use of black testimony in the state courts only to cases that involved another black as either defendant or victim. Blacks were segregated on public transportation, and the railroads were required to run special cars for black passengers. The legislature also enacted laws regulating labor contracts that gave the employer strong control over his workers, provided fines for neglect of duty and other nebulous wrongs, and placed primary responsibility for settling difficulties between employer and employees with the employer. An apprentice law and a vagrant law aimed at blacks also received approval. The act defining the rights of freed slaves prohibited Negroes from holding office, serving on juries, voting, testifying in court cases except those involving other blacks, and marrying whites. Unionists condemned these acts as counter to the wishes of the loyal men of the country and an attempt by the Conservatives to degrade labor in the state. [17]

In addition to the public acts they regarded as disloyal, Unionists opposed the private acts of the Eleventh Legislature and censured its members for alleged personal interest in bills that incorporated and extended state benefits to railroad, navigation, bridge, and other companies. They believed these acts created monopolies detrimental to the interests of the people of the state. Unionists also accused the legislature of needlessly expanding the state government by creating useless positions with which to reward the Confederate faithful, pointing up as the chief example of this action the creation and funding of the office of superintendent of public education at a time when the state had neither public schools nor the money necessary to create them.[18]

The Unionist loss in the state elections of 1866 and the subsequent actions by the governor and the state legislature forced those who had supported Governor Hamilton and his policies into a reassessment of their political attitudes. They had exhausted the means available to them under presidential reconstruction to prevent their old antagonists from securing power. They now searched for other means to make certain that the people who had led the state into secession in 1861 would be excluded from the government. At Washington, Hamilton had hoped to convince President Johnson to change his policies toward the South and exclude the old Secessionists, but he found the president intractable. Subsequently he met with other Southern Unionists at the capital and worked to develop an alternative political solution that would serve their needs. To facilitate the working out of a Southern Union program, Hamilton, Senator Joseph S. Fowler of Tennessee, Congressman William B. Stokes, and others called for the loyal men of the South to meet at Philadelphia on September 3, 1866 to discuss what might be done.[19]

Hamilton's view on the corrective measures necessary to change the situation in the South slowly developed through the summer of 1866. Reports by his friends in Texas who began to arrive in Washington after the state election hastened this change. Texas Unionists concluded that President Johnson could no longer be supported since the states' rights interpretation of federal powers that he used in reconstructing the Union was largely responsible for their dilemma. Instead they turned to Congress as the only means to protect their rights and to secure their life and property at home. Hamilton undertook leadership in establishing Texas Unionism's connection with Congress, frequently speaking in public on the preferability of congressional policy to that of the president. On July 11 he appeared at a tumultuous session of the Union party's congressional caucus and strongly denounced the president, assuring the congressmen that only unreconstituted rebel governments could ever emerge out of Johnson's work. A week later he addressed the Union League at the capital and attacked the executive for attempting to step beyond the bounds of his power by seeking to readmit the Southern states too hastily. Hamilton insisted to his Republican listeners that only the people, through their representatives in Congress, had that power.[20]

But securing congressional intervention in the reconstruction process could only be the first step toward relieving Southern Unionists. A positive program of steps to insure loyal government then had to be implemented, and the Texans in Washington worked to show Congress what these should be. All could agree that the most important step was the continued presence of federal troops in the state. E. M. Pease met with his old friend Gideon Welles to argue that five-sixths of the people of Texas remained hostile to the federal government and refused to tolerate even the mildest expression of Union sentiment among the other sixth. Because they had been loyal to the Union, Pease believed that the national government was bound to protect them, and that protection could only be secured by army occupation of the state. Welles was not a sympathetic listener and his response only encouraged further alienation of Southern Unionists from the president. The secretary of the navy pointed to the Constitution as a limit on the central government. It prevented intervention; consequently the loyal population had no recourse but to remain passive and to strive quietly and patiently to modify public opinion. For individuals who had believed their course during the war justified by the Northern victory, such sentiments were unacceptable.[21]

By the time of the convening of the Southern Loyalists convention at Philadelphia on September 3, the Texas Unionists had come to agree that another step was necessary for their protection. That step was the extension of the suffrage to the state's black population. Unfortunately for their purposes, general agreement could not be achieved among all the delegates. Whatever individual reasons attracted men to Philadelphia, the central theme of the convention was the hostility of Loyalists to presidential reconstruction. The meeting provoked great excitement and the delegates marched through the streets of the city to the music of brass bands and listened to the harangues of Unionist leaders. The convention hall was filled with symbols reminding the Southern Loyalists that they had pursued the correct course during the war and should be rewarded—a portrait of Abraham Lincoln hung behind the speaker's stand and a sign stretched across the front of the auditorium welcoming those Southerners who had been "Unstained by Rebellion, and Unawed by Treachery!" On the walls were appropriate slogans, including President Johnson's promise that treason was a crime to be punished and made odious. But the sense of grievance did not prove powerful enough to sustain cooperation in the meeting.[22]

The convention moved smoothly until its third day when during the morning session Colonel Charles E. Moss, editor of the *St. Louis Press*, offered a resolution instructing the committee on resolutions to report to the convention a statement favoring impartial and unconditional suffrage, regardless of race or color. Moss argued that the safety of the loyal men of the South depended upon the election of loyal men to office and their election could only be assured with the votes of Negroes. He insisted that while not desired by all, it was a step that had to be taken and could no longer be put off. The resolution threw the convention into an uproar and only the threat by the chairman to adjourn the convention restored order. The chair then promised that no precipitous action would be taken, and that the question would be debated at length when the committee offered its report. The delegates returned to other business to await the committee's action.

During the evening delegates were pressured to produce a moderate position on the suffrage issue. Delegates from the border states, especially West Virginia and Maryland, argued that they would not support such a measure. Northern Congressmen who had come to Philadelphia to observe the convention's proceedings were aware of the tension black suffrage created in their own states, and they also pushed for dropping the issue. The following day the moderation position was supported when J. A. J. Creswell of Maryland reported the resolution committee's "Address" which carefully sidestepped the issue. The committee endorsed a resolution supporting the proposed Fourteenth Amendment to the Constitution then before Congress, although the committee believed it had some inadequacies.[23]

Creswell incensed Loyalists from the deep South, and Lorenzo Sherwood promptly proposed a specific endorsement of Negro suffrage. Led by Creswell the moderates in the convention tabled Sherwood's proposal and pushed for an adjournment of the meeting *sine die*. At this point Hamilton rushed to the speaker's platform and gave an emotional speech that condemned Creswell and the border states for forcing the unreconstructed states to yield too much so that their own self-interests might be protected. Hamilton stated that the convention had met with the purpose of placing the true condition of the South before the people of the North. He did not care whether or not it influenced the election of a representative or two from Maryland; he did care that it lead to action to protect loyal people in the South. In reaction to Hamilton's impassioned plea the convention continued, but it could not reach agreement on the issue. When the delegates finally left for home, observers concluded that if the convention had demonstrated anything it was that the people of the nation were not willing to accept universal suffrage. A Texan at Philadelphia believed that Hamilton's convention had strengthened the hands of the Northern Radicals by giving them an opportunity to disclaim the doctrine of Negro suffrage. The convention had shown that "the *political* abolitionists have done with the negro." [24]

Hamilton and the other Texans in the North, however, had not finished, and they remained there to canvass in favor of candidates for Congress who supported the extension of the suffrage. On September 11 Hamilton and Jesse Stancel, a Union Army veteran from Galveston, appeared at massive Union League rallies in New York City where they argued in favor of allowing blacks to vote. From New York Hamilton canvassed Ohio, Indiana, and Illinois, a tour that ended with a visit to Lincoln's grave at Springfield just before the election. In Connecticut Governor Pease spoke for the cause and in a speech at Hartford told his audience that he and his family had abandoned Texas because they feared for their safety. Everywhere they repeated their accusations that President Johnson's policy made it impossible for a Union man to remain in the South. Black suffrage was necessary to restore loyal government. The summer of 1866 had seen a transformation in the views of Texas Unionists. Their view of the situation at home had forced them into a position that only several months previously would have been to most of them unthinkable. [25]

The shift in the view of blacks held by the Texas Unionists was nowhere more apparent than in the stand of Governor Hamilton. On December 3, 1866, the man who had told the Texas constitutional convention that he thanked God he lived in a white man's government and trusted that it would always be so, addressed the Impartial Suffrage League at Boston's Tremont Temple on the need to integrate the freedmen into state politics. His new perspective was part of the total plan that he believed was necessary if the rebellion was ever to be brought to an end and the Union restored. Hamilton suggested that it was the responsibility of Congress to intervene, and he pointed up four steps that he considered necessary to secure his goal of creating loyal governments in the South. The first was a law granting impartial suffrage in the District of Columbia. As a second step he suggested Congress should declare the former rebel states out of the Union and incapable of participating in the national political process. Afterward he believed Congress should pass an enabling act to permit the organization of loyal governments under the control of loyal citizens of any race and color, with the disloyal excluded. As a final step, he argued for a constitutional amendment to secure equal and impartial suffrage in a way more acceptable than the proposed Fourteenth Amendment.

In his Boston speech Hamilton elaborated on his reasons for seeing Negro suffrage as an integral part of the reconstruction. His most vigorous argument centered on his belief that any society predicated upon the ideas of republican equality and the capacity of people to govern themselves had to integrate all of its free citizens into the political process. Although he had initially favored some form of qualified suffrage in the future, Hamilton had seen that the freedmen were no less capable than other people. He pointed up their intelligence with regard to the everyday affairs of life, their respectful manner and deportment, their faithful labor, their obedience to law, their attachment to family, their desire for improvement, their Christian beliefs, and their "respect, love, and veneration" for the government of the United States as commending them to receive the right to vote. If these were not enough to recommend the extension of the suffrage to the freedmen, however, Hamilton suggested that the fact that granting this right was the only means of securing loyal government in the South should be. He declared:

If we must descend from the high ground of Constitutional debate to the consideration of questions of policy, in determining the great question of impartial suffrage, then I most earnestly insist that it is essential to the reconstruction of local State Governments in the South, to invoke the aid of loyal black men, and that without such aid any governments now existing, or which may be established in the South on any other basis than that of full and entire franchisement of *all loyal* men, will be a failure; that such State Governments will, if the freedmen are excluded, be in the hands of the late rebels . . . who dread nothing so much as the cultivation in the South of a spirit of sincere attachment to the Union, and full and candid inquiry into their motives and purposes in dragging the people of the South into rebellion.[26]

Having shifted their support to Congress and having come to see the need for black suffrage, the Texas Unionists at Washington subsequently worked to develop a specific program of reconstruction and to convince those people in power to intervene in the South to secure the desired goals. To accomplish that end Hamilton, along with other Southern Unionists, organized the Southern Republican Association with the stated purpose of serving as a forum to discuss matters relating to the Southern states and presenting to Congress the wishes and needs of the loyal men of the South. In this body Hamilton helped forge a program that requested Congress to depose the existing state governments and in their place establish territorial commissions governed by United States commissioners in cooperation with the federal district judges. Hamilton wanted this commission to have the authority to prepare a new state constitution to be presented to Congress, one that would have to require universal suffrage. While the Southern lobby agreed upon the program they wanted, they could not find anyone in the North willing to support it. In January 1867, they finally agreed to support a bill to establish civil government in Louisiana introduced by Thomas A. Eliot of the Select Committee on the New Orleans Riot. Eliot's bill had reputedly been written by a member of the Southern Republican Association, R. King Cutler of Louisiana, and thus it reflected what the group wanted in Congress.[27]

The "Louisiana Bill" appeared on February 11, 1867. It reflected Hamilton's ideas, providing for the appointment by the president of a governor and provisional council of nine men to run each Southern state until an election could be held the following June. The governor and council would have the power to appoint state officers until the election and would be responsible for supervising the election. The bill expressed Hamilton's desire to exclude the disloyal from politics through a provision that limited suffrage and officeholding to males over the age of twenty-one who had resided in the state for one year and had never willingly borne arms against the United States (although private soldiers could participate if they could prove that their service had not been voluntary.) The officers elected in June would call a constitutional convention, and the new constitution would be submitted to Congress for approval prior to consideration of readmission. The bill also provided for a military force to support the civil authorities, both federal troops and a militia composed of qualified electors.[28]

On the evening of February 11, the Southern Republican Association met and passed resolutions favoring the "Louisiana Bill," which Eliot had placed in the *Globe*. After considerable parliamentary maneuvering the House passed the bill the following day by a vote of 113 to 47, then sent it to the Senate where Benjamin Wade introduced the bill on February 13. The "Louisiana Bill" quickly passed its first reading but then ran into trouble. Following debate on it the next day its opponents buried it in committee. Hamilton led a meeting of the association on February 18 that called upon the Senate to bring up the Eliot bill and pass it, but it was too strong a measure for the majority in the Senate. Most of the Senators favored the much modified and watered down "Military Bill" of George W. Julian and Thaddeus Stevens, even though the association condemned it as inadequate. The "Military Bill" secured the approval of Congress, and after surviving President Johnson's veto it became the law under which Southerners had to reorganize their states. The "Louisiana Bill" came up one more time, at the end of February, but a vote on adjournment prevented further action on it. As in 1865 Southern Unionists found themselves operating under provisions imposed from the North which they did not believe would fill local needs. Governor Hamilton viewed the Military Bill's passage as a terrible defeat for the hopes of all loyal men in the South.[29]

The bill that received Congressional approval incorporated features desired by the Southern Unionists, but it also contained problems. It theoretically ended presidential reconstruction by declaring legal government nonexistent in the rebel states with the exception of Tennessee. The declaration meant that the state governments created under the presidential plan had no legal basis within the national context, but since the bill did not provide for their disbandment they continued to operate as if they were legal. The "Military Bill" divided the South into five districts directed by a military officer assigned to protect the property rights of all persons in the state, to suppress insurrection, disorder, and violence, and to punish all criminals and disturbers of the peace. While these military commanders had the power to exercise the functions of civil government, most of them initially opted to allow the existing state authorities to continue in order to maintain stability. While the Congress had created a means for alleviating the situation confronted by Southern Unionists, immediate change was slight.[30]

However, the "Military Bill" did reopen the political struggle in the Southern states because of its provisions for readmitting them into the Union. Under its terms each state had to reconvene a constitutional convention with delegates elected by all male citizens above the age of twenty-one years, regardless of race, color, or previous condition, excluding only those disfranchised for their participation in the rebellion or for committing a felony. The convention was to write a new constitution that conformed with the Constitution of the United States and provided for universal adult male suffrage. When the qualified electors of the state had approved the constitution and ratified the Fourteenth Amendment, Congress would examine their action and consider an application for readmission to the Union. The bill allowed the Unionists to try again to prevent their old antagonists from dominating the state government, and this time conditions appeared to favor them. Blacks would participate and they would probably support the Unionist cause. Further, after the passage of a supplementary reconstruction act, March 23, 1867, the federal government excluded the leaders of secession from taking part in the process.[31]

The Texas Unionists who went to Washington in the summer of 1866 had not accomplished all they had sought, but a new opportunity had opened and the travelers returned to gain their political goals. The men who returned to Texas were not of the same mind as they had been when they left. Their Unionism had turned to Republicanism, and they had accepted the need for black suffrage. As a result they would find that their ideas and political hopes provoked stronger opposition from their enemies. They would be forced even further into evaluations of their political strategies and philosophy. For the Unionists the political needs of the postwar era had caused change. By the norms of their society, they had become "radicalized." They had accepted the unacceptable.

CHAPTER 4

Organizing the Republican Party

The Texans who returned from Washington in the spring of 1867 faced a tremendous challenge if they were to gain and hold on to political power in the state: they had to create a biracial political coalition. This posed significant problems. Republicans would have to create a program that appealed to a constituency of freedmen, but at the same time did not alienate the traditional supporters of the Union party. The creation of such a program was particularly problematic since the potential needs of the freedmen differed from those of the white elite that had been represented in the old party. Blacks wanted land and education, and education required public spending. White Unionists wanted railroads and sectional development, items that would also cost money. In an agrarian society, enough capital to finance all of these needs would be difficult to acquire, and thus potential for disagreement over the allocation of resources existed from the first. Probably the whites who first helped to organize the Republican party always assumed that they would control the development of policy and the allocation of funds, but such a situation opened the party to fragmentation whenever another set of leaders could promise the black constituents more participation in government and a greater share of the state's resources.

The development of a party program for Texas Republicanism was not enough to secure power, especially since for the freedmen the advantages to be gained by adhering to the Republicans rather than the Democrats were not immediately clear. White Republican leaders were willing to go further than the Democrats in recognizing emancipation and protecting blacks in their civil rights, but limits existed to how far they would go. Events since the end of the war had shown that white Republicans had many of the same racial prejudices held

by their political opposition, and that even they would be
reluctant to push for complete political equality for freed slaves.
To solidify black support party leaders realized that Republicans would have to be more than simply an agrarian party
in the traditional model. The interests of landless black farm
workers were not the same as those of the white landowners
of the state. Black voters had to be educated to how Republican leaders deserved their support. The best way to accomplish this was organization. In addition political unity provided
blacks with the means to protect themselves against violence.
As a result Republicanism in Texas would reflect a new style
of politics in which party leaders would be managers and ma-
nipulators of a political machine, rather than simply organizers
of ideas or spokesmen for the agrarian elite.

Efforts to build a Republican party in Texas started on
April 27, 1867, when prominent Unionists met at Austin and
called for a convention at Houston to organize a party of loyal
men who favored restoring the harmony of the Union and ac-
cepting the Congressional plan of reconstruction. Colonel John
L. Haynes was the principal instigator of the meeting, along
with other Unionists at Austin such as Attorney General Alexander, Judge Peter W. Gray, Colonel Thomas H. Baker, George
C. Rives, and Leander Brown. The resolutions that the meeting
passed tried to identify the party with a program of development in the newer sections of the state, of meeting needs of
the black community, and of identification with congressional
reconstruction policy. The men at Austin supported the National Republican Union party, approved the acts of Congress, and
acquiesced in military rule. They encouraged the men who
would meet at Houston to adopt a party platform that would
eliminate all restrictions on the rights of freed slaves; safeguard,
increase, and fairly distribute the state's school fund; establish
a free public school system; support railroad construction; hasten immigration to the frontier by backing a homestead law;
and encourage a return to the rule of law in Texas.[1]

At the same time Unionists in Texas' chief port founded
a Galveston National Republican Association. Texans were an
important element in the Galveston association, but the organizers tried to bring newcomers into the party, if they supported
its goals. Typical of the "carpetbaggers" who would play significant roles in the party were Oscar F. Hunsacker and Edwin
M. Wheelock. Hunsacker, the association's first president, was

adjutant general in the Fifth Military District. The association's secretary, Edwin M. Wheelock, was superintendent of schools for the Freedmen's Bureau in Texas. Harvard-educated, a Presbyterian minister and prewar abolitionist, Wheelock left his native Massachusetts to become an officer in the 76th United States Colored Infantry. Arriving with the army in Texas in 1865 he early became interested in local politics. At their first meeting the Republicans adopted resolutions similar to those passed at Austin, especially endorsing congressional reconstruction and the extension of full civil and political rights to all men.[2]

Unionists held other Republican meetings across the state during May. At San Antonio blacks participated at a major political rally for the first time. Isaiah A. Paschal, a Unionist delegate to the constitutional convention in 1866, and Doctors Theodore Hertzberg and M. G. Anderson addressed the meeting which pledged itself to support the Austin platform and endorsed a program for the education of laborers throughout the state. Rev. Frank Green from Colorado County and Scipio McKee from Washington County spoke on the political role for blacks in Texas. On the same day Judge Gray, Major A. H. Longley and Thomas Merry, all prominent Republicans from Austin, held a party rally at Prairie Lea in Caldwell County to organize that area's large Negro population. Judge Andrew J. Evans, another Unionist, led a similar meeting at Waco in McLennan County.[3]

Republicans used these meetings to introduce the secret Union League organization to the black population. Judge James H. Bell had brought plans for starting the League in Texas with him when he returned from Washington in March. Shortly after his arrival at Austin the Conservative press noted that Negroes and whites had joined together in clandestine meetings at the freed slaves' church. Attorney General William Alexander played an important role in these meetings. Jacob Raney, a freedman, appeared to be one of the early political leaders of the black community. The Texas *State Gazette* reported that Alexander and Raney had instructed the Negroes how to vote and informed them that the Republicans were their political friends while the Conservatives were their enemies. The speakers carefully stated, however, that they did not believe the freedmen were yet ready for holding office, although they promised that their time was speedily approaching.[4]

Republican efforts to organize Negro voters drew a quick response from the Conservatives. Governor Throckmorton asked Raney and another local black leader, Anderson Scroggins, to meet with him and discuss the political situation. At their conference Throckmorton advised them that the blacks had best look to the Conservative party for friends because he believed its members had their welfare at heart. He proposed that the two call a meeting of freedmen to hear addresses by Judge John Hancock and Colonel George W. Carter and furnished them with copies of his inaugural message and the acts of the Eleventh Legislature so that they might see his party's concern for Negroes. Instead of calling a rally as the governor suggested, Raney and Scroggins condemned him for his opposition to the franchise bill introduced in the constitutional convention in 1866, his approval of a school bill that excluded freed slaves from its provisions, his failure to prosecute outrages against Union men and Negroes, and his opposition to congressional reconstruction.[5]

The Republican effort and its success exasperated the Conservatives. One prominent leader among them, Guy M. Bryan of Galveston, wrote to an old friend in the North, the future President of the United States Rutherford B. Hayes, that his party was willing to allow Negroes to vote. However, he was uneasy because he believed that "designing white men" were creating a difficult situation in the state. He noted that the Republicans made extravagant addresses to the freedmen, the result of which was that the Negroes turned against their former masters. Bryan believed that the introduction of Negroes into local politics was leading to a war of the races.[6]

Certainly organization of the Negroes had created tensions. Republicans relied on a thorough exposition of the planter's exploitation of the slave in their appeals to the freedmen. At a public meeting in Galveston on May 15 Major Oscar Hunsacker of the city's National Republican Association warned them to be on their guard against the Conservatives who tried to deceive them into believing that they were the black man's best friends. What they really wanted to do, Hunsacker insisted, was reenslave them. Judge D. J. Baldwin of the United States District Court at Galveston appealed for the freedmen to stand up against the Conservatives and stop the men "who once scarred your backs from dissuading you from doing right." Baldwin called upon black men to do their duty and join the state Republican party. In a similar vein Republican propaganda, issued from Galveston, invited Negroes to join Republican clubs, vote Republican, and send delegates to the Republican convention at Houston, reminded them that rebels had massacred Negroes at Fort Pillow, Andersonville, Belle Isle, and Richmond, and begged them never to give their votes to such men. The circular warned, "If they [the Conservatives] carry the elections they will disfranchise every black loyalist, and drive from the State your white friends; they will not allow your children to be educated nor you to discuss your rights." [7]

The rapid organization of the black community provoked unfavorable reactions in the Conservative press, but it also created concern among old Unionists. Ferdinand Flake had been a strong opponent of secession and a faithful Unionist. He was not opposed to black suffrage, but he feared that in appealing to Negroes party leaders were going too far. In his *Bulletin* Flake denounced the May 15 meeting at Galveston as being unrepresentative of the loyal men of the city. He expressed particular opposition to the formation of the Union League among blacks since he feared that it would array the races against one another. Flake believed that men such as Hunsacker were demagogues who sought to use the aspirations of blacks to secure their own advancement. From the beginning, then, the Republicans found the creation of a biracial coalition in the South was a sensitive matter. The varieties of racial views held by whites made agreement on the proper role for blacks in politics nearly impossible. [8]

Despite disagreements, the Republicans made remarkable progress on organizing at the county level. When they assembled at Houston on July 4 almost six hundred delegates, representing at least twenty-one counties, attended the first session at the Harris County courthouse. Even though a significant number of white men attended the convention, the majority of the delegates were Negroes. The election of convention officers and the appointments to committees did not reflect this, even though some blacks received positions of authority. One, George Ruby, served as a vice-president. Only a few carpetbaggers participated in the convention, although none of them served in key places. Most of the leaders of the convention were native Texans or men who came to the state before the war. Former governor Pease presided over the assembly as its president. [9]

Most of the men in attendance were political unknowns,

at least on the state level. Few of them had been politically active before the war. Not many of them continued to play a prominent role in Republican politics in Texas. There were some prominent exceptions that give an idea of the complexion of the convention. Governor Pease, Judge Bell, William Moore, A. J. Evans and Jesse Stancel had already played important roles in postwar state politics. George W. Honey and George Ruby were both carpetbaggers. Honey was a clergyman from Wisconsin who came as a representative of the American Missionary Association to supervise that group's schools among the freed slaves. Ruby was a well-educated black man, originally from Maine, who had come to Texas in 1866 as a teacher with the Freedmen's Bureau. Scipio McKee of Washington County and Stephen Curtis of Brazos typified the freedmen from around the state who constituted the majority of the convention's delegates. Both had emerged from obscurity to work effectively as Republican organizers and continued to represent their constituents throughout the reconstruction period.

The platform drafted by the delegates reflected the interests of the elements in the Republican coalition. For blacks the party promised to back the enactment of a homestead law to allow citizens "without distinction of race or color" to secure portions of the unappropriated public domain and to support the creation of a system of free public schools for the equal benefit of all children in the state. The needs of Unionists appeared in the platform's strong support of the National Republican party, endorsement of the work of local district military commanders, and demand for the removal of all civil officers who had participated in the rebellion or acted in hostility to the acts of Congress. Because they believed that they would naturally move into these offices, the white Unionist leadership of the Republican party could accomplish its goals by supporting Congress. Only the carpetbaggers lacked a group interest to be expressed by the party, although their individual interests could be filled by implementation of the platform's other parts. The Republican platform indicated that the new party had moderate aims—it did not intend to revolutionize society—but it also showed that the Republicans believed that they, not those who were enemies of the national government, had the right to exercise political power in the state. While they denied any intention of dealing harshly with former rebels, the Republicans promised that they would not compromise on their principles. They would not conciliate their enemies.[10]

Having stated their principles, the delegates adjourned and returned home. To continue the organization of the party, however, they created a state central committee to coordinate local efforts. Pease named Colonel John Haynes to serve as party chairman. Haynes's choice was one designed to appeal to the Unionists for he had been a strong one prior to the war, then maintained the cause as the popular commander of the First Texas Cavalry. To work with Haynes, Pease selected Alfred H. Longley, editor of the newly created *Austin Republican*, former attorney general William Alexander, and two black men, Henry Dickinson and Ed. Wilkinson of Austin. Their task was formidable, for although the apparatus of party organization was in operation, the viability of the alliance between whites and freedmen was untested. The question remained open as to how many whites could be brought into a biracial coalition. The state central committee would have to work in the following months to secure patronage rewards for people who came into the party, to register as many of the freedmen as possible for the elections authorized by Congress, and also to attempt to prevent the Throckmorton administration from interfering with their efforts.[11]

One of the most important jobs that confronted the Texas Republicans was securing control of local patronage, the traditional means for building up parties in the United States. The problem was that the opposition held all of the state and local offices, and a hostile president had closed the doors of national patronage. Their only source in the spring and summer of 1867 was the military commander whom Congress had empowered to appoint individuals to fill vacant local offices. Under these circumstances, party leaders courted military officials in the district in an effort to gain access to these positions. Fortunately for the Republicans General Charles Griffin was in charge of the subdistrict of Texas. Griffin was a career officer who had served meritoriously until a crippling wound relegated him to administrative duties. In Griffin the Republicans found a man who viewed the local political situation as much as they did. The general expected the same support and loyalty from the civil authorities of Texas that he looked for from the men under his command. Of course local authorities did not consider themselves to be under his command, and they frequently exercised judgment that took them along courses counter to his wishes. Griffin interpreted these actions as disloyal, and he complained to his superiors of the refusal of state officials to cooperate with him. Soon after taking command in Texas, Griffin had requested Fifth Military District Headquarters at New Orleans to remove Governor Throckmorton and his associates from office. He was particularly incensed at the governor's reluctance to punish men accused of committing outrages and murders among the loyal population. Throckmorton and other officials executed the letter of the law because they had no other choice; Griffin believed they should exercise the law in spirit.[12]

On the initial application to remove Throckmorton General Philip Sheridan, in command of the Fifth District, endorsed the request, but at Washington General Ulysses S. Grant decided to delay. Grant believed that until Congress or the courts settled numerous legal questions concerning the power of the military commanders it was best not to move. But tension continued to build between Griffin and the governor, especially over the registration of voters to participate in the election of delegates to a constitutional convention. The general wanted a quick and peaceful registration, but he felt that Throckmorton hindered all his efforts. In July he once again requested the governor's removal. "I feel great anxiety about the state of affairs in this state, the feeling of hostility towards the General Government is very bitter," he wrote Sheridan, "and I attribute it in a great measure to the inefficiency and temper of the officers whose duty it is to maintain the laws and protect the citizens."[13]

The passage of a third reconstruction act in July clarified the powers of district commanders in the eyes of Sheridan. He succumbed to pressure from Griffin and Texas Republicans who wanted former governor E. M. Pease appointed to replace Throckmorton. Local Republicans had finally found the means to obtain the local offices necessary to reward the party faithful. With the blessings of Griffin and the Republicans in the state, on July 30, in Special Order No. 105, Sheridan removed Governor Throckmorton and replaced him with Elisha M. Pease.[14]

The new provisional governor took over the executive offices on August 8, and immediately sent letters to General Griffin that urged the dismissal of most of the other Conservative officials. The governor noted that they all expected to be removed and he saw no reason to disappoint them. The governor went to Galveston for a personal interview with the commander to reinforce his request and to discuss the manner in which removals and appointments should be handled. After meeting with Pease, Griffin asked Sheridan to oust three district judges who were particularly objectionable to the Republicans. His own scruples concerning his power settled, Sheridan complied with the request and removed all three.[15]

After the initial removals a flood of requests reached the offices of Pease and Griffin. Local Republicans believed that the proper appointments would help them secure a majority of the delegates in the constitutional convention. William Longworth of Karnes County urged rapid replacement of Conservatives, writing: "We will have a tough enough job of it at the next election with the offices in our possession, without them we may miss it." General Sheridan opened the way for massive removals on August 27 when he authorized Griffin to dismiss all county officials who were disloyal or who held office in violation of the provisions of the Reconstruction Act of March 2. Griffin and Pease developed a procedure for handling the desired changes that placed appointments in the hands of the governor and his Republican advisors. Pease assumed the responsibility for obtaining information on the qualifications of all prospective appointees and then forwarding recommendations to Galveston. Although Griffin retained the final decision on such matters, Pease's endorsement appears to have been tantamount to appointment.[16]

A temporary halt to removals came when General Griffin died on September 15, the victim of one of the Texas coast's frequent yellow fever epidemics. General Joseph J. Reynolds, however, proved equally agreeable to the interests of the local Republicans and soon took up the unfinished work of his predecessor. Informed by the secretary of the district's Civil Bureau of Griffin's arrangement with Pease, the new commander began sending names to Austin for the governor to evaluate. From September 21, the date he assumed command, until the end of November, the general and Pease appointed 644 officers to various positions throughout the state. Although 108 of the positions had not been filled previously, 536 required the removal of Conservative officials. However, Republican joy ended when President Johnson replaced Sheridan with a Democratic general, Winfield S. Hancock, who restrained his subordinates from further removals. Hancock expressed open hostility toward congressional reconstruction, and after taking command declared his belief that the civil governments of the state took precedence over the military authority.[17]

Reynold's flurry of activity placed the party in a much better position than that occupied through the summer. For most Republicans, however, the general's work ended before the political miracle for which they hoped. As a committee in the constitutional convention pointed out in 1868, the general election of 1866 had filled 2,377 elective offices and almost all of these positions were in the hands of Conservatives. From the beginning of congressional reconstruction through June 24, 1868, the military appointed only 796 men to office. Of this number almost half, 394, had either refused to take office or failed to qualify, leaving these offices in the hands of the incumbents. For practical purposes only 402 "loyal" men received office from the military, leaving 1,975 of the state's civil positions in the hands of the Conservatives. In better shape because of the military's help, the Republican party in Texas was still far from being politically entrenched.[18]

The machinery of military patronage operated in favor of the Republicans in Texas, and party leaders asserted considerable control over appointments, but it proved of only limited value. Intervention by military superiors and the president prevented either Griffin or Reynolds from fully exploiting this source of power to the advantage of the fledgling Republican party in Texas. Limited interference actually worked to the detriment of the party for it provided the Republicans with less than 20 percent of the state's offices and at the same time connected Republicanism with the spectre of military intervention in local affairs.

Republican success also required the fullest possible registration of voters under the Second Reconstruction Act. General Griffin had opened the registration on April 19, 1867, in an order that provided for a division of the state into registration districts headed by supervisors, clerks, and county boards. He arranged for the lists to remain open until September 1 in order to allow ample time for the largest possible registration. The Conservative press reported that Griffin could not find suitable men for the registration boards, but the general denied these reports. In an interview at Galveston he said that the selection of competent men was proceeding as quickly as possible and he looked for an early election for the constitutional convention.[19]

The registration boards appointed by the general became

the object of serious criticism from the Conservatives. In May, Griffin issued secret instructions to the registrars that listed the classes of men the general believed disqualified from registering by the Reconstruction Acts. He provided a rather broad interpretation of the provision prohibiting the registration of any man who had held a state office prior to February 1, 1861, and had later supported the Confederate government. Griffin defined a state office as everything from governor and lieutenant governor to city surveyor and cemetery sexton. Using Griffin's instructions the boards refused to register men such as Willard Richardson, former mayor of Galveston and editor of the *Galveston News*. In other instances Conservatives complained that local boards had no fixed principles upon which they made decisions. Former governor Throckmorton reported, "It makes no difference what a man done [*sic*] or what office he held before the war if he is a radical man he can register—at least it is so in some counties."[20]

While the Conservatives complained that the boards illegally prevented them from registering, the Republicans accused the Conservatives of illegal interference with operations of the boards. In Washington County registration halted when assailants shot two of the registrars. Blacks refused to serve on the boards in Red River County after whites threatened them with violence. Complaints from Red River finally compelled Griffin to send a calvary unit to Clarksville to maintain order. At Fort Worth the registrars suspended their work because of a rumored attack on their office. The Republican *San Antonio Express* also accused the Conservatives of more devious interference. In many counties employers threatened the freedmen with economic reprisals should they register.[21]

Despite the controversy and violence the Republicans scored an enormous success in getting blacks to register to vote. Approximately 98 percent of the state's male black population over the age of twenty-one registered. After Reynolds ended the second and final supplementary registration in January 1868, 49,497 Negroes had qualified. At the same time, however, only 50 percent of the adult population registered. Still, white registrants outnumbered the blacks by 10,136. The white majority required a cautious Republican strategy for even if every registered Negro went to the polls and voted Republican, the party still needed over 10,000 more votes to carry a state election. These statistics emphasized that the party needed to prevent any effort to draw the race line in politics and required as many white supporters as possible.[22]

Politics among Republican officeholders, however, did not encourage efforts to play down the race issue. The Republicans had found that their Unionism and opposition to Conservatism were not an adequate base for party unity when they had to make policy. A serious fracture developed within Pease's administration over the validity of the constitution of 1866 and the legislation passed following the state's secession in 1861. Governor Pease believed that all state laws not in opposition to the Constitution of the United States or acts of Congress should be held legal and in force. Comptroller Morgan C. Hamilton and Attorney General William Alexander, however, held that the acts of all legislatures meeting in the state after March 1, 1861, including those of the Eleventh Legislature in 1866, were null and void from the beginning or *ab initio*. Contemporaries labeled this dispute the *ab initio* controversy. Such questions as the validity of land granted to corporations, the payment of railroads on their indebtedness to the state school fund, and legislation concerning other major interests in the state complicated the problem.

What was a stake in the controversy has been hidden by the partisan rhetoric used by the contending factions. Pease's adherents accused their opponents of being impractical, unreasonable, and intolerant men who stood in the way of the state's progress. In their newspapers they accused Hamilton and Alexander of unworthy motives, adherence to mere dogma, and political hatred. The comptroller and attorney general were "misanthropic old bachelors" and schemers who wanted to produce disaffection in Unionist ranks. Pease and his supporters controlled the Republican press; the Conservatives had no reason to interfere in a squabble that made their opponents look bad, and therefore made no comment in their papers, so the intent of the *ab initio*-ists has long remained obscured. Historians who have touched upon the affair have accepted the accusations of the Pease faction of the Republican party.[23]

An examination of the events leading up to the break suggests that the partisan interpretation presented at the time was overly simplistic. As a doctrine *ab initio* had first been advanced by Unionists during the constitutional convention of 1866 when they argued against the legality of the ordinance of secession. The issue appeared again in July 1867, when Comptroller Hamilton questioned the validity of the postwar convention and subsequent legislation in a letter accompanying a petition sent to General Griffin. Hamilton asked the military commander to void the acts of the Eleventh Legislature, contending that no legal government had existed in Texas from secession until the establishment of the military government under congressional act in March 1867. Hamilton appears to have been particularly concerned with the "Act to Collect Back Taxes on Land." [24]

Hamilton, the elder brother of Andrew J. Hamilton, was a new man to Texas politics. He had arrived in Texas in 1837 and served with distinction as a clerk in the War Department of the Republic, but after Texas entered the Union in 1845 Hamilton retired from government to devote all his time to a mercantile establishment in Austin. In 1852 he retired from business after having acquired considerable wealth. Much of this wealth was based on land. In addition to large land grants received for his services to the Republic, Hamilton acquired thousands of acres of state lands through the purchase of land certificates and scrip issued by the Republic and the state. During the war he refused to pay taxes on these land holdings. [25]

Because of his land holdings Hamilton's opposition to the implementation of the "Act to Collect Back Taxes on Land" was not surprising. Passed by the Eleventh Legislature on November 12, 1866, that legislation required the payment of all land taxes assessed between 1849 and 1867 on the basis of the specie valuation of the lands at the time payment had been due. For any Unionist who had fled the state during the war or who had refused to pay Confederate taxes, such a law must have seemed a reward for the "rebels" who paid their taxes with deflated Confederate notes and a punishment for the loyalist now forced to pay at specie value. In addition to the tax the act required the payment of a 10 percent per annum penalty fee. The legislature placed the task of compiling back tax lists in the hands of the comptroller. [26]

A month after he failed to obtain Griffin's nullification of the acts of the previous legislature, Comptroller Hamilton asked Pease for permission to suspend the tax audit board and other activities of his office. He reported a large backlog of work and proposed that since the existing tax laws were of questionable validity, his office should be allowed to confine itself to the collection of current taxes. When Pease refused to approve the request it opened a breach between him and his comptroller.

Shortly after the incident Hamilton and Attorney General Alexander made their first public statements on the matter, declaring their belief that the laws enacted by the Eleventh Legislature were null and void.[27]

On October 25 Governor Pease attempted to end the controversy with a proclamation that declared the constitution and the statutes of 1866, subject to some exceptions, "rules for the government of the people of Texas." The comptroller, however, protested to General Reynolds, and Alexander resigned as attorney general. Alexander asserted that he had taken an oath to perform the duties of his office agreeable to the only adopted constitution, that of 1845, and that he could not perform his office under Pease's proclamation. While they had hoped to provoke the intervention of the commanding general, neither Reynolds nor district headquarters at New Orleans offered to intervene. They viewed the matter as a local affair and, implicitly, supported Pease's action.[28]

Despite this reverse, Hamilton refused to abandon his fight. In a further effort to stop the sale of land that had been unassessed or for which taxes had not yet been paid, the comptroller asked Pease on November 14 to suggest to Reynolds that tax sales be suspended. Pease forwarded the comptroller's letter but would not endorse its proposed action. Pease informed Reynolds that he believed such a suspension would benefit only the state's large land holders. The 15,000,000 acres of unrendered lands, the governor suggested, belonged mainly to the most virulent rebels in the Union. To suspend the tax law would only allow these men continued escape from taxation. Reynolds returned the letter to Pease, noting his agreement with the governor and promising that he would not suspend the sales.[29]

This division between Pease and Morgan Hamilton became politically critical when the comptroller decided to carry out his battle in the party. Blocked by the governor, the courts, and the military, he appealed, with the help of Alexander, to the predominantly Negro Union League at Austin. On October 12, 1867, the local chapter endorsed Hamilton's and Alexander's stand and a committee appointed to consider the necessity of amending the original Republican platform proposed five additions. The most important was a resolution supporting the *ab initio* doctrine. The appeal of Hamilton and Alexander to the Union League brought into the open concern among the supporters of Governor Pease about increased assertiveness and demands from the party's Negro element. At Galveston the League had opposed Pease's appointment of Major R. H. Perry as chief of police because of his reputed antagonism toward Negroes. That city's most prominent black politician, George Ruby, reportedly had boasted that he would be elected to the constitutional convention as a representative of his race through the support of the League. Already concerned, the backers of Governor Pease condemned the action by the Austin League in support of Morgan Hamilton. Ferdinand Flake denounced it as an organization composed largely of plantation Negroes, unable to read or write, and incapable of speaking for the Republican party of the state. At Austin, A. J. Hamilton condemned the "smooth faces and beardless youngsters of the Republican party" who attempted to instruct old men in political policy. He warned Negroes to be wary of such men and encouraged them to strive for intelligence but not be too ambitious for office. Premature ambition, he said, would only bring about a war of the races.[30]

When the district commander ordered elections to select delegates to the proposed constitutional convention, the split within the party grew worse. On December 20 the Austin League announced that it would support Morgan Hamilton for the convention rather than his brother. The *Austin Republican*, the administrative newspaper at the capital, accused the comptroller and Alexander of attempting to form a Negro party. It described this movement as one composed of nothing but "white fools, demagogues, or worse . . . and such colored men as they can induce to follow their lead. They assume par excellence the name of Radicals, and are justly entitled to that of Black Republican. Their object is to build up a black man's party; and they err just as much, and perhaps even more, than those misguided conservatives, who would make a white man's party." A correspondent of the *Galveston News* wrote from Austin that only the prospect of a Conservative entry into the election kept the Republicans at the capital from complete disintegration.[31]

Dissatisfaction among Republicans with the course of Morgan Hamilton and his followers offered the Conservatives an opportunity for gaining political converts. Through the fall of 1867 the Conservative leaders pushed voter registration and planned a boycott of the election. By this means they hoped to prevent a convention, since under the reconstruction act one-half of the registered voters had to vote in favor of a convention before it could be called. This policy was risky and when the Republicans began to split, the Conservatives called a convention to meet at Houston on January 20, 1868, to allow party leaders from throughout the state to decide whether or not the situation required a new course of action.[32]

At the same time a group of men in Galveston, calling themselves Conservative Reconstructionists, circulated a letter asking for those who sought an early reconstruction to meet with them at Houston on the same date as the Conservative convention. This movement received its impetus from the prominent Galveston banker and merchant T. H. McMahan and the editor of the *Galveston Civilian* Hamilton Stuart. Both were prominent Union men before the war, and they had not joined the Conservatives with Throckmorton in 1866. They had never found themselves at home in Galveston's Union League Republican party, however, and the split at Austin made them even more unlikely to join the Republican party. If the Conservatives managed an alliance with these men the potential strength of the Republican party in Texas would be more greatly depleted.[33]

Large crowds gathered at Houston on the day the two conventions opened. A. J. Hamilton and his former secretary of state, James Bell, were among the observers. The convention of Conservative Reconstructionists opened the morning of January 20 with A. B. Sloanaker, one of President Johnson's key political operatives in the South, in the chair. The election of George Hancock, brother of Judge John Hancock, as permanent chairman indicated that the Johnson men controlled the convention. Although the leaders made overtures to Hamilton and Bell to join them, the two refused to cooperate with an organization dominated by representatives of the president. After organization, the delegates appointed a committee headed by Hancock to consult with the Conservatives about the possibility of a fusion.[34]

While the Conservative Reconstructionists met at the Hutchins House the Conservatives opened their meeting at the county court house. They also appointed a conference committee, then adjourned until after the representatives of the two conventions discussed the possibility of joining together. That evening the committees met. The Conservatives objected to a proposed resolution that proclaimed the loyalty of the convention but the Unionists refused to strike it out. Judge John Hancock telegraphed from Austin that a combined convention must proclaim its loyalty or he would not support it. The conference adjourned without arriving at an agreement for further cooperation between the two conventions.[35]

Following the failure of the conference committees, the Conservative Reconstructionists adjourned their convention with the delegates divided over whether or not they should affiliate with the Conservatives and the national Democratic party or whether they should temporarily abandon politics. All that they could agree upon was their opposition to Negro suffrage. The Conservatives had pressed the idea that a merger was necessary to save the state from Negro supremacy when they lobbied for fusion and that point had made a deep impression.[36]

When the Conservative convention reassembled on January 22 a large number of delegates from the Conservative Reconstruction convention attended, although Flake reported that many Unionists had gone home rather than attend the meeting. The Conservatives passed seven resolutions that received the approval of the Conservative Reconstructionists. They first promised political support to any man who opposed the Africanization of the state. For the election they recommended the fullest possible registration of voters and a vote against the convention. While voting against a convention the Conservatives noted, however, voters should be sure to vote for convention delegates who opposed Negro suffrage. The remaining resolutions dealt with general matters such as immigration, law and order, protection of personal and property rights, and acceptance of the end of the war. Before adjourning the delegates appointed a central committee that consisted of men from both conventions and charged them with assisting in the organization of county and precinct political clubs for action in the election. This coalition of Conservatives and Unionists who had not bolted with Throckmorton in 1866 formed the basis for a reorganized Democratic party. It was a significant event, for one more segment of potential white support for the Republican party had been cut away. Further, the Republicans would have to struggle with an opposition party daily growing stronger and more assertive.[37]

The reformation of the Democratic party helped make the election for delegates to the constitutional convention one of the most violent in the reconstruction period. Throughout the state Republican candidates received hostile responses from white Texans, especially in eastern counties where people proved particularly murderous. At Marshall on December 31, 1867, the city's chief of police, the sheriff, and the deputy sheriff of Harrison County, in the company of a mob, broke up a Republican rally at the county courthouse. In the ensuing riot the whites attempted to assassinate the Republican candidate for the district, Judge Colbert Caldwell. Following the incident Caldwell refused to continue with the canvass because he believed that his life was endangered. He returned to the campaign later, however, when a former Conservative, Anthony B. Norton, offered to canvass with him and General Reynolds provided him with a military escort. When he resumed the campaign he stopped first at Marshall, this time without incident. In Wood County friction burst into conflict when assailants fired upon a Republican rally at the home of Doctor N. J. Gunter, the party's candidate for the convention. The attackers escaped but they killed and wounded several of the people at the rally.[38]

Freedmen's Bureau records support the contention of Republicans that violence increased in the state during the campaign. Of course the fact that Bureau officials often used their records for political purposes casts some doubt upon their credibility. Agents in the field had been reporting between thirty and forty crimes per month from January to June of 1867. Many of these appear to have been personal rather than political, although the two are difficult to distinguish because in most cases the crimes consisted of attacks by whites against blacks. After Sheridan removed Throckmorton in August the reported crime diminished. In October, however, reports began arriving at state headquarters of increased attacks upon freedmen. By the time the campaign opened in December the level had jumped back to that of the preceding spring.[39]

Freedmen crowded to the polls on February 10, 1868, despite the real and threatened violence. At Houston Republicans provided housing for Negroes from the countryside when they came to the county seat to cast their votes. At Webberville, a small community near Austin, the freedmen went to the polls en masse, armed and on horseback, led by a tall black man with a sabre and carrying the national flag. The Conservative press blasted these activities as an attempt to intimidate and discourage whites from voting. But while the Conservatives complained about the methods used to get out the black vote, the Republicans charged that their opponents used intimidation to keep the blacks from voting. At Bastrop the election board suspended the poll when a crowd led by former lieutenant governor George W. Jones gathered around the polling place and harassed black voters. At other locations the Republicans accused the Conservatives of voting for Negro candidates in an effort to discredit the party and draw the race issue before the public.[40]

The returns from the election showed that whites generally stayed away from the polls. Only 31 percent of those registered cast their votes, just 18,379 men. Of that number 7,757 voted in favor of holding a convention and the remaining number opposed it. However, the black community braved the intimidation in great numbers to insure that the constitutional convention would meet. Almost 82 percent of the blacks who registered voted, and they favored a convention almost unanimously.[41]

While the Republican position triumphed in the election, party leaders must not have been pleased with evidence presented in the results. If the returns in Galveston County are typical, they indicated that the Republicans were not attracting old Unionists and, further, those whites who joined the party were not supporting their black allies. In the election at least 879 blacks voted for a convention, but only 202 whites supported it. In 1859 Houston had received 321 votes in the county, while the Republicans, even with the addition of "carpetbag" voters, could produce only two-thirds that amount of white support. Equally important for the party was the apparent refusal of whites to support the party's black candidate in the election, George T. Ruby. Ruby won handily, but he polled only 900 votes, just 21 more than the total number of Negroes voting in the election. If Ruby had attracted the votes of all the blacks, the returns indicated that less than 20 percent of the white voters could have cast their ballots for him. In Harris County, where the Republican party did not have as much strength among the white community as in Galveston, whites appeared less reluctant to support black candidates. There the vote for the convention suggests that party strength consisted of 1,269 blacks and 62 whites. The black candidate in Harris, Charles W. Bryant, received 1,334 votes, or corresponding closely with the 1,331 votes cast in favor of the convention.[42]

While the returns suggest that whites bolted the party rather than vote for black candidates, they also indicate that

blacks were firmly aligned with the Republican party. Of the
3,024 Negroes voting in Galveston, Harris, and Travis counties
only two opposed the Republican position and voted against
the convention. The election solidified the union between blacks
and the Republican party, an alliance that continued through
the rest of the century. The election demonstrated that Republican organizers had built the black community into a well-
running political machine. But if the election indicated Republican success among blacks, it also showed that the party had
failed in the vital task of building and strengthening a biracial
organization. Only 7,757 whites voted in favor of the convention, a number that probably indicated the white Republican
strength in 1868. The returns told party leaders that they had
not even been able to maintain their hold on the Unionists
who had voted for Pease in 1866, the Republican cause attracting 4,937 fewer votes than the Unionist candidate. Only the failure to vote of large numbers of registered whites allowed the
Republicans to call a convention.[43]

The future success of the Republican party in Texas still
required expansion of its base among whites. At the same time
there could be no erosion of support from the black community.
Even after the election Republicans still believed that they had
a chance to establish themselves in the state. General Edmund
J. Davis wrote to Pease that the party's poor showing among
white voters disappointed him, but he insisted that once state
political battles settled down and the old issues reappeared after
the convention the Unionist voters would march into the Republican column.[44]

Congressional reconstruction provided the opportunity for
the Republican party in Texas to take power. The party's leadership, however, achieved only partial success in their efforts
to maximize party strength and consolidate their hold on the
government of the state. With the aid of the military the Republicans managed to place many of their supporters in state
and local offices, but military patronage proved ineffective in
breaking the Conservative hold on the county governments of
the state. The failure of the military commanders to carry out
a thorough and complete program of removals left the Republicans with only token power at the local level and with less
than one-fifth of the elective offices of the state.

The Republicans achieved the same mixed results in their
efforts to build up a broad-based and biracial party. Organiza-

tion and registration of the freedmen was a success, but the coalition with Negroes caused many old Unionists to stay out of the Republican party. Hamilton's recourse to the blacks in the *ab initio* crisis showed the dangers of such a coalition. Worrying about working with Negroes in state politics, these men sought other avenues through which they might participate in state government. The Whig element that joined the Republican party in other states, only to abandon the party before the Democrats regained control, never aligned with the Republicans in Texas. For the Republicans the critical job of securing support in the white community remained a job for the future.

Congressional reconstruction and the power it gave to the Republicans also confronted the party's leadership with the fact that they presided over a coalition of men holding antagonistic views on many questions of policy. When out of power they had been able to ignore this problem. In control of the state government, however, opposing points of view became a source of constant friction. Party success in the future depended at least in part upon the ability of its leaders to reconcile these internal differences. A major test of the party's leadership and its capacity to create a cohesive party in Texas would develop in the constitutional convention of 1868.

CHAPTER 5

Radicals and Conservatives: Factionalism and the Split of Texas Republicanism

A small group of men controlled the Texas Republican party when the state constitutional convention assembled at Austin in June 1868. Governor Pease and the Hamilton brothers, Jack and Morgan, dominated the party's early existence. Its policies and goals were their own. The two governors had woven together a political organization with patronage and appeals to prewar prejudices. With only a few other individuals, they had assumed leadership on their own. They had never received a statewide mandate, even from members of their own party. Party members from throughout the state appeared at the constitutional convention, however, and for the first time all Republicans would have some say in producing their party's policies. The convention would test the coalition and its leadership.

The variety of interests that had joined the Republican party were apparent at the convention. Most of the delegates were white—all but ten of the eighty-odd Republicans—and this racial composition indicated the dominant role of white leaders in a party where blacks provided most of the votes. Most of the whites were "scalawags," drawn from the ranks of antebellum opponents to the Democrats—Unionists, Know-Nothings, Whigs, and Independent Democrats. They had pursued many different courses during the war: seventeen had fought with the Union Army, eleven with the Confederate. Many of the delegates had joined Governor Hamilton in 1865, and twenty-three of the sixty-four "scalawags" had received offices in his government. The convention would show that they did not have a single set of interests. When joined by black delegates and "carpetbaggers" the Republicans appeared even more varied.[1]

Four major blocs, individuals with similar voting patterns, existed among the Republicans. These reflected the most cohesive factions and the powerful interests, but more indicative of the shifting nature of the Republican coalition is the fact that over one-half of the party's members did not support any one of the four consistently. Because of their movement from bloc to bloc as issues changed, no one faction could dominate the convention. The result was a breach between leaders of the various blocs and continued warfare within Republican ranks. Rather than agreeing to and carrying out a Republican plan of action, the delegates used the convention as a battleground to determine what Republicanism would be and which faction would control it. The situation worked in favor of the Democrats who, although a small minority, could influence the convention's course by casting their votes so as to keep Republicans fighting or to obtain moderate actions whenever possible.[2]

The largest Republican bloc, consisting of seven scalawags, two carpetbaggers, and one black, represented the supporters of Governor Pease. For the most part the administration forces came from the central district of the state and the old Unionist strongholds of Northeast Texas. Former governor A. J. Hamilton led this faction and his role in the convention made him, rather than Pease, the chief representative of the administration's position in the state. The bloc usually sided with the agricultural and commercial groups in the state. It supported development of transportation, settlement of the frontier, restoration of law and order, and protection of the civil rights of blacks. It did not want widespread economic or cultural disorganization, however. On the issue of the legality of wartime and postwar legislation, for example, it favored recognition of private rights acquired through such acts. While an associate justice of the state supreme court, Hamilton had indicated his beliefs. In *Luter* v. *Hunter* he wrote that municipal laws, such as tax levies and the creation of corporate bodies to construct internal improvements, were without political significance and "not void, and such rights as have been fairly acquired under them will be upheld and protected," even if they might have indirectly aided the Confederate war effort. The administration also opposed efforts to divide the state. Governor Pease argued that division would only increase the tax burden and lessen the people's ability "to support a system of education and to give aid and encouragement to the measures that are needed to develop the wealth and resources of the state." These delegates also favored the protection of basic civil and political rights of the freedmen as defined in the federal Civil Rights Act of 1866, but did not envision anything more positive. Most of the administration supporters believed that blacks would continue to provide the chief element in the state's agricultural labor force and saw no great need to meet the demands of blacks for such things as public education. Their goals indicated ties with prewar Unionism and also with the interests of the newer and unsettled portions of the state. However, unlike the old Unionists, they had come to see that their goals could be secured by expanding the existing transportation and commercial enterprises of the state. To them the railroads and merchants of Galveston and Houston no longer appeared as ogres.[3]

The second Republican bloc, led by Major James W. Flanagan of Rusk County, consisted of eight delegates who represented interests usually associated with East Texas. Flanagan was typical, a colorful character who had made a name for himself in the small community of Henderson as a lawyer, land speculator, contractor, railroad financier, and planter. Most of his life had been devoted to the construction of a railroad into eastern Texas that would connect the section with the Mississippi River. Flanagan's railroad goals ran counter to those of many men at Galveston and Houston who were more interested in completing lines to tie their own cities with the state's markets. While Flanagan and the others would favor programs for economic development, and would support the disputed rights of individual railroads in the convention, they did not approve policies that would further the expansion of Central Texas's hegemony over the economic and political life of the state. People in the bloc preferred division of the state, so that each section could use its resources for its own development and thus achieve economic autonomy. Generally, the Flanagan bloc was hostile to the interests of the freed slaves. Coming from an agricultural district they still believed that some sorts of restrictions on blacks were necessary to prevent dislocation of their labor force. For the most part they had not fully accepted federal civil rights definitions and looked for ways to avoid their implementation.[4]

The third bloc in the convention was also sectional, composed of nine "scalawags" who represented counties in the western district, the Fourth Congressional District. Four men led this group: Morgan Hamilton, Edmund J. Davis, James P. Newcomb, and Edward Degener. They had all been Unionists.

Davis had served in the First Texas Cavalry, Newcomb had been run out of the state because of his opposition to secession, Degener had spent the war in a military prison in San Antonio, and Hamilton had stayed in Austin where he refused to pay taxes to the Confederate government. Like Flanagan, these four did not appear to oppose the development of transportation in the state, but they did not see any benefits to their own section as a result of administration policies. Consequently they opposed efforts to relieve railroad debts, backed *ab initio* to force a restoration and reallocation of public funds, and supported division. Of the four, Hamilton was the least favorable to internal improvement schemes, or at least those that used public funds for support. His large land holdings made him always sensitive to matters that increased taxes. Members of this bloc held the broadest view on the rights of blacks among the whites in the convention. They made more concessions in the areas of officeholding and education than the other groups. Their position probably did not derive as much from an enlightened point of view as from the fact that they came from a section where blacks were neither a major portion of the population or work force. E. J. Davis had been able to support universal manhood suffrage in the constitutional convention of 1866 without any fear of causing great concern among his constituents. The same would be true on other matters in 1868.[5]

The first three blocs typified political divisions that had existed in the antebellum years, but the fourth represented something new. Four men, three blacks and a carpetbagger, operated in a manner designed to achieve the interests of blacks. The dominant figure in this bloc was George T. Ruby, the black agent of the Freedmen's Bureau schools who had helped to organize the Union League in the spring of 1867. From his entry into politics until the convention, his power had grown. In the autumn of 1867 he had been able to challenge white control of the Galveston council of the League. When he ran for the convention he campaigned on the promise that he would work for the interests of his race. With a firm base in the Galveston League and with his campaign promises, Ruby easily swept aside his white opponents. On economic questions he was ambivalent. He did want to see the convention adopt strong provisions to insure the rights of blacks. His experiences in being refused first-class passage to New Orleans on a Morgan steamship, despite his ability to pay, made him want to prevent the same thing from happening to others of his race. He also desired public support for education to allow blacks to become more than agricultural workers. Ruby's goals challenged the view of blacks held by most white Texans. They further threatened the power of those who used black laborers or who would be taxed to provide schools. The appearance of this black leader and his associates presented a potential problem to the old coalition, since Ruby was able to shift his support to whatever group would best serve his purposes.[6]

The Republican coalition encountered its first problem in the party caucus called to select a candidate for convention president. They found that they could not agree and after a lengthy discussion adjourned to leave the choice to a vote on the convention floor. The decision was risky. Even though the Democrats could not select a president, they could cast the deciding votes if the Republicans split. An open decision gave the Democrats a chance to influence the selection of a man more favorable to themselves than had they faced a united Republican party. One candidate was Judge Colbert Caldwell, the nominee of A. J. Hamilton and the administration. Morgan Hamilton nominated E. J. Davis. Of the two, Davis appeared the more moderate. Many considered Caldwell a rabble-rouser and one of the organizers of the Union League. In the canvass his enemies had tried to kill him. Caldwell's nomination proved an inept move on the part of the administration, and Davis easily defeated him by a vote of forty-three to thirty-three. Although they later denied it, the Democrats apparently voted for Davis. For the administration Caldwell's defeat was serious, since it placed an outsider in the key presidential chair.[7]

The problem of *ab initio* was the first major issue to appear before the delegates; it was introduced by Andrew J. Evans of McLennan County on June 5. His resolution argued that the people had established the federal government, that no government could exist without the permission of the representatives of the people (the Congress), and, consequently, that all government existing in Texas unsanctioned by Congress from the date of secession to the present was illegal and its acts invalid. Evans had proposed to nullify all acts of the civil government from 1861 to 1866 and Morgan Hamilton appeared to be behind the move, still challenging the Pease administration's efforts to enforce the tax laws of the Eleventh Legislature. In the convention, however, others joined him. Some wanted nullification of a law that granted a potentially lucrative railroad charter to a group of former Confederate officers incorporated as the Houston and Great Northern Railroad. Others wanted land seizures made during the war invalidated. *Ab initio* would also have negated land grants made to fraudulent internal improvement schemes. In the convention, however, the fight centered on the legality of an act passed in 1864 that allowed six of the state's railroads to pay portions of their indebtedness to the state school fund in state and Confederate warrants rather than in specie as required by the enabling legislation.[8]

In 1864 the railroads asked to be allowed to use warrants to pay part of the one million dollars in interest they owed on the two million they had borrowed from the school fund between 1858 and 1861. The legislature passed enabling legislation and the roads paid $320,364 on the interest of the debt with Confederate treasury warrants. Although the warrants were practically worthless the legislature required the treasury to accept the paper at face value. Morgan Hamilton accused the railroad owners of conspiring with members of the legislature to pass the bill so that they could unload their "rebel" money before the end came. Invalidating the law of 1864 and forcing the roads to repay the school fund in specie became the rallying point for the *ab initio* men in the convention.[9]

Connection of the school fund with *ab initio* greatly broadened its appeal in the convention. It brought behind the *ab initio*-ists those blacks who believed restoration of the school fund would hasten the organization of public schools. For West Texans, repayment of the debt restored the school fund and would allow future construction, possibly into their section. Leaders of both the West Texas and black blocs came out in favor of the Evans resolution and Morgan Hamilton, whatever his personal reasons, became the leader of the combination. Hamilton held nightly caucuses at which he planned strategy and tried to win converts. At every opportunity he buttonholed delegates to explain the implications of the *ab initio* doctrine and its application to the individual's interests. His efforts included, when necessary, impugning the motives and the loyalty of the governor, an approach that won him the hostility of administration forces in the convention.[10]

A test of strength among the different factions over newspaper patronage provided the first indicator of the potential success of the Evans resolution, since it indicated the division between administration supporters and their opponents in the convention. Governor Pease wanted to give the entire convention printing to the *Austin Republican*, his official newspaper at the capital. A combination of delegates from East Texas, West Texas, and the black community joined against the Democrats and administration men to block the measure by a vote of forty-three to forty-three. Some observers believed that the East Texans had entered into a permanent alliance with other antiadministration groups, but the activities of Republican factions in the convention proved to be anything but permanent. The vote showed that the administration could count on thirty-three Republican votes, that there were forty-three other Republicans who could not be counted on, and that there were ten Democrats who might be used.[11]

That the Republicans had not lined up permanently into administration and antiadministration blocs became apparent when the delegates took up the Evans resolution after it received a favorable report from the Committee on Federal Relations. Evans spoke before the Committee of the Whole in favor of the measure, then Jack Hamilton presented the administration's response. In a two-day speech Hamilton attacked the motives of the men who supported *ab initio*, characterizing them as "selfish interests." Neither side could manage to put together enough votes to force immediate action on the resolution, however. After ten days of discussion its backers abandoned the fight, and E. J. Davis stepped down from the chair to introduce a substitute. Davis's resolution called for validation, by the convention or a subsequent legislature, of all private acts for meritorious object, such as the establishment of corporations, marriages, transfer and registration of deeds, and private contracts. In principle, however, the resolution claimed the illegality of all acts after secession. After a preliminary skirmish with the administration to block its introduction, the resolution went to Morgan Hamilton's Committee on General Provisions. Reported out of committee on July 8, the *ab initio*-ists decided to postpone action on the resolution until another matter had been taken care of.[12]

On July 11 J. W. Flanagan submitted the report of his Committee on Internal Improvements, which contained a section that would have undercut much of the *ab initio* agitation. The report proposed that the convention recognize the validity of payments made by railroad companies during the war. In addition it recommended that the state foreclose on the Buffalo Bayou, Brazos, and Colorado, the Southern Pacific, and the Texas and New Orleans to secure its loans to those roads, although it suggested no action against the Houston and Texas Central and its branch, the Washington County. If passed, the school fund would have remained bankrupt. The foreclosures represented another way for the railroads to get themselves out of debt. They owed nearly eight million dollars to creditors in the North, in addition to what they owed the state, but Texas had the first lien on the railroad property. Ferdinand Flake believed that Flanagan's purpose was to put the roads up for sale at a time when Northern investors would not appear in Texas to bid on them. Flake thought that the owners could buy their roads back from the state at a fraction of their real value, free from debts and ready for expansion. A number of lobbyists, including former secretary of state James Bell, appeared at Austin to lobby in favor of the report.[13]

The *ab initio*-ists saw the threat and countered with a report from the special Select Committee on Railroads that called for the sale of all the companies indebted to the state and for a declaration that payments made under the law of 1864 were invalid. The two reports came before the convention on August 19. The delegates tabled the Select Committee's report, forty-five to twenty-nine, with East Texans and administration men lined up against West Texans, Democrats, and blacks. The alignment then shifted and they tabled the Flanagan measure too, forty-two to thirty-four. The Republicans who stayed outside the major blocs had chosen to oppose both reports.[14]

On the following day administration men, realizing that they could dispose of Davis's *ab initio* resolution, forced a vote on it. In a roll call that paralleled the tabling of the Select Committee's report, the delegates tabled *ab initio*. Caldwell then introduced an administration measure to recognize the nullity of the acts of the state government after secession, on the condition that it did not prejudice private rights granted by the state. Caldwell's resolution recognized the principle advocated by Evans, Davis, and Morgan Hamilton and preserved the legislation endorsed by the Davis proposal, but it also approved the controversial railroad acts. At this point several delegates who had supported Evans's resolution switched in favor of Caldwell's. Perhaps they realized that nothing more positive could be obtained in the convention and wanted to keep alive the principle. The Democrats who had backed the administration against the Evans and Davis proposals opposed Judge Caldwell's. Despite the Democratic reverse, the administration's measure passed easily by a vote of forty-five to twenty-eight.[15]

Through much of the discussion of *ab initio*, George Ruby and the black delegates who voted with him supported the West Texans in favor of the Evans and Davis resolutions. In return, they found the West Texans allies in their own efforts to press the idea of civil rights being written into the constitution. The Committee on General Provisions, controlled by Morgan Hamilton, provided the means to introduce their measures to the floor. Typical of the work was the fourth section of the proposed Bill of Rights. The fourth section tried to broaden the idea of rights beyond simply equal protection before the law to equal treatment in areas of the private sector. The section declared unconstitutional all discrimination on public conveyances, in places of business and public resort, and in establishments licensed by the state.[16]

Section Four provoked an outraged response among most of the white delegates. Administration forces lined up with East Texans, Democrats, and most of the uncommitted Republicans to oppose the blacks and their West Texas backers. The whites viewed the effort as an attempt to give blacks "social equality." In public they argued that the differences between the two races precluded equal treatment. William Horne of Fort Bend suggested that only by maintaining distinctions between the races could they live in harmony. He went on to argue that if society introduced competition "the negro inevitably goes to the wall, and his hope of mental and moral advancement and of physical well being are at an end." Implicit in his statement was Horne's belief that blacks could not be fully free until they had learned their social duties from whites. Incorporate measures to prevent social discrimination in the Bill of Rights? The delegate from Fort Bend spoke for most of the other whites when he said: "I maintain that in the Bill of Rights there is ample protection to the black men. But, sir, let not the aspirations of the black man be confounded with his rights."[17]

Davis realized that the section could never be passed as written and introduced a substitute designed to keep it intact but give the racists in his party an out. The Davis substitute outlawed racial discrimination, but authorized the owners of the facilities in question to prescribe rules and regulations necessary to secure "comfort, good order and decency." The state would be committed to the idea of equal rights, but the individual could do what he wanted in his own establishment within limited restrictions. The delegates refused to pass even this modified proposal and substituted their own that recognized the "equality of all persons before the law." The Democrats refused to support this more generally acceptable provision and found themselves allied with Flanagan and the East Texans in opposition. It passed, however, fifty-three to twenty-two, an expression of the maximum the Republican majority would give to blacks on civil rights. While the black delegates failed to obtain the Bill of Rights that they wanted, they had found a political ally in the West Texans. The two groups operated together through most of the rest of the convention.[18]

When the delegates considered a public school system the West Texans and black blocs cooperated unsuccessfully again, but their work on the measure helped formulate the school policies of the later Republican administration. Proponents of the school system wanted free public education and realized that in some counties economic and demographic conditions would make it very expensive. These conditions made the establishment of segregated schools almost impossible and, as a result, they wanted the constitution not to take a stand against an integrated system where necessary. The resolution that they introduced would have prevented the legislature from mandating segregation, but they could not get the votes. Most white Republicans were unwilling to accept the idea of blacks and whites going to school together.[19]

The third major question brought before the convention was division. On June 24 the Committee on Division reported a resolution to endorse a plan before Congress that would have divided Texas into three states. The bill had been introduced from the House Committee on Reconstruction by Fernando C. Beaman of Michigan on behalf of numerous Republican businessmen and politicians in West Texas. From the end of the war they had petitioned Congress to create a new state west of the Colorado or Brazos rivers. In December 1866, E. Degener, I. A. Paschal, a prominent banker George W. Brackenridge, and others asked for division. In February 1868, many of the same men repeated the appeal to Thaddeus Stevens. In both petitions the West Texans played upon party sympathies by arguing that a new state was necessary to save them from a disloyal majority that persecuted them for their Unionism or Republicanism. If given the chance they believed a firmly loyal state could be created out of the western counties. But the driving force behind division which united the West with East Texans was economics. In the petition to Stevens the divisionists noted that they wanted to be free of Central Texas and the domination of the coastal cities "so that 'our' credit can be applied toward building 'our' roads, as we are not properly tributary to Houston or Galveston."[20]

Division brought about a different alignment than previous issues. Blacks remained combined with the West Texans, but they had a new ally in the East Texans. The Pease faction stood alone on the issue. Under Jack Hamilton's leadership they worked against the committee report, first by introducing counter proposals designed to play upon the ambitions of different divisionists by altering boundaries. Hamilton's son-in-law, William W. Mills of El Paso, submitted one such resolution that would have given El Paso and much of western Texas to the United States government. The divisionists managed to stay together and vote down each of Hamilton's efforts to split them. Hamilton then turned to parliamentary procedure to stop them. Disregarding the wishes of the majority he halted all business in the convention through skillful use of a "call of the House." Under the rules fifteen members could sustain a call. This suspended business until all members absent without a satisfactory excuse appeared on the floor. By having enough delegates off the floor Hamilton managed to stall business for more than two weeks. With other business pressing, the convention voted to leave the matter to Congress. Hamilton had proved himself an astute parliamentary manager, but his tactics made enemies for him, expecially among the East Texans.[21]

With most of the convention's time devoted to *ab initio*, civil rights, and division, the business of drafting a constitution was left to the committees. Only one other major issue reached the floor and received a full debate—violence. Murder, robbery, and mayhem had taken place in Texas since its first settlement, part of the frontier tradition of the state. The war and subsequent breakup appeared to worsen an already bad situation. Because they believed that much of the violence was directed toward themselves or their constituents, its suppression was a vital concern of the delegates. Violence alone, of all the issues

before the convention, drew all the Republican factions together. When the Committee on Lawlessness and Violence indicated
that some 509 whites and 468 blacks had been murdered in the
state between the end of the war and the opening of the convention and suggested that Congress be asked for the power to
organize a state militia, party members voted almost unanimously to approve the report. They later appropriated $25,000
for the use of Governor Pease in apprehending criminals. To
try to obtain federal intervention in the state, the convention
sent Morgan Hamilton and Colbert Caldwell to Washington
with the committee report and instructions to work for laws
in Congress that would insure the appointment of loyal men
to state offices, the appointment of new voting registrars, and
the authorization of a state militia.²²

By mid-August of 1868 the delegates had not drafted a
new constitution. Political conditions in the state encouraged
many leaders to adjourn the convention until after the autumn
elections and the reassembly of Congress. Increased violence
against Republicans created fear, so that many believed without
stronger congressional intervention their effort was in jeopardy.
Fear had also furthered a split within the Republican ranks that
did not appear to be reconcilable. When General Reynolds reported that the convention had exhausted the funds originally
appropriated to finance it and refused to allocate more money,
any Republicans who had not made up their minds in favor of
adjournment came into line. After resolving to reconvene the
convention on the first Monday in December, after the congressional elections, the delegates left Austin.²³

The violence that provoked such concern among Republicans appeared to be the result of efforts to reorganize the Democratic party in 1868; at least that is what the Republicans
believed. The Democrats always denied any political motivation
behind what was going on. They suggested that it was the upheaval typical of a frontier community, worsened by the social
dislocations caused by the war and subsequent federal interference in local affairs. The Democrats charged the Republicans
with intentional misrepresentation of conditions to prompt further intervention and to justify repressive police measures. According to the Democrats the mobbing of Republicans was not
the result of purposeful violence but of leaderless and spontane-
ous outbursts against hated symbols of the state's defeat and
degradation. The Democratic analysis gained wide acceptance

among contemporaries and later historians, but it is clear that much violence was directed at Republicans, and they had valid reasons for suspecting it was part of a Democratic campaign against them.[24]

In January 1868, the Democrats had started organizing local clubs throughout the state. Party leaders promoted their party's resurgence with a vigorous campaign of racist propaganda. They charged their opponents with wanting to saddle the state with Negro and radical rule. They warned Texans that the result would be disfranchisement of all whites, Negro participation on juries, mixed schools, and ultimately miscegenation. The party executive committee pictured a frightening world in the "shackles" of Negro rule, with radicals "punishing" whites for refusing to abandon the Democratic party or to acknowledge "the African as your equal." At stake in the state's future political battles were the "freedom" and "honor" of the white race. The only solution for whites was joining the Democratic party. They called for "no apathy, no idleness, no discord among those who would save the state from the disgrace and ruin of being ruled by strange adventurers, native demagogues and negro ignorance. Every man who is opposed to the social equality of the negro should commence and continue the earnest work directed towards the success of the conservative party until the troubles of the country are ended."[25]

Whether Democratic leaders intended it or not is not clear, but a large number of Texans translated the "earnest work" as violence against the Republicans. Charles C. Gillespie of the *Houston Telegraph*, later to join the Republican party himself, urged an audience gathered for the thirty-second anniversary of the battle of San Jacinto to lynch the Republicans. "There are grape vines enough in the old battle ground," he said, "to hang every damned one of them; and if I had my way I would have every damned one of them hung as high as Haman before sundown." At the same time others organized secret societies, usually known as the Ku Klux Klan. First noticed in March, the Klan's activities consisted of ghostly parades, publication of cryptic newspaper notices, and midnight meetings in graveyards. Republican newspapers treated these happenings as a joke, a Democratic answer to the Union League, but the amused observations ended when the pranks turned into destruction of property, intimidation, and murder.[26]

In May 1868, an almost systematic attack upon critical

points of the Republican organization, its communications, and its leadership, began throughout the state. The offices of the Freedmen's Bureau and Bureau school buildings, gathering places for blacks, became prime targets for arsonists. At Jefferson terrorists unsuccessfully tried to bomb the offices of A. B. Norton's *Union Intelligencer*. Such disruption interfered with the dissemination of political information among Republicans. Both white and black leaders received threats. In some towns retaliation was in the form of ostracism; in others violence was used. Terrorists singled out black political leaders as the special object of their activities. At Bastrop masked riders kidnapped two delegates to the state convention of the Union League and hanged them. Assassins murdered the influential Negro politician, A. R. Wilson, in Burleson County. At other places black leaders simply disappeared, not to be found again.[27]

By the middle of the summer of 1868 a virtual state of war existed in some areas of Texas. One of the worst incidents took place at Millican in Brazos County where a group of white horsemen who identified themselves as the Ku Klux Klan rode into a small Negro community and lynched the leader of the Union League, Miles Brown. The following day a local black minister, George E. Brooks, gathered a group that attempted to arrest the alleged leader of the whites, William Holliday. That day and the next both groups fought, and on July 17 federal troops arrived, called in by the local Bureau agent, and dispersed the Negro "mob." The army reported that it had killed five blacks, although other reports indicated that as many as sixty may have died on the seventeenth, over a hundred in the four-day battle. After the army scattered the blacks, whites pursued them and dealt harshly with the survivors. They captured Brooks and lynched him. His death, coupled with the murder of Brown, deprived the black community of political leaders and damaged the local Republican organization. Such activities provided ample evidence to Republicans that their political opponents were using violence to turn them out of office.[28]

Violence, especially that directed toward blacks in the Republican party, helped undermine the control exercised by the Pease administration over Union League voters. At the state Union League convention in Austin on June 25 the black delegates were not responsive to the efforts of their president James Bell, the governor's unobtrusive but ever-present advisor. On the first day the rebellious delegates condemned the administration in resolutions that cited its weak stand on civil rights, its hesitation to prosecute white terrorists, and its failure to recognize blacks with offices. George Ruby turned unrest into revolt when he challenged the regular organization and ran against Bell for president. The delegates disregarded the discipline of white leaders and voted for Ruby. The regulars prevented a complete defeat by holding on to some offices, but only because the rebels had not prepared a challenge against all League officials.[29]

Ruby's victory caused discomfort at Austin since it removed the administration's chief mechanism for mobilizing black voters from the governor's control. The Democrats realized what had happened and showed little sympathy. The party press said that Pease had gotten what he had deserved for appealing to "vulgar prejudice" in building a party. He had unchained a tempest and the Negro had proved unmanageable, "a real Tartar" in Texas politics. The *Galveston News* believed that Ruby's election foreshadowed disaster for the white Republican leaders. Its editors wrote: "Unless Governor Pease, A. J. Hamilton and Judge Bell are saved by the success of a better party than the one they have unchained they will at last find themselves insulted and trampled upon by those who once seemed only too proud to be called their political followers and servants."[30]

The black revolt carried over in the Republican state convention at Austin on August 12. This time, however, the administration was prepared. A majority of the delegates were white and the administration controlled enough proxies to prevent blacks from taking over. The administration had not counted, however, on Ruby finding support among whites. On the evening before the first session Ruby met with Morgan Hamilton, Edmund Davis, James Newcomb, and other people dissatisfied with the administration in the convention, to discuss a course of action. The result was an alliance and a decision to support Judge R. P. Crudup of McLennan County for chairman against the regular organization's candidate, James Bell. Their combination was not enough to prevent Bell's election, and the administration then proceeded to fill the committees with its own men.[31]

On the second day of the convention George W. Paschal introduced a proposed platform. It was an innocent enough draft with the usual formal endorsements of the national party platform and candidates. It also restated commitments to the protection of citizens and the carrying out of reconstruction laws. The proposed platform concluded with a statement of belief in the Republican party as the symbol of progress and liberal principles, the organization within which Northern capital and aid necessary to invigorate industry could be obtained. Davis responded with a minority report that offered two additional resolutions to "set at rest questions that are disturbing the Union party, and may possibly cause estrangement among those that should be friends." He asked for a declaration nullifying all legislation passed during the rebellion with the exception of land grants to persons in actual residence. He proposed the annulment of all laws that authorized the use of state warrants to pay debts of the railroads to the school fund. The *ab initio* crisis of the constitutional convention had shown up again.[32]

The Davis resolution received lengthy debate, but the general did not have enough votes in the convention. When it became apparent that he could not get his resolutions passed, Davis and his supporters walked out. The bolters decided to take their appeal to the people, probably realizing that enough dissatisfaction existed among Republicans that they could be successful. On August 15 they met in the Senate chamber and formed a new Republican organization in opposition to the regulars. The platform they adopted included Davis's report to the regular convention, a call for rigid enforcement of the law, and an objection to proscriptive residence requirements for officeholding that blacks believed were leveled at them. Another plank agreed with the party regulars on the importance of manufacturing and internal improvements, but asserted that a free public school system should take precedence and advised the collection of all money owed to the school fund without delay.[33]

With division and *ab initio* bottled up in the constitutional convention and Pease in control of the regular convention, Davis and the West Texans had gone outside the party. Their platform indicated that they hoped for support from the Union League. The key to its endorsement was George Ruby, who wanted a strong commitment to public schools and protection for blacks, and the bolters were ready to give him that. Ruby attended the Davis meeting but did not commit himself to the bolt in advance. After the Committee on Address presented a platform so coincidental with his own interests, the Galveston politician joined with his allies from the constitutional convention in their bolt from the regular party.[34]

The regulars tried to settle their problems with the bolters, but without success. Named by the convention chairman of the regular executive committee, John L. Haynes headed a special group appointed to seek a compromise. The bolters reportedly agreed to give up *ab initio* in return for a promise that the railroads would pay the disputed school debt. Haynes offered in return additions to the party platform that declared the ordinance of secession and subsequent legislation null and void and illegal, but respected those laws enacted for municipal purposes, "the good of society," or creating private rights. Neither side had given anything, and the two sides could not be brought together.[35]

The Republican party had split. Differences among white leaders had furnished the reasons. Dissatisfaction among black leaders and voters had provided the possibility for a successful attack against control of the party by Pease and his associates. Although practically meaningless with regard to the policies of the individual factions, Texans began to call the Davis group Radicals and the forces of the governor Conservatives. Texas had two Republican parties in the field, vying with each other for the limited voting base available to them.

The Radicals threatened Governor Pease with a disaster, especially if they could draw black voters to their cause. To prevent Davis and his ally Ruby from using the Union League to divert blacks away from their party, Pease, Hamilton, Bell, and others began efforts to break up the League. Their chief object was the chapter at Galveston that served as Ruby's base of power. As a first step the Conservatives formed the "Union Club," their stated purpose being to break the hold of the secret Union League on Republican politics in the city and to dispose of Ruby as a political leader. Local white politicians understood that Ruby would not be easy to destroy, but they saw no other course. Ferdinand Flake, reflecting a fear of increasing black power and the type of racism typical among many local Republicans, argued that it would be best not to confront Ruby directly. He proposed that whites withdraw their support of Ruby and the League and leave the "demagogues" in control. Neither they nor the freedmen, in Flake's opinion, had the brains necessary to maintain party power.[36]

The administration was not willing to risk Ruby's lack of brains and began a more direct assault in the local chapter meeting of September 7. Dr. Robert K. Smith, a delegate to the convention, accused Ruby of "political treason." Smith, a physician who had come to Texas with the federal army and then remained as city health officer, charged that "The Ruby" had not represented his black constituents in the convention. He alleged that Ruby had agreed to support A. B. Sloanaker, a Galveston Conservative, in exchange for a bribe of $600. Blacks did not need a traitor or a criminal as their leader. At the Galveston Republican Association meeting two nights later Ruby denied Smith's allegation. When the meeting adjourned, a fight broke out between the two and the police had to pull them apart. Rather than undermining local confidence in Ruby, however, Smith's attack only encouraged greater support. A reporter indicated that had the police not been present during the fight blacks might have killed Smith. After this encounter the administration people in Galveston backed away from Ruby.[37]

While the Conservatives attempted to destroy the power of the League, the Radicals endorsed it as the backbone of the Republican party in Texas. The state executive committee appointed by the bolters included Ruby and other prominent members of the organization. Newcomb defended his group's reliance on the League in the San Antonio newspapers. "The Union Leagues are the only real organizations of the Republican Party in the State," he wrote. "The Union Leagues have brought us one victory, it has the power to give us another and in its power the future destinies of our State are held." As a result the local Leagues began to move behind the Radicals. Spokesmen for the Conservative Republicans found themselves on the defensive at rallies held in the autumn of 1868. At Galveston on September 9 A. J. Hamilton had to explain his vote against requiring public transportation and public houses to be opened to Negroes. In the same city Judge Caldwell begged an audience to ignore the lures held out to them and reminded them that he had always favored unqualified Negro suffrage. The *ab initio* faction was dangerous, he warned, and "the colored man who suffers it to disturb him and plants himself upon it, perils his political safety."[38]

As their support among blacks began to slip, the Conservative Republicans initiated changes in their policies to try to pick up backing elsewhere. The most significant was a change in attitude toward disfranchising former Confederates. On June 3 Governor Pease had asked for the exclusion of enough former rebels to insure that they could never regain control of the state government. Now his spokesmen embraced a policy of universal amnesty and suffrage. At Jefferson Colbert Caldwell said that he believed all whites must be enfranchised, exclaiming that "no power shall degrade or enslave these blue-eyed and fair-haired countrymen of mine." John Haynes wrote in the *Austin Republican*:

Those who are wedded to the policy of disfranchisement will probably appeal to the colored voters of the State to sustain their action. I have never yet deceived this class of our people and can afford to tell them now that such a policy on their part would drive thousands of whites, native and foreign, from their support, and would in all probability, force the formation of parties in this State down to the narrow question of race and color. They cannot afford to approve a system of disfranchisement intended to give them, with a handfull of office-seekers, the control of the State.

When the constitutional convention reassembled, the administration men would be committed to a liberal franchise provision.[39]

When the delegates returned to Austin for the constitutional convention on December 7, 1868, the political situation and issues had changed greatly from what they had been at adjournment. The West Texans had achieved a permanent alliance with the blacks in the new Radical Republican movement. Because they had stripped control of the Union League from Governor Pease, the Radicals could now expect more convention support from delegates sent to Austin by League votes. In addition *ab initio*, a major issue dividing factions in the first session, had been removed from consideration as a result of the *Texas* v. *White* decision by the United States Supreme Court. The *ab initio*-ists had hoped for a decision that clearly defined the illegality of Civil War state government, but they had not received it. Instead the court had accepted the argument of state indestructibility advanced by George W. Paschal, an associate of Pease and Jack Hamilton. Most Texans no longer believed that a blanket declaration of the nullity of the state government after secession was possible. Although not completely dead, *ab initio* no longer served as a point of contention.[40]

During the second session the question of dividing the state became the central object of interest. In the first session a coalition of East Texans, West Texans, and blacks had held a slight majority on the issue, but had not been able to overcome the obstructionist tactics of Jack Hamilton. Bolstered by new adherents as a result of the recess, the divisionists returned with a promise to carry out a sustained fight. The day after the convention reconvened J. W. Flanagan brought up the topic by introducing a resolution to permit taking up the question of division. The resolution failed, however, because a resolution passed during the first session required the convention to wait for action by Congress before considering the question again. Through the month of December the divisionists worked to rescind this resolution, only to face Hamilton's continued delaying moves. Hamilton again deadlocked the convention, and by the middle of January a solution had not been reached. When Davis asked General E. R. S. Canby for a remedy, Canby suggested that the convention should alter the rule allowing calls of the house. The result was a resolution to amend the rule so that a call of the house required only the presence of members who had been in attendance on the preceding five days. When the antidivisionists attempted to block it with a call, Davis ruled that all delegates were present, basing his ruling on the point that the roll call on the amendment should be made in accordance with the proposed change. The result was its passage by a vote of forty-two to twenty-eight and an end to the delay.[41]

Breaking Hamilton's roadblock allowed the convention to consider division. The result was the quick passage of a resolution to send a committee to Washington to ask Congress to divide the state into more convenient units. The passage of the division resolution on January 20 was the result of cooperation among blacks, West, and East Texans. Their action together on this measure would be the basis for later political activity within the Radical Republican faction. After sending the committee to Washington, the divisionists wanted to adjourn the convention, without a constitution. They failed in this, however, and on January 27, after two months of session, the convention took up the constitution for the first time. The various provisions had been worked over in committee and the convention moved rapidly through these sections. Only the question of suffrage qualifications provoked any real dispute. The Radicals had supported a provision that established a system of registration and disfranchisement that excluded all federal and state officers, ministers, and newspapermen who had favored and openly supported the rebellion. It also excluded members of secret orders hostile to reconstruction. The Conservatives joined with the East Texans to offer a substitute that allowed all men to vote except those disqualified by the United States Constitution. The substitute passed and the delegates moved hastily through other measures. They agreed to an appointed judiciary, a system of public schools, and a more powerful executive. Unnoticed in the speed to put together a constitution were provisions that limited the use of school funds and prohibited the appropriation of public lands for the aid of internal improvements. Both would become important in later Republican party struggles.[42]

The radicals opposed the convention's work and protested its compromise on *ab initio* and failure to disfranchise former rebels. On the suffrage question they felt the majority had "deliberately removed from the constitution every safeguard for the protection of the loyal voter, white and black." On the evening of February 5, led by Davis, they attempted to adjourn the convention rather than end it. Both James Newcomb and George Ruby submitted resignations. Ruby protested the continuation of a body whose action would only disgrace the entire country. Still, the majority refused to adjourn.[43]

The next morning the administration's forces met before the appointed time and, trying to prevent an adjournment before finishing the constitution, declared themselves the convention and elected M. L. Armstrong chairman. They sent a committee to consult with General Canby who informed them he was willing to recognize them as the official convention, but only for the purpose of winding up business and nothing else. Work ceased, however, when the regular convention's secretary fled with the papers and deposited them at Canby's office. Unable to proceed, the rump convention agreed to meet again two days later.

Davis protested Canby's decision while the Armstrong group met and the commander reconsidered. He authorized Davis to convene the convention and adjourn it *sine die*. On the evening of the sixth, Davis and several others met in the convention's hall. Davis read Canby's order that directed the adjutant general of the district to take over the archives of the convention and appointed a committee to sift through these papers to prepare a constitution for public consideration. Davis then adjourned the convention while Jack Hamilton and others jeered from the gallery. The administration forces did not believe Canby had authorized Davis to adjourn the meeting, but his decision was made clear on February 8 when the Armstrong delegates returned to find a party of federal troops sitting in the door of the convention hall. Canby's action ended the constitutional convention nine months after it had started and placed the completion of its document in the hands of an appointed committee.[44]

The Republican party emerged from the convention of 1868 split into two parties. Each had its own executive committee and state organization. The Conservative Republicans, supporters of the policies of the Pease administration, had held on to the regular party machinery, but had lost control of the Union League. This loss cut deeply into their ability to attract voters among blacks and created a situation that forced them to explore alternative sources of support in order to maintain power. The hostility of the Democrats to the Republicans and the violence of 1868 made the discovery of votes among whites unlikely, but it was the only direction to pursue. The Conservatives used the second session of the constitutional convention to prepare the way for such a move.

The Radical Republicans consisted of a combination of blacks and West Texans. To secure sectional goals, the West Texans had been willing to make concessions to the blacks, and these formed the basis for political cooperation. Whether the Radicals could attract enough voters to their cause to be a viable party remained to be seen. The issue of race, as it was being drawn by the Democrats, made it difficult for whites to remain in a biracial coalition.

Many Republicans remained outside of either organization. The followers of J. W. Flanagan had cooperated with each faction. They remained to be convinced, however, which group would serve their interests best. The Conservatives opposed Flanagan's project of division and did not support his railroad goals. An alliance with the Radicals, however, would require overcoming a host of racial prejudices and hostilities. The struggles over ratifying the constitution and over the subsequent state election would determine the alignments among Republican factions and would decide which party would direct the subsequent course of reconstruction.

CHAPTER 6

Texas Republicans in the State Election of 1869

The constitutional convention had witnessed the public split among leaders of the Republican party. The subsequent state election would determine which faction would be able to implement its policies. Both had to take into account two major factors in determining their plans of action. Registration figures indicated that the successful group would have to appeal to a biracial electorate. There were not enough blacks to pitch an appeal solely to them. Neither could a faction expect to be elected by making its appeal to whites only. In addition, whatever approach they made to the local electorate, Texas politicians had to consider the needs of officials at Washington and try to appease them in this campaign, since until Texas came back into the Union they possessed the potential to intervene.

The national dimension of the election in 1869 was always a critical part of local Republican thought. Republicans at Washington had the power to insure acceptance or rejection of the proposed constitution. They also were keys to obtaining the black vote. The faction given the blessing of the national leadership received the symbolic approval of the party of Lincoln and the liberating United States Army. It was not surprising, therefore, that the Texas campaign first turned to Washington rather than to the local scene.

The struggle for national recognition took place within the context of an apparent revolt in the constituency of Northern Republicans. By 1869 party leaders faced a growing demand to back down on Negro suffrage and to end reconstruction. As a result Republican positions on these measures had softened considerably. In the national elections Ulysses S. Grant campaigned promising moderation and a retreat from reconstruction. He was portrayed as the peacemaker and he carefully guarded his conservative reputation. While the party did not withdraw its endorsement of congressional reconstruction, Grant sounded the major theme of the campaign in his accept- ance speech when he said: "Let us have peace."[1]

At the same time, Republican leaders did not desire a com- plete collapse of their reconstruction efforts. In addition to ide- ological issues, fear of a return to power by the Democrats if they abandoned the South caused Northern politicians to look warily to events there. Given the right circumstances they could be pushed back into a more radical position. When the Texas convention ended, affairs in other Southern states had already provoked sentiments for a hard line. When Georgia's legislature attempted to expel its black members, Congress had shown its teeth and returned the state to military rule. But while willing to take such measures, congressional Republicans tried to avoid situations that might necessitate them. They wanted to secure rights, but without the use of force. As a result the com- plete loyalty of Southern parties concerned Northern officials.[2]

The Texas groups that went to Washington immediately after the state convention attempted to use Nothern fears to their advantage. Both attacked the motives and policies of their opponents while assuring party leaders of the correctness of their own. Jack Hamilton and his supporters arrived first and opened the attack, claiming they represented the loyal elements in Texas and asking for an early election and rapid readmission of the state. They pictured their opponents as mere office seek- ers who had jumped on issues such as *ab initio* for selfish pur- poses. The Hamilton men focused particularly on Generals Sheridan, Griffin, and Reynolds's opposition to *ab initio* since that seemed to show how the bolters were little more than "as- piring extremists." Given the situation in the North, the charge of extremism represented a major threat to the hope of the bolters.[3]

Supporters of Morgan Hamilton's executive committee fol- lowed the former governor into Washington. On March 7 they met with Benjamin Wade and charged that A. J. Hamilton and E. M. Pease were political traitors who had abandoned the Republican party to ally with the Conservatives. They urged a delay in the election to prevent the alleged alliance from de- stroying Republicanism in the state. They also urged division, if nothing else could be done, so that loyalty could be protected in the western districts. E. J. Davis elaborated on the charges in a letter to R. C. Schenck of the House Select Committee on

Reconstruction: "An arrangement seemed to have been made between some of our conservative Republicans, and the rebel leaders, under which there are to be no disfranchisements. The understanding is that some of the (so called) Republicans are to be elected to Congress because they can take the test oath, while the state is to remain in Conservative hands." These charges aimed at the fears of Northerners who did not want to intervene in the South again.[4]

The immediate purpose of the two factions was to convince the Committee on Reconstruction, which possessed the power to effect delays. That committee provided the bolters with a favorable forum since its chairman, Benjamin Butler, looked unfavorably on the activities of the Texas regulars. Butler considered himself the heir of Thaddeus Stevens in Congress and the special protector of loyal whites and blacks in the South. As a result, he was sensitive to signs of potential disloyalty. Further, he did not trust Jack Hamilton. After testimony before the committee on March 30, then April 1 and 3, Butler wanted the Texas election postponed. Benjamin F. Whitemore of South Carolina introduced a resolution to the House that would have delayed action indefinitely. However, concern over the apparent extremism of the bolters created opposition within the committee.[5]

When the Whitemore report came to the floor of Congress the opponents in the committee managed to force a compromise. Their resolution overrode the convention's election mandate and delayed the vote; however, Congress gave the president power to call an election. This appeared to place the decision in the hands of forces favorable to the regulars, since Grant seemed to favor the cause of Jack Hamilton. The bolters, on the other hand, could count on the president to move slowly and cautiously in the matter.[6]

It is important to note, however, that the president had remained equivocal in his support of Hamilton. General Reynolds was a friend of Grant and had advanced Jack Hamilton's cause before the president. He had persistently opposed division of the state and thus earned the hostility of Davis and Morgan Hamilton. Reynolds had taken the regulars to the White House for an interview to inform the president of events in the state, and they had been received warmly. But Grant avoided giving a definite statement as to when an election would be held in Texas or which faction he favored. The interview pleased the regulars who thought it strengthened their position. However, they were aware of the president's uncertainty on local matters.[7]

After Congress had placed matters in the hands of the president, the local leaders returned home to prepare for what they thought would be an immediate canvass. Jack Hamilton announced that he would campaign for governor along lines designed to build broader support among whites. He hoped to win the support of many of the leaders of the prewar Democratic party. The bolters, on the other hand, turned to the organization of the Union League to secure their own political goals.[8]

The white policy had been broached by Jack Hamilton at Brenham in Washington County shortly before he went to Washington. He was careful in his approach. He did not propose to abandon Republican principles, but he was willing to compromise with the Democrats. The speech contained a defense of his party's actions in the convention that had prevented the disfranchisement of former Confederates, blocked integration of the schools, and prevented the subordination of whites to the rule of white demagogues and Negroes. Hamilton believed these actions merited support for his party and the proposed constitution. He characterized himself as a moderate who had taken a less radical position on the rights of Negroes. He told his listeners: "It was a good deal to make the black man free, but to say that his former master, a man of education, culture, and refinement, shall be placed behind him, disfranchised, would create ill feelings among any men on earth."[9]

Leading Democrats recognized that Hamilton had proposed compromise and responded favorably. The editors of the conservative *Texas State Gazette* at Austin praised his new departure and the *Houston Telegraph* called upon him to run for governor. Each promised him the support of conservative men throughout the state. At the same time the Democrats also circulated a private letter among leading party men that solicited backing for Hamilton. Former postmaster general of the Confederacy, John H. Reagan, typified Democratic sentiment when he wrote Ashbel Smith: "All concur in indicating that true policy makes it proper for us to run him for Governor if he will accept the position. He has shown that he can forget past differences for the public good, and we should not do less."[10]

Hamilton realized that this position among the old Democratic leaders was one of temporary expediency. Certainly their correspondence concerning the position toward Hamilton made clear they believed support for Hamilton was the quickest way to end reconstruction. Ashbel Smith called the election of Hamilton "the shortest road to the ultimate triumph of the Democratic party in the State." Reagan supported him because "he can do more than any other person I know to divide the Republican party and defeat the extreme radicals." Democratic newspaper editors did not hesitate to say the same thing in public. Their support for Hamilton was the choice of a lesser evil. To them he was better than the other likely candidates for governor, particularly E. J. Davis.[11]

What Hamilton hoped to accomplish in such a situation is not clear, although he apparently hoped to draw whites into a permanent alliance from this temporary one. If they could be persuaded to act with him in one election, perhaps they would do so again. The program was risky for it created potential suspicion among white Republicans. After approaching the Democrats the governor reassured his own followers that he was not selling out to the Democrats and would never run for governor as anything but a Republican. His spokesmen in Texas worked to dispel the rumors of a "sellout." Edwin M. Wheelock, a supporter of Pease and editor of the *San Antonio Express*, warned Democrats to "take a back seat" in state politics and not expect to assert their will on Hamilton. While willing to compromise on issues such as civil rights for blacks and disfranchisement of Confederates, Hamilton did not intend to pursue a course that would allow the Democrats to return to power.[12]

Despite Hamilton's reassurances, his efforts at reconciliation with the Democrats stimulated concern among many party members. As a result of this concern a movement for compromise among Republicans grew during the spring. Although aimed in part at Jack Hamilton, the general impetus appears to have been the belief that to go into the election divided into two factions was political suicide. The intent of the movement's leaders was a party convention in which some sort of conciliation could be achieved and a compromise Republican ticket agreed upon.[13]

E. J. Davis believed that the compromise movement was the work of supporters of Governor Pease, since a major Republican behind it turned out to be Pease's supporter at Galveston, Ferdinand Flake. Davis and Morgan Hamilton approached the compromises with caution. Pease denied any ambition to make the canvass, however, and expressed surprise when Republican newspapers continued to express their belief that he would run. Despite his disavowals the men who worked for compromise may have believed that he would make the race if he were convinced his candidacy was necessary to save the party.[14]

The motives behind the movement are probably best seen in the work of James G. Tracy, the forty-five–year–old editor of the *Houston Union*. Tracy was a newcomer to politics. He had come to Texas prior to the war and learned the newspaper trade at the conservative *Houston Telegraph*. An ardent advocate of internal improvements, Tracy joined the Republican party early in 1868 and established the *Union* as a party newspaper in Houston. He was among the party members who believed Pease was the best choice in 1869 and that he could be prevailed upon to run for governor. Hamilton's refusal to seek the nomination in a convention and the policy that he had taken toward the Conservatives particularly concerned Tracy. In a letter to Pease, the editor indicated that the truth of Hamilton's defection was immaterial; what counted was the number of voters who believed the charge. The suspicions among blacks allowed individuals such as George Ruby to reorganize the Union League. Tracy warned Pease: "We are going to have trouble unless Gen. Hamilton is regularly and fairly nominated by a Republican convention."[15]

Tracy received encouragement in his course from Edwin M. Wheelock. Wheelock was a former Union Army chaplain who had come to Texas with the Freedmen's Bureau. He was a friend of Pease. He became editor of the *San Antonio Express* when its owner, A. Siemering, fearing a party disaster, replaced William B. Moore, who had been using the paper against the administration. The new editor pursued policy calling for the party to begin anew. Wheelock held fears similar to those of Tracy. In a letter to Pease, the editor pointed out that he realized the governor was afraid that the party might fall into the hands of such "canaille" as George Ruby and J. P. Newcomb, but despite this Wheelock could not support Jack Hamilton. The editor believed that the party faced an even greater peril if it lost itself among the "rebels."[16]

The compromise movement received a boost when General Reynolds returned to the state and discussed the situation with Tracy. The general's sentiments expressed in their discussion shocked Tracy, who had believed Reynolds firmly behind Hamilton. Reynolds advocated a policy of either harmonizing the existing leaders or dropping them all in favor of new men. While Reynolds did not make his sentiments public, the general convinced Tracy that he was on the right course and should push toward a party convention.[17]

Tracy and Wheelock combined to call for a convention of all Republicans to meet at Houston on may 24, 1869. They asked the bolting committee to revoke its call for a convention at Galveston on May 10 so that reconciliation might be achieved. Although concerned that Morgan Hamilton might try to pack the convention with members of the Union League, they hoped that he would agree not to. Despite their plea the proposed convention received a favorable reception with neither faction. Morgan Hamilton still believed the May 24 movement was a ploy to give Pease the nomination, and he saw the financial aid of party secretary Haynes behind it. Jack Hamilton also opposed the movement and told the organizers that he would spurn the nomination of any convention. Jack Hamilton said that he was a Republican, but wanted to run as a candidate of all the people. A convention would only serve to rekindle old animosities and prevent whites who wanted to join in support of him from doing so. In addition, he indicated that he did not believe his brother Morgan was willing to make concessions on anything.[18]

Although rebuffed, Tracy persisted, and when the Morgan Hamilton convention met at the Galveston Varieties Theatre both he and Wheelock attended. They found the convention packed with members of the reorganized Union League, firmly in the hands of George Ruby. Ruby was irreconcilably opposed to Hamilton who he believed had defected to the enemy. In a Galveston League meeting several days before the convention Ruby denounced Hamilton as being anything that he wanted to be—rebel or loyalist. A black man could not give his support to a person who had gone to Washington to try to convince Congress that no Negroes were being killed in Texas. Ruby urged the delegates at Houston to make nominations in order to be ready for the ensuing election. Despite Ruby's apparent control, Tracy found the delegates generally open to his compromise move. Over Ruby's opposition Tracy secured a resolution from them adjourning their convention in order to consolidate with Tracy's, now reset for June 7.[19]

The ease with which Tracy managed to get a consolidated meeting probably had little to do with Tracy's arguments, but more likely resulted from a change in Morgan Hamilton's view of the potential for harm in compromise. Before the convention at Galveston, Hamilton had observed a meeting in the Twenty-eighth District where Jack Hamilton's supporters had forced Pease to come out in open support of the former governor. Morgan Hamilton believed that this killed the "middle party movement" and eliminated the possibility that Pease could emerge as the candidate of the compromise convention. Without Pease as an active candidate Morgan Hamilton believed that the bolters might be able to compete in such a convention "for the prize." Hamilton's belief that the compromise movement represented only the interest of E. M. Pease would prove to be a disastrous misreading of the movement's meaning, a misunderstanding that would lead to his own disappointment.[20]

With concern growing for compromise, the friends of A. J. Hamilton and those bolters who supported E. J. Davis met to see if something could be worked out between the candidates. One of Pease's friends in Galveston wrote that the representatives had met, and he believed they had reached an accord in which Hamilton would run for governor on a ticket with Davis as lieutenant governor. Pease's correspondent thought that the first legislature would then send Hamilton to the United States Senate. For some reason the accord broke down prior to the June 7 convention and both men denied that they had authorized the deal. The convention would open, therefore, with both major factions still unreconciled.[21]

The delegates who appeared at Houston June 7 seemed ready to compromise. There were only sixty official delegates, representatives from only twenty-one of the state's thirty senatorial districts. Supporters of Jack Hamilton thought that the convention might be taken over without difficulty. Secretary Haynes had urged party regulars to attend the meeting in the event that the governor's forces could control it. Governor Pease and Jack Hamilton showed up and decided, however, that there were not enough supporters in attendance to warrant working in the convention. Consequently, while they stayed to watch the proceedings, they refused to lend their support.[22]

Without contest from Jack Hamilton, Morgan Hamilton's committee took the convention's offices, but they were not able to manage its course. The spirit for compromise was too strong. In their platform the delegates attempted to appeal to as many Republicans as possible. After they endorsed congressional reconstruction, the national party platform, and the Fourteenth and Fifteenth Amendments, the delegates surprised the state when they supported the ratification of the proposed constitution. Such a move had not been expected and suggests how strong the pressure to get along with politics and abandon old factions had become within the party. Even Flake recognized the strength of the compromise sentiment when he reported the convention's abandonment of principle in order to frame a platform that would anger no one and allow as broad a base of support as possible.[23]

Also demonstrating the new mood, the delegates selected as many people from the regular party as possible to run for office. E. J. Davis received the nomination for governor, but James W. Flanagan received that for lieutenant governor. Flanagan was not in Houston, but his supporters had come to the convention and stayed despite the refusal of Pease and Jack Hamilton to participate. Flanagan had opposed the regulars on the question of division, but he had not withdrawn from the regular organization. His appearance on the Houston ticket indicated the desire for compromise. The rest of the ticket reflected an equal concern. They even nominated William D. Price, a friend of Jack Hamilton, for the treasurer's slot. Price later refused to run, but the convention had made a gesture toward unity.

When he accepted the nomination Davis appeared caught up in the new party mood. The nominee asked those who had voted for him to make every effort to bring about a spirit of good feeling among Republicans throughout the state. He hoped that the canvass would ultimately bring about renewed unity and party harmony. "I propose, if possible," he told the convention, "to be the candidate of the whole Republican party, without regard to faction or clique." The proceedings infuriated Morgan Hamilton. He had approved the convention after he thought that his men could control it. The very men he had sent to Houston, however, compromised the principles he espoused in favor of party unity. In disgust Hamilton refused to serve on the newly organized state executive committee. Hamilton did not believe Davis could defeat Jack Hamilton in a general election, and he feared that by endorsing the constitution the party had surrendered the very grounds it held for appealing to Congress after the loss. Endorsement of the constitution meant the end of the Republican party in Texas for Hamilton.[24]

While Morgan Hamilton worried about the convention's actions, President Grant responded favorably. Since the previous spring he had pursued a policy designed to promote some sort of cooperation. The federal patronage had been carefully dispensed in an effort to show favor to no one faction. The Pease-Hamilton group had received Treasury and Post Office positions, while the patronage of the Justice Department went to their opponents. Grant had also made known his desire, to Texans who talked with him at Washington, for the party to heal its internal division. In the East the Houston convention appeared to represent the very action the president desired. Eastern newspapers began calling Davis the regular Republican candidate. George W. Paschal, a friend of Pease and Hamilton, wrote to John Haynes shortly after the Houston meeting that it had created severe problems for Hamilton's candidacy with the administration. In the minds of Republican leaders the bolting committee had come to be thought of as the regular organization.[25]

Grant's concern for cooperation and for clarification of party loyalty developed as a result of the political situation in Virginia where a schism had developed similar to the one in Texas. Gilbert Walker, a Northerner, was running for governor as a moderate Republican and seeking Democratic support. Many national Republican leaders feared that a Walker victory would be a defeat for their party. Grant's delay in calling the Texas election was at least in part due to his concern for the situation in Virginia and his desire to obtain the results before allowing events to proceed in Texas. A Walker victory and the Virginia Democrats gaining control of the state legislature created a situation in Washington not favorable to the candidacy of a man tarred with the suspicion of selling out to the Democrats.[26]

Supporters of the Houston convention worked to capitalize on the administration's concerns. William B. Moore, the outspoken supporter of the bolting committee while editor of the *San Antonio Express*, appeared at Washington to lobby in favor of the Houston ticket and to increase doubt about Jack Hamilton's loyalty. His primary goal was a postponement of the Texas election as long as possible, a goal that would allow the bolters to organize the League. In addition he sought support among cabinet officials and congressmen to remove Hamilton's men from patronage positions. Moore's work was an important part of the ultimate abandonment of Hamilton by the administration.[27]

Jack Hamilton's men at Washington were aware of the

problem created for their candidate by the Houston convention. John Haynes urged Pease to convince Hamilton to call a convention in which he could be fairly nominated, and thus help overcome the advantage Davis's candidacy had achieved. The need to attract the support of Democrats was not easy to explain to national leaders; consequently the appearance of loyalty was all the more important. Rather than call a convention, an act Hamilton refused to do, Pease went to Washington to try to counter Moore's influence, but he arrived too late. National party leaders had already decided the course to take when he showed up. The day after the Virginia election results became known, the chairman of the National Republican Committee instructed the party secretary to recognize the committee appointed by the Houston convention as the regular party organization for Texas. At the same time the president consulted with his cabinet and decided to delay the Texas election until after the canvass in the North. He was particularly concerned with the impact of the Southern disasters on Ohio and Pennsylvania. Delay would work to the advantage of Davis and the bolters. In effect Pease and Jack Hamilton had lost their initial battle to gain the support of the national administration.[28]

Pease's only victory at Washington was to secure promises from the president that Hamilton's friends would not be removed from office and that the president would not intervene in local affairs, despite facing considerable pressure from within his administration on this matter. At a cabinet meeting on July 13 Secretary Boutwell attacked Grant's refusal to take a stand on the party problems in Texas and Mississippi. Boutwell argued that the failure to attack the "pretenders" and "new Movements" was a sign to many voters that the president endorsed the "Conservative" politicians. Secretary of the Interior Jacob D. Cox backed Boutwell and pointed out that he had received pressure from Ohio politicans who wanted the executive to intervene actively against the Conservatives. The president, however, moved carefully and delayed action.[29]

On July 31 the president met with a delegation from Mississippi and appeared to be on the verge of acting against the Conservatives. Grant informed his visitors that he supported the regular party candidates in their state, Tennessee, and Texas. Despite this endorsement of the Davis candidacy, the president still refrained from making removals that Texas Republicans considered necessary. Having taken the step of recognition, he refused to take the final step that would cut the Hamilton party off from national patronage. Grant's tortuously slow course reflected his lack of clarity concerning the political situation in Texas, but for the two contending parties in Texas it was a burden.[30]

The national patronage was a symbol of connection with national power that transcended statements of party recognition. The individual who occupied the Galveston customs house was an important figure on the local political scene. The various jobs at his disposal could be used to reward the local party faithful. More importantly, occupancy of the position indicated some measure of power in Washington. As a result, E. J. Davis adherents made repeated efforts to have the president remove Hamilton men from position and reward Davis's followers. With the support of national leaders of the Union League, the Texans reasserted the charges of disloyalty against these placemen, particularly John L. Haynes who held the customs house at Galveston. One of the most damning criticisms of Haynes came from Davis, who informed Secretary of the Treasury Boutwell that Haynes was using his patronage to destroy the regular Republican party in the state. Davis warned Boutwell that unless stopped, Haynes would insure the election of Jack Hamilton.[31]

The final step in the switch of the national administration to the Davis candidacy came when General Joseph J. Reynolds wrote to Grant of his own concern with the loyalty of Hamilton. Reynold's anxiety was important, for the general was a friend of the president. Although a friend of Pease and his associates, Reynolds had returned to Texas in the spring of 1869 believing that continued party fragmentation was bad. To Reynolds, Jack Hamilton had been the one who had refused to compromise. When Pease and A. J. Hamilton had walked away from the Tracy convention at Houston, they disappointed the general. His growing discontent had been expressed to Pease when he refused to endorse the governor's mission to Washington. Davis's supporters believed that a break had occurred between the general and Pease, but Reynolds refused to make public his misgivings.[32]

On September 4 he finally sent a private letter to Grant stating that his efforts to harmonize the local party had failed and blaming Jack Hamilton for the results. They had not only refused to unite with the "radicals," they had begun to support candidates who were unqualified under reconstruction laws to hold political office. These actions convinced Reynolds of the accuracy of the accusations of the Davis men against their opponents. Given these circumstances, Reynolds concluded the election of A. J. Hamilton would mean the defeat of the Republican party in Texas.[33]

After receiving Reynolds's letter the president informed his cabinet members to use their own discretion concerning political appointees in the state. Immediately Postmaster General John A. J. Creswell and Secretary of the Treasury Boutwell began to remove officeholders hostile to Davis. Among the first to fall was Haynes, replaced by Nathan Patten, a supporter of the compromise movement the previous spring who had given full support to Davis. This manufacturer from McLennan County was a good appointment, for Patten's business career and background added a tone of stability and conservativeness to the Davis group. By the end of September the major postal and treasury offices in the state were in the hands of Davis men.[34]

The turn of the Grant administration against Jack Hamilton could have been a major disaster for his candidacy. His supporters had lost national offices, and with quick work by Reynolds they could also lose all of their state and local jobs. At this point Governor Pease made an astute move that helped to block action by the commanding general. Pease resigned. He had received word from Washington that his own position was in danger and that his removal was imminent. Rather than wait, the governor stepped down from office and in a letter to Reynolds condemned the military's interference in local political affairs. The general was, in Pease's opinion, supporting men who had tried to delay and defeat reconstruction and he wanted no part of the results. With his quick step, Pease made a vote for Davis a vote for military intervention and continued reconstruction. Hamilton's candidacy now represented an end to such measures.[35]

The resignation of Pease and the subsequent uproar took Reynolds by surprise. He had hoped to promote party harmony —indeed his letter may have been an effort to press unification—but he had only succeeded in creating an uproar. Immediately supporters of Davis demanded that he remove some of the three thousand local office holders they believed sympathized with Hamilton. Others pressured him to delay the election until 1870 to give the regulars more time to organize. In the face of this situation Reynolds backed down and refused to cooperate. The general would not postpone the election and he made none of the requested removals. From September until after the election the general removed only two state officers. Local offices, for the most part, remained in the hands of the allies of Hamilton and Pease. Morgan Hamilton wrote of the affair shortly after publication of the Reynolds letter that the general was "almost frightened to death at what he has already accomplished in our behalf and is laboring to counteract the effect." [36]

These events on the national scene provided the background for the active campaign between Jack Hamilton and E. J. Davis that began in earnest in September. It was to be a face-to-face struggle for the two candidates. They traveled across the state, at times meeting together to speak from the same platform, at other times accusing each other of being too frightened to appear in the same town. Wherever they went, both Hamilton and Davis could count on a fair number of hecklers, a platform filled with aspiring local candidates, music, and a large turnout. In a time when the newspapers could not give a day-to-day analysis of the campaign, they safely gave the same speeches over and over, rehashed charges, made countercharges, and put on a good show.

Davis opened his campaign at Galveston on September 22 with a major speech given from the steps of the United States customs house to a crowd gathered in the square below. The papers reported the multitude numbered six hundred persons, more than had gathered for a political rally since before the war. A large bonfire lighted the assembly and a military band serenaded before the appearance of the candidate. At the appointed time Davis stepped to the front of the platform and the band broke into a rendition of "Dixie." The campaign was underway.

At Galveston and in subsequent speeches Davis emphasized three major themes. The first of these was Hamilton's treason to his party and refusal to cooperate with the radicals. The second was the difference between Hamilton and Davis. Hamilton had accused him of radicalism, but Davis asserted the only major policy that separated the two was what should be done to protect the state's school fund. He argued that *ab initio* was a policy designed to protect the school fund and to dispossess speculators of lands gained under the hammer of the Confederate auctioneer. His party wanted to force the railroads to pay what they owed to the school fund and to regain lands that had been fraudulently given out. Davis believed his stand had been moderate; he had offered to validate all just acts passed by the Confederate legislature, but his opponents had refused. They were "shrewder . . . and understood better how to manufacture public opinion." Now they were doing nothing more than obscuring the issues with their accusations of radicalism. Davis's final point was that Hamilton rather than Davis had sold out the people he now pretended to champion, and he did not deserve their support.[37]

Absent in the canvass was any clear statement by Davis or his supporters of their position on race issues. They had adopted a platform that endorsed the Fourteenth and Fifteenth Amendments. In the campaign, however, they played down even this mild commitment in favor of securing the rights of Negroes. Their entire effort revolved around the white voter, and they tried to avoid the radical label. When a black man attempted to secure the party's nomination for the legislature in Galveston, George Ruby intervened because of the impact such a choice would have on the party's propaganda. Ruby informed Newcomb that such candidates had to be prevented because they "threaten credence to the story the enemy assidiously [sic] circulates of a 'Black mans' party."[38]

They made their appeal secretly to blacks through the League. Newcomb as secretary of the League remained in communication with organizers throughout the state, circulating information on the candidate and preparing black voters for the election. They appear to have encountered opposition in their efforts, and their desire to delay the election reflected the Davis party's concern with the slowness of their organizational attempts. As late as November, just before the election, Davis complained that the League had made little headway among blacks in the northeastern counties. There the black population remained essentially unorganized.[39]

Hamilton had been in the field longer, but like his opponent he emphasized only a few major themes. His major point was the moderate course he had pursued in the convention, one he believed had earned him the support of all conservative men in the state. He claimed credit for preventing the disfranchisement of whites. He pledged his administration to the proscription of no man. The "intelligent tax paying citizen" had to be enfranchised. While he had supported the enfranchisement of blacks, he never believed that they should or would control the state. As to his own policies, Hamilton wanted the government to support immigration into the state. Hamilton also assured Texans that his administration would encourage the construction of railroads and other worthwhile internal improvements with liberal aid. His stance on *ab initio* he believed affirmed his concern for the well-being of the state. His opponents had attempted to overthrow legislation which did not contradict the laws of the national government, an activity that would have created chaos; but he had blocked the measures.

His severest criticisms of Davis centered on what he believed was his opponent's effort to build up a Negro party. To his black audiences he urged resistance, to whites opposition. He feared that a Negro party would force whites together into a coalition that would ultimately destroy the Negro race. Accompanied by Scipio McKee, a black supporter, he addressed Negroes whom he urged to break away from the control of the Union League. Davis, he believed, was pursuing a course destined to bring him and the state to ruin.[40]

Hamilton's campaign appeared on the verge of success; certainly his supporters believed that they had victory at hand. Three major problems that worked against his candidacy developed as the canvass progressed, however. The first was the refusal of Democrats to come to his support. The second was the effort among the Conservatives to occupy minor positions on the ticket. The last was the appearance in the field of a third party designed to draw voters away from Hamilton.

The slowness of Democrats to enter the Hamilton campaign was a major problem since its success depended on a good-sized white vote to counter what appeared to be an en masse black vote for Davis. But Hamilton suffered from repeated rebuffs. The previous June his backers had planned a political rally to start a Conservative Republican club at Houston. The meeting was to coincide with the annual assembly of the Grand Masonic Lodge of Texas. The organizers hoped to present Hamilton's program to the powerful Democratic members of the Grand Lodge and secure their endorsement. The mass meetings scheduled for June 16 fizzled, however, when most of the Democrats in attendance refused to sign the address in support of Hamilton adopted by the meeting. The *Galveston News* endorsed the address as "moderate, conciliatory, and commending itself to a majority of the white citizens." Still most of the white citizens would not sign it.[41]

Another reverse came when a group of Democratic newspaper editors met at Brenham in September and recommended that their party run candidates for all offices. This meeting nominated Hamilton Stuart, editor of the *Galveston Civilian*, to head such a ticket. Jack Hamilton's supporters accused the editors of trying to help Davis by drawing Democratic voters from their candidate. Others believed that Stuart ran in an effort to discredit the notion that Hamilton was a Democrat. According to Stuart, he entered to block Hamilton because he believed the governor and his associates had been responsible for the overthrow of the Throckmorton government in 1867, and he was not ready to forgive them for that. He also did not like their railroad interests. To Stuart, Davis was the lesser evil and he was willing to draw away some votes from Hamilton in order to prevent his election. Stuart wrote: "We know of no more thoroughly corrupt men than Jack Hamilton, Pease, Bell and Paschal." [42]

The most threatening problem developed when Republican voters who might have voted for Hamilton began to fear that the Conservative party he proposed was dangerous. The Hamilton coalition required considerable manipulating at the local level if each faction within it was to be represented for local offices. The Republicans found, however, that the Democrats were not willing to cooperate. Democratic intransigence forced many to reconsider the possibilities of a coalition and to move into the Davis camp. In no instance was this more apparent than in the campaign for Congress in the Third Congressional District.

The Third was a stronghold of the Union League after that organization was introduced in 1867. Over 98,000 blacks lived there, approximately 39 percent of the Negro population of the state. Because they represented about 45 percent of the total population, they had the potential for a political majority. The League was well-drilled and in August had selected William T. Clark as their candidate. The League controlled the convention and George Ruby, state League president, not only chaired the assembly but managed Clark's nomination. Clark was a carpetbagger, a native of Connecticut who had come to Texas with the Union Army. After being mustered out in 1866, he had remained to open the First National Bank of Texas in partnership with a former Confederate general. The combination of League support and Clark's drawing power appeared to give the Davis candidate a runaway victory. Clark's promise to work for federal aid to Galveston harbor, railroads, and a system of inland waterways, attracted white businessmen of both Houston and Galveston.[43]

Clark was not unopposed. Too many candidates had entered the race. John Haynes had attempted to assure concerted action, but two Democrats and two Conservative Republicans had appeared to contest Clark for the position. In June, Haynes believed that he had secured the promise of all four to withdraw in favor of a compromise candidate, General Benjamin G. Shields, a prominent Republican planter from Falls County. As the election approached, however, two of the candidates, Jacob Eliot, a Democrat, and Tom Ochiltree, a Conservative Republican, refused to withdraw in favor of Shields. On November 13 Shields met with Ochiltree and agreed that the Conservatives must unite or default the election to Clark, and they asked Eliot to meet them at Houston to determine who should withdraw. Eliot refused to submit his claims to the race in such a conference because he believed that in a meeting between two Republicans and one Democrat he had no chance. After much more discussion Eliot finally agreed to a plan in which friends of the candidates would first decide between Shields and Eliot, then select between the winner and Ochiltree. At the first stage of negotiations, however, Shields and Eliot could not agree and two days later Shields withdrew completely from the race, charging the Democrats had dealt in bad faith. Since he had entered the race on the assurance that all other parties would withdraw, Shields decided that he would not continue.[44]

Eliot's apparent refusal to submit his case to arbitration outraged Republicans in the district. Ferdinand Flake informed his readers that when faced with the alternative of an outright Democrat and a Republican, they had no choice but to support the Republican. Flake believed that such acts by the Democrats severely hurt Hamilton's chances, for they lent credence to reports that the candidate had made a deal with the Democrats. To the Galveston editor it appeared the Democrats had indeed agreed to support Hamilton but were working to elect their own men to Congress, place a Democrat as lieutenant governor, and "save the legislature." He believed this course was driving hundreds of Hamilton Republicans into the Davis camp. Officials both at Galveston and Austin received reports of this shift toward Davis. Their action was forced, according to Flake, "not because they like Davis or prefer proscription, but because they have nowhere else to go." By the time of the election the likelihood of a Jack Hamilton victory was no longer as sure.[45]

The polls opened in the state on November 30. General Reynolds had sent out over six hundred of his troops to prevent violence and insure the peaceful operation of the election. A Texas norther, a cold front accompanied with ice and freezing winds, blew during the four days of the polls. Although Democratic newspapers complained that whites allowed conditions to keep them away from the polls, about 53 percent of the registered white voters turned out, some 41, 500 voters. At the same time 66 percent of the registered blacks voted, nearly 37, 400 men. Reports from around the state indicated good turnouts among the German-Americans and Mexican-Americans.[46]

Davis took an early lead over Hamilton as the first returns reached Reynolds's offices at Austin. In the black belt counties of the Third District he piled up heavy majorities. The counties of the Second District in northern Texas reported more slowly than others and Hamilton's backers believed their candidate would receive a large enough vote there to counter the early victories for Davis. As the polling continued, however, Davis's lead held up. Hamilton made gains, but never enough to push him in front of his opponent. When all of the returns were received, military officials announced that Davis had received 771 more votes than Hamilton, 39,831 to 39,060. The returns filed at district headquarters showed an even greater majority for Davis. Hamilton Stuart's campaign had attracted little support. He received only 308 votes.[47]

Davis carried many of his supporters into office with him, although only by thin majorities. George W. Whitmore, a supporter of Davis in the constitutional convention, carried the congressional race in the First District. In the Third, W. T. Clark easily defeated the Democratic candidate Eliot. In the Fourth District, where Davis's candidate E. Degener was supposed to have had an easy victory, John L. Haynes ran a good race. Ultimately Degener's victory depended upon the invalidation of returns in Bell and El Paso counties. In the Second District the Davis ticket was defeated, although the meaning of the vote there is not clear since the Democrats ran as their candidate a carpetbagger, former Union Army officer John C. Conner.

The closeness of the Davis victory was particularly apparent in the races for other state offices. George W. Honey became state treasurer, A. Bledsoe, comptroller, and Jacob Keuchler, commissioner of the general land office, without much difficulty. James W. Flanagan, however, narrowly averted a defeat in the race for lieutenant governor. He drew only 35,511 votes, more than 400 less than his running mate, and only the refusal of his opponents to agree on a single candidate secured a victory for him. The one Democrat and two conservative Republicans who ran against Flanagan polled a combined total of 36,296 votes.

The structure of the legislature remained in doubt, and only its assembly would reveal its composition. Davis's supporters feared that many men elected as Republicans could not be counted on to support the governor, since the exact meaning of a Republican label on the local level was not always clear. To make sure that Davis's opponents did not infiltrate the legislature, his supporters discussed with military authorities the propriety of administering a loyalty oath to each new member. In public the Conservatives claimed that they had achieved control, but in private they admitted that they knew little more about the situation than their opponents. John Hancock, a strong supporter of Hamilton in the election, believed that Davis had been successful. He calculated for the governor a majority in the Senate of from fifteen to fourteen members, and an even larger one in the House.[48]

The election returns suggest something of the nature of the voters who put Davis and his men into power. As they had planned, the key to their victory had been the mobilization of black voters through the League. Some 37,370 blacks voted in 1869, and although all of them probably did not support Davis, the returns suggest that a large majority of them did. In the thirty-one counties in which more blacks voted than whites, Davis won easily in all but three. A strong statistical correlation existed between the Davis vote and the black population.

Davis and his supporters discovered a problem with their reliance upon black votes, however, that did not bode well for the future. Despite the presence of the United States Army, enough violence broke out to indicate that black voters would have to be protected if they were to continue to be a political force. In Navarro County the election board refused to accept Negroes' ballots and the military had to close the poll. When blacks went to vote in Milam County a riot ensued in which one man was killed. The army again had to move in and suspend the election. Backers of Hamilton complained that these counties would have voted for their candidate. However, registration statistics suggest that more probably a free election would have helped Davis since blacks were in the majority. Throughout the state Davis's supporters saw different forms of intimidation being used against blacks. Their fears may have been justified, for three thousand fewer blacks voted in 1869 than had voted in 1868, and the percent of registered black voters who went to the polls dropped from 82 to 66 percent.[49]

Black votes alone, however, were not sufficient for victory, and Davis received at least 4,451 white votes.[50] The majority of these came from the Fourth District, Davis's own. All of the counties in which Davis received more than 50 percent of the white vote were located there. Although the fact that two Republican candidates were in the field may have created the results, the returns indicated the increasingly sectional nature of the successful faction's white support. Where Pease had managed to secure support from throughout the state, Davis drew few white votes outside his own section. Nowhere was this problem more striking than in the Northeast where the old Unionists did not come out strongly for Davis. Instead, there was a negative correlation between prewar Unionist strength and the Davis vote.

Among ethnic groups in the state, reports from poll observers suggested that Davis appealed to German-Americans and Mexican-Americans, although since the majority of these lived in the Fourth District it is not clear if their votes represented ethnicity or sectional interest. A statistical correlation existed between the Davis vote and the population strengths of each of these groups. But the correlation was not strong and did not appear to insure victory. Of the twenty-one counties with sizeable German minorities, Davis managed to carry only fifteen. A correlation with Mexican-American voters presents a problem, since the significance is not clear. Throughout this period these votes tended to be voted by major landowners in the area whose interests would be better served with a Davis victory.

Perhaps the most significant trend evidenced in the election was Davis's inability to attract a majority of the whites who may have tended toward Republicanism. Davis polled almost eight thousand fewer votes than Pease in 1866; thus Hamilton had attracted almost two-thirds of the potential white Republican vote. If these Republican whites would not go with Davis despite fears of Democratic resurgence, it was not clear that the

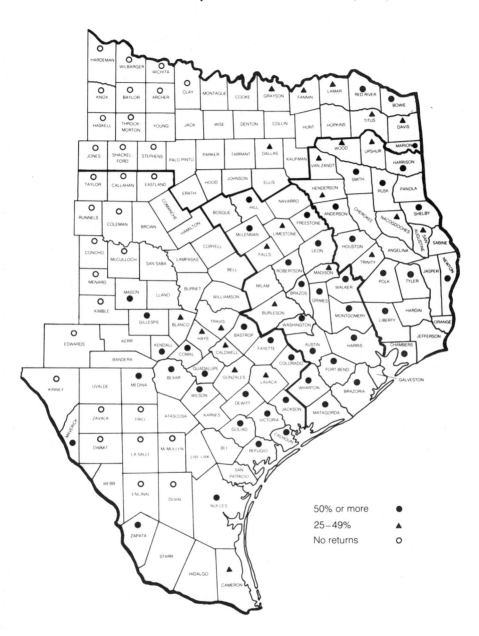

MAP 4. Vote for Davis, 1869

newly elected governor could ever gain their support. Davis and his followers were aware of the problem, and the policies they would undertake in the future would always keep in mind the need to somehow attract these potential white voters.

With the vote in, General Reynolds indicated a desire to move as rapidly as possible for restoration of civil government. Despite complaints made about the suspension of the election in Milam and Navarro, Reynolds refused to order new elections for those counties. Instead he announced the victory of Davis and in a special order issued on January 8, 1870, he ordered Davis and the other newly elected officials to take their offices immediately as a provisional government. The continuation of civil government concerned Reynolds and he asked each person to hold office until Congress readmitted the state to the Union. He thus filled the vacancies caused by resignations the previous autumn and stepped out of the picture himself.[51]

Reynolds also ordered the newly elected legislature to assemble provisionally to act on the Thirteenth, Fourteenth, and Fifteenth Amendments. The members met for a short time and quickly approved the amendments and elected United States senators. Considerable interest accompanied their proceedings since rumors had spread that Reynolds's endorsement of Davis had been part of a "corrupt bargain" in which the general withdrew his support from Hamilton with the promise from Davis that he would then be elected United States senator. The *San Antonio Express* noted that this bargain and the general's ambitions probably existed more in the minds of Davis's enemies than in fact. Reynolds denied his interest in the office and his name never came up. The party caucus decided to support J. W. Flanagan and M. C. Hamilton for the positions, and the legislature quickly confirmed these choices. Hamilton received two terms, serving until 1877, and Flanagan drew the term that ended in 1873. After taking these actions the legislature adjourned to await the governor's call for a regular session.[52]

With the groundwork out of the way, Reynolds sent the results of the Texas election to Congress for action. Congress did not take up the matter until March 1870, and by then Jack Hamilton was already at the capital to contest the results. While he carried petitions and complaints, he received little encouragement in his goals. On March 7 Oliver P. Morton of Indiana introduced a bill to readmit Texas, and while there

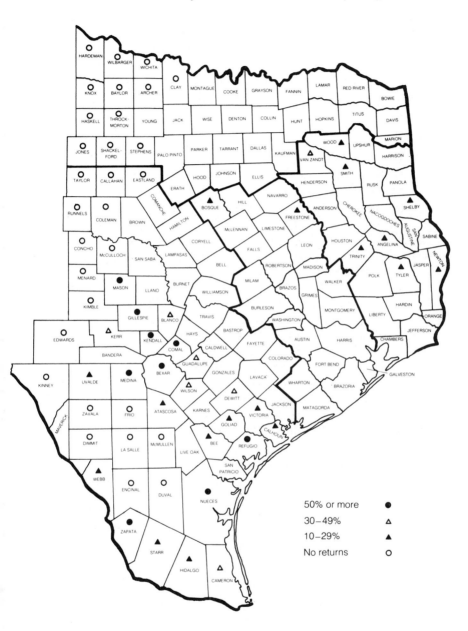

MAP 5. White Vote for Davis, 1869

were some objections, it quickly passed. In the House the provisions of the new constitution that prohibited the state from granting land to any but actual settlers raised concern, but the opposition was not large enough to block the measure. On March 30, President Grant signed the readmission bill. General Reynolds issued orders that turned over civil functions to the newly elected officials on April 16, 1870. The military reconstruction of Texas was at an end.[53]

Readmission found the Texas Republicans still divided into two factions. Pressure from home and from Washington failed to reconcile the rival leaders. The election had shown, however, that such a situation was not safe for the party since it split up the available white votes. The Democrats were moving back toward power, and with a white population that amounted to almost three-fourths of the total population of the state, they would regain control of the government unless some sort of cooperation could be achieved. The Davis government had either to reconcile itself with the Hamilton Republicans or strip the unsuccessful leaders of their white support, if they were to maintain control or even have a chance at controlling the state for more than one term.

While Davis had to seek a broader coalition, the Jack Hamilton wing of the party had little incentive to make peace. The former governor retained his belief that an alliance could be achieved with the moderates in the Conservative party. Although no longer in control of the League and without a voice in Washington, Hamilton persevered in his opposition to Davis and the new administration. In part this intransigence grew from a lesson learned in the campaign. Davis had achieved success in part through his resort to outside authority, and the same ploy might work again. Rather than work things out among themselves, party members would appeal to the precedent already established and seek outside intervention. Interference by federal officials made possible an escape from compromise and reconciliation, and consequently allowed the Republicans to remain factionalized. By the time they would ultimately realize the need for united action, their opponents would have become too powerful and their own resources too weak to prevent their fall from power. The state election of 1869 contributed an important component to the failure of local Republicanism by providing the experience that helped develop this tendency.

Andrew Jackson Hamilton
From Dudley G. Wooten, ed., *A Comprehensive History of Texas,
1685 to 1897* (Dallas: William G. Scarff, 1898), courtesy of the Barker
Texas History Collection.

Elisha M. Pease
Courtesy of the Barker Texas History Collection.

Edmund J. Davis
Courtesy of the Barker Texas History Collection.

James Winwright Flanagan
From the Brady-Handy Collection, courtesy of the Library of Congress.

Morgan C. Hamilton
From the Brady-Handy Collection, courtesy of the Library of Congress.

William T. Clark
From the Brady-Handy Collection, courtesy of the Library of Congress.

Edward Degener
From the Brady-Handy Collection, courtesy of the Library of Congress.

George W. Whitmore
From William Horatio Barnes, *The Forty-First Congress of the United States, 1869–1871* (New York: W. H. Barnes and Co., 1872), courtesy of the Library of Congress.

CHAPTER 7

The Price of the Republican Coalition: The Radicals and the Twelfth Legislature

The victorious Radical Republicans faced a difficult task as they took office. They were a splinter faction and still had to build a party. Key elements that provide unity and direction to a political movement were either absent or undeveloped. The Radicals did not have a well-defined set of common principles and policies to provide identity and command loyalty. They did not possess a constituency committed to their leadership through habit and tradition. The party's lines of organization were so weak that state leaders could not insure support for their goals among local politicians. The lack of organization was particularly a problem when the governor made appointments, for without correct information on conditions in the counties he could not distinguish between his friends and enemies. The Radicals were little more than a collection of individuals and groups struggling to realize their goals through government when they appeared at Austin in the spring of 1870. A party would develop, however, forged from the battles of the Twelfth Legislature, the strife among its members, and the struggles between them and Governor Edmund J. Davis. Efforts to develop a Radical program would help to define more precisely the nature of Republicanism in Texas.

When the Twelfth Legislature met at Austin in April for a special session, the array of ambitions and interests that would create the party's program was apparent. Those of Governor Davis would play a major role, since he, along with his advisors, would initiate many of the measures the legislature considered. Born in Florida in 1827, he came to Texas when he was about twenty years old. His family settled at Galveston where he studied law and entered the bar. In the mid-1850s, Davis moved to Corpus Christi in the southern portion of the state, where he set up his legal practice. Early in his career he showed political ambition and in 1857 won his first elected office, district attorney. A year later he advanced to the position of district judge. Davis made close contacts with local political leaders, especially Colonel Forbes Britton whose daughter he married, and prior to the outbreak of the Civil War appeared to be one of the region's up-and-coming young politicians.

From the beginning of his career Davis linked himself to the sectional interests of southwestern Texas. He retained that connection throughout his life. With others, he believed that the settled areas of the state had neglected the protection and development of the frontier sections. As a result he advocated state military aid against the Indians and supported efforts to construct a railroad that would tie his section to the rest of the state. The divisionist panacea that would have solved the frontier problem by creating a separate state in the Southwest also attracted him, and as a delegate to the constitutional conventions in 1866 and 1868 he had backed efforts to create a new state.

The governor's Civil War experiences added new dimensions to his character. In the secession crisis he adopted the Unionist sentiments of his section, and in 1862 fled the state. Not one to sit out the war, Davis helped organize the First Texas Cavalry, U.S.V., and led the unit along the Texas-Mexican border. The war reinforced his love of the Union and reassured him of the correctness of his own stand. He emerged from the conflict a staunch supporter of the national government and its programs of reconstruction.

The governor's loyalty to the national government and the Union perhaps accounts for an enigmatic part of his career—his position regarding freedmen. It is not exactly clear when and why he adopted his views, but Davis became one of the first Texans to advocate extending the franchise to blacks and insuring them equal treatment before the law. His stand became apparent in the first constitutional convention after the war, and he reasserted it in the next. Although Davis shared the white culture's general racist views, unlike his contemporaries he wanted to give blacks an equal chance. In an interview with a correspondent of *Flake's Bulletin* that he gave shortly after taking office, the governor stated the position that he had held and could continue to hold: "I do not want to see white or black named in any law whatsoever."[1]

Davis would subsequently exercise a critical role in determining the Radical Republican program, but the members of the Twelfth Legislature would be equally important. They would take the executive's basic programs, reject some, modify others, and add their own. The impact they would make was not clear when the legislators assembled. The Radicals controlled both houses, but the precise number of their majority was not known. *Flake's Bulletin* indicated that the margin in the Senate was seventeen to thirteen, but early voting suggested that the initial Radical majority was eighteen to twelve. The same newspaper put Radical strength in the House at fifty to forty. Some of the opposition may not have appeared, however, since the Radicals usually outvoted their opponents fifty to thirty. The fact that a legislator's statement of party affiliation meant little contributed to the ambiguity of the situation. To be a Republican had only limited meaning with respect to local issues. The Radical element was a heterogeneous group composed of many different interests.[2]

The lack of clear lines distinguishing legislators was more apparent in the Senate than in the House. The representatives tended to follow the lead of the governor and his spokesmen. As a result they were more cohesive and put up little struggle. In the Senate, however, Davis and his program would encounter a hard fight. Moving legislation through the Senate forced compromises out of Davis that would lead to the creation of a Radicalism that amounted to much more than the wishes of a single individual.

The men in the Senate with whom the governor would work were, for the most part, whites who had been born in Texas or had settled in the state prior to the war. Senators George Ruby and A. J. Fountain were two exceptions. They were carpetbaggers. Ruby had come with the Freedmen's Bureau schools and Fountain had arrived with the federal army of occupation in El Paso. Two of the senators were black, Ruby and a former slave, Matthew Gaines. As a group the Radical Republicans were not remarkably different from their Democratic opponents. Among them were farmers, professionals, and businessmen, the major occupations in postwar Texas. Some had been Unionists, others Democrats. Radicals had fought for the Union and the Confederacy. A few had refused to fight. They represented a variety of interests, both old and new to the state's political life.[3]

The railroads had representatives among the Radicals. Sev-

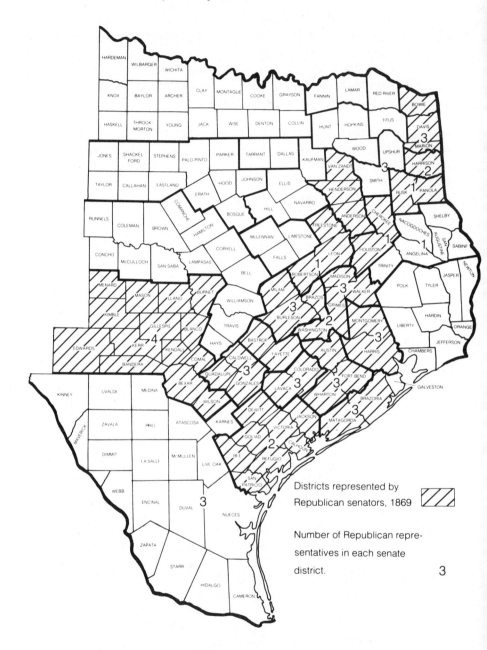

MAP 6. Republicans in the Twelfth Legislature, 1870

eral members had ties with roads that were seeking concessions or relief. General William H. Parsons, an ardent Secessionist and a veteran of the Confederate Army, was an advocate of the construction of a Southern Pacific railroad and had ties to the Houston and Texas Central. Parsons had become a Republican so that he could "act upon convictions of individual duty to self, family, and State." In the Senate he would be a strong supporter of internal improvements. Supporting him would be Webster Flanagan, another former Confederate in the Republican camp, Thomas Baker, John G. Bell, and Don Campbell, president of the Senate.[4]

The frontier interests were still trying, in 1870, to secure aid and protection for that section. In the Twelfth Legislature a carpetbagger, Albert J. Fountain, would be the primary spokesman for the Westerners. Fountain was a New Yorker who had come to the state with the First California Volunteer Infantry. When mustered out at El Paso in 1864 he decided to stay. In his adopted city he practiced law and served as a deputy collector of customs under W. W. Mills, El Paso's delegate to the constitutional convention.[5]

Agrarian interests also returned to the political arena. Farmers and planters had been the strongest economic group before the war, and their political influence had been responsible for the limited government that had existed. Landowners did not want taxes and, as a result, public service had suffered in Texas. Within the Republican party Morgan Hamilton had been the major spokesman of these interests, and he continued that role through men in the Senate. B. J. Pridgen of Victoria, a farmer with considerable property, united with E. L. Alford of Bastrop and E. Petit of Anderson in support of agrarian measures.[6]

In addition to railroads, frontier protection, and agriculture, new interests emerged among the Radicals that had not been important in the prewar years. The Germans in Texas had existed on the periphery of power, but now they had Senator Theodore Hertzberg, a physician from San Antonio, in the Senate. Hertzberg belonged to a German element that believed they should exercise some political power as an ethnic group. They had organized before the war and urged a program of reform that included a graduated income tax, an inheritance tax, and popular election of public officers. They had also opposed slavery and argued for its abolition by the states. Hertzberg had been active in this movement and he now appeared as a Republican senator. The Republican party could become a permanent home for the Germans if it responded to their needs.[7]

More important in terms of potential voting strength, blacks were ready for a share in determining their party's direction. Their interests were complex, however, and they cannot be considered as constituting a single group. Most of them were farmers, and although interested in public schools and protection, they were not sympathetic to higher taxes. The agrarian blacks had Matthew Gaines as their spokesman. A former slave himself, he identified with his constituents. While he had become a minister after freedom, he still farmed in Washington County. Characterized as a dull, plodding, honest politician at the beginning of the session, by the end he would be seen as a keen, shrewd, wirepuller. But there were black workers in urban areas for whom Gaines could not speak. For them there was George Ruby.[8]

George T. Ruby was becoming a very important figure within the Republican party. In the Twelfth Legislature he would be the administration's chief spokesman. He was president of the Union League, but his chief source of power was the black labor force on the Galveston docks. From the day he arrived in the state he had worked to organize them. In 1869 he established the Colored National Labor Convention to speak for blacks other than those on the farms. A man to be reckoned with, Ruby's appearance was striking. *Flake's Bulletin* described him as a medium-sized man with a light olive complexion. His face was sharp and incisive, his nose like a hawk's. Many people thought that his face exuded aggressiveness. Given the situation in the Senate he would need all of the aggressiveness that he could muster.[9]

The session began on April 28 with the inauguration of Governor Davis. The Radicals celebrated before getting down to the tough business. The First Texas Cavalry, the governor's old unit, held a reunion in his honor and gave him a barbecue. The *Galveston News* reported that "all the world hereabouts were in attendance." When he appeared before a joint session of the legislature, Davis called for "a fresh departure in political affairs," a departure by sensible men who "agree to accept the situation as they find it." The governor did not believe that there could be room for debate over the place of blacks

in politics, the question of states' rights, or the supremacy of
the national government. He welcomed all men who accepted
these new realities to join forces with him, set aside party differences, and work together for the welfare of the entire state.[10]

With the pleasantries out of the way, the legislature met
the following day to receive the governor's message. They then
set about dealing with his program as it came before them.
Davis's address and the subsequent administration bills provided an outline for the package of legislation that he wanted. The
central thrust was to reestablish law and order, but the governor
also wanted legislation to provide for public schools, internal
improvements, frontier protection, and adequate financial
support.

The legislation proposed to secure law and order included
bills to organize a state militia, establish a state police force,
expand the district court system, put into operation the county
and justice of the peace courts, restrict the carrying of firearms,
and insure the conduct of political officers. The creation of a
state police was the keystone of the governor's effort. The state
had operated a police agency of sorts, the Texas Rangers, in
the antebellum years, but its use had been restricted to the
frontier. Governor Pease used the Rangers in Karnes County,
where whites had been attacking Mexican teamsters, and set a
precedent for their use as a civil police. Governor Davis envisioned a force designed primarily to preserve civil law. The
bill his supporters introduced provided for a force of 258 men,
including 12 officers under the command of the state adjutant
general. The adjutant general was to head both the police and
a restored militia and insure their coordination in civil emer-
gencies. The measures desired by the administration included
a provision for the subordination of local peace officers to the
command of the chief of state police and the governor when
the execution of criminal processes demanded it. District judges
were to be empowered to call the police in to their aid when
such action appeared necessary. In all, the proposed state police
bill included a great increase in the central power of the state.[11]

The Militia Bill was a complement to the state police legislation. The basic organization did not differ greatly from that
of the antebellum militia, but Davis wanted the power to ac-
tivate this force in the event of "resistance of civil process,
breach of peace or imminent danger thereof." As written, the
bill gave the governor the power to declare martial law in coun-

ties where lawless forces obstructed justice. To pay for the militia's operations, the bill allowed the state to assess any county where it was used. In the event of a declaration of martial law, the governor could suspend the civil law and appoint courts martial for the duration of the emergency. When combined with other bills concerned with the courts, the use of firearms, and the duties of officials to uphold the civil rights of all men, the state police and militia measures provided a comprehensive attack upon disorder in the state.[12]

In his message to the legislature Davis had indicated, however, that he believed the only ultimate solution to the problem of violence was education. As a result he urged the legislature to set up a system of free public schools as provided for by the constitution. These schools, he believed, would insure the success of republican institutions and universal suffrage. In the legislature the administration introduced a school bill that provided for a highly centralized system. A board of education, consisting of a superintendent of public instruction, the attorney general, and the governor, would direct the schools. Their instructions would be implemented by thirty-five appointed district supervisors and local school boards appointed by the supervisors. While the supervisors watched over educational programs the board would hire teachers, levy and collect school taxes, construct buildings, and make sure students attended classes for four months a year.[13]

A man of the Southwest, Davis also wanted his administration to secure the frontier from attack by Indians. Davis urged the legislators to authorize "minute companies" to track down Indian raiders and exterminate them. The governor believed that the only solution was the total conquest of these peoples. He scorned those individuals who believed that Indian raids were savage ways of redressing wrongs inflicted on them by whites. Such views were held only by "philanthropic people, throughout those parts of the nation were Indian reminiscences exist only in romantic stories." The administration bill before the legislature authorized the recruiting and equipping of twenty companies of rangers, about twelve hundred men, to serve for twelve-month periods at the call of the governor. The proposal allowed financing to be accomplished through a special bond issue.[14]

On the issue of internal improvements the governor urged judicious encouragement of "honest and feasible" enterprises

through special favors, such as tax breaks. He was not interested in direct subsidies and asked, instead, for a bureau of immigration, a bureau for the collection of statistics on economic
matters, and a geological survey. Such measures would, in his
opinion, encourage private investors to enter the state. His
supporters introduced legislation to gain these ends. Davis understood, however, that many of the men of his party were
not as cautious concerning grants to railroads, and he insisted
that if they went ahead, they insure the safety and fair treatment
of passengers as well as reasonable rates. He also encouraged
them to limit their support to only one road. The one he favored
was a line connecting the Rio Grande with the Red River and a
national railroad system.[15]

The governor understood that what he wanted to do would
cost money. He believed that the programs he wanted would
cost one and a half million dollars and he warned the legislators
that additional items would raise this cost. While taxes would
increase for everyone, Davis thought that by revising the system
of revenue collection the tax burden would be spread more equi-
tably. The administration proposed a bill that shifted the work
of assessing and collecting taxes to the justice of the peace and
the sheriff of each county. This would have ended the practice
of assessments being made in the county of the landowner, a
procedure that had led to considerable fraud. In addition the
governor's backers proposed the raising of revenues through a
1.5 percent tax on real and personal property, a 1 percent
tax on the receipts of railroad and telegraph companies, and
occupation and license taxes.[16]

Considering their later attacks on Davis for increasing the
power of the state government and for raising taxes, the Conservatives greeted the governor's program in its early stages
with surprising approbation. When he sent his message to the
legislature they praised its content and its tone, although they
did express some reservations about the proposed state police
and militia. For many of them the message indicated that the
governor was a conservative and high-minded individual who
would not use the government against the people of the state.
Even the Jack Hamilton Republicans praised the message, calling it an able state document that deserved wide approval.[17]

In the legislature, however, the administration program
ran into trouble from the beginning, and the governor had to
make compromises. Some legislators believed that the gover-

nor's railroad policy was too conservative and expressed their concern in the election of the president of the Senate. Davis wanted General Parsons of Galveston in the position. He was a railroad man, but one who could probably be controlled. Parson's choice, however, drew the opposition of Webster Flanagan who wanted Donald Campbell, a friend of his father. Davis was not completely opposed to Campbell—he had earlier appointed him as a district judge—but someone so close to Flanagan was not his first choice. The two Flanagans had too many railroad schemes brewing not to be expected to try to push something through the legislature. Instead of fighting the elder Flanagan, however, Davis agreed to his choice, and Campbell received the party nomination. Morgan Hamilton and other agrarians in the party believed that the administration had lost its first confrontation in the Twelfth Legislature and saw the incident as foreshadowing difficulties ahead.[18]

The encounter over the Senate leadership quickly faded as Republicans began a new struggle over a racial matter. In order to get public schools working as quickly as possible, the governor appointed Joseph W. Talbot to the position of superintendent of public instruction and sent his name to the Senate for its consent. Talbot appeared to be a sound choice, as he had chaired the education committee in the constitutional convention and had demonstrated a good grasp of school problems. When Davis selected him, general sentiment approved the choice. In the Senate, however, Talbot's position on integration of the schools came into question. The senators did not want to create a racially mixed system, and neither did Davis's nominee, but he realized that maintaining a dual system of public schools was impossible financially. He argued to the senators that Texas should not be committed to a segregated system and refused to declare himself opposed to integrated schools in all cases. The senators asked Davis to withdraw Talbot's name; Davis refused and threatened to keep his candidate in office without the Senate's approval. In a showdown on May 11 four Republicans joined with the Democratic minority to deny consent. The administration had lost its second battle, and its ability to keep party members in line on racial questions was in question.[19]

After the Talbot episode several senators refused to participate in the Republican caucus. This put other party legislation in jeopardy, for both the Senate and House had taken up bills to form the state police, the militia, and the frontier ranging companies. Objections existed to all three among both Democrats and Republicans. Among the latter the chief complaint was cost. When considering the rangers Senator Alford spoke for the party members concerned with limiting government expenses when he urged that the federal government take up the cost of pacifying the Indians. Even Senator Parsons had some problems with appropriating money for the companies, and he said: "I do not myself propose to weigh the gold of the treasury by the side of our frontier settlers. It is not, sir, a mere question of cost. . . ; but I regard it simply as to whether the end could not be consummated in a more direct manner, and with no expenditure to our State by the action of the Congress of the United States." Republicans could not safely vote the bill down, however, and it passed both houses. The old issue of restricted government had reappeared.[20]

The militia and the state police raised stronger objections. The problem of cost was part of the reason Republicans opposed these institutions. The Democrats added arguments against their constitutionality and condemned the measures for giving the governor too much authority and local officials too little. While the Democrats may have had constitutional scruples, the fact that the bills provided for the enrollment of blacks in both groups also concerned them. Senator Matthew Gaines believed that the race issue was at the heart of their opposition. They engaged in rhetoric, according to Gaines, designed to cover up their real hostility to "the idea of gentlemen of my color being armed and riding around after desperadoes."[21]

Neither piece of legislation had difficulty in the House, but in the Senate they encountered opposition. The House passed the militia bill on May 21 by a vote of fifty-three to twenty-seven and the police bill sixteen days later by a similar vote, fifty-four to twenty-three. How the Senate would act on the bills was not clear. In the Republican caucus on May 12 Senators B. J. Pridgen and E. L. Alford announced that they refused to support the proposed forces and would not consider the bills party measures. Each voiced his belief that the militia bill was not necessary for the party's welfare and echoed Democratic arguments concerning its constitutionality. At a subsequent caucus meeting on May 17 the majority expelled both Pridgen and Alford after they refused to submit to party discipline. With their votes unsure, the governor's law and order program faced a challenge.[22]

Fearing a loss in the Senate, Davis tried to use other measures to whip Senators into line. The major tool in his possession was patronage, and the constitution of 1869 had given him control over numerous positions, including district judgeships and offices in various public institutions. While the Senate debated the police and militia, Davis refused to make appointments. Conservatives alleged that he could not find competent Republicans, but the governor may have delayed in order to insure that the greatest political good would be served when he filled offices. Senator J. S. Mills, who had withdrawn from the caucus after the expulsion of Pridgen and Alford, had a father who was a doctor. Davis offered Dr. Mills the position of superintendent at the blind asylum, and shortly afterwards Senator Mills announced that he had decided to support the governor's bills. When questioned about his change of mind, the senator replied that his constituents had convinced him of the necessity of some police measures. Senator Mijamin Priest, another Republican who had refused to enter the caucus, received a promise that he would be nominated for a district judgeship, and he also came into line.[23]

Davis used his control of the House, in addition to the patronage, as a lever to force his bills through the Senate. While the Senate considered the police and militia, his men in the House stopped considering private legislation and indulged in a debate over the state printing. To make sure that business halted, the governor also announced that he would veto any private bills that appeared before he received his police legislation. Even if enough votes could have been mustered to continue action in the House, nothing could be passed over a veto. Two important railroad bills fell idle before this strategy—the Southern Pacific bill, involving the interests of Senator James W. Flanagan, and a relief bill for the Houston and Texas Central. Both roads involved powerful people who might be manipulated to use their influence in the governor's behalf.[24]

Proponents of both bills needed quick action and the delay caused trouble. The Southern Pacific bill sought to organize a new road and give it the charter of the old Memphis, El Paso, and Pacific to get around the constitutional prohibition against land grants to private corporations. Although of doubtful legality, incorporation of the Southern Pacific and state support were necessary to attract private investors in the North. The Houston and Texas Central bill sought to relieve that road from its indebtedness to the state school fund, and again Northern support was at stake. Since the state held the first lien on the road's property, it could not draw financial aid as long as the state debt question was unresolved.[25]

Through the governor's manipulations the Senate achieved a compromise. Webster Flanagan offered to support the militia bill in return for passage of the Southern Pacific bill. Representatives of other local roads offered their support to lobby for the administration measures, and lobbyists received instructions that they should not aid efforts to defeat them. In an investigation of attempted bribery the chairman of the state's Democratic executive committee testified that men that he knew had been unable to raise $2,000 to buy the vote of Senator Fountain to block the police bills. The lobbyists had apparently refused to act against Davis. It is not clear if the governor accepted the deal forged by his men in the Senate, but administration supporters there appeared happy to exchange the police and militia bills for railroad bills.[26]

On June 16 the Senate took up the militia bill. The substitution of a Senate bill for the administration-backed House version provided an early test of strength, and the governor won by a vote of fifteen to fourteen. Senators Thomas Baker and John G. Bell who were associated with the Texas Central voted for the substitute. Senators Mills and Priest also appeared in the aye column. Of all the Republicans who had wavered in their support, only Webster Flanagan voted against the administration's position. The lines had been drawn, and Davis had won his first victory in the Senate.[27]

The governor's opponents were not ready to concede victory, and they moved to eliminate by amendment the powers given to the executive by the militia bill. The Republican majority held firm and voted down the first effort at changing the bill, fifteen to fourteen. Judge John Hancock and J. W. Throckmorton offered Senator William A. Saylor money to change his vote, but the deal fell through when the intermediary turned out to be a private detective hired by Davis to spy on the legislature. Unable to disrupt Republican ranks, thirteen members of the Senate walked out to break the quorum and prevent the first reading of the bill. President Campbell ordered them arrested and the sergeant-at-arms brought them back. After excusing four so that the Senate could proceed on the militia bill, Campbell suspended the rest until a special committee could consider the case.[28]

The arrest of the bolters and the administration's pressure

on Republican Senators paved the way for the passage of both police measures. On June 22 the Senate passed the militia bill by a vote of fifteen to five, and the governor signed it the following day. The police bill passed six days later. At this point, realizing the unpopularity of expelling the senators, Republican leaders in the Senate released those arrested, after they disclaimed any premeditation in walking out. In the House the Southern Pacific bill came up, out of order, and passed quickly. On June 30 C. J. Stockbridge, one of the Davis men in the House, introduced the Houston and Texas Central relief bill and it also passed. The governor moved now to release his nominations for the Senate's consent. Among the interesting nominees was Senator Mijamin Priest, named as judge of the Fourth Judicial District.[29]

After the successful passage of the militia and police bills, a new crisis developed when Davis returned both the Southern Pacific and H & TC bills to the legislature with his veto. Although his role in the legislative deal is not clear, when the railroad measures came before him he found them outside the bounds of the constitution. The Southern Pacific had been given land (despite the effort to hide this fact by calling the road a perpetuation of the Memphis, El Paso, and Pacific), and the new constitution prohibited land grants. The Texas Central bill provided for school funds to be invested in Central bonds, and that conflicted with a provision preventing the investment of school money in any security other than United States bonds.[30]

Had Davis dealt in bad faith, or had he not been a party to what his men in the legislature had done? The governor may have given in to pressure from the agrarian elements of his party to veto the bill. He had been warned by Senator Morgan Hamilton that the Southern Pacific and other roads wanted to rob the treasury and bankrupt the state. Hamilton's associate, Chauncey B. Sabin, argued that the party could gain nothing by making agreements with the railroads. Aid to the roads, Sabin feared, would create a tremendous tax burden and would aid the party's opponents by giving credence to charges of corruption and unfair taxation. Even his secretary of state, James Newcomb, counseled the governor to veto these particular bills. His advisors indicated that open support for the railroads would not be politically wise for Davis.[31]

If he had moved to block desertions among one element of his party, the railroad vetoes only precipitated a revolt from another. Senator James W. Flanagan informed Davis that if he had known he would hold to the doctrine announced in his vetoes, he would never have to run on the same ticket with him. The loss of Flanagan was not unexpected since he had been critical of the Davis program after he went to Washington. In order to secure his railroad projects Flanagan would shift his alliances in whatever way he could achieve his ends. Morgan Hamilton complained that Flanagan had "done nothing on the face of the earth since he has been here but log roll on railroad matters and hand in disability petitions." In the legislature the Senate passed both bills over the veto, and the House tried but fell short of the two-thirds needed. Using the governor's tactics, House members blocked action on the budget until Davis reconsidered what he had done.[32]

Flanagan's course had little impact on the Texas Republicans, but the situation in the House led to meetings between the governor and members of both the House and Senate. Davis's spokesmen urged the legislators to let railroad matters lie over until the next session and promised them that the administration would work to amend the constitution to allow land grants to corporations. The railroad men did not want a delay, however, and opposed the idea. In the meantime another proposed line entered the picture. Backers of a railroad along the line envisioned by Governor Davis, connecting the Southwest with major trunk lines, wanted a charter. Known as the International, the road had the support of important businessmen such as T. W. House of Galveston and Richard King, as well as New York investors. On August 5 the negotiators agreed to a compromise in which the governor's program would be acted upon in return for his agreement to allow the state to guarantee railroad bonds with its own. Following the railroad settlement, the legislators passed the Houston and Texas Central bill over the veto. They also chartered the International, promising $10,000 in state bonds for each mile of track placed in service between Fulton, Arkansas and Laredo. For the six hundred miles the company would receive a total of $6,000,000 in bonds. Davis would not agree, however, to the resurrection of the Memphis, El Paso, and Pacific in the form of the Southern Pacific, and action on it had to await the next session.[33]

After dealing with the railroads the legislature worked on the administration's package. They passed a law that restricted the right to carry weapons in areas away from the frontier. Bills organizing both the district and county courts received approval. A new election law that provided for registration and supervision went through. On some matters, however, the legislators modified the governor's program. The public school bill that they approved placed total control of the free schools in the hands of local authorities, contrary to Davis's wishes. The governor believed that as written the bill made a system impossible. In addition, the legislature failed to create the government bureaus that Davis wanted to promote the development of the state. The governor received most of the laws that he wanted, although not all. With the railroads he got more.[34]

The interaction of Davis and the legislature created a pattern of Republican policy that reflected the party's constituency. It did not reflect a radical departure from traditional political goals of Texans, although it did try to secure these ends for a broader segment of the population. Public schools had been a goal of Texans since the days of the Republic, and the Republicans now tried to obtain them, not simply for whites but for blacks also. Internal improvements had been started in the 1850s, but now the new party sought to back construction throughout the state rather than just in the plantation region. The problem with the program as a whole was that it cost money. The legislature trimmed several items from the governor's requested budget, but they still appropriated $442,481.61, double the appropriation of 1861. In addition they had approved the issue of bonds to finance the ranging companies and to back the railroads. The schools, the militia, the state police, the rangers, the district courts required staff. The number of state employees increased drastically and they had to be paid. The cost of Republicanism in Texas would be one of its greatest weaknesses.[35]

The administration's opponents watched the proceedings of the legislature and waited for an opportunity to capitalize on Republican mistakes. In June, while the legislators considered the police and militia bills, Pease went to Galveston to arrange with Flake for a newspaper campaign against the governor. On July 4 *Flake's Bulletin* printed a "Declaration of Wrongs Suffered by the People of Texas" and called upon all men to join together in opposition to the party that had tyrannized the legislature and obstructed justice in order to pass bills that authorized an unconstitutional army. In addition, despite the fact that no action had been taken on railroad matters, the *Bulletin* charged the Republicans with giving away millions of dollars to railroad rings and speculators. In a speech at Brenham, Jack Hamilton joined in the attack and condemned Davis and the legislature as schemers and thieves. The moves of Pease and Hamilton were the first steps against the governor. They proposed public meetings in every county to denounce the administration.[36]

The Conservative Republicans believed that the issues of tyranny and high taxes could be the basis for a fusion with moderate Democrats, and on July 9 Ferdinand Flake suggested united action. Flake believed that the Democratic party had made progress since the war, although there were still a few states' rights antiquarians. The editor suggested that "nothing but the bare name separates, or soon will separate them from moderate Republicans. . . . The Democrats are now moderate Republicans, and ought, in all honesty assume the name." The *Austin Republican*, still in the hands of the Conservative Republicans, joined with Flake in appealing for fusion. Its editor advocated the organization of men of all parties "who love their state" into political opposition to Governor Davis.[37]

Democratic leaders noticed the efforts of the Conservatives and at a meeting in Austin on July 9 party chairman William Walton discussed such a union with other members of his party. They agreed to cooperate in drafting a platform that appealed for a bipartisan alliance. To indicate a willingness to cooperate, the Democrats agreed to a joint chairmanship of the platform committee by Benjamin Epperson, a Unionist who had become a Democrat, and A. J. Hamilton. The committee's members included Republican senators Pridgen and Webster Flanagan and the former chairman of the Republican party, John L. Haynes.[38]

The fusion received general endorsement from the Democratic press. The *Bastrop Advertiser* encouraged all men to "unite to save our State from the threatened bankruptcy and ruin." The *Southern Banner* expected all "liberal minded gentlemen" to work together. The *Galveston News* advocated concessions to the Conservative Republicans by Democrats. Its editor asked if it was reasonable on the part of Democrats "to expect old line Whigs and Conservative Republicans to repudiate opinions long and honestly entertained." He concluded that it was not and urged the abandonment of party feeling.[39]

As a result of the efforts of Conservative Republicans and Democrats, a bipartisan meeting convened at Austin on July 16 and achieved a fusion of sorts. The delegates adopted a list of grievances that incorporated those in Flake's "Declaration of Wrongs." Their chief complaint was that the legislature had invested too much power in the executive, particularly with regard to law enforcement, voter registration, and appointments. However, most other Republican legislation received some criticism. The fusionists were particularly afraid that the financial policies of Davis threatened the state with an enormous debt. To combat "tyranny" they urged public meetings to draw up petitions directed to the governor and Congress for the repeal of the repugnant laws. Asking for openness rather than the resort to secret societies, the delegates established a committee on petitions cochaired by John Haynes and William Walton, to receive the local petitions and see to their publication. The fusion movement was underway and its battlecry was tyranny and taxation.[40]

The goal of the fusionists was to win special elections that had been ordered for the following November to fill vacancies in the legislature. At stake were two seats in the Senate, one Democratic and one Republican. In the House there were two Democratic, three Republican, and two previously unfilled seats. The Republican majority in the House would not be challenged by the election, but the narrow margin of the party in the Senate could be changed. If the Republicans could not fill the position vacated by M. Priest with another member of the party, they would lose their majority.

With the autumn election in mind, the Republicans started their own efforts to combat their opponents and retain control of the legislature. Reorganization of the Union League had begun in April in conjunction with the League's preparation for the congressional elections of 1870. On May 15 it held a meeting of the Grand State Council and elected secretary of state James Newcomb as president to replace Ruby. Newcomb sent representatives into the state to start councils in previously unorganized counties and to harmonize disputes in existing councils. By the middle of July his efforts had met with success across the state.[41]

While Newcomb worked on the League the chairman of the party's state executive committee, J. G. Tracy, started a reorganization of the party machinery. In much of the state the Republicans had no formal organization, and the chairman asked local leaders to establish executive committees in each county and judicial district. Tracy gave district committees the responsibility of guiding the work in counties and asked for periodic reports on their progress. While he wanted an open organization, he did not believe that it was practical in every area and aided Newcomb's retooling of the League in those places where a Republican organization could not flourish openly.[42]

The administration contributed to the preparations for the campaign by advancing an active defense of its policies in the pages of party papers, particularly the *Houston Union*. It denied that Republicans had approved massive railroad subsidies or had any part in the corruption rumored to have taken place on the railroad bills. The administration asserted that the Democrats were responsible for what had taken place and for the possibility of higher taxes. "Why the Democrats are the very men that are seeking to emburden our people with heavy taxes," the editor of the *Union* wrote. "Who are the railroad monopolists? Do they not belong to the 'old set?' Are they not Democrats?" Party leaders pointed out that the governor had vetoed the Southern Pacific bill, and yet only two Democrats in the Senate voted to sustain him. Chauncey Sabin accused the Democrats and Conservative Republicans of conspiring to raise taxes in order to create an issue to use against the governor.[43]

Republican campaign efforts received a setback shortly before the election when Senator Hamilton addressed an open letter to the *State Journal* and repudiated the administration. Hamilton believed that Davis had made too many concessions to the railroad men and accused the governor of encouraging an assault on the state treasury by using railroad legislation as a means to secure the militia and police bills. Behind the administration's deviation Hamilton saw Tracy who he believed had led the party away from "principles" and into the quagmire of compromise.[44]

Hamilton's break with the administration reflected the growth of his own isolation from it. Tracy had brought outsiders into the party and they did not always advocate the same policies as the senator. Tracy himself, for example, wanted a more liberal railroad policy because he thought "the broad and liberal spirit of Republicanism, which has rescued this country

from all its perils and placed it upon the high road to prosperity" required it. The appearance of such men created conflicts of interest with Hamilton. When the governor opposed
his efforts to fill a vacancy in the Federal Court for the Eastern
District of Texas, the Senator knew that his "enemies" had
secured Davis's ear. As a result they engaged in a time-consuming and costly fight that Hamilton lost. He complained to Newcomb late in the summer of 1870: "It seems I am not to be
consulted about any measure, however important to the party,
the country or myself as touching ... railroad bounties, and
expenditures on jobs, not to have any opinion of my own, but
to shout the cry of the party leaders for the times, whether it
be the Governor or some new recruit who has but just got warm
in his nest." [45]

The opposition of Hamilton, added to the fusion of Conservative Republicans and Democrats, made winning the election more difficult, but Davis urged Republicans to stronger
efforts. Emphasizing how important he believed the elections
were, he sent Newcomb and Adjutant General James Davidson
to help with party organization in the disputed districts. "The
carrying of the vacant senatorial districts is of so much importance," the governor informed Newcomb, "that I willingly
spare you both. Only do your work thoroughly." The governor
did not want any more Democrats in the legislature or any
more men interested in "chicken pie." [46]

Internal problems and violence added to campaign rhetoric
in deciding the election. In the Twenty-sixth District an outbreak of hostility between blacks and Germans prevented cooperation and provided an indication of future party problems.
In the Twenty-fifth, campaign workers found local Republicans
inactive. They were like "drones in the hive, they don't like
to work but are anxious to eat the honey after it is gathered."
In the Eighteenth District violence flared up and the sheriff
of Leon County complained that Ku Klux Klan outlaws tried
to drive freed slaves from their farms around Cotton Gin. In
the Third District an observer found the Union men thoroughly
cowed and disoriented by threatened violence by the Democrats. Governor Davis sent Thomas Sheriff of the state police
to Nacogdoches as a result, but the investigator concluded that
intimidation there was carried out in a manner that precluded
criminal prosecution. The governor could not prevent blacks
and whites from being driven away from the polls. [47]

Considering all of their problems, the Republicans did well

at the polls when they opened on November 28. In the Twenty-fifth, R. P. Tendick, a German merchant from Columbus, defeated Wells Thompson, a prominent lawyer and landowner, to give the Republicans the Senate seat of A. R. Foster, a Democrat who had died during the session. In the other Senate race in the Third, however, Priest's place went to a Democrat, J. E. Dillard. In the House, although Democrats defeated the Republican candidates for two vacant seats and one that had been unfilled, the Republicans managed to pick up the remaining seats. The results left the two parties at virtually the same strength as before and the Republican control of the Senate was maintained. Numerous county and city elections took place at the same time, but what happened in them is not clear. Republicans reported some success.[48]

The Twelfth Legislature reconvened for its first regular session on January 10, 1871, with Republicans heartened by the election. Davis renewed efforts to secure his program and asked for modification of many of the acts passed in the preceding session. He wanted more arms for the militia and more men for the state police. Changes had to be made in the school law to meet the state needs, and he once again advocated passage of a bill similar to the one originally introduced. He requested more stringent restrictions on the carrying of weapons in order to insure law and order. The legislature still needed to create immigration and geological bureaus. In his address to the legislators at the beginning of the session, the governor praised them for their work and urged them to finish the program. He realized that he was asking for a greater expansion of services and higher taxes, but the welfare of the state required that sacrifice.[49]

The legislature met for five months and during that time the Republicans exhibited a solidarity that they had not demonstrated in the special session. Democratic newspapers predicted that the Republican legislators would be more antagonistic toward the governor's programs, but they proved more agreeable. They sent to Davis each piece of legislation requested in his message and in the form he desired. In turn, despite the governor's official position, the executive proved more open to state subsidies for railroads. The Southern Pacific received a charter with the same support given to the International. Although the governor vetoed the bill, both houses easily overrode it. The railroad crisis that had been so important in the previous legislature was not duplicated.[50]

The passage of the Southern Pacific charter suggests something about the operations of the Davis administration and the governor's views on railroad matters. Following the creation and funding of the frontier ranging companies, Davis had tried to dispose of the $750,000 in bonds that had been authorized. Because of the state's bad credit and threats that the state debt would be repudiated, he could find no one to buy the bonds. Jay Cooke & Co. refused to act as the Texas agent since it was involved in a law suit against the First National Bank of New York initiated by the state to recover indemnity bonds disposed of by the Confederate state government. Davis sent Newcomb to New York to try to sell the bonds. Through Congressman Clark, Newcomb met with Marshall O. Roberts, head of the boards of both the Southern Transcontinental and Southern Pacific railroads, who sent the secretary of state to the Farmers Loan & Trust Company. Farmers Loan, whose directors were associated with the Texas and Pacific organization, agreed to become the agent of the state in New York and agreed to make loans to the state based on the bonds. Davis might veto railroad measures, but his agents could work with the backers of the roads.[51]

Morgan Hamilton believed that Davis had made a deal with the Southern Pacific interests to gain backing for his bonds, and subsequent actions seemed to support him. When the bill that subsidized the two Roberts railroads passed through the legislature the governor adhered to his stated opposition and vetoed it. The Republican majority, however, refused to sustain his action and Davis's strongest backers voted to pass the bill over the veto. The action of the Republicans suggested that the administration did not oppose the bill as unalterably as the veto might indicate. In the Senate only two Republicans voted against overriding the veto and the bill passed twenty-three to four.[52]

If the Republican leadership had made a deal with Roberts it had been done with considerable astuteness. Because their party contained a strong agrarian and antirailroad faction, a Republican governor could not openly endorse the subsidy without provoking a revolt. By allowing the legislature to pass the bills while the governor stood steadfast against railroad "monopoly" and "raids on the treasury," Davis managed to retain some claims to the loyalty of the agrarian element. Davis had to be a man for the whole party. The votes of individual members of the legislature were less critical to Republican unity.

When the legislature adjourned on May 31 it had completed the governor's program. The legislation may have been more beneficial to the state as a whole than to the party that initiated it. It secured law and order, created schools, and built new railroads, but the tax collector dug deeper into the property owner's pocket. The party placed demands for capital upon an agricultural community that had fought to avoid taxes in the past and may not have had the ability to meet these demands. Opponents certainly saw Republican policies as a threat that necessitated a response with all the means at their command.

The battles to secure the Republican program also created deep fissures within the party. The governor found that he could satisfy neither the antirailroad "agrarians" nor the railroad "monopolists." The defections of Morgan Hamilton and James Flanagan altered the coalition that had secured power in 1869. In addition, the Twelfth Legislature had demonstrated the insensitivity of white Republicans to the needs of their black constituents. While willing to accept blacks as voters and to provide services such as education, they did not consider them to be equals and were not interested in doing anything that would change their position in society. This attitude would produce discontent among blacks that would add to the party's basic instability.

CHAPTER 8

Tyranny, Taxes, and Corruption: Crisis of the Radical Coalition

The organization of the forces hostile to the Davis administration in the summer of 1870 outlined the grounds for future political battles in Texas. While the Twelfth Legislature met in its first regular session early in 1871, the opponents of the governor's brand of Republicanism started their preparations for a major political test, the Congressional elections that would be held the next autumn. Charging Davis and his administration with tyranny, high taxes, and corruption, a combination of Democrats and dissident Republicans would force modifications in the programs and goals of the party regulars. The congressional elections of 1871 would result in changes to the identity of Texas Republicanism.

The elections marked the first time since 1866 that a strong Democratic party had been in the field. At the beginning of congressional reconstruction the Democrats had divided into two major factions concerning the proper course with regard to national politics. The conservative-secessionist wing, which had seized the initiative in 1866 and been responsible for the constitution written that year, lost control to a group of moderates. The chief of the new leaders was party chairman William Walton, whose political philosophy was closer to that of Unionists like Governor Throckmorton than to the old Secessionists of his own party. Walton pursued a careful policy toward the Republicans, even considering fusion with the followers of Jack Hamilton and Pease when political gains could be made. Walton's control over the Democratic party, however, had become more tenuous as congressional pardons and migration to Texas from the rest of the South swelled the ranks of his party.

In the special elections of 1870 a revolt against Walton and the moderates spread through the local organizations. This dissatisfaction increased in the county conventions of 1871, and conservatives demanded an end to Walton's fusion policies and a return to "straight out" Democracy. The conservatives blocked an effort to nominate a former Unionist for Congress in the Fourth Congressional District and raised charges that Walton was trying to destroy the Democratic party. The Democratic *State Gazette* at Austin indicated the changing temper of the party. Its editors demanded that the next state convention be for Democrats and Democrats only. The editors wrote: "Those who expect to break bread and eat salt with us must have on the wedding garments."[1]

At the Democratic state convention on January 23, 1871, the "straight out" element was in control. Rather than fight them, the moderates gave in, and Walton called for renewed party unity. The result was a party platform that the *Jefferson Radical* argued would drag every Southern Unionist from his "bloody grave" in opposition. The document reaffirmed the doctrine of states' rights, protested federal interference in state elections, complained against restrictions on the suffrage, and attacked the policies of the Davis administration. The convention indicated that the Democratic party intended to run its candidates for Congress on the issue of state policies rather than the merits of the individual candidates. If the Republican congressmen had not been directly involved in forming the Davis administration's programs it did not matter; they were guilty by association.[2]

Following their meeting at Austin, the Democrats held district conventions where, in each case, they selected "straight out" candidates to run for Congress. In the Third District, to oppose William T. Clark, they chose Dewitt C. Giddings who, although denying that he was a "rawhead and bloody bones Democrat," did not claim to be a "milk and water" one either. The latter were as much a curse to Texas as the Radicals, he asserted. In the Second, Congressman John C. Conner, the carpetbag Democrat, took a conservative position that got him renominated over the opposition of powerful moderates such as Throckmorton. Conner claimed to be an unswerving Democrat and was a vociferous advocate of a renewed and "straight out" Democratic party in Texas. To oppose George Whitmore in the First District, the Democrats selected W. S. Herndon, another "straight out" party man. Only in the Fourth District, where Unionism had been strong and Republicanism had a hold, could the moderates name a candidate, and they chose John Hancock to oppose Degener.[3]

The resurgence of old-style Democratic activity in Texas

was made possible by the "New Departure" movement that had taken place in the party in the North. In Ohio Clement L. Vallandigham had called for the forging of a new party based upon acceptance of the results of the Civil War and a return to the principle of states' rights. Vallandigham, whose arrest for declaring sympathy with the enemy in 1863 had made him a hero of the Democratic party, argued that to continue to try to fight the implementation of the Thirteenth, Fourteenth and Fifteenth Amendments was a waste of time. He urged Democrats to turn to civil service reform, revenue reform, universal amnesty, changes in the tariff, return to specie payment, taxation of wealth rather than people, and an end to land grants to private corporations. The Texas Democrats could not agree on Vallandigham's specific measures, but they could adhere to his call for a return to the "original theory and character of the Federal government." At a party rally at Galveston, congressional candidate Giddings said: "The government of the Union should be limited and controlled by the Constitution, each branch of the Government within its sphere being independent of the others, each limited by the powers delegated, which should be strictly construed, the largest liberty being accorded to the citizens consistent with the rights of the whole, recognizing as still binding the late amendments to the Constitution, which have been declared adopted by the constituted authorities." The moderate *Galveston News*, whose policies had been toward fusion, stated its approval of the new course. The tendency toward centralization had ruined the country, according to its editors. Now, they wrote: "We must have a confederation of States opposed to a consolidated nation or we will never be a free people." [4]

In the face of the greater reluctance of the Democrats to cooperate with them, the followers of Hamilton and Pease were not certain what to do. Colonel John L. Haynes broke with the fusionists, saying that he could never support a party that adopted a states' rights platform. "I cannot sacrifice those principles of government to sustain which I took up arms during the late war," he wrote, "to retain the good will of those who supported me." But Hamilton and the others continued to look for alternatives to returning to the regular party. Rumors that a third party movement was developing in the North encouraged them to remain independent. In May, Horace Greeley came to Galveston for the state agricultural fair, but he also met with Hamilton, Pease, and Ferdinand Flake. Greeley's encouragement led them to believe that fusion might still be possible if centered on a program of ending corruption and bringing men of ability to public office. As a result, while calling themselves liberals, these Republican outsiders continued their opposition to the governor and his administration and cooperated, where possible, with the Democrats.[5]

The strategy of the Radical Republicans, in response to their opponents, was to try to attract more whites to the party. Simply the growth of the white population had made such a course necessary, and the party's chairman, James Tracy, believed that avoiding a racial identity was essential to success. In an interview at Houston he said, "The Republican party of Texas is composed of various races and nationalities. It is true in this district the colored element predominates, but it is equally true that in some of the other districts the white element outnumbers the colored." For Tracy, Republicanism was a political movement that should have meaning to both races, and he set for himself the task of making the party biracial.[6]

The party chairman, as well as members of the administration, believed that a major impediment to the movement of whites into the party was the power of the secret Union League. Many whites refused to join because they believed they would have little voice in such an organization. As a result, a key element of Tracy's efforts in 1871 was to break up the power of the League. The state executive committee encouraged the formation of new, open groups such as the Grand Army of the Republic or simple county Republican clubs. Newcomb, party secretary and president of the state League, used his authority for the same goal and issued new charters to break up powerful local chapters.[7]

Opposition developed quickly to Tracy and Newcomb's attack upon the League. Because the admission of whites to local councils and the deemphasis of the League as a political instrument threatened the control of bosses over local politics, the instructions on reorganization touched off a general revolt. The uprising of local leaders presented a severe challenge to the ability of the state officers to move the party in directions they thought more useful for the future. The resulting battle would indicate one of the weaknesses or limits to the flexibility of Southern Republicanism.

Matthew Gaines, the outspoken black senator from the

Sixteenth District, was one of the men threatened by Tracy and Newcomb. He was personally ambitious and wanted the seat in Congress occupied by William T. Clark. Because of the hostility toward him of many party leaders, however, the only chance that he had for gaining the nomination was through manipulation of the district convention and the Union League. When Tracy demanded that more whites be brought into the party he lessened the chances Gaines had of getting to Congress. As a result the senator attacked the chairman and accused him of betraying the black people of the state. In Gaines's eyes the party no longer responded to the needs of the vast majority of its constituents and its leadership needed to be changed.[8]

Another man thwarted by the new policy was Major Louis W. Stevenson. He had come to Texas with the army of occupation in 1865 and stayed on as an agent of the Freedmen's Bureau. In 1867 he had joined the Republican party and had become one of the organizers of the Union League in the black belt counties. Through these activities he established strong ties with the black community. By 1871 he believed that he should be allowed to run for Congress in the Third District. He was, however, no better choice than Gaines to officials at Austin. Because his strength lay solely with blacks, whites refused to associate with him and party leaders believed that Stevenson could never help them broaden their base of support. When the major indicated that he would try to secure the nomination for Congress, Newcomb responded that he would block any attempt that he might make in the convention. Stevenson indicated that he would not submit to the will of the leadership and informed the secretary, "If it becomes necessary to make war, so be it, but the field will not only be where you have been firing missiles [the newspapers], it will be transferred to Africa [the black belt counties]."[9]

The effort to reduce the power of the League also had meaning for Congressman Whitmore in the First District. Whitmore had not been a strong backer of Davis while at Washington, and party officials at Austin wanted to replace him with someone less critical of the governor and his policies. Whitmore's power rested on the local chapters of the League, and his men controlled them. When Newcomb started issuing charters to new chapters during the spring, Whitmore, like Gaines and Stevenson, saw it as a direct attack upon himself.[10]

The three men undermined by the reorganization of the

party were each in a position to take advantage of growing sentiment among blacks that the state leaders were not adequately rewarding their black constituency with patronage or nominations. Frank Webb, the black editor of the *Galveston Republican* had warned: "We daily see subordinate offices that hundreds of colored men in our midst could fill creditably, given to white men of very questionable republicanism, and who cannot command a single vote, beside their own, or exercise the slightest influence among the colored people, who after all are *the* Republican party." Matthew Gaines expressed similar sentiments when he complained about the immigration policies of the party, especially its efforts to promote the introduction of more German settlers into the state. In a speech in his home district Gaines condemned what had been done: "They pay a man a salary of $3,500 per annum to bring Dutch here to work the land that we cut the trees from and pulled the stumps out of. They sell land to the Dutch on credit with ten per cent interest, but a colored man cannot buy it on four months or forty months at fifty per cent interest." Such antagonism offered individuals under attack by the administration a base upon which to build their own counterattack.[11]

Whitmore took the initiative by sending a political protegé, George H. Slaughter, to Austin. After appealing to Newcomb, Slaughter used his post as vice-president of the state League to call a meeting of all dissatisfied Republicans. When the group assembled on May 18, Slaughter declared it a formal meeting of the executive council of the Union League and managed to get those attending to call a state League convention to replace Newcomb as president. Slaughter manipulated another resolution through the assembly that favored his acting as head of the League until the state convention. Both Gaines and Stevenson jumped to the support of this bolting organization.[12]

Slaughter's work received added impetus when Senator Morgan Hamilton lent his support to it. Hamilton backed William B. Moore in the publishing of an antiadministration newspaper at Austin called *The Reformer*, and Moore supported Slaughter's League organization and Stevenson's candidacy for Congress. When Newcomb took over the Travis County League, Moore helped form a competing one. At Houston another close friend of the senator, Judge Chauncey Sabin, placed his own support behind Stevenson. While Hamilton was not a great friend of any of the bolters, he saw their effort as a tool to regain control of the party from the railroad "monopolists" and Tracy, who he believed was their agent. With Hamilton's shift into this "reform" movement, the regulars had a full-scale revolt on their hands. Hamilton's leadership would make the opposition into something more than the howling of disappointed office seekers or an expression of black discontent. Hamilton made it into a reform movement.[13]

The combination of Whitmore, Slaughter, Stevenson, Gaines, and Senator Hamilton forced Tracy and Newcomb to move away from their reorganization. They realized how dangerous dissatisfaction among their black constituents could be, especially since they had used it in 1869 to wrest control of the party from Jack Hamilton; consequently Tracy urged Newcomb to use a liberal allocation of police and school positions to blacks to defuse the situation. Newcomb consulted with the newly appointed school superintendent, Jacob DeGress, and urged him to fill the post of school supervisor to make the greatest political impact. Typical of the superintendent's work was the appointment of Captain William H. Griffin at Galveston. After taking his office Griffin immediately named George Ruby, N. Wright Cuney, Nathan Patten, and F. C. Mosebach, all strong party regulars, to the school board in Galveston County. Senator Ruby advised Newcomb that he believed Griffin was a wise choice and that he would be of great service in the coming campaign.[14]

Congressman Clark hurried home to do his own part in suppressing the "reform" movement and in mending his fences. Now that he faced defections of blacks from his support, Clark came to Ruby to secure support that he had not previously solicited. After a meeting with Tracy and Ruby, the congressman began appearing at Republican meetings in the black counties. He consulted with Negro legislators and county officials. Showing that he was as much a representative of his black constituents as of the white railroad men and bankers at Galveston, Clark joined the Emancipation Day celebration at Houston on June 19 where he presided over the festivities and played in the afternoon baseball game. Unfortunately for Clark, while he worked hard to establish his links with the black community and its political leaders, his efforts made him less acceptable to the businessmen whose favors he had been currying.[15]

Newcomb moved to cut off any possibility that the bolters might receive recognition from the national League by summoning a meeting at Austin which passed resolutions condemning the legality of the Slaughter movement. After reaffirming their support of Newcomb, the League members who came to Austin read out Slaughter and the others who had participated with him. Newcomb informed the national League secretary, Thomas G. Baker, that he still represented the regular organization and that the bolt was nothing more than an effort by "soreheads" and party "outs" to overthrow the existing leadership. Newcomb urged the national council to stay out of the affair and predicted that, if ignored, the Texas reformers would quickly fall apart. The result was favorable to the Davis administration, for Baker promised not to intervene. When representatives from the Slaughter group asked for recognition, they received word that national officials intended to keep their hands out of Texas affairs. Through prompt action Newcomb avoided one of the blunders that had led to the overthrow of Jack Hamilton in 1869.[16]

Left to settle their own fight, the reformers and the regulars first confronted one another at the National Labor Convention of the Working Men of Texas. This meeting had been called by the Negro Longshoremen's Benevolent Association, a part of Ruby's political machine, and had grown out of the Republican party's efforts to counter the National Labor Union's attempts to organize blacks into the National Labor Reform party. Stevenson and his supporters appeared at Houston hoping to take over the convention and secure its endorsement. Support from the NLC would give the bolters a stronger appeal to black voters and also provide a better case for securing national support. Unfortunately for the reformers, the regulars appeared at the meeting in force and managed to prevent the convention from making any political endorsements. Ruby secured the chair of the executive committee for a young associate, Norris Wright Cuney, and, consequently, kept control of the permanent organization as well.[17]

The failure before the NLC at Houston did not deter the bolters, who held a Grand Council of the Union League at Austin on July 3. Poor attendance forced Slaughter to postpone it four days, but then, despite the poor turnout, the delegates met and issued resolutions condemning Newcomb for letting the League disintegrate. After expressing their beliefs that Newcomb no longer represented the interests of the Union League, the delegates approved his suspension and elected a new president, Justice of the Peace Johnson Reed, a black man from Galveston. The Grand Council meeting was something of a last gasp for the reformers.[18]

When the Third District convention met, Davis forces had matters in hand. The reformers had made few inroads into the county conventions where the regular party organization had maintained control. The delegates who showed up at Houston appeared to be aligned firmly behind Clark, although two of four from Washington County expressed a preference for Stevenson. A local party official, however, informed Newcomb that a little "greesing" could change that. Only in Galveston had Stevenson managed to attract any strength, but the administration had stifled it. Prior to the county convention in Galveston the Stevenson forces had seized control of the League, but Newcomb retaliated with the issue of a new charter and the naming of N. Wright Cuney as its head. With Cuney in control, the Stevenson movement had been blocked.[19]

Stevenson still believed, however, that he could win the nomination. In most counties his men had chosen alternate delegates to contest those for Clark, and the candidate believed that these challengers could gain control over the convention if allowed on the floor. George Ruby, working as temporary chairman, stopped this maneuver by using the state police to keep any of the Stevenson delegates from reaching the floor until after the credentials committee had decided their cases. While the committee was out, Ruby went ahead with the organization and managed the election of James Tracy as permanent chairman. The choice of Tracy insured Clark's nomination. Stevenson and the six delegates who supported him walked out. Although Clark received the convention's endorsement, Stevenson refused to withdraw, and he decided to run on his own. Governor Davis worked to bring about some sort of compromise, but neither man would agree to one and the Republicans entered the canvass with two candidates in the field, a regular and a reformer. Stevenson had gotten the battle to Africa, however, and the regulars had been forced to back away from their attempt to limit the role of the Union League.[20]

Having fought out their internal battles, the Republicans turned to their other opponents. Pease and Hamilton were still hoping for some sort of fusion and they finally managed to put together a combination of Democrats and "reform" Republicans for a taxpayers' convention to discuss political conditions in the state. Unable to capture the regular organization, Morgan Hamilton reconciled himself with his brother and Pease and joined them in their efforts. While the taxpayers' convention offered them a forum for their attacks upon the administration, the Republicans who met in it found that no political coalition could be achieved. Morgan Hamilton's *Reformer* reported that most Republicans had been disgusted with the bad faith of the Democrats who had refused to allow any blacks to attend. Further, the Democrats had treated the Republican rank and file with indifference. "Judging from what we have seen of the concern," the editor wrote, "we should say that a Republican has as little show in it as a cat would have in perdition without claws." One associate of Pease, Hans Teichmueller of La Grange, indicated that he did not see the possibility of action by the people regardless of party.[21]

Although called as a nonpartisan assembly, the taxpayers' convention actually initiated the Democratic canvass for the congressional seats. The delegates drafted two reports concerning the state administration that became the basis for the Democratic campaign. The first charged the governor and his administration with an unprincipled lust for power and with using every means to concentrate authority in central hands. To sustain their accusations, the delegates catalogued the laws and actions they believed served as proof—the Enabling Act that gave the governor the power to fill local vacancies, firearms control laws, the state police, the militia, and Davis's declarations of martial law. The second report focused on state financial conditions and charged the governor with reckless use of the taxpayers' money. It showed that from 1866 to 1870 the cost of government had increased almost 400 percent, going from about a half million to over two million dollars. The committee pointed out that the legislature had provided for an *ad valorem* tax of .225 per hundred dollars and a $1 poll tax to finance the state government in 1866. In 1871 the tax burden had mushroomed to 2.175 on the hundred with a $2 poll tax to help pay for schools and major road improvements. The delegates argued that an *ad valorem* tax of .333 for state purposes and .166 for the counties was sufficient, and that more was excessive and unrealistic.[22]

Members of the Davis administration responded to the meeting as though it were simply a campaign ploy. The *State Journal* called the delegates "tax-howlers . . . [who] can't pay their taxes, but have money enough to travel hundreds of miles and pay heavy bar room bills in order to add a little fuel to the Ku Klux disaffection and hostility that disfigures and disgraces the state." When the convention adjourned, Davis led the Republicans of Austin around the capitol building to symbolically purify the legislative halls of the ideas of states' rights heretics.[23]

The Democrats could not be put down so easily. Taxes, tyranny, and corruption became their battle cry, one repeated again and again. In their canvass the two Hamiltons and E. M. Pease served them well, for they added to the speakers travelling about the state in opposition to Davis. Their presence perhaps indicates that the governor and his supporters had misread the extent of concern over fiscal policy in the state. Morgan Hamilton condemned in particular the expenses of the government and argued that they had not resulted in greater services but in a larger bureaucracy. Taxes, in the senator's opinion, had reached the point that they were confiscatory in the case of men who owned large amounts of unproductive lands on the frontier. Jack Hamilton explained his brother's hostility toward Davis in a speech at Galveston: "My brother sided with the authorities, but on his return [to Texas from Washington] he found an argument *ad pocketum*, for though my brother, he has now to pay about $3,000 in taxes. He does not like to be robbed in a day."[24]

The tack of the Democrats compelled the governor to tour the state and defend his policies. The congressional campaign had turned into a referendum on his administration and Newcomb, Adjutant General James Davidson, and Superintendent Jacob DeGress joined him on the hustings. Administration spokesmen addressed themselves to the charges of the Democrats and denied either the intention of assuming despotic powers or the unreasonableness of state taxes. They argued that the Enabling Act had been an emergency measure designed to fill offices where occupants had refused or failed to qualify after the election of 1869, and it was a nuisance that they were happy to be through with. The police measures were defended as necessary to insure law and order. For the various measures intended to put down civil disturbances, they offered no apologies and suggested that the decrease in crime in the state proved both the need and effectiveness of the laws.[25]

Republicans took great care in the defense of their use of

state monies. Davis did not deny that his administration had cost more than previous ones, but he argued that the reforms initiated by him had been more expensive. At Galveston on August 16 the governor told the crowd: "If you live in a hut and sleep under a Mexican blanket, it will cost you less than if you fabricate an elegant building. If you have no government it will cost you nothing. If you have public schools and law and order, you must pay for it." The opposition raised by men such as Morgan Hamilton particularly incensed Davis, for the senator had been a longtime supporter of free public schools. When it was clear that he would have to carry a share of the tax burden to support them, however, he had moved to the forefront of those opposing the administration. While admitting that expenses and taxes were higher than they had been, Republican leaders denied that they were excessive. They charged the Democrats with trying to mislead the public, since the figures they presented were inaccurate in some cases and misstatements of existing conditions in others. The Democrats, for example, charged the Republicans on the basis of maximum tax limits rather than on the basis of those actually collected.[26]

As the campaign developed, Davis became convinced that his opponents intended to use more violence than usual in addition to their rhetoric. When the Democrats planned "barbecues" in county seats during the election, the governor responded with a proclamation forbidding the gathering of large numbers of people for the purpose of interfering with the election. As a further hindrance to violence the proclamation contained a provision that prohibited the sale of liquor and the carrying of firearms in any town with a poll. Under the state police law Davis assumed control over all local peace officers and Adjutant General Davison authorized and appointed special police to look over the polling. When several citizens of Galveston protested, Davis replied that he would not withdraw his proclamation. "The right of some people to assemble together," he wrote, "must be subordinate to that of other people to exercise the privilege of franchise peaceably and without hindrance or intimidation."[27]

At Groesbeck in Limestone County a crisis developed when a man named Gallagher appeared and made public statements denouncing local Republican officials and the state police. The Republicans charged the Democrats with sending him, and the Democrats asserted that he was an agent sent by Governor Davis to provoke an incident. Whoever he was, the local mayor sent the police to arrest him. They found Gallagher protected by a mob and when they tried to arrest him one man, an auctioneer for the Texas Central Railroad, pulled a gun and a policeman shot him. A riot ensued, the mob seized the arresting officers, then more police moved in to free them. A period of quiet followed, but the whites organized and planned to gather at the county seat on election day. Governor Davis believed that they intended to prevent a fair vote from being taken and declared martial law. On October 9 the militia moved into the county and arrested twenty-five whites whom they accused of inciting a riot. The military commission that investigated the affair charged "organized political societies" with using the killing of the auctioneer as a pretext to arm and using violence to influence the election. Although tried, none were convicted, and the uproar that had taken place accomplished their goal as well as more direct intimidation. The Republican vote dropped from 297, the number of votes cast for Davis in 1869, to 1.[28]

Any hope that the Republicans had of carrying the election disappeared as the first reports filtered into Austin. Fuller results indicated a disaster. In the Second District the Democrat Conner easily defeated Judge Anthony M. Bryant. Bryant improved on the vote received by the Republican candidate in 1869, but the growth in the Democratic column left him with only 29 percent of the total. The election was closer in the First and Fourth Districts, although not enough to allow the manipulation of votes. In the First, Whitmore received 2,973 more votes than he had in 1869, but his opponent, W. S. Herndon, attracted 9,214 more than his predecessor and carried the district by over 5,000 votes. In the Fourth District where Degener had won by a narrow margin in 1869, the incumbent increased his vote by 41 percent, but the Democrat John Hancock received 92 percent more votes. This time Degener lost and by over 4,000 votes. The only close contest was in the Third District where the Democrat, Giddings, led Clark by only 135 votes.[29]

Faced with the loss of all four congressional seats, party leaders at Austin looked over the results to see if anything could be salvaged. While the Democrats had resorted to intimidation of Republican voters, in most cases they had refrained from open violence, and local leaders complained to Newcomb that they had provided neither enough grounds for criminal prosecution or for throwing out the election. Further, some Republicans feared that charges against their opponents would only lead to countercharges. A party member in Anderson County expressed the situation of party members when he informed the administration: "Although we believe there were at least two hundred who voted with them who were with us if left to their own choice and voted with them through intimidation, yet we do not think that a criminal prosecution could be sustained against them, and beside there was a good deal of intimidation practiced by the colored men in our party and if we would commence proceedings against them they would retaliate."[30]

While the state returning board certified Conner, Herndon, and Hancock, its members delayed in the case of Giddings after the governor concluded that enough fraud had taken place to warrant an investigation. The board decided to reject the votes from Limestone and Freestone counties because of reported violence against Republicans. Bosque County votes were rejected on the grounds that the board had received no official results from the county. In Brazos and Washington counties the board refused to include in the tally ballots that had been "illegally marked" or received at a "white man's box." The altered returns appeared to give the seat to Clark, so the board issued him a qualified certificate. While Giddings decided to contest the case, Davis believed that the incumbent would be seated with little difficulty.[31]

Giddings appealed first to the Federal Court for the Western District of Texas, filled with officers with connections to the Democratic party. On January 31 the grand jury indicted Davis, Newcomb, and Attorney General Alexander for "willfully, unlawfully and feloniously [making] a false and untrue tabular statement of the votes cast by the legal voters of the Third Congressional District." Even though the federal circuit court found the defendants not guilty of the charges, the indictments and prosecutions of the governor and other state election officials helped the Democrats convince people in the North that Davis's administration was corrupt. The court action also interfered with Clark's efforts to gather affidavits in his favor for a congressional hearing on the election. Clark complained that threatened legal action discouraged people from filing statements in his behalf. When Congress took up the disputed election, Giddings appeared with volumes of testimony supporting his cause, while Clark had little but the statements of party officials. The congressman asked the House for an extension of time to gather more testimony, but the House Committee on Elections introduced a resolution in favor of Giddings. The House adopted the committee report and swore Giddings in.[32]

The Republicans had lost all four of the state's seats in Congress, but this loss was only one of the consequences of the election. In the Twelfth Legislature the results produced a panic. The legislature had convened in its second session in September 1871, but its members had refrained from action while they awaited the outcome of the elections. Although they produced a law designed to prevent racial discrimination on public carriers, Republican legislators began backing away from the administration and started efforts to dismantle its program. Through vetoes and careful manipulation the governor managed to prevent the repeal of important elements, but he realized that he could not stop the attack. It was clear that Davis could no longer count on the legislature for support.[33]

The election also created a financial crisis for the state government. Sensing the inevitable victory of the Democrats and tax relief, Texans started withholding their taxes in defiance of the Republican administration. When this revolt presented the governor with the possibility that he would not have enough money in the treasury to meet operating expenses, he resorted to the sale of bonds to finance operations. In turn the Democrats threatened to repudiate them, and Davis found little market for their sale. Across the North, rather than support, the governor found general acceptance of the accusations made by Democrats and of their efforts to undermine his administration. The Republican *Chicago Tribune* printed inaccurate charges that Davis had increased the state debt to $50,000,000 and raised taxes to $7,000,000 per year and suggested taxpayers band together to issue a warning that the debt would be repudiated when "the People" returned to power. The *New York Tribune*, organ of Horace Greeley, warned Texas Republicans to squelch their embryo Tweeds or meet a just defeat at the hands of the people of their state.[34]

The election of 1871 had uncovered several weaknesses of Texas Republicanism. No matter what benefits might exist as a result of their programs, the majority of Texans found them too expensive, and the Democrats had managed to use the issue of taxes to achieve a victory for themselves. Without some changes in the party's programs, the Republicans could not hope to attract the white voters necessary to regain a majority position. When party leaders attempted to reorganize to bring in more whites, however, they opened themselves to accusations that they were abandoning their chief source of strength, the black voters. The need to insure the support of blacks imposed a limit on how far the state leadership could go in its appeal to other groups. In 1871 efforts by the "reformers" to strip black support away from the regulars forced the regulars to reconsolidate their position and drop their attempts to create a more racially balanced party. The party needed white support; it could not afford to lose its backing among blacks. Some way to achieve both had to be found.

CHAPTER 9

"We Have Met the Enemy and We Are Theirs": The 1872 General Election

Another campaign after the congressional disaster of 1871 forced the Texas Republicans to regroup almost immediately. They faced a general election called by the Twelfth Legislature for the following November, and a victory was critical for the party's future. Texans would vote for half of the places in the state Senate and all in the House; thus the Republican control of the legislature was in jeopardy. Also at stake were two new seats in the United States House of Representatives that had been created in the redistricting of the state after the recent census. Equally important for the local party was the presidential race, where Grant faced a major revolt within Republican ranks as well as a powerful Democratic opposition. Reelection of the president was necessary to the local party if it was going to retain any influence over federal patronage or hope for national support. The importance of the patronage and keeping people in office who were friendly to the administration already had been demonstrated by the problems created for Davis by the actions of the federal district court in the previous election. Grant had to be sustained in the autumn canvass, but particularly in the national convention. That spring, state Republican party officials began work to secure solid support for the president and a good showing in November.

An important goal for the Republicans, if they hoped to do well in the general election, was to expand their base of support among whites. After the war the white population of Texas had grown rapidly, boosted by immigration from other Southern states. This growth had made the success of any party based primarily on black voters impossible. Whites might be attracted, however, if their interests could be served within the Republican party. To win greater white support, Republican leaders tried to demonstrate how they could meet individual needs by manipulating the federal patronage and creating a more moderate program.

The offer of jobs was the most direct way the administration could reward people who came to their support. The most lucrative positions at the party's disposal were those of the federal government, and leaders worked to demonstrate not only that they could control these offices but also could deliver them to the right individuals. The most important recent convert for the Davis administration had been John L. Haynes, who had abandoned the Hamilton group after their fusion with the Democrats in 1871. A post for Haynes would be an important indication that the governor did not hold grudges and might attract other Unionists who had not gone along with him in 1869. Davis went to Washington personally to secure the removal of the collector of customs at Brownsville and the appointment of Haynes in his place. Despite the failure of local Republicans in the congressional elections and Morgan Hamilton's opposition to the appointment, Davis managed to get Haynes named to the post. It appeared that the governor was the chief arbiter in local patronage matters, and for any ambitious politician the rewards possible from supporting Davis were clear.[1]

Party chairman James Tracy believed that it was also necessary to change the party's basic policies. The administration and the legislature had produced a program that had greatly expanded the activities of the state government. Tracy believed that its measures had been good and necessary, but they had proved too costly to attract the kind of support the party needed. The congressional election had indicated the extent to which these measures had become a political liability. While the taxpayer's revolt had involved more than economic factors, it did reflect genuine concern that the Republican government was pursuing a ruinous fiscal policy. If the party was to become the voice for progressive business interests, as Tracy hoped, it had to cut back and bring tax relief.

There was little disagreement with the party chairman over the need to cut taxes among Republicans, but there was no consensus on how to do it. The party's program had reflected the various needs of its constituency and to change any part of it risked a revolt. That had been the result when Tracy tried to bring about a change the year before. In April, Tracy informed Newcomb that he intended to work for curtailment of the police system and repudiation of the militia laws. These two items had not only been costly, but they had burdened Republicanism with the charge of tyranny. Support to internal improvements and free public education could be maintained if the police measures were abandoned. The move was risky since the state police and the militia were the primary means to protect black voters. Not only was there a real possibility of intimidation, but Tracy's effort might also convince blacks that the administration was abandoning them. Congressional passage of three "force bills" in 1870 and 1871 provided possible relief, however, since these laws appeared to put the federal government into the business of protecting black voters. If the laws did work and if blacks could be convinced that they had not been abandoned, Tracy's effort to create a party program more acceptable to whites was feasible.[2]

As Harold Hyman has pointed out, concern for election reform in Northern cities and for protection of voters in the South had led Congress to pass three statutes that addressed fraud in federal elections. The first was that of May 31, 1870, which placed in the federal courts those cases involving the use of force, bribery, or intimidation to prevent citizens from voting. As a means of insuring clean elections, however, it was virtually useless since it did not protect voters before the fact. The law of February 28, 1871, moved toward protection by placing federal elections in the hands of supervisors appointed by federal circuit judges, and by giving these officials police power to prevent election fraud and keep the peace at the polls. More direct in its impact was the Ku Klux bill of April 20, 1871, which defined activities such as those of the Klan as criminal and authorized the president to suspend the privilege of *habeas corpus* to suppress such activities. The Klan bill aimed not only at officials but also at any persons who deprived others of their constitutional rights. Texas officials had not used these laws in 1871, but they were available and allowed the state to decrease its own efforts in the area.[3]

The use of federal protection in Texas required changes in local court officers, especially in the western district where the only prosecution that had taken place under the statutes had been that of Governor Davis for violations in Congressman Clark's district. District Attorney C. T. Garland, U.S. Marshal Thomas J. Purnell, and Judge Thomas H. Duval were actively working against the governor and his administration. In addition to the charges against Davis, Garland had arraigned numerous Republican registrars before a friendly grand jury. Senator A. J. Fountain, a critical vote maintaining the administration's power in the Senate, was under indictment for forgery. The governor's own efforts to secure indictments against the Klan had resulted in no arraignments. Davis believed the court was in the hands of the Democrats, and with good reason. If the court's record was not sufficient, Garland demonstrated his political tendencies by calling upon Jack Hamilton and Democratic party chairman William "Buck" Walton to help him prosecute the case against the governor.[4]

Garland and Purnell had to be removed if the Republican party was to abandon the use of the state police and the militia. With hostile parties running the grand jury and packing it with Democrats, the federal law would not protect black Republicans, so Davis worked to bring about a change before the election. Senator Morgan Hamilton objected to the removals because he believed Davis was trying to halt prosecution of the election law cases. Davis, however, urged the president and the attorney general to move quickly so that he could call members of the Ku Klux Klan before the district court prior to its adjournment. If the Klan could be actively prosecuted, the coming election would be more peaceful. Purnell managed to hang on to his office, but Garland lost his to A. J. Evans, the governor's nominee. While Purnell could still fill the grand jury with people opposed to the administration, Evans could begin actions desired by the governor. The Evans appointment looked promising. In the election cases the administration was acquitted, and Evans then began to prosecute individuals under the Ku Klux act. The Republicans had managed to secure order, or at least it appeared so, at no cost to the state.[5]

If the Texas Republicans were going to maintain their control over federal patronage, the renomination of Grant by the national party was essential. Davis had been tarred with charges of corruption; he could expect little from the president's opponents. As a result, the regular Republicans worked as much to keep the Texas party united behind Grant as to prepare for the autumn election. Because of the attraction of many of the German members to the national Liberal Republican movement, the administration's ability to insure a pro-Grant delegation was not clear. Rather than risk taking delegates hostile to the president to Philadelphia, Tracy announced that he intended to appoint the delegation rather than have it elected in a state convention. When asked to explain such a move, he indicated that in a state as large as Texas and with a constituency as poor as his party's, frequent meetings were impractical. In 1868 the party had allowed its chairman to appoint delegates rather than have them elected. Now Tracy had decided to save money and adopt the policy of his predecessor. When informed of this decision, William Chandler immediately responded with a strong recommendation to hold a meeting and elect delegates. The word of the secretary of the national committee was enough to change Tracy's mind, and he ordered a convention at Houston for May. The need to elect delegates forced local officials into a strenuous effort to make sure that those elected favored President Grant.[6]

A complete reorganization of the local party was the first step taken toward controlling the state convention. Tracy had tried the same thing in 1871, but with limited success. The reason for this effort was that the Union League, the principal party unit at the local level, could not always be relied on. The League had become the base for strong county and district machines whose bosses acted practically independent of the state leadership. That freedom had worked to the disadvantage of the administration, since it allowed men like J. W. Flanagan to oppose the governor without fear of political consequences in their home districts. Officials at Austin could never be sure of the loyalty of the county League organizations, and they did not possess the means to demand it. As in the previous year, the reorganization tried to undermine the local groups by creating alternatives, principally the National Guards and the Sons of Liberty. They were similar in style to the League, with military organization and elaborate rituals, but they were not secret and they did not have the same reputation as the League. If successful, they promised to deliver greater control over county-level politics to state officials. Administration backers had high hopes for them and Congressman Clark believed that if properly organized the Republicans would finally have "the infidel on the hip."[7]

Party officials had another weapon working for them in 1872, one that had not been available before: a fully organized public school system. The centrally supervised schools created by the Twelfth Legislature provided the administration with an enormous patronage. The law allowed the governor to appoint a state superintendent of public instruction. Together with the attorney general these two had a hand in naming district school supervisors and county school boards. Through these groups the governor even played a role in the employment of individual teachers. In short, the school system could be filled entirely with people who owed their jobs to the governor and would work for him. School jobs provided the administration with a way to secure reliable information on county politics and a means to reward party loyalty. The system provided party officials with an apparatus they could control that worked at the local level. That spring, Superintendent Jacob DeGress worked in the president's cause and reported his efforts to party secretary Newcomb. DeGress coordinated local efforts and instructed his subordinates. The result was extensive activity among school officials. The *San Antonio Express* complained of the "flock of office holders" moving about the state apparently engaged in public duties. Their real purpose, according to the editor, was "securing county conventions which will select delegates whose only purpose will be to perpetuate the powers of their masters."[8]

The work of the school officials turned out to have mixed results for the administration since it was often heavy-handed. In several counties their active intervention created a furor. In San Antonio, where Newcomb wanted to be included among the delegates, the Liberal Republicans were particularly strong and presented a challenge to the Grant forces in the county convention. A. Siemering, chairman of the Bexar County executive committee, was typical of the Germans attracted to the Liberals. When Siemering called a county convention for April 13 and then postponed it, Newcomb's agent worked to rid themselves of the chairman. They agreed to the original call, but ignored the postponement and gathered anyway. Their meeting passed resolutions in favor of Grant and Davis, selected a pro-Grant delegation, and elected a new county committee comprised of friends of Newcomb and the governor. In Travis County, Newcomb carried out a similar action. Party members in San Antonio demanded that Davis fire Newcomb. At Austin they protested the secretary of state's interference because it distracted the party from real issues and divided those who should work together. The administration produced delegations favorable to Grant for Houston, but it was making enemies at the same time.[9]

When the delegates appeared for the state convention the administration had matters firmly in hand. They easily agreed to endorse Grant and sent a delegation to Philadelphia committed to his renomination. But differences between Tracy and Newcomb over party programs remained to be worked out. Railroads and schools had won out over the state police and the militia in the spring of 1872, but it was not clear that the state could even support the two remaining measures completely. Tracy was primarily a railroad and internal improvements man, while Newcomb was an advocate of the public schools. Each realized the need to cut costs, but each wanted the cuts at the expense of the other. Initially the school forces appeared to be in command. The *Houston Union* reported that fifteen counties were represented by Superintendent DeGress while another fifty were in the hands of his officers and appointees. However, hostility toward the school "clique" united a majority of delegates behind Tracy, and he appeared to control the convention. The first sign of Tracy's supremacy was the election of Robert H. Taylor to the chair. Taylor was an old Unionist and a friend of prominent railroad men, and he had not participated actively in the party since its organization. His selection reflected Tracy's efforts to move the party more firmly into the hands of "progressive" whites and businessmen. In fact, another old Unionist, A. B. Norton of Dallas, noted that a large number of his old comrades were at Houston. Tracy appeared on the verge of recapturing elements of the old Union party.[10]

Tracy's work was also apparent in the platform adopted by the delegates. After traditional statements of loyalty to the philosophy of the national party and approval of the administrations of Grant and Davis, the delegates addressed local matters. They renewed the party's pledge to free public education, although now with the condition that it be "at the smallest cost possible to the people." Further, they promised rigid economy and the best administrative experience possible in running these schools. The platform had not abandoned education, but it indicated party leaders had moved to more qualified support. At the same time, however, the delegates stated their desire for continued support of internal improvements by "reasonable state aid." The law and order position of previous platforms had been almost completely abandoned. The Republican party appeared to be in Tracy's hands, and he was fishing for white support.[11]

While the Republican regulars prepared for the renomination of Grant and the subsequent campaign, their opponents faced some confusion. Their course of action had been obscured by the appearance in the North of a possible third party movement. The course of political events, particularly the disappearance of ideological issues, had prompted a coalition of individuals and groups unable to accept the change. Journalists and politicians whose constituencies had been broken up with the disintegration of the wartime Union Republican coalition were among the principal supporters of Liberal Republicanism. Dissatisfaction with the Grant administration had been apparent for some time, but in January 1872, various groups joined to organize a new party in Missouri and to call for a national convention at Cincinnati the following May.[12]

The followers of Governors Pease and Hamilton had watched Northern events with some interest since the Liberal Republican movement offered them some possibilities for political success. They did not know, however, whether they should risk active involvement with a third party rather than simply trying to reform the existing one. Ferdinand Flake wanted people to know about military despotism, fraudulent elections, and corruption, but he urged his old friend Pease against a party revolt unless absolutely necessary. A group of Republicans, including the two former governors, finally called for a convention at Austin to determine what their position would be with regard to Liberal Republicanism.[13]

The convention met on April 6 and attracted a large number of people. They endorsed the Missouri platform and the call for the Cincinnati convention. The sixteen men who went to Cincinnati did not go expecting a third party, but once there they heartily endorsed its formation and the nomination of Horace Greeley as their candidate for president. Judge Chauncey Sabin, who had supported the "reform" candidacy of Louis W. Stevenson in 1871, welcomed Liberal Republicanism as a continuation of his work to bring good government back to the state and joined in its support. The movement, he wrote, represented "a grand swell among the people of this nation in the interest of fraternity and good government, rising above faction and packed associations." Jack Hamilton also believed the new party promised a return to good government. Hamilton indicated that he thought the old party had come to stand for power and plunder rather than representative government, and he could not support it longer. The Texas Liberals placed themselves on the side of reform and an end to misrule.[14]

Of course the motivation behind these activities was complex. Their opponents in the regular organization believed that the reform issue was a ruse to cover up their real purposes—to grab power. James Newcomb characterized the sponsors of Liberalism in Texas as the political outs, men who had lost all influence in state and federal government. In a letter to William Chandler he called Jack Hamilton a "broken down salivated politician," motivated by personal grievances and a thirst for public office. He accused Pease of trying to reopen the gates of the capitol that had been shut to him by the Davis administration. The Liberals were, in the opinion of the secretary of state, "the dead beats of all parties and factions." Whether prompted by the motives ascribed to them by Newcomb or not, the Liberals did hope that the national upheaval against Grant would give them the leverage to drive Davis and his administration from power at home.[15]

The principal goal of the Texas Liberals appears to have been a fusion between themselves and the Democrats, or at least the moderate members of that party. Fusion offered something for everyone. The Democrats appeared on the verge of recapturing the state government on their own, but their position would be awkward since the Republicans would retain control of the government at Washington. The occupation of local federal offices by men hostile to the Democratic party could hinder the operation of the government. If Greeley became president, however, he would reward the Liberals in Texas who had supported him, and the federal posts would be filled, if not by Democrats, at least by their political allies. Fusion would make it easier for the Democrats to take over the government. It would also secure public offices for the Hamilton group. The moderate Democrats appeared willing to accept cooperation, and the *Galveston News* welcomed the choice of Greeley as the strongest one possible for defeating President Grant. Jack Hamilton was bold enough to propose a ticket for local offices with both Liberal Republicans and Democrats on it.[16]

The Liberal Republicans and the moderate Democrats had not counted on the power of the "straight out" Democrats to block their coalition. Rather than cooperation, the nomination of Greeley provoked an outright revolt among some Democrats. Congressman John Hancock presented the case against fusion when he asserted that the Cincinnati movement amounted to an endorsement of every principle to which his party objected. For Hancock it was not enough to replace thieves with economical and honest men when the same party was returned to power. The differences between Greeley and Grant, in his opinion, were not over measures but how to carry them out. A "Democrat" provided a different view of the same matter in a letter to the *Galveston News* when he suggested that standing aside and allowing Republican reformers clear sailing would only insure a Radical triumph. He wrote that "no ticket, headed by what is known as Republican reformers, or composed of that class of men, will succeed in getting one-half the Democratic vote in this state." The "straight out" line taken by prominent party men such as Hancock helped undermine the move toward cooperation and frustrate the Liberal Republicans.[17]

The state's Democratic convention at Corsicana on June 17 would settle the matter. The moderates urged support of Greeley, while their opponents pushed for a Democratic ticket and platform. Because the moderates occupied key positions in the convention, they managed to secure an endorsement of the Cincinnati movement as a commendable effort at reform, but they could not bring about cooperation with the Texas Liberals. The Democrats ran their own ticket in the state while urging the election of Greeley at the national level. The Liberals believed that they had been betrayed, but even the moderate *Galveston News* indicated that the Democrats had decided that there could never be fusion as long as they remained Republican. While Pease and Hamilton might want public office, the Democrats would not cooperate to give it to them as long as they were Republicans. If they wanted to work with the Democrats in the future, wrote the editors, "just let them cut loose from old relations and join. . . . When they have joined the true old orthodox church and become full disciples, then they shall be partakers in the triumph of the State as well as the National Administration." The uncompromising stance of the Democrats forced the Liberals to reassess their position. Although they would still oppose Davis, and factions would be formed that would persist in later years, most of the Liberals returned to the ranks of the regular party after 1872.[18]

While their opponents argued over the possibilities of fusion, the regulars attempted to get the campaign underway as quickly as possible. From the start, however, they encountered problems similar to those that they had experienced in previous elections, although the show of strength by the Democrats the year before made these worse. Individuals and groups within the party moved frantically to maintain some hold on their political power. Factionalism, ethnic spirit, race, and even religion helped create division within the Republican group. When these worked together with inadequate funds and Democratic violence, the party's possibilities in 1872 did not seem very good.

The most ominous sign of trouble from within came when Congressman E. Degener refused to run as a presidential elector on the regular party ticket. Degener's reason was that he could not appear on the ticket of a party that had endorsed the Davis administration. In a letter to Tracy, Degener argued that the party had mistakenly made national issues accessories to local and, consequently, doomed the chances of the president to carry the state. Among the faults of the governor and his supporters Degener cited their meddling in county affairs, intrigues against federal officials, and use of representatives of the state and school department to interfere in local politics. Degener complained: "The financial blunders committed since the ascendency of the Republican party in Texas would have been forgotten, the increased taxation forgiven, in view of the advantages arising therefrom, had the people been left to govern themselves instead of being treated like a set of school boys, by strangers sent among them." Although the governor did not like Degener and the congressman had not supported the administration well, the German leader's attack created problems for Davis in the election. Degener was a respected member of the German community, and his abandonment of the party opened up the possibility of a wholesale German renunciation of the governor.[19]

Dissatisfaction with the party among the Germans became more apparent as the campaign progressed. This was especially true in the black belt counties where Negroes had been moving to gain greater control over local party affairs. The battle in the Twenty-fifth District was typical. There blacks were in the majority and thought that they deserved at least two of the district's three seats in the House. The Germans, always ill at ease in their coalition with blacks, and now concerned with their party's general programs, responded negatively. The party appeared ready to split and Col. J. R. Burns, Republican elector-at-large who was canvassing the state, informed Newcomb that the German members of the party were ready to "accept *one* colored man as a matter of policy, but not two." Burns urged Newcomb to provide an office to one of the black House nominees so that he would withdraw and allow the district executive committee to nominate a more generally acceptable slate.[20]

While white Republicans were concerned with black demands for office, blacks were concerned that whites blocked them from achieving office. Throughout the state, black political leaders were more assertive than in previous elections. At the district convention of Senator Matthew Gaines's Sixteenth, blacks went so far as to demand an all-Negro slate, since they formed the party's voting strength. DeGress, in an attempt to prevent what appeared to be a destructive move, argued that it would destroy the party's chances in the district. Since the blacks outnumbered the whites, however, the delegates selected a slate composed completely of Negroes. Concerned with the state party's neglect of their situation and their ambitions, blacks at the local level moved to take over the party for themselves.[21]

In some cases blacks were ready to see what kind of deal they could make with the Democrats. In the Thirteenth District the Democrats supported Walter Burton, the Negro sheriff of Fort Bend County, for the state Senate in opposition to a German. The Democrats reasoned that encouraging straight black tickets would work to alienate many white voters from the Republican camp. They also believed that men such as Burton would be easier to control once in office. A correspondent of the *Galveston News* encouraged the growth of hostility between white and black Republicans in Fort Bend by suggesting that many Democrats believed Sheriff Burton to be far superior to any white nominee that the Republican party might present for election. Although such activity was not widespread, it did occur elsewhere, and indicated the increased difficulties party leaders faced in keeping together their coalition.[22]

As the Republicans faced fragmentation of the black-white alliance, they also encountered a threat in another area. The Fourth Congressional District with its large foreign population had always been the strongest base of Republicanism in the state. Party power there was threatened not only by the German revolt, but also by the growth of opposition to Republicanism by the Catholic Church. Many feared the secularizing influence of the public schools, and priests worked among Polish immigrants and Mexicans to discourage them from voting for Republican candidates. Catholic priests helped the Democrats in their canvass at the Polish community of Pana Maria, and in El Paso a Father Borajo threatened to excommunicate any Catholic who voted the Republican ticket. In the case of Borajo, party officials protested to the priest's bishop and thought they had him removed from his parish. Borajo, however, refused to abandon his pulpit and continued up to the election in a house-to-house campaign against the Republican party.[23]

Although encountering severe problems, the Texas Republicans put together a well-organized campaign. In the larger cities the party formed Grant and Wilson Clubs, popularly known as Tanner's Clubs. These were uniformed in oilcloth capes colored tan, with portraits of Grant painted on in white. Another club also appeared, the Boys in Blue, distinguished by their blue uniforms. While not extensive, these semimilitary organizations helped to create interest in the election in cities such as Galveston and Austin, and aided the effort of state officials to undermine the League. While serving a practical political purpose, these clubs also added to the color of the state's first presidential canvass in twelve years.[24]

Governor Davis personally campaigned throughout the state in favor of the national and state candidates. The Texas Central Railroad served as the chief route of Republican speakers, who appeared at rallies along its line. Davis and the other speakers directed themselves to several key issues. Republicanism, in their opinion, represented free speech and an end to violence in Texas. The party was the only one with principles. According to Governor Davis, the Republican and Democratic parties had reversed their roles, and his had taken up the tradition of Andrew Jackson and become the rightful representative of common people. The party's appeal was to the small farmer, the individual who might consider himself left out of the politics that had long been typical of the state. To blacks, speakers repeated the role of Republicanism in destroying the rebellion and liberating the slaves. For the unrepresented white, the party offered a home. For black men, support of Grant, Davis, and the party was a duty.[25]

Campaigns cost money, however, and the lack of funds hindered Republican operations in the state. Galveston provided most of the party's operating capital, but only $2,000 could be raised there. As the campaign progressed, the lack of money became critical. J. K. McCreary of the customs house at San Antonio informed Newcomb that he had to collect money from his employees to further the party in his district. The funds that he raised had been spent to pay for transporting some voters to the polls and to provide a fund for registering poor men, but more was needed. Senator Fountain wrote from El

Paso for state officials to "send us the *means*" to pull off a deal with the Democrats for a seat in the House. In an appeal to the secretary of the national party in March, Tracy reminded the people at Washington that the local organization had never received money from them. Now it needed support. Tracy received no funds, not even a speaker to aid his efforts. In the summer, Tracy requested the help of Grenville E. Dodge of the national committee in securing at least $10,000 to help finance the campaign. Dodge sent the request to William Chandler for a decision. The party secretary returned the letter to Dodge with the endorsement: "We cannot yet say that Texas is sufficiently hopeful to make it advisable to promise them money or to call on Dodge for any for that State." [26]

As the election approached, the Democrats appeared confident. Their campaign centered on the issues of taxation and corruption once again. In addition they worked to pry foreign voters away from the Republicans by giving a full airing to the connection of James Newcomb with the old Know-Nothing party. Statements by the governor of Illinois and Senator Wilson of Massachusetts against Germans, Irish, and Catholics received play in the newspapers. Editors of the *Galveston News* asked how it was possible for foreigners to affiliate with a party composed of such a "conglomerate of isms . . . not the least of which was Know-Nothingism." At the same time, the Democrats used fraud and intimidation to diminish the black vote for the Republicans. O. H. Bounnelle wrote to Newcomb from Wharton County that the Democrats were selling worthless lands to Negroes and then claiming black votes as their due. Bounnelle complained: "They make Political capital . . . Saying Who, but us, sold you lands and furnished you homes? Are we not your friends? did we not stop the collection of the obnoxious school tax in Wharton Co.?" [27]

The Democrats had reason for their confidence. The result of the campaign was another Republican defeat. A friend of Newcomb wrote from San Antonio: "We have met the enemy and we are theirs." While the Democratic vote was not as large as in 1871, it was sufficient for a complete victory. The state was among only seven which gave a majority to the Liberal Republican candidate Horace Greeley. Asa H. Willie and Roger Q. Mills easily defeated their Republican congressional opponents, A. B. Norton and A. J. Evans. The greatest disaster, however, was the loss of both houses of the legislature. In the House of Representatives, Republican strength dropped from a fifty-seat majority to a twelve-seat minority. In the Senate the party lost four of their seventeen seats. Only a large number of Republican holdovers left the party in a position to prevent a complete reversal of the administration's legislative programs, since the governor could veto actions and the Senate could not override him. Given the total nature of the election, however, the ability of Davis to sustain his veto was not much consolation.[28]

For the Republicans the trends established the previous year continued to be apparent. Their vote was declining. They turned out almost three thousand fewer voters than they had in 1871. In not a single district did the party improve its performance. Local candidates tended to do worse than President Grant. Only in the Fourth District did they manage to do better than the president. While the Democrats had suffered a similar decline in voting strength, the Republicans had become a clear minority with only 42 percent of the popular vote.[29]

To party leaders ample evidence indicated what was going wrong. From El Paso a correspondent complained of intimidation and violence. He informed Newcomb that the election was "a deep fraud, mixed with bribery, evil and corrupt influences of every character, threats of violence and various classes of intimidation of which the affidavits of different persons of good standing and forwarded you by this mail will abundantly show you." Without control of the courts, however, the Davis administration could not stop such activity. It was not politically expedient to use the state police and the militia.[30]

At the same time the problems with the German voters had taken a toll. In the Fourth District, the district with the largest German population, Grant received 14 percent fewer votes than Degener had received the previous year. The chief of police at San Antonio complained to Newcomb that the Germans had voted against the Republican ticket. Outraged, he hoped they would be denied political rewards and wrote, "Let us have Americans, Irishmen or Mexicans for our Marshals, and policemen, but not a single German." Without the Germans, Republicanism would be confined largely to black men. The election had shown that a party based on race alone was not viable.[31]

CHAPTER 10

The Last Fight

The period following the election of 1872 comprised a moment of relative quiet in Texas politics. The Democrats believed that their triumph was inevitable and expressed willingness to wait for the next gubernatorial election without agitation. The *Galveston News* cautioned patience to party firebrands: "Davis is harmless with a Democratic legislature. An effort to unseat him would only invite the intervention of General Grant. Such a situation would produce uneasiness not only with our own citizens, but with the capitalists of the North, who are now investing their means in the construction of railroads and other internal improvements, and would certainly stop the flow of immigration that is coming in from every quarter of the Union as well as Europe." At the same time the governor did not appear ready for a fight. He appeared to realize the hopelessness of the situation, and observers noted that he acted like a different man. In February he went to Galveston for that city's Mardi Gras on a special train provided for members of the legislature. He made the rounds on the cars, joking and exchanging pleasantries with his political enemies. "For once," noted one observer, "he left the shell that has for a long time hid his good qualities—and I believe he has many—from all but his closest friends." [1]

In his message to the Thirteenth Legislature Davis spoke in favor of reconciliation. He recognized the opposition to his party's program and stated his willingness to compromise on parts of it. He hoped, however, that everything that had been done would not be destroyed. He suggested that the public school system be modified to let each county elect its board of directors, thus ending his own power to appoint them. The governor agreed that portions of the militia and police laws should be changed, but he hoped that the two would remain in existence to provide peace. Davis believed that many Democratic complaints could be ended if the legislature took steps to distribute the tax burden more equally. Taxes, he believed, fell mainly on those too honest or too weak to evade them, and he asked for a law to change assessment practices. Those that existed had led to underassessments such as the Western Union Telegraph Company's claim to have property valued at $3,800. Under administration scrutiny it had raised its claim to $62,300, but the governor believed that many other companies, especially the railroads, had similar underevaluations. Not only a new assessment law, but provisions to penalize tax delinquents, had Davis's endorsement. The governor pointed out that one-third of the taxes assessed in 1871 remained uncollected, and the state had no means to collect them other than through the courts. Even if eventually collected there could be no penalty.

The governor's message contained a defense of his actions and a justification for the party's measures. The school system was the jewel of the Republican program, and he reported that over half of the state's school-age children had attended its schools in 1871. Davis also claimed that his administration had placed the state in good financial condition. The debt was only a million and a half dollars and much good work had been accomplished. While the state's credit in the Northern bond markets was low, he thought that it was not due to a realistic assessment but to the slanders of men trying to defeat his party. During his three years in office there had been only one major act of corruption. Adjutant General Davidson had misappropriated $30,000 in funds allocated to the state police, but the state was trying to recover the money and Davis believed it had an excellent chance to do so. The governor contended that all the state had benefited from Republican work.[2]

The legislature, despite the Democratic party's decision not to push Davis too far, decided that the Republican program had not helped the state and started dismantling it. Although the governor attempted to veto some of their actions, the Democrats found enough anti-Davis Republicans in the Senate to overturn most of the measures. They modified the militia law in such a way as to divest the governor of most of his power and repealed the police law. Their new school law destroyed the free public schools. While cutting back in the areas of protection and education, the Democrats incorporated sixteen new railroads and gave each sixteen sections of public land for each mile of track they laid, despite the constitutional provisions against it. By the end of their session the legislature had undone almost completely the Republican legislative program. One of their last acts was to start the campaign that would end the Republican control over the executive; they provided for a general election in December 1873, to select both a new legislature and new state officials.[3]

Realizing the inevitability of defeat, Republican leaders could not decide on the best course. On May 28 the party's executive committee met at Austin to discuss the matter, and Tracy suggested they should not make nominations for the 1873 election. Senator Fountain agreed with Tracy. They argued that throwing their support to independent candidates might allow them to maintain some control. Fountain believed that without an active Republican ticket the Democrats would fall out among themselves, since differences on internal improvements had emerged within their party. Davis opposed the move, however, and received support from Superintendent DeGress. The governor argued that the Republican party might still beat the Democrats. Even if they could not, he wanted to see the "ship of Republicanism" go down with its flags flying. The two views could not be reconciled, and they made no final decision. Instead, they called a party convention for Dallas to decide what to do.[4]

The executive meeting at Austin revealed differences among Republicans. Senator Fountain left the meeting to try to put together enough opposition to prevent Republican nominations. Fountain found support among some federal officeholders and former members of the Liberal Republican movement. In a letter to President Grant, several federal officials wrote that Governor Davis's course had been unwise and injudicious. The governor had succeeded in "alienating many good men from the Republican party and preventing many conservative men from joining who really had no sympathy with its enemies." They appealed to Grant to permit federal officers freedom to oppose Davis without fear of being removed.

What had Davis done wrong? Why not run a Republican ticket? The Fountain movement clearly thought that the governor's unwillingness to abandon the party's black constituents was destroying Republicanism. Without a Republican ticket blacks could not be marched to the polls, and a new party based on men with similar economic views might be formed.[5]

Davis moved rapidly against his opponents. On a trip to

Washington to push the sale of state bonds and talk about Indian problems, the governor met with Grant to discuss what could be done to make the federal bureaucracy provide more support to his administration. He argued that they had been of little help in 1872; they drew their money and pocketed it rather than helping the party. Davis wanted new men in office who would help him reorganize for the general election. In particular he wanted W. T. Clark removed as postmaster at Galveston and charged that the former congressman had made a deal with the Democrats—he had not pushed his fight to retain his congressional seat in return for their support for the job in the state's wealthiest post office. Backing the governor the *San Antonio Express*, once more in the regular camp, wrote, "It is undeniable that the Federal appointments in Texas have not generally been made with a view to encourage the Texas Republicans in the unequal contest they have to wage in defense of their natural rights against those embittered opponents of all law and order, the Texas Bourbon Democracy. . . . It is therefore in a sense the duty of the Central Government to protect and aid those who are acting in harmony and engaged in a common cause with the National Republican Party."[6]

At Washington, however, sentiments were not in favor of Davis. A changing situation in the North made Grant less interested in giving in to the governor's demands. The president referred the complaints to the heads of departments without recommendation. Although Davis believed that he had Grant on his side, no removals took place, and by the middle of July he believed nothing could be accomplished. Rebuffed in his efforts to change officeholders, he also could not sell his bonds. Northern businessmen feared repudiation of bonds issued by any Southern state, and the market was dead. Davis needed help, but Northerners no longer believed the state Republican governments could succeed. Davis informed Newcomb that he intended to return home. "I have had enough to discourage and thwart me," he wrote.[7]

While Davis had failed at Washington, his supporters in Texas had been more successful in putting the grass roots party machinery in operation. George Ruby called a convention of the black people of Texas to consider "moral, commercial and political interests of their race." In fact it was to mobilize black support for the governor. Ruby controlled the meeting, and his associate Wright Cuney received the permanent chairmanship.

With the leadership of Ruby and Cuney, the delegates issued resolutions that denounced men who bartered the rights of blacks and used power for personal gain, citing Republican legislators and federal officeholders. Conservative newspapers believed that the convention had overthrown the Radical leadership of the Republican party; in fact it had unified blacks behind it. The delegates unanimously approved the programs of Davis, especially the free public schools. Indicating the unity of blacks behind the governor, Matt Gaines, a man with whom Davis had never gotten along well, introduced a resolution that endorsed him as a friend of the colored citizens of the state.[8]

A. Siemering, another one-time enemy, helped promote a similar meeting among German citizens at Austin in August. Again the regular Republican organization was in control. The Germans adopted a platform that called for free public schools, protection of civil liberties, a general incorporation law, and the honoring of the state debt. In addition they pledged to support men for office because of their honesty and capacity rather than party. The programs they approved were those of Governor Davis. While claiming to be nonpartisan, the Germans provided more support for his administration.[9]

Administration workers also managed the district conventions, a fact made obvious when the delegates met at Dallas. Despite efforts by federal officials to obtain anti-Davis members, his advocates filled the hall. When the governor appeared to make an address, they greeted him as a hero. He told them that it was their duty to nominate candidates or they would play into the hands of the enemy, and the delegates responded with cheers of approval. As one body they rose and shouted "Never!" to any suggestion that a Republican ticket not enter the election. With the renomination of Davis as the party's gubernatorial candidate, the convention turned into a celebration of unity. Senator Saylor, alienated from the governor over legislative problems, pushed his way through a throng of joyous delegates to shake hands with Davis and promise his support. The Flanagans watched the delegates from their own county cast a unanimous vote for their enemy, and then joined in offering their support.[10]

The convention's platform laid out the grounds for the coming campaign. It stressed the Republicans as an alternative that would work for all of the people. The Democratic Thirteenth Legislature had increased taxes and added $500,000 to the state debt. They had given away eighty million acres of public lands to the railroads. The return to power by the Democracy had opened the state to violence and resulted in the destruction of the school system. The Republicans promised to restore the schools, protect the civil rights of all citizens, and reduce taxes. The platform also tried to take advantage of a split that had developed among the Democrats over the validity of the bonds issued by the Republican administration. The Republicans promised to honor the state debt in all its forms.[11]

The Democrats had their own "agrarian" and "railroad" factions. The former had taken advantage of general discontent with the Republican administration to agitate for repudiation of the bonds issued to various railroads by the Twelfth and Thirteenth Legislatures. Accusing the International Railroad of bribery and corruption, one Democratic candidate suggested that the road should be made to suffer and its support withdrawn. The repudiationists received added strength from the Granger movement that was just forming in the state. Although avowedly nonpolitical, the Grangers intended to become involved in politics. They did not like the price of support to internal improvements. A Granger from Fort Worth warned the Democrats that they would vote their economic interests and said, "Farmers are tired of being taxed." On the other hand Democrats like John H. Reagan believed repudiation would be disastrous for the state's credit. Following the war, the former Postmaster-General of the Confederacy had not been politically active except as a lobbyist for the International Railroad, but he now worked with J. W. Throckmorton to insure that the Democratic candidate would be in favor of honoring the state debt. Throckmorton made a personal speaking tour to deprecate "agrarian" hostility to the state's railroad enterprises.[12]

Unfortunately for Republican hopes, the railroad men among the Democrats managed the nomination of Richard Coke, a candidate favorable to their interests, and forced a strong plank against repudiation into their platform. Further, at the convention they required all delegates to pledge themselves to support the Democratic nominees to make sure that the Republicans could not exploit the internal differences on the debt question. In his acceptance speech Coke indicated that repudiation was a minor issue compared to whether or not the state would have four more years of tyranny. The Democratic party represented the people, and it was time to put the people back in power. Coke's rhetoric only thinly disguised the fact that the "people" he was talking about were white. He was using the issue of race to unify his party despite disagreements on the debt question.[13]

The Democratic press picked up Coke's lead and avoided the railroad issue. Instead the editors filled their columns with the usual charges of corruption and tyranny. The Democratic campaign emphasized, in addition, the racial "demagoguery" of the Republicans. The *Texas Observer* at Cherokee asserted that the Radical party was in the hands of the dirt of the land and deserved the scorn of the community. The Radicals had created a party based upon racial unrest; they had spread "sedition" among blacks. Throughout the campaign they reinforced Coke's theme that all white men with property had a community of interest that should keep them together against the Republican evil.[14]

Davis countered the charges with his own—that the Democratic party represented only those "titled gentlemen" who had held themselves above the citizenry. He repeatedly held up his party and himself as champions of the little people of the state. In a full page newspaper advertisement in major cities, the governor asserted that the people included immigrants, blacks, small farmers, mechanics, laboring men, and taxpayers as well as planters and big businessmen. The interests of these people would be served best by reelecting E. J. Davis. The governor tried to get Coke to debate him on the railroads in particular and tried to present himself as the man who had kept the Democrats from completely robbing the people of their state money and public lands. When the two finally got together at Crockett, however, Coke refused to address this issue and dwelled instead on his own connection with the people. When the people decided to secede in 1861 Coke, unlike his opponent, had been proud to support their will. Davis could not turn the campaign toward the issues that he thought were important.[15]

State party leaders at Austin could not put together a clear impression of what was going on at the local level. Some reports indicated that many old Unionists had returned to the party, including A. J. Hamilton, who decided to run for the state senate. The experiments of the Germans with fusion or a third party appeared to be over. The Republicans seemed unified for the first time since 1869. The good news was countered by information that the Democrats were active against blacks.

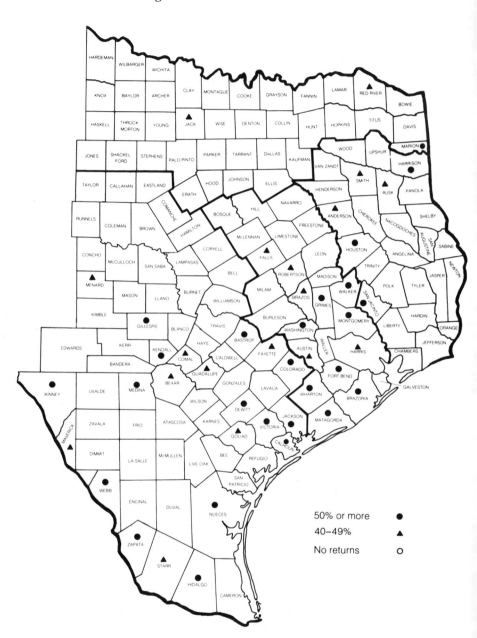

MAP 7. Vote for Davis, 1873

Because of the arrangements for the election, voting would take place in precincts rather than at the county seat, and Republicans feared there would be more intimidation. Their fears were well-founded. In Liberty County officials arrested and tried Harris Stewart, a Republican organizer, for "exciting Negroes to acts of hostility to whites." The jury ordered him to leave the county under pain of death, but Stewart continued preparations for the election. Subsequently county authorities arrested him and "disposed" of him. A white mob in Smith County seized another black man, Jack Johnson, and lynched him. Johnson had been implicated in a murder and the lynching had no connection with politics, according to whites, but the fact that local authorities had no control over a mob provided an easily understood lesson to any black politicians. In Colorado County two freedmen "disappeared," only to be found dead later. The incident resulted in the arming of four hundred blacks for self-defense, but when whites discovered it, they moved to stop them. In the riot that followed "several" blacks died and others fled the county. Federal authorities investigated the problem but could find no one willing to file affidavits. Increased violence did not serve Republican needs.[16]

In the election the Democratic candidate swamped Davis. Coke polled 100,415 votes to 52,141 for the incumbent. The Democrats showed a 36 percent increase over the vote for the party candidate in 1871 while the Republicans showed only 3 percent. The Republican showing in the congressional districts indicated that for the first time violence had made inroads against black voters. In the First and Third districts, the two with the largest Negro population, the Republicans showed a loss of strength. In Liberty County, where Stewart had been eliminated, the Republican vote dropped from 255 in 1869 to 0. Republicans lost Falls for the first time in the postwar years. In Austin, Brazos, Hill, McLennan, and Navarro, they suffered severe cuts in strength. For the districts as a whole, Davis received 928 fewer in the Third than had Clark in 1871, 169 fewer in the First than Whitmore. Contemporaries support the conclusion that blacks did not turn out in 1873. A Democrat at Galveston who took his servant to vote remarked that the election judges reported a poor turnout among blacks. The election of 1873 marked the first time since enfranchisement that the Republicans lost strength in the black belt counties.[17]

Davis recognized that his term was over. Despite the intimidation he decided not to contest the results and expressed his willingness to abide by the election. The governor began preparing to turn over the government to Coke when his term expired on April 28, the following spring. Other members of his party, however, still hoped to prevent the return of the Democrats to power. They decided to challenge the constitutionality of the election, using a technical problem in the election law. The constitution had provided that "all elections . . . shall be held at the county seats of the several counties until otherwise provided by law; and the polls shall be open for four days." The Thirteenth Legislature allowed polling at precinct boxes and also limited the election to one day. The people who wanted to challenge the election believed that the semicolon made the two clauses independent; thus the legislature could not change the length of time for the election. Davis did not know what to do. He had no personal intention of continuing in office, but a question had been raised concerning the legitimacy of the legislative and executive succession, and the governor took such problems seriously.[18]

The Democrats believed that Davis planned on using the constitutional issue to prevent them from taking power, despite his assertions to the contrary. Not trusting him, the Democrats demanded that Davis resign in January 1870, and clear the way for their party to organize the government. They asserted that he had actually become governor when Reynolds appointed him to the position, rather than when he took over the restored civil government. Another constitutional issue had been raised, and Davis refused to step down. As a result Democratic leaders caucused. Coke directed a group of lawyers at Galveston to prepare contingency plans. They first proposed to allow Davis to continue as governor until April, if he recognized the legitimacy of the Fourteenth Legislature. Coke thought such a course would only lead to friction. Party leaders finally decided to assemble the legislature, inaugurate Coke, and continue until in control of the government or faced with federal bayonets.[19]

While Democratic pressure increased, Davis awaited a court decision on the election. The state supreme court had taken into consideration the case of Joseph Rodriguez who had been arrested for voting more than once in the election, and their decision promised a statement on the constitutional matter. Rodriguez's defense was that he had not committed a crime since he had not violated a constitutional law. Attorney General

Alexander and A. J. Hamilton agreed to the validity of this point, and the state asked for the case to be dismissed. In the hands of Republican appointees, the court agreed and gave Rodriguez his freedom. The decision made the election invalid and tied the governor's hands. On January 6 Davis, Newcomb, Tracy, Jack Hamilton, and other Republicans met to discuss the decision. Judges Richard Walker and Wesley Ogden favored a call for federal intervention if the Democrats tried to inaugurate Coke. Tracy suggested that the Thirteenth Legislature be called together to order a new election, although Jack Hamilton believed it would lead to the impeachment of the governor. The group ultimately decided to look for federal help, and Hamilton went to Washington while Newcomb travelled to San Antonio for a conference with the local military commander. Davis sent a formal telegram to the president on January 11 that asked for military support to keep the peace until a solution could be found.[20]

Grant would not intervene; Northern Republicans would no longer support the Davis regime. Grant replied to the governor's request for assistance that domestic violence, as defined in the Constitution, did not exist in Texas and he could not send troops. Further, Davis received a lecture: "The act of the Legislature of Texas providing for the recent election having received your approval and both political parties having made nominations and having conducted a political campaign under its provisions would it not be prudent, as well as right, to yield to the verdict of the people as expressed by their ballots." Davis replied that he admitted troops could not be called under the Constitutional provision, but he did not know what to do and implored the president for aid. "My request was made to secure peace, and as a preventive of such violence threatened here as a result of foolish counsels and inflamed public opinion," he wrote. "I do not propose personally, as I wrote you, to make any objection to the late election, but do not perceive how I can with propriety disregard the decision of the Supreme Court."[21]

Without federal support Davis's cause was hopeless. On January 17 Attorney General George H. Williams telegraphed Davis that, after considering the claims of the contending parties, the president believed the governor's right to office was doubtful enough not to warrant the use of federal troops. Faced with Democrats who refused to give in and a federal administration that would not back him, Davis resigned on the morning of January 19. In a letter to his private secretary he wrote:

"The President of the United States on application made to him by me, having declined to sustain the State Government against the usurpation now attempted here, leaving me only the alternative of defending the constituted authorities against violence by means which I am unwilling to adopt because they would produce great public disturbance and injury to the prosperity of the State, you are authorized under this, my protest, to relinquish the office and archives." The national government, the instrument that had placed the Republicans in power some seven years before, thus tacitly endorsed the Democratic revolution. Tired of their commitment to Southern Republicans, national party leaders abandoned the Texans rather than continue the fight.[22]

Davis's resignation did not bring the Republican experiment to an end. Denied state power, the party continued to operate in the counties for several decades. The loss of the state, however, meant that nothing could be done to stop the local violence that undermined Republican strength. In addition Democratic legislatures began in 1872 to carry out programs that would legally undercut local Republican power. They gerrymandered voting districts and passed new voting laws that hindered Republican operations. Where this work did not accomplish the desired results, local white citizens did not hesitate to seize power by force. The collapse of the Republican county officials before violence in Fort Bend County in 1888 marked the fall of one of the last local party strongholds in the state. The trends set in motion by the return of the Democrats to power could be seen by the end of the century, when of some 650,000 potential black voters only 25,000 qualified. The Democrats had undermined Republican voting strength and doomed the party for the time being.[23]

The Democratic resurgence benefited in part from the policies of both the Grant and Hayes administrations. Grant had refused to intervene actively in the state. President Hayes initiated an effort to develop a white man's Republican party and practically abandoned blacks. He courted Conservative Unionists, Liberal Republicans, and Democrats in Texas, trying to build a new organization. E. M. Pease received the important Galveston customs house and the president consulted with Democrats in all of his appointments. The result was a federal bureaucracy that supported the new national policy, but no party. Pease could command the respect of important Democratic politicians, but he could not deliver Republican votes.

The policies of national administrations had helped to create two Republican parties in Texas, one that occupied federal offices, the other the grass roots organization.[24]

Despite frequent efforts by federal officeholders to remove him, Governor Davis maintained control of the Republican executive committee and over party voters until his death in 1881. He believed that the national leaders had abandoned him and in 1876 he wrote to Newcomb: "I am convinced . . . that they don't care for the wishes of Republicans here, and don't care much whether we have any Republican party at all, or not." But Davis continued to work on building a viable party, and he moved in whatever direction he thought would bring victory. In 1876 he adopted the policy of his advisors in 1873 and endorsed the independent G. W. "Wash" Jones for Congress. In 1878 he led the party in support of the Greenbackers. Tracy, DeGress, and Kuechler typified the Republicans who actively worked for fusion in 1878. In 1880, however, Davis returned to Republicanism in the hopes that a new administration would help his cause. The party's identity changed, but as long as dissatisfaction existed with the dominant Democratic party, a chance existed to return to political power.[25]

Republicanism appeared on the upswing after Garfield's death and Chester Arthur's move into the presidential office. Davis died before he could take personal advantage of the new situation. His rival Pease shortly followed him. However, a new man, Wright Cuney, the young protegé of George Ruby, continued the Davis policies of trying to build a party out of a local constituency and conditions. The Republican party persisted in the work begun in 1865, to build an alternate political force to the dominant Democratic party. The people who controlled it and the ends they looked for, however, were no longer the same.

Unionism, with the addition of black voters, had been the basis for the movement. It had started as an effort to secure a variety of sectional, economic, and personal goals. At times these were antithetical, but outside of power all could work for political office, and internal differences were not important. In the postwar era the Unionists had found acceptance of black suffrage to be a means to gain their ends after their old opponents had denied them power, and emancipation had opened up the possibility of the political use of the freedmen. Whites viewed their political alliance in a one-sided manner. Few believed that blacks would play an active role. Their preconceived ideas about the coalition and their prejudices toward blacks could be seen in their definitions of the rights of their allies. They had justified their advocacy of political rights for blacks on constitutional grounds—they did not believe legal restrictions should hinder an individual. But without land or education, such a definition doomed blacks to a perpetual role as hired agricultural labor. Except for limited aid to education, white Republicans willingly offered little to aid blacks to change their social or economic status.

White Republican views of blacks created an unstable internal situation. The great mass of Republican voters were never fully satisfied with what white leaders offered them. This provided the opportunity for the emergence of black leaders to represent them. It also opened up the possibility for their manipulation by white leaders who would or could give them more than others. When Morgan Hamilton could not get what he wanted within the regular party, he undercut his brother and Governor Pease with more concessions to blacks. So long as the white Republicans were unable to go the full distance in recognizing the aspirations and political goals of blacks, however, they had to fight to keep blacks' votes from being drawn away. The result was a party of constant internal conflict that could never marshal its full strength against its opponents.

The internal struggle created another problem for Republicans as a successful political party. It created a more radical program. While part of a legitimate political process that attempted to put together a program acceptable to the party's constituency, given the social and economic context of postwar Texas it proved unacceptable. Expanded recognition of the rights of blacks and their inclusion into party programs opened Republicans to Democratic challenges based upon racist arguments and the taxpayers' pocketbooks. Given the numerical dominance of whites in Texas, race and taxes proved an insurmountable barrier to Republican success. Only the threat of Northern intervention prevented an even more rapid collapse of the party. When the federal government withdrew its support there was no chance. Except for a few white leaders such as Davis, the Republicans became a party of blacks and federal officeholders. Cuney's rise to power foreshadowed that course.

APPENDIX 1

Returns on Selected Elections, 1859–1873

TABLE I. Election Returns for Governor, 1859

Counties	Total	Houston	%	Runnells	%
		District 1			
Anderson	1,104	672	61	432	39
Angelina	258	200	78	58	22
Chambers	147	88	60	59	40
Cherokee	1,644	933	57	711	43
Hardin[a]	—	—	—	—	—
Harrison	1,055	560	53	495	47
Henderson	491	300	61	191	39
Houston	805	451	56	354	44
Jasper	307	192	63	115	37
Jefferson	74	25	34	49	66
Liberty	366	152	42	214	58
Nacògdoches	1,011	705	70	306	30
Newton	160	130	81	30	19
Orange	168	122	73	46	27
Panola	859	426	49	433	51
Polk	610	298	49	312	51
Rusk	1,886	918	49	968	51
Sabine	180	156	87	24	13
San Augustine	366	265	72	101	28
San Jacinto[a]	—	—	—	—	—
Shelby	729	454	62	275	38
Smith	1,257	801	64	456	36
Trinity	252	184	73	68	27
Tyler	585	233	40	352	60
Upshur	1,098	560	51	538	49
Van Zandt	380	200	53	180	47
Wood	646	404	63	242	37
District totals	16,438	9,429	57	7,009	43

TABLE 1—*Continued*

Counties	Total	Houston	%	Runnells	%
		District 11			
Bowie	389	110	28	279	72
Cass-Davis	1,204	578	48	626	52
Collin	1,183	701	59	482	41
Cooke	306	223	73	83	27
Dallas	974	545	56	429	44
Delta [a]	—	—	—	—	—
Denton	652	517	79	135	21
Ellis	616	357	60	259	40
Erath	178	169	95	9	5
Fannin	1,218	748	61	470	39
Grayson	1,068	639	60	429	40
Hood [a]	—	—	—	—	—
Hopkins	1,084	584	54	500	46
Hunt	852	403	47	449	53
Jack	109	93	85	16	15
Johnson	421	303	72	118	28
Kaufman	649	383	59	266	41
Lamar	1,014	474	47	540	53
Marion [b]	—	—	—	—	—
Montague [a]	—	—	—	—	—
Palo Pinto	113	113	100	0	0
Parker	717	598	85	119	15
Raines [b]	—	—	—	—	—
Red River	889	474	53	415	47
Rockwall [a]	—	—	—	—	—
Tarrant	712	594	73	118	27
Titus	1,042	554	53	488	47
Wise	338	310	92	28	8
District totals	15,728	9,470	60	6,258	40

TABLE 1—*Continued*

Counties	Total	Houston	%	Runnells	%
		District III			
Austin	914	405	44	509	56
Bosque	178	147	83	31	17
Brazoria	427	120	37	307	63
Brazos	279	201	72	78	28
Burleson	694	423	61	271	39
Falls	290	211	73	79	27
Fort Bend	364	188	52	176	48
Freestone	427	234	55	193	45
Galveston	783	321	41	462	59
Grimes	719	465	65	254	35
Harris	1,455	829	57	626	43
Hill	411	250	61	161	39
Leon	782	421	54	361	46
Limestone	586	272	46	314	54
McLennan	231	231	100	0	0
Madison	280	190	68	90	22
Matagorda	229	79	34	150	66
Milam	548	330	60	218	40
Montgomery	452	299	66	153	34
Navarro	679	402	59	277	41
Robertson	419	259	62	160	38
Walker	814	470	58	344	42
Waller[a]	—	—	—	—	—
Washington	1,352	745	55	607	45
Wharton	207	93	45	114	55
District totals	13,520	7,585	56	5,935	44

TABLE 1—*Continued*

Counties	Total	Houston	%	Runnells	%
		District IV			
Atascosa	96	32	33	64	67
Bandera	45	17	38	28	62
Bastrop	769	363	47	406	53
Bee[a]	—	—	—	—	—
Bell	585	338	58	247	42
Bexar	1,761	1,038	59	723	41
Blanco	149	100	67	49	33
Brown	26	25	96	1	4
Burnet	370	302	82	68	18
Caldwell	572	283	49	289	51
Calhoun	356	163	46	193	54
Cameron	429	97	22	332	78
Colorado	620	345	56	275	44
Comal	385	39	10	346	90
Comanche	78	70	90	8	10
Coryell	278	216	78	62	32
DeWitt	521	241	46	280	54
El Paso	450	25	5	425	95
Fayette	1,130	604	53	526	47
Frio[a]	—	—	—	—	—
Gillespie	265	165	62	100	38
Goliad	367	225	61	142	39
Gonzales	902	493	55	409	45
Guadalupe	538	251	47	287	53
Hamilton[a]	—	—	—	—	—
Hays	238	164	70	74	30
Hidalgo	230	3	1	227	99
Jackson	203	143	70	60	30
Karnes	233	165	71	68	29
Kendal[a]	—	—	—	—	—

TABLE I—*Continued*

Counties	Total	Houston	%	Runnells	%
Kerr[a]	—	—	—	—	—
Kinney[a]	—	—	—	—	—
Lampasas	285	220	77	65	23
Lavaca	678	336	49	342	51
Live Oak	106	58	55	48	45
Llano	141	92	65	49	35
Mason	31	21	68	10	32
Maverick[a]	—	—	—	—	—
Medina	238	40	17	198	83
Menard[a]	—	—	—	—	—
Nueces	410	240	59	170	41
Refugio	150	74	49	76	51
San Patricio	57	17	30	40	70
San Saba	167	158	95	9	5
Starr	260	69	27	191	63
Travis	993	590	59	403	41
Uvalde	113	66	56	47	44
Victoria	306	123	60	183	40
Webb	329	110	33	219	67
Williamson	666	488	73	178	27
Wilson[a]	—	—	—	—	—
Zapata	88	0	0	88	100
District totals	16,614	8,609	52	8,005	48
Statewide totals	62,300	35,093	56	27,207	44

[a]Unincorporated county.
[b]No official returns.

TABLE 2. Vote on Secession, 1861

Counties	Total	For	%	Against	%
	District 1				
Anderson	885	870	98	15	2
Angelina	323	139	43	184	57
Chambers	84	78	93	6	7
Cherokee	1,144	1,106	97	38	3
Hardin	229	167	73	62	27
Harrison	930	886	95	44	5
Henderson	449	400	89	49	11
Houston	590	552	94	38	6
Jasper	343	318	93	25	7
Jefferson	271	256	94	15	6
Liberty	432	422	98	10	2
Nacogdoches	411	317	77	94	23
Newton	181	178	98	3	2
Orange	145	142	98	3	2
Panola	562	557	99	5	1
Polk	572	567	99	5	1
Rusk	1,511	1,376	91	135	9
Sabine	161	143	89	18	11
San Augustine	265	243	92	22	8
San Jacinto[a]	—	—	—	—	—
Shelby	361	333	92	28	8
Smith	1,199	1,149	96	50	4
Trinity	214	206	96	8	4
Tyler	421	417	99	4	1
Upshur	1,014	957	94	57	6
Van Zandt	308	181	56	127	44
Wood	642	451	70	191	30
District totals	13,647	12,411	91	1,236	9

TABLE 2—*Continued*

Counties	Total	For	%	Against	%
	District II				
Bowie	349	268	77	81	23
Cass-Davis	455	423	93	32	7
Collin	1,353	405	30	948	70
Cooke	358	137	38	221	62
Dallas	978	741	76	237	24
Delta[a]	—	—	—	—	—
Denton	587	268	77	319	23
Ellis	699	527	75	172	25
Erath	195	179	92	16	8
Fannin	1,127	471	42	656	58
Grayson	1,364	463	34	901	66
Hood	—	—	—	—	—
Hopkins	1,012	697	69	315	31
Hunt	755	416	55	339	45
Jack	90	14	16	76	84
Johnson	562	531	94	31	6
Kaufman	616	461	75	155	25
Lamar	1,216	553	45	663	55
Marion	467	467	100	0	0
Montague	136	50	37	86	63
Palo Pinto	107	107	100	0	0
Parker	596	535	90	61	10
Raines[a]	—	—	—	—	—
Red River	631	347	55	284	45
Rockwall	—	—	—	—	—
Tarrant	589	462	78	127	22
Titus	686	411	60	275	40
Wise	154	76	49	78	51
Young	197	166	84	31	16
District totals	15,279	9,175	60	6,104	40

TABLE 2—*Continued*

Counties	Total	For	%	Against	%
	District III				
Austin	1,037	825	80	212	20
Bosque	314	233	74	81	26
Brazoria	529	527	99	2	1
Brazos	259	215	83	44	17
Burleson	506	422	83	84	17
Falls	297	215	72	82	28
Fort Bend	486	486	100	0	0
Freestone	588	585	99	3	1
Galveston	798	765	96	33	4
Grimes	916	907	99	9	1
Harris	1,228	1,084	88	144	12
Hill	439	376	86	63	14
Leon	616	534	87	82	13
Limestone	534	525	98	9	2
McLennan	777	586	75	191	25
Madison	223	213	96	10	4
Matagorda	251	243	97	8	3
Milam	603	468	78	135	22
Montgomery	416	318	78	98	22
Navarro	411	317	77	94	23
Robertson	467	391	84	76	16
Walker	551	490	89	61	11
Waller[a]	—	—	—	—	—
Washington	1,174	1,131	96	43	4
Wharton	251	249	99	2	1
District totals	13,671	12,105	89	1,566	11

TABLE 2—*Continued*

Counties	Total	For	%	Against	%
		District IV			
Atascosa	236	145	61	91	39
Bandera	65	33	51	32	49
Bastrop	687	335	49	352	51
Bee	155	139	90	16	10
Bell	693	495	71	198	29
Bexar	1,536	827	54	709	46
Blanco	256	86	34	170	66
Brown	75	75	100	—	—
Burnet	407	159	39	248	61
Caldwell	622	434	70	188	30
Calhoun	292	276	98	16	2
Cameron	637	600	94	37	6
Colorado	914	584	64	330	36
Comal	325	239	74	86	26
Comanche	90	86	96	4	4
Coryell	348	293	84	55	16
DeWitt	521	472	91	49	9
El Paso	873	871	99	2	1
Fayette	1,206	580	48	626	52
Frio [a]	—	—	—	—	—
Gillespie	414	16	4	398	96
Goliad	316	291	92	25	8
Gonzales	882	802	91	80	9
Guadalupe	336	314	93	22	7
Hamilton	87	86	99	1	1
Hays	281	166	59	115	41
Hidalgo	72	62	87	10	13
Jackson	225	147	66	78	34
Karnes	154	153	99	1	1
Kendal [a]	—	—	—	—	—
Kerr	133	76	57	57	43
Kinney [a]	—	—	—	—	—
Lampasas	160	85	53	75	47
Lavaca	628	592	94	36	6
Live Oak	150	141	94	9	6
Llano	206	134	65	72	35

TABLE 2—*Continued*

Counties	Total	For	%	Against	%
Mason	77	2	3	75	97
Maverick[a]	—	—	—	—	—
Medina	347	140	40	207	60
Menard[a]	—	—	—	—	—
Nueces	184	142	77	42	23
Presidio[a]	—	—	—	—	—
Refugio	156	142	91	14	9
San Patricio	59	56	95	3	5
San Saba	173	113	65	60	35
Starr	182	180	99	2	1
Travis	1,154	450	39	704	61
Uvalde	92	16	17	76	83
Victoria	401	313	78	88	22
Webb	70	70	100	0	0
Williamson	829	349	42	480	58
Wilson	113	92	81	21	19
Zapata	212	212	100	0	0
District totals	18,031	12,071	67	5,960	33
Statewide totals	60,628	45,762	80	14,866	20

[a]Unincorporated county.

TABLE 3. Election Returns for Governor, 1869

Counties	Total	Davis	%	Hamilton	%
		District 1			
Anderson	1,406	803	57	603	43
Angelina	297	72	24	225	76
Chambers	138	73	53	65	47
Cherokee	1,156	247	21	909	79
Hardin	58	0	0	58	100
Harrison	2,417	1,847	76	570	24
Henderson	528	193	37	335	63
Houston	1,268	790	62	478	38
Jasper	286	13	5	273	95
Jefferson	131	23	18	108	82
Liberty	504	255	51	249	49
Nacogdoches	789	388	49	401	51
Newton	196	108	55	88	45
Orange	151	5	3	146	97
Panola	672	63	9	609	91
Polk	680	459	68	221	32
Rusk	1,817	1,059	58	758	42
Sabine	341	5	1	336	99
San Augustine	489	157	32	332	68
San Jacinto[a]	—	—	—	—	—
Shelby	449	248	55	201	45
Smith	1,669	1,017	61	652	39
Trinity	289	136	47	153	53
Tyler	297	158	53	139	47
Upshur	953	402	42	551	58
Van Zandt	335	191	57	144	43
Wood	440	213	48	227	52
District totals	17,756	8,925	51	8,831	49

TABLE 3—*Continued*

Counties	Total	Davis	%	Hamilton	%
		District II			
Bowie	441	264	60	177	40
Cass-Davis	997	436	44	561	56
Collin	751	28	4	723	96
Cooke	503	99	20	404	80
Dallas	881	289	33	592	67
Delta[a]	—	—	—	—	—
Denton	314	9	3	305	97
Ellis	604	99	16	505	84
Erath	128	13	10	115	90
Fannin	794	287	36	507	64
Grayson	758	253	33	505	67
Hood	290	1	1	289	99
Hopkins	743	134	18	609	82
Hunt	505	1	1	504	99
Jack	109	4	4	105	96
Johnson	469	4	1	465	99
Kaufman	555	105	19	450	81
Lamar	1,231	348	28	883	72
Marion	1,379	1,021	74	358	26
Montague	104	2	2	102	98
Palo Pinto	70	0	0	70	100
Parker	451	93	21	358	79
Raines[a]	—	—	—	—	—
Red River	1,286	780	61	506	39
Rockwall[a]	—	—	—	—	—
Tarrant	622	54	9	568	91
Titus	842	228	27	614	73
Wise	122	0	0	122	100
District totals	14,949	4,552	30	10,397	70

TABLE 3—*Continued*

Counties	Total	Davis	%	Hamilton	%
	District III				
Austin	1,480	998	67	482	33
Bosque	195	50	26	145	74
Brazoria	1,037	603	58	434	42
Brazos	1,237	795	64	442	36
Burleson	819	385	47	434	53
Falls	956	362	38	594	62
Fort Bend	1,157	986	85	171	15
Freestone	1,262	668	53	594	47
Galveston	2,122	1,010	48	1,112	52
Grimes	2,034	1,664	82	370	18
Harris	2,335	1,427	61	908	39
Hill	495	322	65	173	35
Leon	1,043	569	55	474	45
Limestone	666	297	45	369	55
McLennan	1,403	797	57	606	43
Madison	406	180	44	226	56
Matagorda	429	402	94	27	6
Milam [b]	—	—	—	—	—
Montgomery	835	479	57	356	43
Navarro [b]	—	—	—	—	—
Robertson	958	516	54	442	46
Walker	1,459	1,028	70	431	30
Waller [a]	—	—	—	—	—
Washington	2,994	2,035	68	959	32
Wharton	626	577	92	49	8
District totals	25,948	16,150	62	9,798	38

TABLE 3—*Continued*

Counties	Total	Davis	%	Hamilton	%
	District IV				
Atascosa	255	51	20	204	80
Bandera	110	11	10	99	90
Bastrop	1,305	781	60	524	40
Bee	54	11	20	43	80
Bell	461	50	11	411	89
Bexar	1,519	929	61	590	39
Blanco	91	38	42	53	58
Brown	33	1	3	32	97
Burnet	167	10	6	157	94
Caldwell	765	352	46	413	54
Calhoun	418	249	60	169	40
Cameron	548	220	40	328	60
Colorado	1,903	1,175	62	728	38
Comal	615	360	59	255	41
Comanche	41	1	2	40	98
Coryell	259	0	0	259	100
DeWitt	589	367	62	222	38
El Paso	458	336	73	122	27
Fayette	1,701	1,174	69	527	31
Frio[a]	—	—	—	—	—
Gillespie	355	277	78	78	22
Goliad	302	172	57	130	43
Gonzales	989	476	48	513	52
Guadalupe	844	516	61	328	39
Hamilton	44	0	0	44	100
Hays	397	120	30	277	70
Hidalgo	63	14	22	49	78
Jackson	254	197	78	57	22
Karnes	176	31	18	145	82
Kendal	171	122	71	49	29

TABLE 3—*Continued*

Counties	Total	Davis	%	Hamilton	%
	District IV				
Kerr	136	60	44	76	56
Kinney	15	0	0	15	100
Lampasas	130	7	5	123	95
Lavaca	832	382	46	450	54
Live Oak	84	1	1	83	99
Llano	76	1	1	75	99
Mason	66	34	52	32	48
Maverick	52	35	67	17	33
Medina	240	230	96	10	4
Menard[a]	—	—	—	—	—
Nueces	374	231	62	143	38
Presidio	34	19	56	15	44
Refugio	104	72	69	32	31
San Patricio	40	10	25	30	75
San Saba	111	0	0	111	100
Starr	96	14	15	82	85
Travis	1,391	593	43	798	57
Uvalde	37	8	22	29	78
Victoria	540	338	63	202	37
Webb	133	23	17	110	83
Williamson	562	14	2	548	98
Wilson	256	151	59	105	41
Zapata	40	31	78	9	22
District totals	20,236	10,295	51	9,941	49
Statewide totals	78,889	39,922	51	38,967	49

[a]Unincorporated county.
[b]Returns not counted.

TABLE 4. Election Returns for Congress, First District, 1871

Counties	Total	Whitmore	%	Herndon	%
Anderson	2,603	918	35	1,685	65
Angelina	423	73	17	350	83
Chambers	202	51	25	151	75
Cherokee	2,099	636	30	1,463	70
Hardin[a]	66	0	0	66	100
Harrison	3,332	2,216	67	1,116	33
Henderson	1,007	270	27	737	73
Houston	1,789	912	51	877	49
Jasper	465	144	31	321	69
Jefferson	301	101	34	200	66
Liberty	693	303	44	390	56
Nacogdoches	1,492	429	29	1,063	71
Newton	292	97	33	195	67
Orange	152	25	16	127	84
Panola	1,216	284	23	932	77
Polk	470	120	26	350	74
Raines	220	10	5	210	95
Rusk[a]	3,014	1,363	45	1,651	55
Sabine	500	229	46	271	54
San Augustine	829	396	48	433	52
San Jacinto	618	392	63	226	37
Shelby	999	358	36	641	64
Smith	3,119	1,470	47	1,649	53
Trinity	474	109	23	365	77
Tyler	420	105	25	315	75
Van Zandt	836	375	45	461	55
Wood	782	186	24	596	76
District total:	28,413	11,572	42	16,841	58
Returns as adjusted	15,333	10,209	67	15,124	33

[a]Complete returns were rejected in this county because of intimidation at the polling place.

TABLE 5. Election Returns for Congress, Third District, 1871

Counties	Total	Stevenson	%	Clark	%	Giddings	%
Austin	2,676	6	—	1,322	49	1,348	51
Bosque[a]	534	—	—	77	14	457	86
Brazoria	1,266	30	2	850	67	386	31
Brazos[b]	2,283	—	—	1,050	46	1,233	64
Burleson	1,307	—	—	478	37	829	63
Falls	1,893	2	—	960	51	931	49
Fort Bend	1,552	—	—	1,207	78	345	22
Freestone[c]	1,855	—	—	708	38	1,147	62
Galveston	2,326	329	14	304	13	1,693	73
Grimes	2,991	—	—	1,698	57	1,293	43
Harris	3,654	—	—	2,033	56	1,621	44
Hill	1,104	—	—	455	41	649	59
Leon	1,626	1	—	598	37	1,027	63
Limestone[c]	1,182	1	—	28	2	1,153	98
McLennan	2,682	—	—	1,162	43	1,520	57
Madison	590	—	—	161	27	429	73
Matagorda	458	3	1	304	66	151	33
Milam	1,275	—	—	299	23	976	77
Montgomery	1,139	—	—	543	48	596	52
Navarro	1,981	—	—	981	49	1,000	51
Robertson	2,530	13	1	1,144	45	1,373	54
Walker	1,586	18	1	848	53	720	46
Washington	2,645	—	—	2,535	70	110	30
Wharton	1,382	—	—	525	38	857	62
District total:	42,517	403	1	20,270	48	21,844	51
Returns as adjusted by state returning board	38,048	403	1	19,459	51	18,748	48

[a]No official returns received at Austin.

[b]Total includes some ballots marked illegally or cast in an unauthorized "white man's" box and rejected by state returning board.

[c]Complete returns rejected by state returning board because of intimidation at the polling places.

TABLE 6. Election Returns for President, 1872

Counties	Total	Grant	%	Greeley	%
	District 1				
Anderson	2,002	910	45	1,092	55
Angelina	433	120	28	313	72
Chambers	303	169	56	134	44
Cherokee	1,340	372	28	968	72
Hardin	51	17	33	34	67
Harrison	3,149	2,374	75	775	25
Henderson	942	229	24	713	76
Houston	1,563	757	48	806	52
Jasper	551	241	44	310	56
Jefferson	191	64	34	127	66
Liberty	542	274	51	268	49
Nacogdoches	1,191	419	35	772	65
Newton	247	90	36	157	64
Orange	137	55	40	82	60
Panola	899	3	1	896	99
Polk	392	134	27	258	73
Rusk	2,709	1,335	49	1,374	51
Sabine	379	150	40	229	60
San Augustine	647	377	58	270	42
San Jacinto	748	440	59	308	41
Shelby	725	240	33	485	67
Smith	2,530	1,302	51	1,228	49
Trinity	440	113	26	327	74
Tyler	396	115	29	281	71
Upshur	1,404	596	42	808	58
Van Zandt	796	253	38	543	62
Wood	864	253	29	611	71
District totals	25,571	11,402	45	14,169	55

TABLE 6—*Continued*

Counties	Total	Grant	%	Greeley	%
		District II			
Bowie	661	309	47	352	53
Cass-Davis	1,348	512	38	836	62
Collin	843	176	21	667	79
Cooke	419	32	8	387	92
Dallas	1,500	403	27	1,097	73
Delta	288	59	20	229	80
Denton	559	56	10	503	90
Ellis	695	76	11	619	89
Erath	262	16	6	246	94
Fannin	970	351	36	619	64
Grayson	1,031	320	31	711	69
Hood	442	0	0	442	100
Hopkins	753	161	21	592	79
Hunt	569	74	13	495	87
Jack	201	101	51	100	49
Johnson	922	1	1	921	99
Kaufman	752	117	16	635	84
Lamar	1,342	455	34	887	66
Marion	1,819	1,041	57	778	43
Montague	152	28	18	124	82
Palo Pinto	142	5	4	137	96
Parker	579	111	19	468	81
Raines	345	25	7	320	93
Red River	1,551	790	51	761	49
Rockwall[a]	—	—	—	—	—
Tarrant	689	115	17	574	83
Titus	967	227	23	740	77
Wise	203	39	19	164	81
District totals	20,004	5,600	28	14,404	72

TABLE 6—*Continued*

Counties	Total	Grant	%	Greeley	%
		District III			
Austin	2,100	947	45	1,153	55
Bosque	484	39	8	445	92
Brazoria	1,263	1,019	81	244	19
Brazos	1,893	874	46	1,019	54
Burleson	908	257	28	651	72
Falls	1,708	866	51	842	49
Fort Bend	1,222	1,006	82	216	18
Freestone	1,424	603	42	821	58
Galveston	3,665	1,252	34	2,413	66
Grimes	2,557	1,510	59	1,047	41
Harris	4,039	2,150	53	1,889	47
Hill	937	152	16	785	84
Leon	1,413	485	34	928	66
Limestone	1,464	445	30	1,019	70
McLennan	2,469	1,116	45	1,353	55
Madison	601	222	37	379	63
Matagorda	500	365	73	135	27
Milam	1,017	182	18	835	82
Montgomery	1,148	622	54	526	46
Navarro	1,562	439	28	1,123	72
Robertson	2,272	1,084	48	1,188	52
Walker	1,723	979	57	744	43
Waller[a]	—	—	—	—	—
Washington	4,171	2,359	57	1,812	43
Wharton	837	728	87	109	13
District totals	41,377	19,701	48	21,676	52

TABLE 6—*Continued*

Counties	Total	Grant	%	Greeley	%
	District IV				
Atascosa	175	32	18	143	82
Bandera	130	21	16	109	84
Bastrop	1,995	941	47	1,054	53
Bee	83	0	0	83	100
Bell	592	154	26	438	74
Bexar	1,558	682	44	876	56
Blanco	196	36	18	160	82
Brown	22	0	0	22	100
Burnet	231	50	22	181	78
Caldwell	1,080	485	45	595	55
Calhoun	387	199	51	188	49
Cameron	419	163	39	256	61
Colorado	2,325	1,175	51	1,150	49
Comal	568	187	33	381	67
Comanche	265	1	1	264	99
Coryell	576	21	4	555	96
DeWitt	644	258	40	386	60
El Paso[b]	—	—	—	—	—
Fayette	2,338	1,144	49	1,194	51
Frio	48	0	0	48	100
Gillespie	398	183	46	215	54
Goliad	574	249	43	325	57
Gonzales	1,344	473	35	871	65
Guadalupe	1,310	589	45	721	55
Hamilton	122	2	2	120	98
Hays	598	191	32	407	68
Hidalgo	136	57	42	79	58
Jackson	316	201	64	115	36
Karnes	201	28	14	173	86
Kendal	162	94	58	68	42
Kerr	182	53	29	129	71

TABLE 6—*Continued*

Counties	Total	Grant	%	Greeley	%
Kinney	202	147	73	55	27
Lampasas	169	8	5	161	95
Lavaca	1,153	353	31	800	69
Live Oak	122	1	1	121	99
Llano	150	3	2	147	98
Mason	156	61	39	95	61
Maverick	204	94	46	110	54
Medina	184	144	78	40	12
Menard[a]	—	—	—	—	—
Nueces	645	272	42	373	58
Presidio[a]	—	—	—	—	—
Refugio	184	8	4	176	96
San Patricio	87	8	9	79	91
San Saba	148	6	4	142	96
Starr	277	149	54	128	46
Travis	2,477	1,195	48	1,282	52
Uvalde	101	6	6	95	94
Victoria	890	414	47	476	53
Webb[c]	—	—	—	—	—
Williamson	665	170	26	495	74
Wilson[c]	—	—	—	—	—
Zapata	99	61	62	38	38
District totals	26,888	10,769	40	16,119	60
Statewide totals	113,840	47,472	42	66,368	58

[a]Unincorporated county.
[b]Returns rejected by state returning board.
[c]No returns received at Austin.

TABLE 7. Election Returns for Governor, 1873

Counties	Total	Davis	%	Coke	%
		District 1			
Anderson	2,051	916	45	1,135	55
Angelina	578	116	20	462	80
Chambers	257	49	19	208	81
Cherokee	2,013	527	26	1,486	74
Hardin	156	20	13	136	87
Harrison	3,238	2,239	69	999	31
Henderson	1,012	249	25	763	75
Houston	2,072	1,058	51	1,014	49
Jasper	466	121	26	345	74
Jefferson	348	71	20	277	80
Liberty[a]	—	—	—	—	—
Nacogdoches	1,382	395	29	987	71
Newton	361	96	27	265	73
Orange	215	44	20	171	80
Panola	1,382	268	19	1,114	81
Polk	606	159	26	447	74
Rusk	3,098	1,302	42	1,796	58
Sabine	452	112	25	340	75
San Augustine	759	378	49	381	51
San Jacinto	702	441	63	261	37
Shelby	1,078	402	37	676	63
Smith	2,928	1,339	46	1,589	54
Trinity	520	70	13	450	87
Tyler	569	13	2	556	98
Upshur	1,771	605	34	1,166	66
Van Zandt	895	244	27	651	73
Wood	850	169	20	681	80
District totals	29,759	11,403	38	18,356	62

TABLE 7—*Continued*

Counties	Total	Davis	%	Coke	%
		District II			
Bowie	898	268	41	530	59
Cass-Davis	1,259	396	31	863	69
Collin	1,973	282	14	1,691	86
Cooke	1,185	57	5	1,128	95
Dallas	2,964	336	11	2,628	89
Delta	436	40	9	396	91
Denton	1,367	118	9	1,249	91
Ellis	1,651	123	7	1,528	93
Erath	434	58	13	376	87
Fannin	2,090	559	27	1,531	73
Grayson	2,760	495	18	2,265	82
Hood	805	32	4	773	96
Hopkins	2,064	193	9	1,871	91
Hunt	1,605	136	7	1,469	93
Jack	195	84	43	111	57
Johnson	1,442	35	2	1,407	98
Kaufman	1,212	142	12	1,070	88
Lamar	2,326	602	26	1,724	74
Marion	2,213	1,195	54	1,018	46
Montague	477	51	11	426	89
Palo Pinto	265	3	1	262	99
Parker	1,139	184	16	955	84
Raines	291	40	14	251	86
Red River	2,260	939	42	1,321	58
Rockwall	262	33	13	229	87
Tarrant	1,958	138	7	1,820	93
Titus	1,952	250	13	1,702	87
Wise	650	66	10	584	90
District totals	38,133	6,855	18	31,178	82

TABLE 7—*Continued*

Counties	Total	Davis	%	Coke	%
	District III				
Austin	1,815	902	49	913	51
Bosque	844	89	11	755	89
Brazoria	1,428	1,092	76	336	24
Brazos	2,013	816	41	1,197	59
Burleson	1,666	581	35	1,085	65
Falls	1,572	738	47	834	53
Fort Bend	1,420	1,159	82	261	18
Freestone	1,672	602	36	1,070	64
Galveston	3,517	1,025	29	2,492	71
Grimes	2,929	1,600	55	1,329	45
Harris	5,135	2,169	42	2,966	58
Hill	1,460	148	10	1,312	90
Leon	2,065	462	22	1,603	78
Limestone	1,568	337	21	1,231	79
McLennan	2,509	878	35	1,631	65
Madison	626	177	28	449	72
Matagorda	574	388	68	186	32
Milam	1,135	138	12	997	88
Montgomery	1,397	708	51	689	49
Navarro	1,674	462	28	1,212	72
Robertson	2,162	1,000	46	1,162	54
Walker	1,651	877	57	774	43
Waller	1,103	670	61	433	39
Washington	4,021	2,324	58	1,697	42
Wharton [a]	—	—	—	—	—
District totals	45,956	19,342	42	26,614	58

TABLE 7—*Continued*

Counties	Total	Davis	%	Coke	%
	District IV				
Atascosa	420	31	7	389	93
Bandera	183	27	15	156	85
Bastrop	2,234	1,144	51	1,090	49
Bee	121	7	6	114	94
Bell	2,060	198	10	1,862	90
Bexar	3,066	1,234	40	1,832	60
Blanco	266	64	24	202	76
Brown	172	5	3	167	97
Burnet	582	108	19	474	81
Caldwell	1,220	480	39	740	61
Calhoun	445	227	51	218	49
Cameron	654	221	34	433	66
Colorado	2,304	1,304	57	1,000	43
Comal	677	314	46	363	54
Comanche	514	14	3	500	97
Coryell	1,166	45	4	1,121	96
DeWitt	1,097	552	51	545	49
El Paso	493	46	9	447	91
Fayette	3,208	1,531	48	1,677	52
Frio	82	13	16	69	84
Gillespie	452	344	76	108	24
Goliad	516	225	44	291	56
Gonzales	1,469	415	28	1,054	72
Guadalupe	1,698	810	48	888	52
Hamilton	193	6	3	187	97
Hays	677	152	22	525	78
Hidalgo	132	72	53	60	47
Jackson	408	244	60	164	40
Karnes	273	88	32	185	68
Kendal	270	200	74	70	26

TABLE 7—*Continued*

Counties	Total	Davis	%	Coke	%
	District IV				
Kerr	220	77	35	143	65
Kinney	208	114	55	94	45
Lampasas	388	13	3	375	97
Lavaca	1,397	400	29	997	71
Live Oak	148	13	9	135	91
Llano	115	7	6	108	94
Mason	123	41	33	82	67
Maverick	122	52	43	70	57
Medina	402	326	81	76	19
Menard	128	54	42	74	58
Nueces	512	313	61	199	39
Presidio[a]	—	—	—	—	—
Refugio	158	19	12	139	88
San Patricio	103	12	12	91	88
San Saba	293	2	1	291	99
Starr	197	97	49	100	51
Travis	3,573	1,406	39	2,167	61
Uvalde	170	22	13	148	87
Victoria	967	517	53	450	47
Webb	603	512	85	91	15
Williamson	1,395	268	19	1,127	81
Wilson	423	93	22	330	78
Zapata	111	62	56	49	44
District totals	38,808	14,541	37	24,267	63
Statewide totals	152,656	52,141	34	100,415	66

[a] No returns in Secretary of State's files.

APPENDIX 2
Correlations of Political and Ecological Data

TABLE 8. Pearson's r for Unionist and Select Data

	1	2	3	4	5	6	7	8	9	10
1. Houston vote, 1859	1.00	.19	-.33[a]	-.08	-.52[a]	-.22	.01	-.18	-.20	-.25
2. Prounion Vote, 1861	.19	1.00	.38[a]	-.36[a]	-.14	.30[a]	-.36[a]	-.20	-.05	-.17
3. Pease Vote, 1866	-.33[a]	.38[a]	1.00	-.41[a]	.44[a]	.55[a]	-.49[a]	-.18	-.15	.04
4. % Black, 1870	-.08	-.36[a]	-.41[a]	1.00	-.30[a]	-.11	.89[a]	.59[a]	.44[a]	.01
5. % Mexican, 1870	-.52[a]	-.14	.44[a]	-.30[a]	1.00	-.08	-.39[a]	-.10	.01	.35[a]
6. % German, 1870	-.22	.30[a]	.55[a]	-.11	-.08	1.00	-.19	-.03	-.02	-.07
7. % Slaveowners, 1860	-.01	-.36[a]	-.49[a]	.89[a]	-.39[a]	-.19	1.00	.56[a]	.41[a]	.04
8. Av. Farm Value, 1860	-.18	-.20	-.18	.59[a]	-.10	-.03	.56[a]	1.00	.73[a]	.52[a]
9. Av. Farm Value, 1870	-.20	-.05	-.15	.44[a]	.01	-.02	.41[a]	.73[a]	1.00	.34[a]
10. Av. Farm Acreage, 1860	-.25	-.17	.04	.01	.35[a]	-.07	.04	.52[a]	.34[a]	1.00

[a] Correlation significant at the level of .001.

TABLE 9. Pearson's *r* for Republican and Select Political and Ecological Data

	1	2	3	4	5	6	7	8	9	10
1. Davis Vote, 1869	1.00	.63[a]	.68[a]	.60[a]	-.04	.36[a]	.50[a]	.44[a]	.26	.12
2. Grant Vote, 1872	.63[a]	1.00	.83[a]	.66[a]	.11	.20	.54[a]	.45[a]	.44[a]	.10
3. Davis Vote, 1873	.68[a]	.83[a]	1.00	.51[a]	.23	.42[a]	.40[a]	.47[a]	.34[a]	.18
4. % Black, 1870	.60[a]	.66[a]	.51[a]	1.00	-.30[a]	-.11	.89[a]	.59[a]	.44[a]	.01
5. % Mexican, 1870	-.04	.11	.23	-.30[a]	1.00	-.08	-.39[a]	-.10	.01	.35[a]
6. % German, 1870	.36[a]	.20	.42[a]	-.11	-.08	1.00	-.19	-.03	-.02	-.07
7. % Slaveowners, 1860	.50[a]	.54[a]	.40[a]	.89[a]	-.39[a]	-.19	1.00	.56[a]	.41[a]	.04
8. Av. Farm Value, 1860	.44[a]	.45[a]	.47[a]	.59[a]	-.10	-.03	.56[a]	1.00	.73[a]	.52[a]
9. Av. Farm Value, 1870	.26	.44[a]	.34[a]	.44[a]	.01	-.02	.41[a]	.73[a]	1.00	.34[a]
10. Av. Farm Acreage, 1860	.12	.10	.18	.01	.35[a]	-.07	.04	.52[a]	.34[a]	1.00

[a]Correlation significant at the level of .001.

TABLE 10. Pearson's *r* for Unionist and Republican Data

	1	2	3	4	5	6
1. Houston Vote, 1859	1.00	.19	-.33[a]	-.39[a]	-.36[a]	-.40[a]
2. Prounion Vote, 1861	.19	1.00	.38[a]	-.19	-.11	-.08
3. Pease Vote, 1866	-.33[a]	.38[a]	1.00	.15	.09	.28[a]
4. Davis Vote, 1869	-.39[a]	-.19	.15	1.00	.63[a]	.68[a]
5. Grant Vote, 1872	-.36[a]	-.11	.09	.63[a]	1.00	.83[a]
6. Davis Vote, 1873	-.40[a]	-.08	.28[a]	.68[a]	.83[a]	1.00

APPENDIX 3

Delegates to the Constitutional Convention of 1866

TABLE 11. Biographical Data on the Convention of 1866

Name[a]	Occupation	Wealth[b]	Offices, Politics	Wartime Experience
		Members of the Union Caucus		
Armstrong, Micajah L. 61, Tenn.	Farmer	—	Whig	District clerk
Bacon, W. P. —, —	Real estate agent	—	—	—
Camp, Lafayette B. 60, Ky.	Rancher	$ 3,600	House, 8th Legislature	Refugee
Davis, Edmund J. 39, Fla.	Lawyer	0	District judge	General, U.S. Army
Degener, Edward. 57, Germany	Wholesale grocer	—	—	Prisoner
Flanagan, James W.	Planter, lawyer, merchant	$148,590	House, 4th, 6th Leg.	Major, C.S. Army

Name	Occupation	Wealth	Legislative/Service	Other
52, Va.	Lawyer, editor	0	Dist. judge	Captain, C.S. Army
Jones, William E. 56, Ga.	Farmer	$ 42,812	House, 3rd Leg.; Tx. Congress	—
Latimer, Albert H. 58, Tenn.	Lawyer	$ 1,200	—	Lieutenant, C.S. Army
Ledbetter, William H. 32, Tenn.	Lawyer, planter	$ 18,000	—	County judge
McCormick, Andrew P. 33, Tex.	Land agent	$ 12,000	—	—
Murchison, Daniel. 53, Tenn.	Editor	$ 8,000	House, 7th, 8th Leg.	Refugee
Norton, Anthony B. 45, Norway	Lawyer	$ 25,000	—	—
Parker, F. J. 45, Mass.	Lawyer	$106,250	House, 7th Leg.	—
Paschal, Isaiah A. 58, Ga.				

TABLE 11—Continued

Name[a]	Occupation	Wealth[b]	Offices, Politics	Wartime Experience
Ranck, James E. 34, Ind.	Merchant	—	—	House, 10th Leg.
Saunders, X. B. 34, Tenn.	Lawyer	$ 7,830	—	—
Shields, Benjamin G. 55, S.C.	Planter	$ 73,380	House, 26th Cong., from Alabama	At home
Smith, Alex. —, —	Lawyer	—	—	County judge (Lamar)
Taylor, Robert H. 41, S.C.	Lawyer	$ 45,000	House, 3rd, 4th, 5th, 8th Leg.	C.S. Army
Thomas, G. B. 48, Del.	Merchant	$ 15,000	—	—
Varnell, William M. 66, Ala.	Farmer	—	—	—
Young,	—	—	—	—

M. William. 32, Ky.				
Anderson, William R. 32, Miss.	Farmer	$ 12,360	—	—
Ball, A. J. 33, Ky.	Lawyer	$ 2,500	—	—
Benge, George C. 66, Tenn.	Woolcarder	$ 2,000	—	—
Bradshaw, Amzi. —, —	—	—	—	—
Bryan, King. 42, La.	Farmer	$ 13,000	—	—
Bumpas, J. K. 36, N.C.	Farmer	$ 5,000	—	—
Burke, John. 70, Va.	Land agent	—	House, 5th Leg.	Adj. Gen. Texas
Camp, John L. 38, Ala.	Lawyer	$ 14,500	—	—

TABLE 11—*Continued*

Name[a]	Occupation	Wealth[b]	Offices, Politics	Wartime Experience
Dalrymple, William C. 52, N.C.	Rancher	$ 2,000	House, 6th, 7th Leg.	C.S. Army
Davis, Jack. 40, Ala.	Lawyer, farmer, editor	$ 39,000	House, 6th Leg.; Unionist	—
Dickson, David. 51, Mass.	Physician	$ 18,000	House, 1st, 4th, 6th, 9th, 10th Leg.	Captain, C.S. Army
Drake, Orin. —, —	—	—	—	—
Frazier, C. A. 43, Ky.	District judge	$ 14,000	Dist. judge	—
Gentry, Abram M. 45, Ind.	Merchant	—	—	C.S. Army
Giddings, Dewitt C. 39, Pa.	Lawyer	$ 15,000	Unionist	Lt. Col., C.S. Army
Gillock, Braxton W. 55, Ky.	Hotelkeeper	$ 5,000	—	C.S. Army

Name, Age, State	Occupation	Wealth	Office / Political	Military
Halbert, J. L. 33, Ala.	Lawyer	$ 7,000	—	Captain, C.S. Army
Hancock, John. 42, Ala.	Lawyer	$ 85,000	Dist. judge, Unionist	Refugee
Harwood, Alex. 45, Tenn.	Farmer	$ 4,500	Marshal, U.S. Census, 1860	—
Henderson, James W. 49, Tenn.	Lawyer	$ 90,000	House, 1st, 2nd Leg.; Lt. Gov.	Captain, C.S. Army
Hunt, Zimri. 45, N.C.	Lawyer	$ 18,000	—	—
Hurt, James M. 36, Tenn.	Lawyer	$ 2,055	—	C.S. Army
Ireland, John. 39, Ky.	Lawyer	$ 30,000	Mayor, Seguin; Delegate, Secess. Conv., 1861	Lt. Col, C.S. Army
Johnson, Joshua F. 42, Tenn.	Farmer, clergyman	$ 38,650	House, 3rd Leg.; Del., Secess. Conv., 1861	—
Johnson, Middleton T. 56, S.C.	Merchant	—	Del., Secess. Conv., 1861	C.S. Army

TABLE II—*Continued*

Name[a]	Occupation	Wealth[b]	Offices, Politics	Wartime Experience
Jones, George W. 38, Ala.	Lawyer	$ 19,000	Dist. atty., 1856	Colonel, C.S. Army
Lane, Robert H. 51, N.Y.	Lawyer	$ 35,500	—	C.S. Army
Mabry, Hinche P. 37, Ga.	Lawyer	$ 17,000	House, 7th, 8th Leg.	Brig. Gen., C.S. Army
Middleton, W. B. —, —	—	—	—	—
Nelson, H. W. —, —	—	—	—	—
Norris, James M. 47, S.C.	Lawyer	$127,350	—	Colonel, C.S. Army
Parsons, Jesse H. 43, Tenn.	Lawyer	$ 2,500	House, 6th, 8th Leg.	House, 9th, 10th Leg.
Perry, J. M.	Lawyer	$ 25,000	—	—

Name, age, state	Occupation	Wealth		
Alexander ... 62, N.Y.			—	
Porter, J. S. 39, Tenn.	Farmer	$ 800	—	
Randolph, Benton. 34, Ala.	Lawyer	$ 800	—	
Record, J. K. P. 31, Tenn.	Lawyer	$ 3,500	—	
Reeves, Reuben A. 44, Ky.	Lawyer	$ 28,000	Dist. judge	Assoc. justice, st. supreme ct.
Richardson, J. O'Brian. 41, Tenn.	Farmer	$ 948	—	
Roberts, Oran M. 51, S.C.	Lawyer	$ 21,500	Dist. judge; Supreme Ct.; President, Secess. Conv.	Colonel, C.S. Army
Runnels, Hardin R. 46, Miss.	Planter	$108,560	House, 2nd–5th Leg.; Lt. Gov.	—
Saufley, William P. 43, Ky.	Merchant	$ 17,000	Unionist	—

TABLE 11—*Continued*

Name[a]	Occupation	Wealth[b]	Offices, Politics	Wartime Experience
Selman, B. T. —, —.	—	—	—	—
Shepherd, James E. —, —.	—	—	—	—
Shuford, A. P. —, —.	—	—	—	—
Slaughter, Richard A. 37, Tenn.	Lawyer	$ 7,907	—	—
Smith, George W. 43, Ky.	Lawyer	$ 76,000	Dist. judge	—
Smyth, George W. 63, N.C.	Teacher	—	Texas Cong.	—
Spaight, Ashley W. 45, Ala.	Lawyer	$ 84,000	Alabama Leg. 1846–47	Colonel, C.S. Army
Stuart, Hamilton.	Editor	$ 8,000	Mayor, Galveston; U.S. customs col.	—

[a]	Occupation	[b]		Political	Military
William M. 49, Ohio					
Thomas, W. S. 32, Ala.	Farmer	$ 2,000	—		—
Thompson, A. Wells. 29, Ala.	Lawyer, planter	$ 65,000	—		Captain, C.S. Army
Throckmorton, James W. 41, Tenn.	Lawyer, doctor	$ 9,500	House, 4th–9th Leg.; Unionist		Brig. Gen., C.S. Army
Tyus, Ben. R. 36, Va.	Land agent	$ 21,500	—		—
Walker, Richard S. 42, Ky.	Lawyer	$ 26,050	Dist. atty. 1856–58; Ct. reporter		—
Waul, Thomas N. 53, S.C.	Lawyer	$ 55,000	—		C.S. Army
Whitfield, John W. —, —	Land office & Indian agent	—	—		Captain, C.S. Army
Wilson, Samuel A. 31, Tex.	Lawyer	$ 32,000	—		—

[a] Name, age, and place of birth.
[b] Real and personal wealth from manuscript census returns for 1860.

Delegates to the Constitutional Convention of 1868–1869

TABLE 12. Biographical Data on the Convention of 1868–1869

Name [a]	Occupation	Wealth [b]	Postwar Offices	Wartime Experience
Adams, Pleasant P. 51, W., Va., D.	Doctor	$ 6,724	—	—
Armstrong, James T. 56, W., Ky., D.	Farmer	—	—	—
Armstrong, Micajah L. 62, W.. Tenn., R.	Farmer	$ 900	Const. Conv. 1866; Voting registrar	—
Bell, John. 48, W., Fla., R.	Hotelkeeper	$ 10,350	County treasurer, 1865	—
Bellinger, Edmund. 66, W., S.C., R.	—	—	—	—
Bledsoe, A.	Farmer	$ 3,250	County judge, 1865	—

	Occupation	Value	Office, 1865	Military
N. V. 65, W., Va., R.				
Boyd, J. B. 34, W., N.C., D.	Lawyer	—	Assessor-collector, 1865	C.S. Army
Brown, James. 50, W., Va., R.	Carpenter	$ 11,000	—	—
Bryant, Anthony M. 49, W., Ky., R.	Farmer	$ 13,000	County judge, 1865	C.S. Army
Bryant, C. W. 38, B., Ky., R.	Minister	—	—	—
Buffington, Anderson. 62, W., S.C., R.	Merchant	$ 1,250	Dist. clerk, 1865	—
Burnett, James R. 25, W., —, R.	Lawyer	—	—	Captain, U.S. Army
Butler, James P. —, W., N.Y., R.	Teacher	—	—	U.S. Army
Carter, W. Frank. 46, W., Mass., R.	Miller	$ 5,000	County judge, 1865	—

TABLE 12—*Continued*

Name[a]	*Occupation*	*Wealth*[b]	*Postwar Offices*	*Wartime Experience*
Caldwell, Colbert. 46, W., Tenn., R.	Lawyer	$ 5,500	Dist. judge, 1865	Refugee
Cole, D. Washington 58, W., Ky., D.	Merchant	—	County judge, 1865	—
Coleman, C. E. —, W., —, D.	—	—	—	—
Constant, D. C. —, W., —, R.	—	—	—	—
Curtis, Stephen. 62, B., Va., R.	Laborer	—	—	—
Davis, Edmund J. 41, W., Fla., R.	Lawyer	—	Const. Conv., 1866	Gen, U.S. Army
Degener, Edward. 59, W., Ger., R.	Merchant	$ 6,000	Con. con., 1866	Prison
Downing, Andrew.	Merchant	$ 2,700	—	—

Name	Occupation	Wealth	Office	War service
Andrew J. 33, W., S.C., R.		—	—	Refugee
Evans, Lemuel D. 58, W., Tenn., D.	Lawyer	$ 7,000	County judge, 1867	—
Fayle, William R. 48, W., G.B., R.	Minister	—	Const. Conv., 1866	Major, C.S. Army
Flanagan, James W. 63, W., Va., R.	"Capitalist"	$ 7,000	County judge	General, C.S. Army
Flanagan, Webster. 36, W., Ky., R.	Lawyer	$ 1,000	—	C.S. Army
Fleming, William H. 52, W., N.C., R.	Farmer	—	—	—
Foster, H. H. 28, W., Tex., R.	Farmer	$ 4,000	—	C.S. Army
Gaston, M. A. 36, W., Ga., D.	Doctor	—	—	Captain, C.S. Army
Glenn, Marshall. —, W., —, D.	—			

TABLE 12—*Continued*

Name[a]	*Occupation*	*Wealth*[b]	*Postwar Offices*	*Wartime Experience*
Gray, B. W. —, W., —, R.	Lawyer	—	Dist. judge	Dist. judge
Grigsby, Aaron. —, W., —, R.	Minister	—	Assessor-collector, 1865	—
Goddin, Mortimer H. 41, W., Va., R.	Lawyer	—	Justice of peace, 1865	—
Hamilton, Andrew J. 53, W., Ala., R.	Lawyer	—	Prov. gov., 1865	—
Hamilton, Morgan C. 59, W., Ala., R.	"Capitalist"	—	Comptroller, 1867	—
Harn, C. T. D. 26, W., Ala., R.	Farmer	$ 15,000	—	—
Harris, L. P. 59, W., Mass., R.	Carpenter	$ 800	—	—
Horne, William F.	Lawyer	$ 2,100	—	—

Name	Occupation	Property	Office	Military
H. E. —, W., —, R.		—	—	—
Johnson, S. M. —, W., —, R.	—	—	Notary public, 1867	—
Johnson, Wiley. —, B., Ark., R.	Shoemaker	—	—	—
Jordan, A. P. H. —, W., —, R.	Doctor	—	—	—
Kealy, Thomas. 59, W., N.Y., R.	Mechanic	$ 5,830	—	—
Keigwin, William. —, W., —, R.	Farmer.	—	—	—
Kendal, Mitchell. 50, B., Ga., R.	Blacksmith	$ 2,400	—	—
Keuchler, Jacob. 45, W., Ger., R.	Surveyor	$ 2,200	—	C.S. Army
Kirk, Allen L. 37, W., —, D.	Farmer	$ 6,000	County clerk, 1865	—

TABLE 12—*Continued*

Name[a]	Occupation	Wealth[b]	Postwar Offices	Wartime Experience
Klappenback, George. 57, W., Ger., R.	Farmer	—	County judge, 1865	—
Lieb, J. G. —, W., —, R.	—	—	—	—
Lindsey, Livingston. 62, W., Va., R.	Lawyer	$ 17,000	Supreme Court, 1867	U.S. Army
Lippard, John H. —, W., —, R.	—	—	—	U.S. Army
Long, Ralph. 25, B., Tenn., R.	Farmer	—	—	—
McCormick, Andrew P. 36, W., Tex., R.	Lawyer	—	County judge, 1865; Con. con., 1866	C.S. Army
Mackey, John. 46, W., La., R.	Farmer	$ 2,200	—	—
McWashington, J.	Farmer	$ 500	—	—

Name	Occupation	Wealth	Office	Military
William W. [—] 32, W., Ind., R.	Merchant	—	—	—
Munroe, Armisted T. 50, W., Va., R.	Merchant	—	—	—
Morse, John. —, W., —, R.	—	—	—	Captain, C.S. Army
Muckleroy, David. 45, W., Tenn., D.	Farmer	$ 1,600	—	—
Mullins, Shepherd. —, B., —, R.	—	—	—	Captain, C.S. Army
Mullins, W. H. 34, W., Tenn., D.	Merchant, lawyer	$ 1,750	—	—
Mundine, Titus H. 43, W., Ala., R.	Merchant	$ 5,922	Justice of peace, 1865	—
Newcomb, James P. 31, W., Canada, R.	Newspaper owner	—	—	—
Oakes, William E. —, W., —, R.	—	—	County judge, 1867	Captain, U.S. Army

TABLE 12—Continued

Name[a]	Occupation	Wealth[b]	Postwar Offices	Wartime Experience
Patten, Nathan. 45, W., N.Y., R.	Manufacturer	—	—	—
Pedigo, Henry C. 53, W., Va., R.	Lawyer	$ 10,500	Dist. judge, 1865	—
Phillips, William J. 42, W., Va., R.	Merchant	$ 5,000	Assessor-collector, 1865	C.S. Army
Phillips, William. 51, W., Tenn., R.	Merchant	$ 7,000	—	—
Posey, W. H. —, W., —, R.	Merchant	—	—	U.S. Army
Rogers, Edwin C. 61, W., Tenn., R.	Doctor	$ 3,800	—	—
Ruby, George T. 27, B., N.Y., R.	Teacher	—	Freedmen's Bureau	—
Schuetze, Julius.	Lawyer	—	County judge, 1865	—

Name	Occupation	Wealth	Previous office	Military service
J. R. —, W., —, R.				
Slaughter, George H. 23, W., Ohio, R.	Farmer	$ 4,000	Clerk, Supreme Court, 1867	U.S. Army
Smith, George W. 33, W., N.Y., R.	Merchant	—	—	Captain, U.S. Army
Smith, Robert K. 43, W., Pa., R.	Doctor	$ 8,000	Tax collector, 1865	Surgeon, U.S. Army
Sorrell, G. M. L. —, W., —, R.	—	—	—	—
Stockbridge, Charles J. 35, W., Pa., R.	Farmer	$ 1,000	—	U.S. Army
Sumner, Fred W., Sr. 34, W., Vt., R.	Watchmaker	$ 14,600	—	—
Talbot, Joseph W. —, W., —, R.	Rancher	—	—	—

TABLE 12—*Continued*

Name[a]	Occupation	Wealth[b]	Postwar Offices	Wartime Experience
Talbot, Richard E. 49, W., N.Y., R.	Farmer	$ 13,000	Registrar, 1867	—
Thomas, James W. 42, W., Mo., R.	Editor	$ 3,500	—	U.S. Army
Varnell, William M. 68, W., Ala., R.	Farmer	—	Registrar, 1867; Const. Conv., 1866	—
Vaughn, F. A. —, W., —, R.	—	—	—	Captain, U.S. Army
Watrous, Benjamin O. 37, B., Tenn., R.	Minister	$ 600	—	—
Whitmore, George W. 44, W., Tenn., R.	Lawyer	$ 27,930	Dist. atty., 1865	—
Williams, Benjamin F.	Laborer	—	—	—

Erwin N. 58, W., Tenn., R.	—	—	C.S. Army
Wilson, John H. —, W., —, R.	—	$ 11,000	County judge
Wright, Arvin. 69, W., N.C., R.	Farmer	—	—
Yarborough, George. 46, W., Ala., R.	Merchant	$ 5,200	—

^aName, age, race, place of birth, and party affiliation when elected to the convention in 1868.

^bReal and personal income taken from manuscript census returns for 1870.

Cluster Analysis of the Constitutional Convention of 1868–1869

Description of the Analysis

Cluster analysis is a relatively old technique that may be used to identify voting blocs in legislatures or other bodies that keep a record of individual voting. Stuart A. Rice introduced the method in the 1920s. It requires the calculation of an index of agreement for every pair of legislators in the subject assembly. These indices are then used to construct a matrix grouping together members who share a minimum level of agreement. Because of the time-consuming nature of computing the required indices, cluster analysis has received relatively little use by historians. The development and the availability of the computer has made this work easier, and thus provides a useful tool for the student of history. (For a more extensive discussion of cluster analysis see Charles M. Dollar and Richard J. Jensen, *Historian's Guide to Statistics: Quantitative Analysis and Historical Research* [New York: Holt, Rinehart and Winston, Inc., 1971], pp. 106–116.)

The examination of the Texas Constitutional Convention of 1868 undertaken in Chapter 4 used a standard Rice index of cohesion. The examination used the cluster analysis for two purposes. First, it was used to isolate and identify the members of the most cohesive blocs. Second, it was used in an effort to determine the cohesiveness of the Republican coalition, and the bases for its unity. After developing several matrices, an index of cohesion of .70 was chosen as the one best demonstrating the convention's major blocs. The chosen index was high enough to indicate a strong measure of cohesion, and it also appeared to be a natural plateau.

A sample of 150 roll calls served as the basis for this analysis. The total population from which the sample was chosen was approximately 900. The sample was chosen on the basis of content. A more systematic sample was not used because of the nature of the data. Disproportionate numbers of roll calls on certain issues weighted the index of agreement toward clusters based on those issues rather than all issues, and thus precluded, for my purposes, use of the total population of votes. The desire to include votes on certain roll calls that were considered important because of the analysis of subjective data also necessitated the abandonment of a true random sample.

TABLE 13. Agreement Matrix for Administration and East Texas Blocs

	1	2	3	4	5	6	7	8	9	10	11	12	13	14	15	16	17
1. W. Fleming	1.00	.80	.79	.77	.74	.70	.82	.81	.79	.80							
2. T. Kealy		1.00	.75	.77	.76	.71	.81	.78	.83	.71				.70			
3. T. Mundine			1.00	.78	.76	.70	.87	.83	.84	.77	.73						
4. C. T. D. Ham				1.00	.83	.70	.79	.84	.86	.73							
5. Erwin Wilson					1.00	.77	.85	.85	.88	.72							
6. Ben. O. Watrous[a]						1.00	.78	.78	.90	.81							
7. C. Stockbridge							1.00	.92	.91	.86	.72	.71					
8. A. J. Hamilton								1.00	.93	.88	.70	.70					
9. C. Caldwell									1.00	.97	.73	.80					
10. Wm. E. Horne										1.00	.73	.74	.77	.84	.70	.76	.74
11. J. R. Burnett											1.00	.74	.76	.82	.70	.72	.70
12. W. Frank Carter												1.00	.72	.82	.71	.75	.73
13. P. P. Adams[b]													1.00	.70	.76	.76	.78
14. Wm. J. Philips														1.00	.74	.81	.72
15. N. V. Board															1.00	.81	.79
16. J. W. Flanagan																1.00	.87
17. Web. Flanagan																	1.00

[a] Black.

[b] Elected to the convention as a Democrat.

TABLE 14. Agreement Matrix for West Texas and Black Blocs

	1	2	3	4	5	6	7	8	9	10	11	12	13
1. William Oakes	1.00	.90	.90	.88	.86	.84	.84	.70	.77	.81	.81	.79	.73
2. J. P. Newcomb		1.00	.83	.85	.86	.81	.81	.73	.76	.77	.79	.80	.78
3. J. Lippard			1.00	.86	.85	.91	.83	.79	.77	.80	.83	.82	.80
4. N. Patten				1.00	.89	.81	.77	.75	.77	.80	.82	.78	.76
5. E. Degener					1.00	.85	.87	.80	.79	.82	.86	.78	.76
6. H. E. Hunt						1.00	.82	.86	.83	.86	.84	.83	.83
7. J. Keuchler							1.00	.76	.75	.76	.81	.84	.80
8. J. P. Butler								1.00	.77	.74	.79	.80	.71
9. E. J. Davis									1.00	.80	.81	.76	.76
10. G. T. Ruby[a]										1.00	.85	.89	.87
11. A. Downing											1.00	.81	.85
12. R. Long[a]												1.00	.97
13. S. Mullins[a]													1.00

[a] Black.

TABLE 15. Agreement Matrix for Democratic Bloc

	1	2	3	4	5	6	7
1. J. B. Boyd	1.00	.83	.79	.76	.83	.83	.80
2. Wm. Keigwin		1.00	.76	.74	.85	.83	.80
3. W. H. Mullins			1.00	.74	.88	.83	.80
4. A. L. Kirk				1.00	.86	.77	.77
5. G. M. L. Sorrel					1.00	.84	.81
6. M. Glenn						1.00	.86
7. M. A. Gaston							1.00

Notes

Introduction

1. *Galveston News*, July 30, 1870.
2. William A. Dunning, *Reconstruction, Political and Economic, 1865–1877* (New York: Harper & Brothers, 1907), pp. 203–219, 266–280. For an excellent discussion of the historiographic literature on reconstruction and pertinent Dunning studies of politics in individual states see J. G. Randall and David Donald, *The Civil War and Reconstruction* (Lexington, Mass.: D. C. Heath and Company, 1969), pp. 811–813, 817–824.
3. David Donald, "The Scalawag in Mississippi Reconstruction," *Journal of Southern History*, 10 (1944): 447–460. See also Thomas Alexander, "Whiggery and Reconstruction in Tennessee," *Journal of Southern History*, 16 (1950): 291–305; idem, "Persistent Whiggery in Alabama and the Lower South, 1860–1867," *Alabama Review*, 12 (1959): 35–52.
4. Allen W. Trelease, "Who Were the Scalawags?" *Journal of Southern History*, 24 (1963): 445–468; idem, *Reconstruction: The Great Experiment* (New York: Harper & Row Publishers, 1971), Chapters 7, 8. Trelease's class analysis has origins in W. E. B. DuBois, *Black Reconstruction in America, 1860–1880* (New York: Atheneum, 1970), and James S. Allen, *Reconstruction: The Battle for Democracy* (New York: International Publishers, 1937).
5. Charles W. Ramsdell, *Reconstruction in Texas* (New York: Columbia University Press, 1910); William C. Nunn, *Texas under the Carpetbaggers* (Austin: University of Texas Press, 1962). For modifications of the traditional view that the Texas Republicans were vindictive and irresponsible see Edgar P. Sneed, "A Historiography of Reconstruction in Texas: Some Myths and Problems," *Southwestern Historical Quarterly*, 72 (1969): 435–448; Dale A. Somers, "James P. Newcomb: The Making of a Radical," *Southwestern Historical Quarterly*, 72 (1969): 449–469; James A. Baggett, "Beginnings of Radical Rule in Texas:

The Special Legislative Session of 1870," *Southwestern Journal of Social Education*, 2 (1972): 28–39; William L. Richter, "'We Must Rubb Out and Begin Anew': The Army and the Republican Party in Texas Reconstruction, 1867–1870," *Civil War History*, 19 (1973): 334–352; Philip Avillo, Jr., "Phantom Radicals: Texas Republicans in Congress, 1870–1873," *Southwestern Historical Quarterly*, 77 (1974): 431–444.

Chapter 1. Texas in 1865

1. James D. Richardson, *A Compilation of the Messages and Papers of the Presidents* (Washington, D.C.: Bureau of National Literature and Art, 1908), 6:321–323, 310–311.
2. Phillip S. Paludan, *A Covenant with Death: The Constitution, Law, and Equality in the Civil War Era* (Urbana: University of Illinois Press, 1975), pp. 10–15; Eric L. McKitrick, *Andrew Johnson and Reconstruction* (Chicago: University of Chicago Press, 1960), pp. 91–92.
3. Michael Les Benedict, *A Compromise of Principle; Congressional Republicans and Reconstruction, 1863–1869* (New York: W. W. Norton, 1974), pp. 41–48; Morton Keller, *Affairs of State: Public Life in Late Nineteenth Century America* (Cambridge, Mass.: Belknap Press of Harvard University Press, 1977), pp. 55–56.
4. U.S. Bureau of the Census, *Population of the United States in 1860*, 1:486–487; *Manufactures of the United States in 1860*, 2:594; *Agriculture of the United States in 1860*, 3:149.
5. U.S. Bureau of the Census, *Agriculture of the United States in 1860*, 3:149; *Texas Almanac for 1867* (Galveston: W. Richardson & Co., Publishers, 1866), p. 199; *Texas State Gazette*, quoted in *De Bow's Review*, 21 (1856):263.
6. Frederick Law Olmsted, *The Cotton Kingdom: A Traveller's Observations on Cotton and Slavery in the American Slave States* (New York: Modern Library, 1953), pp. 294, 301; idem, *A Journey through Texas* (New York: Dix, Edwards & Co., 1857), p. 415; Charles Sydnor, *The Development of Southern Sectionalism, 1819–1848* (Baton Rouge: Louisiana State University Press, 1948), p. 415.
7. The discussion of labor in this paragraph is based upon Ulrich B. Phillips, *American Negro Slavery* (Baton Rouge: Louisiana State University Press, 1966), pp. 395–397; Kenneth M. Stampp, *The Peculiar Institution: Slavery in the Ante-Bellum South* (New York: Vintage Books, 1956), pp. 84–85, 45–46; Karl E. Ashburn, "Slavery and Cotton Production in Texas," *Southwestern Social Science Quarterly*, 14 (1934):261; average production time from Robert W. Fogel and Stanley L. Engerman, *Time on*

the Cross: The Economics of American Negro Slavery (Boston: Little, Brown and Company, 1974), 1:42.

8. D. E. E. Braman, *Braman's Information about Texas* (Philadelphia: J. B. Lippincott & Co., 1857), pp. 80, 83; Olmsted, *Journey through Texas*, p. x.

9. St. Clair Griffin Reed, *A History of the Texas Railroads and of Transportation Conditions under Spain and Mexico and the Republic and the State* (Houston: St. Clair Publishing Company, 1941), p. 733; John S. Spratt, *The Road to Spindletop: Economic Change in Texas, 1875–1901* (Austin: University of Texas Press, 1955), pp. 61–63; Olmsted, *Journey through Texas*, p. xi.

10. U.S. Bureau of the Census, *Statistics of the United States in 1860*, 4:508; Edmund T. Miller, *A Financial History of Texas* (Austin: Texas Historical Association, 1916), pp. 92, 106; Charles S. Potts, *Railroad Transportation in Texas* (Austin: University of Texas Press, 1909), p. 93; Frederick Eby, *The Development of Education in Texas* (New York: Macmillan Company, 1925), pp. 121–125.

11. Randolph B. Campbell and Richard G. Lowe, *Wealth and Power in Antebellum Texas* (College Station: Texas A & M University Press, 1977), pp. 136, 122; Richard Lowe and Randolph Campbell, "Wealthholding and Political Power in Antebellum Texas," *Southwestern Historical Quarterly*, 79 (July 1975):29.

12. U.S. Bureau of the Census, *Agriculture of the United States in 1860*, 3:148; Captain Flack, *The Texas Rifle Hunter or Field Sports in the Prairies* (London: John Maxwell and Company, 1866), p. 330; Viktor Bracht, *Texas in 1848* (San Antonio: Naylor Printing Co., 1931), p. 75; Olmsted, *A Journey through Texas*, p. 414; Ralph A. Wooster, "Wealthy Texans, 1860," *Southwestern Historical Quarterly*, 71 (October 1967):163–180.

13. Olmsted, *Journey through Texas*, p. 415–430; *Galveston News*, July 26, 27, 28, 1865.

14. Olmsted, *Journey through Texas*, p. 431.

15. Ibid., pp. 163, 160, 164, 245.

16. The importance of sectionalism in Texas politics has long been recognized, although not applied to the postwar era. The following analysis is based for the most part on Olmsted's observations. See also Weston J. McConnell, *Social Cleavages in Texas* (New York: Columbia University Press, 1925); D. W. Meinig, *Imperial Texas* (Austin: University of Texas Press, 1969); Roger A. Griffin, "Intrastate Sectionalism in the Texas Governor's Race of 1853," *Southwestern Historical Quarterly*, 76 (1972); 142–160; Floyd F. Ewing, Jr., "Origins of Unionist Sentiment on the West Texas Frontier," *West Texas Historical Association Year Book*, 32 (October 1956):21–29.

17. *Texas State Gazette*, June 25, 1853.

18. Speech of Sam Houston at Nacogdoches, July 9, 1865, in Amelia W. Williams and Eugene C. Barker, eds., *Writings of Sam Houston, 1833–1863* (Austin: University of Texas Press, 1943), 7: 343–367; C. W. Raines, ed., *Six Decades in Texas, or the Memoirs of Francis Richard Lubbock* (Austin: Ben C. Jones & Co., 1900), pp. 247–254; Stephen B. Oates, ed., *R. I. P. Ford's Texas* (Austin: University of Texas Press, 1963), p. 218.

19. Roberts in Dudley G. Wooten, ed., *A Comprehensive History of Texas, 1685 to 1897* (Dallas: William G. Scarff, 1898), 2:83; E. W. Winkler, ed., *Journal of the Secession Convention of Texas, 1861* (Austin: Austin Printing Company, 1912), pp. 88–90.

20. Ramsdell, *Reconstruction in Texas,* p. 23; Ernest Wallace, *Texas in Turmoil* (Austin: The Steck Company, 1965), pp. 125–127, 301; Robert Delaney, "Matamoros, Port for Texas during the Civil War," *Southwestern Historical Quarterly,* 58 (April 1955), pp. 473–487.

21. *Galveston News,* June 16, May 28, 31, 1865; Buck Walton, *An Epitome of My Life: Civil War Reminiscences* (Austin: Waterloo Press, 1965), p. 93.

22. Testimony of Ben Truman, April 5, 1866, House Committee on Reconstruction, U.S. Congress, *House Reports,* 39th Cong., 1st Sess., no. 30 (Serial 1273), p. 138; Children of Moritz Riedel to A. J. Hamilton, March 9, 1866, R. Hunt to Hamilton, July 6, 1865, B. F. Barkley to Hamilton, October 30, 1865, D. B. Lucky to Hamilton, October 16, 1865, Governor's Papers, Texas State Archives, Austin; Thomas Wilson, *Sufferings Endured for a Free Government; or, A History of the Cruelties and Atrocities of the Rebellion* (Washington D.C.: Thomas L. Wilson, 1864), pp. 131, 133–134, 161, 258–262.

23. *Galveston News,* September 27, 1865; Sam Acheson and Julia A. H. O'Connell, eds., *George Washington Diamond's Account of the Great Hanging at Gainesville, 1862* (Austin: Texas State Historical Association, 1963); D. B. Lucky to A. J. Hamilton, October 16, 1865, John L. Haynes to Hamilton, August 29, 1865, Governor's Papers, Texas State Archives.

24. Lawrence D. Rice, *The Negro in Texas, 1874–1900* (Baton Rouge: Louisiana State University Press, 1971), p. 153; George P. Rawick, ed., *The American Slave: A Composite Autobiography,* 19 vols. (Westport, Conn.: Greenwood Press, 1972), 4: 52, 16.

25. *Flake's Bulletin,* September 13, 1865; Claude Elliott, "The Freedmen's Bureau in Texas," *Southwestern Historical Quarterly,* 56 (July 1952):1–24; Alton Hornsby, Jr., "The Freedmen's Bureau Schools in Texas, 1864–1870," *Southwestern Historical Quarterly,* 76 (April 1973):397–418.

26. *Galveston News,* September 23, 1865; Baker quoted in *Galves-*

ton News, September 3, 1865; *Tri-Weekly Houston Telegraph*, February 26, 1866; see also statements of Caleb M. Forshey before the Joint Committee on Reconstruction, United States Congress, *House Reports*, 39th Cong., 1st Session, no. 30 (Serial 1273), p. 131.

Chapter 2. The Unionist Origins of Texas Republicanism

1. *New York Tribune*, June 19, 1865; Howard K. Beale, ed., *Diary of Gideon Welles* (New York: W. W. Norton, 1960) 2:315, 316; Ferdinand Flake to E. M. Pease, July 5, 1865, Pease-Graham-Niles Papers, Austin Public Library; William Alexander to Francis P. Blair, Sr., June 8, 1865, Andrew Johnson Papers, Library of Congress; J. W. Throckmorton to Ben Epperson, August 6, 1865, Ben Epperson Papers, University of Texas Archives.
2. Roy P. Basler, *Collected Works of Abraham Lincoln* (New Brunswick: Rutgers University Press, 1953–1955), 5:357, 492; 6:465–466; 8:103; Beale, ed., *Diary of Gideon Welles*, 2:162–163, 167; John L. Waller, *Colossal Hamilton of Texas* (El Paso: Texas Western Press, 1968), pp. 1–20.
3. Andrew J. Hamilton to Andrew Johnson, July 24, 1865, Andrew Johnson Papers, Library of Congress; *Flake's Bulletin*, July 22, 24, 1865.
4. Executive Record Book, No. 281, pp. 192–194, Texas State Library Archives; Richardson, *Messages and Papers of the Presidents*, 6:310–312; *Flake's Bulletin*, July 26, 1865; *Galveston News*, July 27, 1865.
5. Andrew J. Hamilton to Andrew Johnson, July 24, 1865, Andrew Johnson Papers, Library of Congress; Ferdinand Flake to Andrew J. Hamilton, July 30, 1865, Governor's Papers, Texas State Library Archives.
6. Election Register, No. 260, p. 33, Texas State Library Archives; Ben Epperson to A. J. Hamilton, July 15, 1865, Governor's Papers, Texas State Library Archives; Waller, *Colossal Hamilton*, pp. 66–67.
7. Proclamation printed in *Galveston News*, August 25, 1865; for the kinds of difficulties encountered in the registration see Robert H. Taylor to James H. Bell, August 18, 1865, Governor's Papers, Texas State Library Archives.
8. Ferdinand Flake to E. M. Pease, July 5, 1865, Pease-Graham-Niles Papers, Austin Public Library; *Flake's Bulletin*, May 15, 1865; William Alexander to Francis P. Blair, Sr., June 8, 1865, Andrew Johnson Papers, Library of Congress; William Alexander to Editor, September 1, 1865, in *Galveston News*, September 30, 1865.

9. A. J. Hamilton to Andrew Johnson, November 27, 1865, Andrew Johnson Papers, Library of Congress; *Galveston News Supplement*, August 6, 1865; *Galveston News*, September 20, 1865; Circular of James H. Bell, in U.S. Congress, *House Reports*, 39th Cong., 1st Sess., no. 30 (Serial 1273), p. 95; E. M. Pease to James H. Starr, August 19, 1865, J. H. Starr Papers, University of Texas Archives.

10. J. W. Throckmorton to Ben Epperson, August 6, 1865, Epperson Papers, University of Texas Archives.

11. James W. Throckmorton to Ben Epperson, August 6, 27, 1865, Epperson Papers; Ben Epperson to James W. Throckmorton, June 24, 1865, Throckmorton Papers, all in the University of Texas Archives; Richard S. Hunt to A. J. Hamilton, July 3, 1865, Governor's Papers, Texas State Library Archives.

12. Walter P. Webb, ed., *The Handbook of Texas* (Austin: Texas State Historical Association, 1952), 1:763; Ralph A. Wooster, "An Analysis of the Texas Know-Nothings," *Southwestern Historical Quarterly*, 70 (January 1967):415, 420–421; *Galveston News*, May 25, 1865; J. W. Throckmorton to Ben Epperson, August 6, 1865, Epperson Papers, University of Texas Archives.

13. *Flake's Tri-Weekly Bulletin*, June 17, 1865; T. H. Duval to E. M. Pease, November 18, 1865, Pease-Graham-Niles Papers, Austin Public Library.

14. *Flake's Tri-Weekly Bulletin*, June 17, 1865; *Flake's Bulletin*, June 22, 1865; A. J. Hamilton to Andrew Johnson, July 24, 1865; James H. Bell, E. M. Pease, Thomas Duval and others to Andrew Johnson, August 30, 1865; E. M. Pease to Andrew Johnson, September 14, 1865; Lorenzo Sherwood to Andrew Johnson, July 12, 1865, Andrew Johnson Papers, Library of Congress.

15. *Flake's Tri-Weekly Bulletin*, June 17, 1865; Report of meeting in Fort Bend County led by David G. Burnet, in *Galveston News*, September 26, 1865; Beale, *Diary of Gideon Welles*, 2:332; *Galveston News*, September 9, 14, October 17, 1865.

16. A. J. Hamilton to Andrew Johnson, September 23, 1865, in Andrew Johnson Papers, Library of Congress; T. H. Duval to E. M. Pease, November 18, 1865, Pease-Graham-Niles Papers, Austin Public Library.

17. A. J. Hamilton to Andrew Johnson, October 21, 1865, Andrew Johnson Papers, Library of Congress.

18. Circular of James H. Bell and Testimony of Lt. Col. H. S. Hall in U.S. Congress, *House Reports*, 39th Cong., 1st Sess., no. 30 (Serial 1273), pp. 93–94, 95, 49; Circular of I. A. Paschal, *Daily Herald*, December 25, 1865.

19. W. C. Dalrymple to the People of the 56th District in U.S. Congress, *House Reports*, 39th Cong., 1st Sess., no. 30 (Serial 1273),

p. 92; Speech of John Hancock in *Galveston News*, December 19, 1865; *Journal of the State Convention, Assembled at Austin, February 7, 1865* (Austin: Southern Intelligencer Office, 1866), p. 21.

20. James Armstrong to Editor, *Texas State Gazette*, October 12, 1865; Henry Ware to the People of Harrison County, *Harrison Flag*, December 28, 1865.

21. Benjamin C. Truman to Andrew Johnson, February 8, 1866, Andrew Johnson Papers, Library of Congress.

22. *Journal of the Texas State Convention*, p. 6.

23. Ibid., pp. 11–13.

24. Ibid., pp. 13–14; *Flake's Bulletin*, February 16, 1866; Testimony of Benjamin C. Truman in U.S. Congress, *House Reports*, 39th Cong., 1st Sess., no. 30 (Serial 1273), p. 138.

25. *Journal of the Texas State Convention*, pp. 25–26; A. J. Hamilton to Andrew Johnson, November 27, 1865, Andrew Johnson Papers, Library of Congress.

26. *Journal of the Texas State Convention*, pp. 13, 35.

27. Ibid., pp. 103, 136, 94–95, 97, 198–199.

28. Ibid., pp. 35, 147, 163; C. A. Frazier, *Speeches of the Hon. C. A. Frazier in the Texas State Convention, Convened February 7, 1866* (Marshall, Texas: *Texas Republican* Office, 1866); *Texas State Gazette*, March 20, 1866.

29. *Journal of the Texas State Convention*, p. 117.

30. Ibid., pp. 336–337; Report of E. M. Pease and Swante Palm, August 1865, Governor's Papers, Texas State Archives; Condensed Report in Appendix to Texas Legislature, *House Journal: Eleventh Legislature* (Austin: Office of the Texas State Gazette, 1866).

31. *Journal of the State Convention*, p. 160; *New York Tribune*, June 12, 1866; *Galveston News*, April 11, 1866; Waller, *Colossal Hamilton*, p. 93.

32. William Alexander to Lorenzo Sherwood, February 26, 1866, Andrew Johnson Papers, Library of Congress.

Chapter 3. From Unionism to Republicanism

1. *Southern Intelligencer*, April 5, 1866; *Galveston News*, April 4, 7, 11, 1866; *Texas Republican*, April 17, 1866; Claude Elliott, *Leathercoat: The Life History of a Texas Patriot* (San Antonio: Standard Printing Co., 1938), p. 120.

2. *Galveston News*, April 3, 7, 1866; *Flake's Bulletin*, April 11, 1866.

3. J. W. Throckmorton to Ben Epperson, April 17, 1866, Epperson Papers, University of Texas Archives; *Galveston News*, April

3, 1866; E. W. Winkler, ed., *Platforms of Political Parties in Texas* (Austin: University of Texas Press, 1916), pp. 98–99.

4. J. W. Throckmorton to Ben Epperson, May 30, 1866, Epperson Papers, University of Texas Archives.

5. *Galveston News*, April 3, 1866; Columbus Citizen to Editor, June 1, 1866, C. C. Herbert to Editor, June 3, 1866, in *Galveston News*, June 8, 1866.

6. Speech at Grayson County, in J. W. Throckmorton to Ben Epperson, May 30, 1866, Epperson Papers, University of Texas Archives; Speech at Gainesville, May 12, 1866, *Dallas Weekly Herald*, June 16, 1866.

7. *Galveston News*, April 4, 7, May 25, June 2, 16, 1866; G. J. Clark to O. M. Roberts, April 16, 1866, Roberts Papers, University of Texas Archives; John Hancock to Gen. W. B. Knox, April 4, 1866, in *Galveston News*, April 19, 1866; *New York Tribune*, May 5, 1866.

8. *Flake's Bulletin*, May 9, 11, 1866; *Galveston News*, April 15, May 11, 15, 1866; John H. Potts and A. T. Monroe to A. J. Hamilton, Governor's Papers, Texas State Library Archives.

9. *Galveston News*, May 11, 16, 1866.

10. J. W. Throckmorton to Ben Epperson, April 17, 25, 1866, Epperson Papers, University of Texas Archives; E. J. Davis to E. M. Pease, July 14, 1866, E. H. Cushing to E. M. Pease, March 24, 1866, in Pease-Graham-Niles Papers, Austin Public Library; *Marshall Republican*, in *Galveston News*, June 29, 1866; *Flake's Bulletin*, August 26, 1865.

11. Ben Epperson to J. W. Thomas, April 26, 1866, quoted in *Galveston News*, June 15, 1866; A. H. Latimer to E. M. Pease, April 2, 1866, Alex Rossey to E. M. Pease, May 8, 1866, E. J. Davis to E. M. Pease, July 14, 1866, in Pease-Graham-Niles Papers, Austin Public Library; Elliott, *Leathercoat*, pp. 124–125.

12. John H. Potts to E. M. Pease, July 7, 1866, Pease-Graham-Niles Papers, Austin Public Library; Secretary of State's File, Election Returns, 1865–1866, Texas State Library Archives. For a statistical analysis of the election returns see Appendix 1.

13. T. H. Duval to E. M. Pease, August 9, 1866, Pease-Graham-Niles Papers, Austin Public Library; Texas Legislature, *Journal of the House of Representatives, Eleventh Legislature* (Austin: Office of the *State Gazette*, 1866), pp. 18–25.

14. R. K. Gaston to O. M. Roberts, August 24, 1866, D. M. Short to O. M. Roberts, August 24, 1866, W. M. Neyland to O. M. Roberts, September 29, 1866, Roberts Papers, University of Texas Archives; *Flake's Bulletin*, August 23, 1866.

15. *Flake's Bulletin*, September 6, 1866; John L. Haynes to E. M. Pease, November 28, 1866, Pease-Graham-Niles Papers, Austin Public Library; Texas Legislature, *General Laws of the State of*

Texas Passed by the Eleventh Legislature (Austin: Office of the *State Gazette*, 1866), pp. 26–29.

16. John L. Haynes to E. M. Pease, November 27, 1866, William Alexander to E. M. Pease, September 6, December 20, 1866, Pease-Graham-Niles Papers, Austin Public Library.

17. Texas Legislature, *General Laws of the State of Texas Passed by the Eleventh Legislature*, pp. 59, 97, 76–79, 61–63, 102, 131; William Alexander to E. M. Pease, August 17, 1866, John L. Haynes to E. M. Pease, October 4, November 28, 1866, Pease-Graham-Niles Papers, Austin Public Library.

18. William Alexander to E. M. Pease, September 6, 1866, November 8, 1866, M. C. Hamilton to E. M. Pease, November 9, 28, 1866, John L. Haynes to E. M. Pease, November 28, 1866, Pease-Graham-Niles Papers, Austin Public Library.

19. *New York Times*, July 12, 1866; on Johnson's policies see McKitrick, *Andrew Johnson*, pp. 153–174; Keller, *Affairs of State*, pp. 57–60; LaWanda Cox, *Politics, Principle, and Prejudice, 1865–1866* (New York: Atheneum, 1969), pp. 172–194.

20. *New York Times*, July 12, 1866; *New York Tribune*, July 12, 20, 1866; *Flake's Bulletin*, July 29, 1866; Beale, ed., *Diary of Gideon Welles*, 2:552.

21. Beale, ed., *Diary of Gideon Welles*, 2:568; *Flake's Bulletin*, June 19, 1866.

22. *New York Times*, September 4, 5, 1866; *New York Tribune*, September 4, 5, 1866; James G. Blaine, *Twenty Years of Congress* (Norwich, Connecticut: Henry Bill Publishing Company, 1886), 2:225.

23. *New York Times*, September 6, 7, 1866; *New York Tribune*, September 6, 7, 1866; David Donald, *Politics of Reconstruction, 1863–1867* (Baton Rouge: Louisiana State University Press, 1965), pp. 45–49; Benedict, *Compromise of Principle*, pp. 196–198. Benedict suggests that the moderation among Republicans was in part an effort to undermine Johnson's efforts to attract votes to his third party movement.

24. *New York Times*, September 8, 1866; *New York Tribune*, September 8, 1866; J. S. Thrasher to Guy M. Bryan, September 9, 1866, Guy M. Bryan Papers, University of Texas Archives.

25. *New York Tribune*, September 12, 1866; *Houston Telegraph*, September 26, 1866, clipping in Pease-Graham-Niles Papers, Austin Public Library; *Tribune Almanac*, 2:1867, pp. 49–67; Henry C. Warmoth, *War, Politics, and Reconstruction* (New York: Macmillan Company, 1930), p. 50.

26. A. J. Hamilton, An Address on "Suffrage and Reconstruction," *The Duty of the People, the President, and Congress, Delivered before the Impartial Suffrage League, December 3, 1866* (Boston: Impartial Suffrage League, 1866), pp. 25, 34, 38.

27. *Flake's Bulletin*, December 6, 10, 16, 1866; *New York Trib-*

une, December 6, 8, 13, 1866; *Galveston News*, February 9, 12, 1867; Beale, ed., *Diary of Gideon Welles*, 2:641.

28. *Congressional Globe*, 39th Congress, 2d Session, p. 1128.

29. Ibid., pp. 1128, 1171, 1175, 1223, 1323, 1518; *Galveston News*, February 21, March 27, April 5, 1867; *New York Tribune*, February 20, 1867; Benedict, *Compromise of Principle*, pp. 210–221; McKitrick, *Andrew Johnson*, chapter 14; Donald, *The Politics of Reconstruction*, chapter 3.

30. *Statutes at Large*, 14:428.

31. Ibid., 15:2.

Chapter 4. Organizing the Republican Party

1. *Flake's Bulletin*, May 5, 1867; *Galveston News*, May 16, 1867.

2. *Flake's Bulletin*, April 30, May 2, 1867; Manuscript biography of Wheelock's prewar career in Edwin M. Wheelock Collection, University of Texas Archives.

3. *Flake's Bulletin*, May 16, 22, 1867; *Galveston News*, May 23, 1867.

4. Illegible to A. J. Hamilton, November 29, 1867, Hamilton Papers, University of Texas Archives; *State Gazette*, quoted in *Galveston News*, May 1, 1867.

5. Jacob Raney and Anderson Scroggins to J. W. Throckmorton, May 3, 1867, in *Flake's Bulletin*, May 14, 1867.

6. Guy M. Bryan to Rutherford B. Hayes, May 18, 1867, Guy M. Bryan Papers, University of Texas Archives.

7. *Flake's Bulletin*, May 16, June 10, 11, 1867; *Galveston News*, May 16, June 10, 11, 1867.

8. *Flake's Bulletin*, May 16, 17, 29, June 4, 10, 1867.

9. *Flake's Bulletin*, July 5, 1867; *Galveston News*, July 5, 1867; no official record of the convention could be found and the newspaper accounts are hostile and apparently both inaccurate and incomplete in listing delegates. The *Galveston News* reported only twelve whites present, but an examination of the officers, committee members, and delegates shows at least thirty-two whites present.

10. *Flake's Bulletin*, July 5, 6, 7, 1867; *Galveston News*, July 5, 6, 1867.

11. *Flake's Bulletin*, July 7, 1867.

12. Charles Griffin to Major George A. Forsyth, March 28, 1867, Civil Bureau, Letters Sent, Fifth Military District, Record Group 393, National Archives (hereafter referred to as R.G.); *Flake's Tri-Weekly Bulletin*, September 17, 1867; Ezra J. Warner, *Generals in Blue: Lives of the Union Commanders* (Baton Rouge: Louisiana State University Press, 1964), pp. 190–191.

13. N. Prime to H. L. Johnson, June 7, 1867, Civil Bureau, Letters Sent, Fifth Military District, R.G. 393, National Archives; *Galveston News*, April 9, 1867; Charles Griffin to P. H. Sheridan, July 15, 20, 1867, Sheridan Papers, Library of Congress.

14. George W. Paschal to P. H. Sheridan, June 24, 1867; John L. Haynes to Charles Griffin, July 16, 1867, Civil Bureau, Letters Received, Fifth Military District, R.G. 393, National Archives; Charles Griffin to P. H. Sheridan, July 20, 1867, Sheridan Papers, Library of Congress; "M" to Editor, July 15, 1867, in *Galveston News*, July 20, 1867; Special Order No. 105, July 30, 1867, in *Galveston News*, July 31, 1867.

15. E. M. Pease to Charles Griffin, August 8, 1867; Charles Griffin to P. H. Sheridan, August 14, 1867, Civil Bureau, Letters Received, Fifth Military District, R.G. 393, National Archives; T. H. Duval to John Hamilton, August 9, 1867, Hamilton Papers, University of Texas Archives; Special Order No. 153, August 15, 1867, in *Galveston News*, August 20, 1867.

16. William Longworth to Joseph Spence, August 19, 1867; C. B. Sabin to E. M. Pease, August 9, 1867; A. H. Latimer to Charles Griffin, August 12, 1867; Lt. Albert A. Meitzner to Capt. James C. Devine, August 16, 1867; G. T. Ruby to E. M. Pease, August 16, 1867; E. J. Davis to J. T. Kirkman, August 16, 1867; James Towne to J. T. Kirkman, August 19, 1867; Philip Howard to Charles Griffin, August 20, 1867; P. H. Sheridan to Charles Griffin, August 27, 1867, Governor's Papers, Texas State Library Archives; N. Prime to J. J. Reynolds, September 17, 1867, Civil Bureau, Letters Sent, Fifth Military District, R.G. 393, National Archives.

17. N. Prime to J. J. Reynolds, September 17, 1867; N. Prime to E. M. Pease, September 27, 1867, Civil Bureau, Letters Sent, Fifth Military District, R.G. 393, National Archives; U.S. Congress, *House Exec. Documents*, 40th Cong., 1st Sess., no. 58; McKitrick, *Andrew Johnson*, pp. 494–500; William L. Richter, "The Army in Texas during Reconstruction," Ph.D. dissertation, Louisiana State University, 1970, pp. 127–128.

18. Texas Constitutional Convention, *Journal of the Reconstruction Convention Which Met at Austin, Texas, June 1, A.D., 1868* (Austin: Tracy, Siemering & Co., Printers, 1870), 1:201.

19. *Flake's Bulletin*, April 21, 1867; *Galveston News*, April 23, 1867; Ramsdell, *Reconstruction in Texas*, p. 162.

20. J. W. Throckmorton to Ben Epperson, September 5, 1867, Epperson Papers, University of Texas Archives; *Galveston News*, July 14, 1867, January 14, 18, 1868; *Flake's Bulletin*, June 27, 1867; Ramsdell, *Reconstruction in Texas*, pp. 164–165.

21. Charles Griffin to P. H. Sheridan, June 15, 1867, Sheridan Papers, Library of Congress; *Flake's Bulletin*, July 20, 1867; B. F.

Barkley to E. M. Pease, August 20, 1867, Governor's Papers, Texas State Library Archives; *San Antonio Express* in *Galveston News*, July 20, 1867.

22. U.S. Congress, *Senate Executive Documents*, 40th Cong., 2d Sess., no. 53 (Serial 1317); see also *Triweekly Austin Republican*, November 27, 1867, for registration at end of September; *Flake's Bulletin*, February 8, 1868, for registration at end of January. The percentages shown here are based on the population given in the census of 1870 and the premise that the ratio of black to white males over 21 was essentially the same as the ratio of the total population of black to white males, 1 : 2.36.

23. T. H. Duval to John Hamilton, August 9, 1867, Hamilton Papers, University of Texas Archives; D. J. Baldwin to E. M. Pease, October 23, 1867, Governor's Papers, Texas State Library Archives; A. J. Hamilton to E. M. Pease, October 28, 1867, Pease-Graham-Niles Papers, Austin Public Library; *Austin Republican*, December 24, 1867; *Flake's Bulletin*, December 26, 1867; Ramsdell, *Reconstruction in Texas*, pp. 167–176; Webb, *Handbook of Texas*, 1 : 3; Richter, "The Army in Texas during Reconstruction," p. 149.

24. M. C. Hamilton to Charles Griffin, July 30, 1867, Civil Bureau, Letters Received, Fifth Military District, R.G. 393, National Archives; Ramsdell, *Reconstruction in Texas*, pp. 95–97.

25. Waller, *Colossal Hamilton*, p. 7; Webb, *Handbook of Texas*, 1 : 760.

26. Texas Legislature, *General Laws of the State of Texas Passed by the Eleventh Legislature* (Austin: Office of the *State Gazette*, 1866), pp. 204–206.

27. M. C. Hamilton to E. M. Pease, September 5, 1867, Governor's Papers, Texas State Library Archives.

28. *Flake's Bulletin*, November 3, 1867; M. C. Hamilton to J. J. Reynolds, October 29, 1867, Civil Bureau, Letters Received, Fifth Military District, R.G. 393, National Archives; Texas Attorney General, *Letter of Resignation of William Alexander*, October 28, 1867; A. Gentry to J. J. Reynolds, November 23, 1867, Governor's Papers, Texas State Library Archives. Both Reynolds and Griffin acted to avoid taking a stand on an issue that was in the courts. In Texas, by 1867, several cases had been heard and varying decisions reached on the question of *ab initio*. In the autumn of that year Judge J. J. Thornton of the Second District had ruled in a tax case that all laws passed between secession and 1867 were invalid and that foreclosures on property for nonpayment of taxes during the war had been illegal. In October, however, in the case of *Texas* v. *Spillers* the state supreme court ruled that the state estray laws, suspended by the Confederate state legislature in 1863, had never been

suspended and that all laws passed not in aid of the rebellion were legal and in force. The Supreme Court decision in the case of *Texas* v. *White* in 1869 offered strong reinforcement to the latter decision. The court ruled that the states were indestructible components of the Union, although outside their proper relationships as a result of secession. Nonetheless, the decision gave sanction to the legality of the actions of the states during the war. *Galveston News*, September 24, October 2, 1867; *Texas* v. *Spillers*, 30 *Texas Reports*, pp. 517–518 (1867); *Texas* v. *White*, 7 Wallace, pp. 700–743 (1868); Harold M. Hyman, *A More Perfect Union* (New York: Alfred A. Knopf, 1973), p. 518.

29. M. C. Hamilton to E. M. Pease, November 14, 1867; E. M. Pease to J. J. Reynolds, November 14, 1867; Governor's Papers, Texas State Library Archives.

30. *Austin Republican*, December 21, 1867; *Texas State Gazette*, October 19, 1867; *Flake's Bulletin*, October 24, 25, 27, November 22, December 8, 19, 21, 1867.

31. *Austin Republican*, in *Flake's Bulletin*, December 26, 1867; *Austin Republican*, December 21, 1867, clipping in William Alexander biographical file, Austin Public Library; Special Order No. 213, December 18, 1867, in *Galveston News*, January 5, 1868; Anon. to Editor, December 25, 1867, in *Galveston News*, January 5, 1868.

32. *Galveston News*, January 5, 7, 1868; *Flake's Bulletin*, January 5, 1868; *Houston Telegraph* quoted in *Flake's Bulletin*, January 17, 1868.

33. *Flake's Bulletin*, January 5, 1868.

34. Ibid., January 21, 22, 23, 1868; M. H. Brewster to Elihu B. Washburne, February 19, 1868, Elihu B. Washburne Papers, Library of Congress.

35. *Flake's Bulletin*, January 22, 1868; *Galveston News*, January 22, 1868.

36. *Flake's Bulletin*, January 23, 1868; *Galveston News*, January 23, 1868.

37. *Flake's Bulletin*, January 23, 24, 1868; *Galveston News*, January 23, 24, 1868.

38. Allen W. Trelease provides an excellent account of the Marshall riot in *White Terror: The Ku Klux Klan Conspiracy and Southern Reconstruction* (New York: Harper & Row, 1971), pp. 105–106; C. Caldwell to A. H. Longley, January 2, 1868, Governor's Papers, Texas State Library Archives; *Galveston News*, January 10, 11, 15, February 4, 13, 1868; *Flake's Bulletin*, January 10, 20, 1868; *Austin Republican*, January 8, 15, 1868.

39. U.S. Congress, *House Misc. Documents*, 40th Cong., 2d Sess., no. 127 (Serial 1350).

40. *Galveston News*, February 13, 1868; *Flake's Bulletin*, February 15, 18, 1868.
41. *Flake's Bulletin*, February 17, 1868; U.S. Congress, *Senate Executive Documents*, 40th Cong., 2d Sess., no. 53 (Serial 1317).
42. *Flake's Bulletin*, February 16, 17, 18, 1868; U.S. Congress, *Senate Executive Documents*, 40th Cong., 2d Sess., no. 53 (Serial 1317).
43. U.S. Congress, *Senate Executive Documents*, 40th Cong., 2d Sess., no. 53 (Serial 1317); *Flake's Bulletin*, February 18, 1868; *Galveston News*, February 18, 1868.
44. E. J. Davis to E. M. Pease, March 8, 1868, Governor's Papers, Texas State Library Archives.

Chapter 5. Radicals and Conservatives

1. *Galveston News*, April 2, June 7, 9, 1868; *Flake's Bulletin*, March 6, 1868; biographical data are presented in Appendix 3 and are based upon the manuscript census returns for 1860 and 1870, Webb, *Handbook of Texas*, and county, city, and state studies listed in the bibliography.
2. Historians have seen the Republicans in the convention as being divided into two factions. In his study of reconstruction Charles Ramsdell noted a division of the party into Radicals and Ultra-Radicals, and more recent scholars such as Betty J. Sandlin and John P. Carrier have agreed with the analysis, although describing them as Radicals and Moderates. While applicable to the division of the party that took place in August 1868, this two-faction model does not appear to fit the situation in the convention. This study uses the technique of "cluster analysis" to discover groups of delegates who voted together. The results, presented above, suggest that Republicanism in Texas consisted of more than two factions. See Ramsdell, *Reconstruction in Texas*, pp. 200–201; Betty J. Sandlin, "The Texas Reconstruction Constitutional Convention of 1868–1869," Ph.D. dissertation, Texas Tech University, 1970; John P. Carrier, "A Political History of Texas during the Reconstruction, 1865–1874," Ph.D. dissertation, Vanderbilt University, 1971, pp. 250–251.
3. *Luter v. Hunter*, 30 *Texas Reports*, pp. 692–712 (1868); *Galveston News*, December 21, 1867, June 16, 1868; *Flake's Bulletin*, December 21, 1867; Waller, *Colossal Hamilton*, pp. 76–77, 109–110; Texas Constitutional Convention, *Journal of the Reconstruction Convention Which Met at Austin, Texas, June 1, A.D., 1868* (Austin: Tracy, Siemering & Co., 1870), 1:12–17.
4. Garland R. Farmer, *The Realm of Rusk County* (Henderson:

The Henderson Times, 1951), pp. 29–30, 77; Llerena B. Friend, *Sam Houston: The Great Designer* (Austin: University of Texas Press, 1954), p. 306; Texas Legislature, *House Journal of the Fourth Legislature, Regular Session*, p. 876; Texas Constitutional Convention, *Journal of the Texas State Convention, . . . 1866*, p. 135.

5. *Galveston News*, September 8, 1865, April 26, 1867, November 21, 1873; *Flake's Bulletin*, September 8, 1865; *Weekly Freedman's Press* (Galveston), July 25, 1868, clipping in E. J. Davis biographical file, Barker Texas History Center, University of Texas; *New York Tribune*, July 1, 1869; Dale A. Somers, "James P. Newcomb: The Making of a Radical," *Southwestern Historical Quarterly*, 72 (April 1969):449–469; Webb, ed., *Handbook of Texas*, 2:275; 1:482; *Biographical Dictionary of the American Congress, 1774–1970* (Washington, D.C.: Government Printing Office, 1971), p. 843. For examples of regional dissatisfaction see U.S. Congress, *House Misc. Documents*, 39th Cong., 2d Sess., no. 35 (Serial 1302), pp. 1–4; E. Degener to Thaddeus Stevens, February 27, 1868, Stevens Papers, Library of Congress.

6. *Flake's Bulletin*, May 14, 16, July 5, September 5, December 19, 22, 1867; *Flake's Evening Bulletin*, April 22, 1868; *Houston Union*, July 30, 1870.

7. Texas Constitutional Convention, *Journal of the Reconstruction Convention*, 1:3; *Flake's Bulletin*, June 5, 1868; *Galveston News*, June 5, 1868.

8. Texas Constitutional Convention, *Journal of the Reconstruction Convention*, 1:28.

9. Texas Comptroller, *Biennial Report of the Comptroller of Public Accounts, State of Texas, from September 1, 1867, to August 31, 1869* (Austin: Tracy, Siemering & Co., 1870), p. 5, Tables 2, 18–23.

10. *Flake's Bulletin*, June 13, 17, 1868.

11. Texas Constitutional Convention, *Journal of the Reconstruction Convention*, 1:49–59, 59, 61–63.

12. Ibid., pp. 53, 126–128, 134, 138, 143, 150, 154, 157, 188, 241–242, 632; A. J. Evans, *Speech of Hon. A. J. Evans, Delivered in the Convention at Austin, Texas, June 17, 1868* (n.p., [1868]); *San Antonio Express*, June 21, 1868; *Galveston News*, June 20, 25, 1868; M. C. Hamilton to J. P. Newcomb, July 2, 1870, Newcomb Papers, University of Texas Archives.

13. Texas Constitutional Convention, *Journal of the Reconstruction Convention*, 1:270–283; *Flake's Bulletin*, July 28, August 6, 1868.

14. Texas Constitutional Convention, *Journal of the Reconstruction Convention*, 1:790–792.

15. Ibid., pp. 797, 848.
16. Ibid., p. 235.
17. *Galveston News*, August 22, 1868.
18. Texas Constitutional Convention, *Journal of the Reconstruction Convention*, 1:696–697.
19. Ibid., p. 912.
20. Ibid., p. 146; *Congressional Globe*, 40th Congress, 2d Session, p. 2971; U.S. Congress, *House Misc. Documents*, 39th Cong., 2d Sess., no. 35 (Serial 1302), pp. 1–4; Circular, February 24, 1868, in papers of the House Select Committee on Reconstruction, Legislative Records, R.G. 233, National Archives; E. Degener and others to Thaddeus Stevens, February 27, 1868, Stevens Papers, Library of Congress.
21. Texas Constitutional Convention, *Journal of the Reconstruction Convention*, 1:160–162, 174–175, 180, 190–191, 205, 407–408, 410–411; *San Antonio Express*, July 17, 1868.
22. Texas Constitutional Convention, *Journal of the Reconstruction Convention*, 1:111–112, 137, 212–213, 221–224.
23. Ibid., pp. 858, 851–853, 860.
24. Ibid., pp. 672–679; Ben H. Procter, *Not Without Honor: The Life of John H. Reagan* (Austin: University of Texas Press, 1962), p. 83; Sandlin, "The Texas Reconstruction Constitutional Convention of 1868–1869," pp. 65–94. Sneed, "A Historiography of Reconstruction in Texas," p. 445, concluded that the problem "has not been adequately studied."
25. *Galveston News*, January 23, 24, April 15, May 26, June 2, 24, July 2, 1868; *Flake's Bulletin*, January 23, 24, May 6, 1868; Allen W. Trelease, *White Terror*, p. 51.
26. *Galveston News*, April 12, 22, 23, 1868; *Houston Telegraph*, July 14, 1868; *Houston Journal* in *Galveston News*, May 25, 1868; *San Antonio Express* and *Houston Democrat* in *Flake's Bulletin*, April 29, 1868, see also March 20, April 9, 15, 23, 28, 29, 30, May 6, 1868.
27. General Orders No. 1, General Orders No. 7, Bureau of Refugees, Freedmen and Abandoned Lands, in *Galveston News*, May 5, July 14, 1868; U.S. Congress, *House Executive Documents*, 40th Cong., 3d Sess., no. 1 (Serial 1367), pp. 704–705; John W. Alvord, *Semi-Annual Report on Schools and Finances for Freedmen*, 6 (July 1868):42; *Union Republican* in *Flake's Bulletin*, May 8, 1868, see also June 17, 19, 1868; Don Campbell to E. M. Pease, May 6, 1868, E. M. Pease to J. J. Reynolds, June 26, 1868, Governor's Letter Press, both in Governor's Papers, Texas State Library Archives; *Galveston News*, May 20, 24, July 16, 1868.
28. Report of Lt. N. R. Randlett, in *Galveston News*, August 13, 1868, see also July 17, 18, 21, August 12, 13, 27, 1868.

29. *Flake's Bulletin*, June 28, 1868; *Galveston News*, June 23, 1868.
30. *Galveston News*, July 1, June 23, 1868.
31. Republican State Executive Committee, *Proceedings of the Republican State Convention Assembled at Austin, August 12, 1868* (Austin: Daily Republican Book & Job Office, 1868), pp. 3–8; *Austin Republican*, August 13, 22, 1868; *Flake's Bulletin*, August 16, 1868.
32. Republican State Executive Committee, *Proceedings of the Republican State Convention . . . 1868*, p. 9; *Austin Republican*, August 15, 1868; *Flake's Bulletin*, August 19, 1868.
33. Republican State Executive Committee, *Proceedings of the Republican State Convention . . . 1868*, p. 10; *Flake's Bulletin*, August 13, 15, 19, 1868; *Austin Republican*, August 15, 1868; *Galveston News*, August 15, 1868; *San Antonio Express*, August 21, 1868.
34. *Galveston News*, August 15, 22, 1868; *Austin Republican*, August 15, 1868.
35. Republican State Executive Committee, *Proceedings of the Republican State Convention . . . 1868*, p. 11–12; *Flake's Bulletin*, August 19, 1868.
36. *Flake's Bulletin*, August 15, 22, 1868.
37. Ibid., September 9, 10, 24, 1868.
38. Ibid., September 20, 25, October 22, November 3, 1868; *Galveston News*, September 20, 1868; *San Antonio Weekly Express*, October 15, 1868, clipping in Newcomb Papers, University of Texas Archives.
39. *Jefferson Jimplecute* and *Austin Republican* in *Galveston News*, November 20, December 9, 1868.
40. 7 Wallace, 726–743; Hyman, *A More Perfect Union*, pp. 517–518.
41. Texas Constitutional Convention, *Journal of the Reconstruction Convention*, 2:278–288, 302; *Galveston News*, January 17, 1869. Extensive narratives of the division fight during the second session appear in Ramsdell, *Reconstruction in Texas*, pp. 242–260; Sandlin, "The Texas Reconstruction Constitutional Convention of 1868–1869," pp. 119–131.
42. Texas Constitutional Convention, *Journal of the Reconstruction Convention*, 1:569, 2:303–304, 325, 343–346, 483; *Austin Republican*, January 23, 1869.
43. Texas Constitutional Convention, *Journal of the Reconstruction Convention*, 2:518–519, 527–529; *Flake's Bulletin*, February 7, 1869; *Galveston News*, February 14, 1869.
44. *Flake's Bulletin*, February 9, 1869; *Galveston News*, February 14, 1869.

Chapter 6. Texas Republicans in the State Election of 1869

1. Martin E. Mantell, *Johnson, Grant, and the Politics of Reconstruction* (New York: Columbia University Press, 1973), pp. 63–67, 129; Charles H. Coleman, *The Election of 1868: The Democratic Effort to Regain Control* (New York: Octagon Books, 1971), p. 305; Keller, *Affairs of State*, pp. 81–82; Benedict, *Compromise of Principle*, pp. 265–270; Michael L. Benedict, "The Rout of Radicalism: Republicans and the Election of 1867," *Civil War History*, 18 (1972):334–344.

2. Alan Conway, *The Reconstruction of Georgia* (Minneapolis: University of Minnesota Press, 1966), p. 161; John Hope Franklin, *Reconstruction after the Civil War* (Chicago: University of Chicago Press, 1961), pp. 130–133.

3. *Statement and Memorial in Relation to Political Affairs in Texas by Members of the State Convention and other Citizens of the State, Addressed to Hon. B. F. Butler* (Washington, D.C.: McGill & Witherow, Printers, 1869); *Galveston News*, March 20, 1869.

4. E. J. Davis to R. C. Schenck, January 27, 1869, Papers of the House Select Committee on Reconstruction, Legislative Records, R.G. 233, National Archives; *Memorial to the Senators and Representatives of the Forty-First Congress from the Commissioners Elected by the Reconstruction Convention of the State of Texas to Represent the Condition of the State and the Wants of the Loyal People* (Washington, D.C.: J. L. Pearson, 1869); *Galveston News*, March 2, 3, 4, 11, 1869; *Flake's Bulletin*, February 17, March 11, 1869.

5. Minutes, March 30, April 1, 3, 1869, "List of Questions to be Asked to Members of A. J. Hamilton's Committee," Papers of the House Select Committee on Reconstruction, Legislative Records, R.G. 233, National Archives; *Galveston News*, April 4, 6, 1869; Hans L. Trefousse, *Ben Butler: The South Called Him Beast* (New York: Twayne Publishers, 1957), pp. 212–215.

6. Minutes, April 6, 1869, House Select Committee on Reconstruction, Legislative Records, R.G. 233, National Archives; *Congressional Record*, 41st Cong., 1st Sess., pp. 633–637, 662, 699; U.S. Congress, *Statutes at Large* (Boston: Little, Brown & Co., 1871), 16:40–41; *Galveston News*, April 7, 9, 1869.

7. *Galveston News*, March 2, 3, 4, 1869; *Flake's Bulletin*, February 17, 1869; James R. Burnett to Mark Miller, March 12, 1869, Governor's Papers, Texas State Library Archives.

8. *Austin Republican*, March 20, 24, April 1, May 22, 1869; A. J. Hamilton to Ferdinand Flake, March 18, 1869, in *Galveston News*, March 19, 1869.

9. *Austin Republican*, February 23, 1869; *Galveston News*, Febru-

ary 18, 19, 1869; *Tri-Weekly State Gazette*, February 24, 1869.

10. *Tri-Weekly State Gazette*, February 24, 1869; *Houston Telegraph*, in *Flake's Bulletin*, February 12, 1869; Ashbel Smith and others to Oran M. Roberts, February 12, 1869, Roberts Papers, University of Texas Archives; John H. Reagan to Ashbel Smith and others, February 23, 1869, Ashbel Smith Papers, University of Texas Archives; J. W. Throckmorton to Editor, *McKinney Enquirer*, in *Tri-Weekly State Gazette*, March 8, 1869; *Galveston News*, March 31, 1869.

11. Ashbel Smith to Oran M. Roberts, February 12, 1869, Roberts Papers, University of Texas Archives; John H. Reagan to Ashbel Smith, February 23, 1869, Ashbel Smith Papers, University of Texas Archives; see newspaper comment from around the state in *Galveston News*, March 11, 12, 13, 17, 19, 20, 1869.

12. James H. Bell to E. M. Pease, February 22, 1869, Pease-Graham-Niles Papers, Austin Public Library; *San Antonio Express*, in *Galveston News*, March 20, 1869; *Flake's Bulletin*, March 20, 1869.

13. William Phillips to E. M. Pease, February 23, 1869; John A. Purnell to E. M. Pease, April 9, 1869, James R. Butler to E. M. Pease, March 23, 1869, Governor's Papers, Texas State Library Archives; J. G. Tracy to E. M. Pease, April 8, 1869, E. M. Wheelock to E. M. Pease, April 11, 1869, Pease-Graham-Niles Papers, Austin Public Library; A. Siemering to J. P. Newcomb, March 11, 1869, Newcomb Papers, San Antonio Public Library; *Austin Republican* in *Flake's Bulletin*, March 23, 1869; *Flake's Bulletin*, March 13, 1869.

14. M. C. Hamilton to J. P. Newcomb, April 30, May 14, 1869, Newcomb Papers, University of Texas Archives; E. J. Davis to J. G. Tracy, May 3, 1869, in *Flake's Bulletin*, May 8, 1869; John A. Purnell to E. M. Pease, April 9, 1869, Governor's Papers, Texas State Library Archives; *Tri-Weekly State Gazette*, April 23, 1869; *Flake's Bulletin*, April 25, 1869; *Galveston News*, April 25, May 2, 1869; *Austin Republican*, April 21, 1869.

15. J. G. Tracy to E. M. Pease, April 8, 1869, Pease-Graham-Niles Papers, Austin Public Library; Chauncey B. Sabin to Edward McPherson, March 6, 1869, Edward McPherson Papers, Library of Congress.

16. E. M. Wheelock to E. M. Pease, April 11, 1869, Pease-Graham-Niles Papers, Austin Public Library; A. Siemering to E. M. Pease, March 8, 1869, Governor's Papers, Texas State Library Archives.

17. J. G. Tracy to E. M. Pease, April 8, 1869, Pease-Graham-Niles Papers, Austin Public Library.

18. *Houston Union* in *Flake's Bulletin*, April 29, 1869; *Galveston News*, April 29, 1869; M. C. Hamilton to J. P. Newcomb,

April 30, May 14, 1869, Newcomb Papers, University of Texas Archives; A. J. Hamilton to E. M. Wheelock, May 16, 1869, in *Austin Republican*, May 22, 1869; *Houston Times* and *Houston Union*, in *Galveston News*, May 6, 9, 1869.

19. *Flake's Bulletin*, May 4, 11, 12, 1869; *Galveston News*, April 18, May 11, 1869; *Austin Republican*, May 14, 31, 1869; M. C. Hamilton to J. P. Newcomb, May 14, 1869, Newcomb Papers, University of Texas Archives.

20. M. C. Hamilton to J. P. Newcomb, May 14, 1869, Newcomb Papers, University of Texas Archives; *Galveston News*, May 15, 1869.

21. James R. Kean to E. M. Pease, May 28, 1869, Pease-Graham-Niles Papers, Austin Public Library; E. M. Wheelock to E. M. Pease, June 11, 1869, Governor's Papers, Texas State Library Archives; *San Antonio Express*, in *Flake's Bulletin*, June 10, 1869; James R. Kean tc J. L. Haynes, May 29, 1869, in *Austin Republican*, June 12, 1869.

22. N. Patten to J. P. Newcomb, May 17, 1869, Newcomb Papers, University of Texas Archives; A. J. Evans to E. M. Pease, May 21, 1869, Thomas H. Stribling to E. M. Pease, May 1869, Pease-Graham-Niles Papers, Austin Public Library; *Galveston News*, June 3, 4, 11, 1869.

23. *Galveston News*, June 8, 1869; *Flake's Bulletin*, June 8, September 24, 1869; *Austin Republican*, June 12, 1869.

24. M. C. Hamilton to J. G. Tracy, June 16, 1869, in *Austin Republican*, July 6, 1869; M. C. Hamilton to J. P. Newcomb, June 19, 26, July 25, 1869, George C. Rives to J. P. Newcomb, June 18, 19, 1869, M. C. Hamilton to E. Degener, June 28, 1869, Newcomb Papers, University of Texas Archives.

25. G. W. Paschal to John L. Haynes, June 20, 1869, John L. Haynes to E. M. Pease, June 29, 1869, Pease-Graham-Niles Papers, Austin Public Library; *Flake's Bulletin*, April 7, 8, 9, 11, 14, 1869; *Galveston News*, July 1, April 4, 7, 1869; *New York Tribune*, May 24, 1869.

26. *New York Tribune*, May 21, 24, July 8, 14, 1869; *New York Herald*, in *Galveston News*, May 23, 20, 1869; *Baltimore Gazette*, in *Galveston News*, August 15, 1869, see also July 10, 11, 13, May 23, 1869; Jack P. Maddex, *The Virginia Conservatives, 1867–1879* (Chapel Hill: University of North Carolina Press, 1970), pp. 73–81.

27. W. B. Moore to N. P. Banks, July 7, 1869, N. P. Banks Papers, Library of Congress; John L. Haynes to Thomas L. Tullock, June 10, 1869, Appointment Papers, Treasury Department, R.G. 56, National Archives; *Flake's Bulletin*, July 13, 1869.

28. C. Caldwell to E. M. Pease, July 3, 1869, Pease-Graham-Niles Papers, Austin Public Library; E. M. Pease to John L. Haynes,

July 12, 1869, in *Austin Republican*, July 30, 1869, and July 14, 1869; *New York Tribune*, July 10, 13, 1869; *Galveston News*, July 13, 1869.

29. *New York Tribune*, July 14, 15, 16, 1869; *Baltimore Gazette*, in *Galveston News*, July 21, 1869; Allan Nevins in his *Hamilton Fish: The Inner History of the Grant Administration* (New York: Charles Scribner's Sons, 1936), p. 290, mentions this cabinet meeting and cites as his source the Fish diary in the Library of Congress. I could find no mention of the meeting, however, in the manuscript diary.

30. *New York Tribune*, August 10, 1869; *Galveston News*, August 4, 1869; *Flake's Bulletin*, August 1, 11, 1869; Morgan C. Hamilton to J. P. Newcomb, August 17, 1869, Newcomb Papers, University of Texas Archives.

31. *Galveston News*, July 20, 1869; Charles W. Godard (President of the Union League) to George S. Boutwell, July 23, 1869, Thomas G. Baker (Secretary of Union League) to G. S. Boutwell, July 28, 1869, John W. Glenn to G. S. Boutwell, July 19, 1869, J. G. Tracy to U. S. Grant, July 19, 1869, E. J. Davis to G. S. Boutwell, August 2, 1869, all in Appointment Papers, Treasury Department, R.G. 56, National Archives; Thomas G. Baker to William E. Chandler, July 24, 1869, William Chandler Papers, Library of Congress; Wm. E. Chandler to B. F. Butler, August 10, 1869, Butler Papers, Library of Congress; C. Schurz to G. S. Boutwell, August 14, 1869, Carl Schurz Papers, Library of Congress.

32. J. G. Tracy to E. M. Pease, April 28, 1869, Pease-Graham-Niles Papers, Austin Public Library; M. C. Hamilton to J. P. Newcomb, July 25, 1869, Newcomb Papers, University of Texas Archives; J. J. Reynolds to U. S. Grant, September 4, 1869, in *Flake's Bulletin*, October 5, 1869.

33. J. J. Reynolds to U. S. Grant, September 4, 1869, in *Flake's Bulletin*, October 5, 1869. Accusations that Reynolds supported Davis in return for the candidate's promise of a seat in the United States Senate circulated during this period and most historians have accepted them as factual; see Ramsdell, *Reconstruction in Texas*, pp. 274–278 and Richter, "Army in Texas during Reconstruction," p. 160. There is no proof of the allegations. In fact supporters of Davis seemed as surprised as those of Hamilton by the general's letter. See M. C. Hamilton to J. P. Newcomb, October 16, 1869, Newcomb Papers, University of Texas Archives.

34. *Flake's Bulletin*, September 25, 26, 28, 1869; *Galveston News*, September 25, 27, October 6, 1869.

35. George W. Paschal to E. M. Pease, September 28, 1869, Pease-Graham-Niles Papers, Austin Public Library; E. M. Pease to J. J.

Reynolds, September 30, 1869, Letters Received, Civil Bureau, Fifth Military District, R.G. 393, National Archives.

36. George C. Rives to J. P. Newcomb, September 30, October 3, 1869, M. C. Hamilton to J. P. Newcomb, October 16, 1869, Newcomb Papers, University of Texas Archives; M. C. Hamilton to J. J. Reynolds, November 8, 1869, E. J. Davis to J. J. Reynolds, November 8, 10, 1869, William Alexander and others to J. J. Reynolds, November 2, 1869, Letters Received, Civil Bureau, J. J. Reynolds to U. S. Grant, November 2, 1869, J. J. Reynolds to E. J. Davis, November 11, 1869, Letters Sent, Civil Bureau; Vol. 81, Civil Appointments, Civil Bureau, Fifth Military District, R.G. 393, National Archives.

37. E. J. Davis to J. P. Newcomb, July 4, 1869, Newcomb Papers, University of Texas Archives; *Flake's Bulletin*, September 24, 24, 1869; *Galveston News*, September 25, 1869; *Austin Republican*, September 27, 29, 1869.

38. G. T. Ruby to J. P. Newcomb, May 6, 1869, Newcomb Papers, University of Texas Archives.

39. E. J. Davis to J. J. Reynolds, November 8, 10, 1869, Letters Received, Civil Bureau, Fifth Military District, R.G. 393, National Archives; G. T. Ruby to J. P. Newcomb, September 12, 1869, Newcomb Papers, University of Texas Archives; *Galveston News*, August 1, June 10, August 10, 1869.

40. *Galveston News*, May 24, 25, July 6, September 16, October 10, 1869; *Flake's Bulletin*, May 30, July 4, September 22, 1869; *Tri-Weekly State Gazette*, July 2, 1869.

41. *Flake's Bulletin*, June 18, 1869; *Galveston News*, June 18, 1869.

42. *Galveston Civilian*, August 23, 1870, in *Flake's Bulletin*, August 25, 1870; See also *Flake's Bulletin*, September 30, October 1, 2, 3, 12, 1869; *Galveston News*, September 2, 30, October 1, 8, 10, 13, 1869; E. J. Davis to J. P. Newcomb, September 5, 1869, J. G. Tracy to A. Siemering, October 2, 1869, Newcomb Papers, University of Texas Archives.

43. *Galveston News*, August 1, 5, 6, 1869; *Flake's Bulletin*, August 6, 1869; *Biographical Directory of the American Congresses, 1774–1961* (Washington, D.C.: Government Printing Office, 1961) p. 745.

44. John L. Haynes to E. M. Pease, June 21, 24, 1869, Pease-Graham-Niles Papers, Austin Public Library; B. G. Shields and Thomas P. Ochiltree to Jacob Eliot, November 15, 1869, Jacob Eliot to B. G. Shields and Thomas P. Ochiltree, November 16, 1869, in *Galveston News*, November 19, 1869; Thomas P. Ochiltree to the Citizens of the Third Congressional District, November 19, 1869, in *Galveston News*, November 24, 1869; *Galveston News*, July 23, November 19, November 20, 1869; *Flake's Bulletin*, June 13, November 21, 1869.

45. *Flake's Bulletin*, November 17, 21, 28, 1869; *Sherman Courier*, October 23, 1869, in *Galveston News*, November 5, 1869; C. Caldwell to E. M. Pease, September 7, 1869, Pease-Graham-Niles Papers, Austin Public Library.

46. *Galveston News*, October 27, December 1–4, 9, 1869; *Flake's Bulletin*, December 1–4, 14, 1869; *New York Tribune*, December 7, 1869. Voters indicated their race on the ballot for or against the proposed constitution. Nine counties did not provide this data when they reported. In order to obtain an approximation of the total number of blacks and whites voting in the election for these 9 counties I divided the vote in each into the same proportion as blacks and whites in the population. The estimate corresponded loosely with the division of the vote between Davis and Hamilton and suggested that it was at least partially valid for these cases. Adding these figures to the recorded data for the other 111 counties I obtained my estimate of the vote.

47. Manuscript election returns, Civil Bureau, Fifth Military District, R.G. 393, National Archives; *Flake's Bulletin*, December 8, 14, 1869; *Austin Republican*, December 8, 18, 1869; *Galveston News*, December 14, 1869; E. J. Davis to J. P. Newcomb, December 12, 1869, Newcomb Papers, University of Texas Archives; Joseph Welch to J. P. Newcomb, December 18, 1869, Newcomb Papers, San Antonio Public Library.

48. M. B. Walker to James A. Garfield, December 20, 1869, E. J. Davis to E. R. Hoard, December 27, 1869, Robert K. Smith to B. F. Butler, December 30, 1869, in papers of the House Select Committee on Reconstruction, Legislative Records, R.G. 233, National Archives; John Hancock to Ben Epperson, December 20, 1869, Epperson Papers, University of Texas Archives; *New York Tribune*, December 18, 21, 1869; *Galveston News*, December 21, 1869; *Flake's Bulletin*, December 8, 18, 1869.

49. Lt. Charles E. Morse to Post Commander, Waco, November 30, December 1, 1869, Lt. Charles E. Morse to J. J. Reynolds, December 7, 1869, in Civil Bureau, Letters Sent, E. J. Davis to J. J. Reynolds, December 11, 1869, E. J. Davis to J. J. Reynolds, December 12, 1869, J. G. Tracy to J. J. Reynolds, December 11, 1869, in Civil Bureau, Letters Received, Fifth Military District, R.G. 393, National Archives; *Galveston News*, December 5, 15, 21, 30, 1869; *New York Tribune*, December 24, 29, 1869.

50. White votes were computed by subtracting the number of blacks who voted in the election from the number of votes received by Davis. This method assumes that all blacks voted for Davis, not a probability, but it does provide a figure that suggests the

minimum strength of the Radical candidate among white supporters.

51. Special Order No. 6, in Governor's Papers, Texas State Library
    Archives.

52. *San Antonio Express* in *Flake's Bulletin*, February 18, 1870,
    see also January 27, February 8, 1870; *New York Tribune*,
    February 14, 1870; Texas Legislature, *Journal of the Senate,
    Provisional Session of 1870*, pp. 37–38, 42; Texas Legislature,
    Journal of the House, Provisional Session of 1870, pp. 55–56.

53. *New York Tribune*, February 11, 12, 1870; *Flake's Bulletin*,
    January 27, 1870; *Galveston News*, March 9, 1870; "Call for a
    Republican Convention to Meet at Austin, January 18, 1870,"
    broadside in E. M. Pease Collection, University of Texas Ar-
    chives; *Galveston News*, March 9, 30, 31, 1870; Minutes,
    March 15, 1870, House Select Committee on Reconstruction,
    Legislative Records, R.G. 233, National Archives.

Chapter 7. The Price of the Republican Coalition

1. *Flake's Bulletin*, May 13, 1870; *Tri-Weekly Houston Union*,
   July 27, 1870, clipping in Appointment Files (Morgan C. Ham-
   ilton), Justice Department, R.G. 90, National Archives; *New
   York Tribune*, July 1, 1869; *Flake's Bulletin*, September 8, 1865;
   Galveston News, September 8, 1865, November 21, 1873.

2. *State Journal*, May 26, 1870; *Flake's Bulletin*, January 14, 1870.

3. For discussion of the members of the House see *Flake's Bulletin*,
   May 3, 1870; *Galveston News*, April 29, 1870, *State Journal*,
   April 29, 1870. They indicate that there were 33 Radicals, 26
   Republicans, 17 Democrats, 10 Conservatives, 1 Whig, and 1
   Independent. There were 11 black legislators, 73 whites. An
   occupational analysis indicated 23 planters and farmers, 19 law-
   yers, 10 merchants, and 9 physicians. Eleven carpetbaggers sat
   in the House along with 66 white Southerners.

4. Speech of Gen. W. H. Parsons, in *Galveston News*, March 9,
   1870; *Flake's Bulletin*, May 13, 14, 1870, November 8, 1871;
   Webb, *Handbook of Texas*, 1:609; *Dictionary of American
   Biography*, 6.

5. *Galveston News*, December 16, 1871.

6. This assessment is based upon the performance of the three individuals in the Senate in 1870.

7. Rudolph L. Beisele, *The History of the German Settlements in
   Texas, 1831–1861* (Austin: Press of Von Boeckmann-Jones Co.,
   1930), pp. 197–198.

8. *Flake's Bulletin*, May 18, 1870, February 24, 1871; J. Mason
   Brewer, *Negro Legislators of Texas and Their Descendants*

(Dallas: Mathis Publishing Co., 1935), pp. 51–52, 31–49. For information on blacks in the House and Senate see Monroe N. Work, "Some Negro Members of Reconstruction Legislatures: Texas," *Journal of Negro History*, 5 (January 1929): 111–113; Arthur Z. Brown, "The Participation of Negroes in Reconstruction Legislatures of Texas," *The Negro History Bulletin*, 20 (January 1957): 87–88; Manuscript Census Returns, 1870; Brewer notes nine blacks in the House. I find eleven: Mitchel Kendall, Richard Allen, R. Goldsteen Dupree, Silas Cotton, Henry Moore, Shep Mullins, B. F. Williams, J. F. McKee, Jeremiah J. Hamilton, Richard Williams, and John Mitchell. See *Flake's Bulletin*, January 14, 1870.

9. *Flake's Bulletin*, June 16, 1868, November 30, 1869, May 18, 1870, October 7, 1870; *Flake's Evening Bulletin*, April 22, 1868; *Houston Union*, July 30, 1870.

10. *Galveston News*, April 9, 29, May 10, 1870; *Flake's Bulletin*, May 4, 1870; Texas Legislature, *House Journal of the Twelfth Legislature, Called Session* (Austin: Tracy, Siemering & Co., 1870), pp. 14–16.

11. Texas Legislature, *House Journal of the Twelfth Legislature, Called Session*, pp. 17–21; *General Laws of the Twelfth Legislature, Called Session*, pp. 19–21; Walter P. Webb, *The Texas Rangers: A Century of Frontier Defense* (Austin: University of Texas Press, 1965), pp. 127–192, 191.

12. *General Laws of the Twelfth Legislature, Called Session*, pp. 11–16, 21–23, 63, 87–112.

13. Texas Legislature, *House Journal of the Twelfth Legislature, Called Session*, pp. 20–21; *General Laws of the Twelfth Legislature, First Session* (1871), p. 58.

14. *General Laws of the Twelfth Legislature, Called Session*, pp. 5–8, 45–46, 64; Texas Legislature, *House Journal of the Twelfth Legislature, Called Session*, pp. 26–28.

15. Texas Legislature, *House Journal of the Twelfth Legislature*, pp. 21–26.

16. Ibid., pp. 29–30; *General Laws of the Twelfth Legislature, Called Session*, pp. 119–124, 199–201.

17. *Galveston News*, April 30, 1870; *Austin Republican*, May 2, 1870; *Flake's Bulletin*, May 1, 1870.

18. M. C. Hamilton to J. P. Newcomb, May 15, 1870, J. P. Newcomb Papers, University of Texas Archives; *Flake's Bulletin*, April 28, 1870, November 8, 1871; *Galveston News*, April 27, 1870.

19. Texas Legislature, *Senate Journal of the Twelfth Legislature, Called Session* (Austin: Tracy, Siemering & Co., 1870), pp. 82–83; *Flake's Bulletin*, May 7, 12, 14, 1870; *Galveston News*, May 1, 15, 1870.

20. *State Journal Appendix* (Tracy, Siemering & Co., 1870), pp. 24, 45.
21. Texas Legislature, *Senate Journal of the Twelfth Legislature, Called Session*, pp. 63, 85; Texas Legislature, *House Journal of the Twelfth Legislature, Called Session*, pp. 60, 154; *State Journal Appendix*, pp. 82, 81–84.
22. Texas Legislature, *House Journal of the Twelfth Legislature, Called Session*, pp. 179, 211–212, 313–314; *Flake's Bulletin*, May 14, 18, 1870; *Galveston News*, May 14, 15, 18, 1870.
23. *Flake's Bulletin*, May 13, 22, June 7, 8, July 3, 1870; *Galveston News*, May 22, 24, June 7, 10, 1870.
24. M. C. Hamilton to J. P. Newcomb, June 26, 1870, Newcomb Papers, University of Texas Archives.
25. Texas Legislature, *Senate Journal of the Twelfth Legislature, Called Session*, pp. 92, 108, 194–195; *State Journal*, May 4, 6, 18, 1870; *Galveston News*, May 7, 27, 1870; Waller, *Colossal Hamilton*, pp. 101–102.
26. Texas Legislature, *Senate Journal of the Twelfth Legislature, Called Session*, p. 359; *Flake's Bulletin*, May 24, July 2, 1870; *Houston Times*, in *Galveston News*, June 23, 1870, see also May 29, June 16, 1870.
27. Texas Legislature, *Senate Journal of the Twelfth Legislature, Called Session*, p. 211.
28. Ibid., pp. 335–359, 247–251, 352–356.
29. Ibid., pp. 250–251, 279, 332–333, 366, 316; Texas Legislature, *House Journal of the Twelfth Legislature, Called Session*, pp. 444, 462, 487; *Galveston News*, July 21, 1870.
30. Texas Legislature, *Senate Journal of the Twelfth Legislature, Called Session*, pp. 381–384, 391–394.
31. C. B. Sabin to E. J. Davis, July 20, 1870, Governor's Papers, Texas State Library Archives; M. C. Hamilton to J. P. Newcomb, July 17, 1870, W. T. Clark to J. P. Newcomb, July 26, 1870, Newcomb Papers, University of Texas Archives; *Galveston News*, August 2, 1870.
32. J. W. Flanagan to E. J. Davis, July 21, 1870, in *Flake's Bulletin*, August 6, 1870; M. C. Hamilton to J. P. Newcomb, June 13, 1870, Newcomb Papers, University of Texas Archives; Boulds Baker to E. J. Davis, August 6, 1870, Governor's Papers, Texas State Library Archives; Texas Legislature, *House Journal of the Twelfth Legislature, Called Session*, pp. 789, 836, 877, 889, 895, 915, 937, 954, 999; *Lavaca Commercial*, in *Flake's Bulletin*, June 5, 1870; *Flake's Bulletin*, July 30, August 3, 1870.
33. *Flake's Bulletin*, August 2, 3, 4, 1870; *Galveston News*, August 2, 3, 4, 19, 1870; J. G. Tracy to *Houston Union*, August 8, 1870, in *Flake's Bulletin*, August 9, 1870; *Special Laws of the Twelfth Legislature, Called Session*, pp. 104–110, 325–331.

34. *General Laws of the Twelfth Legislature, Called Session*, pp. 63, 21–23, 82–112, 24–31, 113–118.
35. Ibid., pp. 119–124, 45–46.
36. *Houston Union*, July 6, 1870; *Flake's Bulletin*, July 3, 1870; *Columbus Reporter*, in *Flake's Bulletin*, July 9, 1870; *Galveston News*, July 13, 1870.
37. *Flake's Bulletin*, July 9, 1870; *Austin Republican*, in *Galveston News*, July 16, 1870.
38. *Flake's Bulletin*, July 11, 21, 29, 1870; Elliott, *Leathercoat*, p. 191.
39. *Bastrop Advertiser*, in *Galveston News*, July 16, 1870; *Galveston News* and *Southern Banner*, in *Flake's Bulletin*, July 15, 1870.
40. *Flake's Bulletin*, July 28, 29, August 12, 1870; *Galveston News*, July 20, 30, August 9, 10, 1870.
41. *Flake's Bulletin*, May 10, 15, 1870; *Galveston News*, May 10, 1870; Louis W. Stevenson to J. P. Newcomb, June 4, August 6, 9, 28, 1870, Thomas G. Baker to J. P. Newcomb, June 20, 1870, Stephen A. Hackworth to J. G. Tracy, June 23, 1870, William Waddell to J. P. Newcomb, July 2, 1870, J. H. Wilson to G. T. Ruby, July 7, 1870, Daniel D. Claiborne to J. P. Newcomb, August 10, 1870, Newcomb Papers, University of Texas Archives.
42. *Flake's Bulletin*, June 22, 1870.
43. *Houston Union*, July 30, 1870; C. B. Sabin to Editor, in *Houston Union*, July 31, 1870; L. W. Stevenson to J. P. Newcomb, August 6, 28, 1870, Newcomb Papers, University of Texas Archives.
44. M. C. Hamilton to Editors of the *State Journal*, in *Galveston News*, November 25, 1870; M. C. Hamilton to A. Bledsoe, in *Galveston News*, July 14, 1870; C. B. Sabin to Ferdinand Flake, November 30, 1870, in *Flake's Bulletin*, December 1, 1870; M. C. Hamilton to J. P. Newcomb, June 13, 26, July 2, 4, 1870, Newcomb Papers, University of Texas Archives.
45. M. C. Hamilton to J. P. Newcomb, August 10, July 2, 17, 1870, Newcomb Papers, University of Texas Archives; J. W. Flanagan to U. S. Grant, April 28, 1870, E. J. Davis to Amos T. Ackerman, July 27, 1870, also letters in files of C. B. Sabin, A. Morrill, J. C. C. Winch, N. Appleton, Appointment Files, Justice Department, R.G. 90, National Archives.
46. E. J. Davis to J. P. Newcomb, September 30, 26, 1870, G. D. Morris to J. P. Newcomb, October 30, 1870, Newcomb Papers, University of Texas Archives; Robert Zapp to E. J. Davis, September 30, 1870, Governor's Papers, Texas State Library Archives.
47. J. S. Bacheldor to E. J. Davis, August 31, 1870, Robert Zapp to E. J. Davis, September 30, 1870, Daniel D. Claiborne to E. J.

Davis, September 10, 1870, M. L. Bates to E. J. Davis, August 16, 1870, W. H. Howard to E. J. Davis, September 1, 1870, Thomas Sheriff to E. J. Davis, January 21, 1871, Governor's Papers, Texas State Library Archives; James King to J. P. Newcomb, August, 1870, A. N. B. Tompkins to J. P. Newcomb, September 19, 1870, Newcomb Papers, University of Texas Archives; *Galveston News*, September 6, October 12, 1870; *Flake's Bulletin*, September 29, 1870.

48. *Galveston News*, November 29, 30, December 2, 1870; *San Antonio Express*, November 30, December 3, 9, 1870.

49. Texas Legislature, *Senate Journal of the Twelfth Legislature, First Regular Session*, pp. 23–39.

50. *Flake's Bulletin*, December 31, 1870, January 10, 1871; *Galveston News*, January 11, 1871; Texas Legislature, *Senate Journal of the Twelfth Legislature, First Regular Session*, p. 533; *General Laws of the Twelfth Legislature, First Session (1871)*, pp. 88–89, 57–60, 25, 71, 127–128; *Special Laws of the Twelfth Legislature, First Session (1871)*, pp. 297–299.

51. E. J. Davis to J. P. Newcomb, December 6, 1870, J. P. Newcomb to W. S. Huntington, January 7, 1871, Marshall O. Roberts to W. T. Clark, January 26, March 7, 1871, Newcomb Papers, University of Texas Archives; *State Journal*, February 7, 1871; *Galveston News*, February 8, 1871.

52. M. C. Hamilton to E. M. Pease, May 21, 1871, Pease-Graham-Niles Papers, Austin Public Library; *Galveston News*, March 22, 1871; Texas Legislature, *Senate Journal of the Twelfth Legislature, First Regular Session*, p. 1222.

Chapter 8. Tyranny, Taxes, and Corruption

1. *Lavaca Commercial* and *Texas State Gazette*, in *Galveston News*, October 21, 1870, January 4, 1871.

2. *Jefferson Radical* in *San Antonio Express*, March 31, 1871; *Galveston News*, January 24, 1871; *New York Times*, February 2, 1871; Winkler, *Platforms of Political Parties in Texas*, pp. 124–127.

3. *Galveston News*, May 26, July 8, 12, 1871; M. G. Anderson to J. P. Newcomb, July 19, 1871, Newcomb Papers, San Antonio Public Library.

4. *Appleton's Annual Cyclopedia*, 11 (1871), 609–610; *Galveston News*, March 3, June 28, August 4, July 23, 27, 1871; Joel H. Silbey, *A Respectable Minority: The Democratic Party and the Civil War Era, 1860–1868* (New York: W. W. Norton, 1977), p. 237.

5. John L. Haynes to A. H. Longley, February 12, 1871, in *San Antonio Express*, March 5, 1871; *State Journal*, January 31,

1871, in *Galveston News*, March 8, 1871; *Flake's Bulletin*, September 28, 1870, May 20, 21, 1871; *Galveston News*, May 20, 21, 28, 1871; William K. Foster to J. P. Newcomb, March 23, 1871, Newcomb Papers, University of Texas Archives.

6. *Galveston News*, July 9, 1871.
7. J. G. Tracy to J. P. Newcomb, June 1, 1871, Newcomb Papers, University of Texas Archives; *Flake's Bulletin*, June 22, 1871; *San Antonio Express*, May 28, 1871.
8. Matthew Gaines to the Republicans of the Union League of America, March 30, 1871, in *Galveston News*, April 5, 1871; *Flake's Bulletin*, May 18, 1870, February 24, 1871.
9. L. W. Stevenson to J. P. Newcomb, May 26, February 12, 13, 1871, Joseph M. Gibbs to J. P. Newcomb, April 30, 1871, Newcomb Papers, University of Texas Archives.
10. H. C. Hunt to J. P. Newcomb, June 17, 1871, Newcomb Papers, University of Texas Archives.
11. *Galveston News*, February 14, 1871; *Flake's Bulletin*, June 30, February 24, 1871; *San Antonio Express*, April 21, 1871; S. A. Hackworth to J. P. Newcomb, June 24, 1871, Newcomb Papers, University of Texas Archives.
12. *Galveston News*, May 21, 27, 1871; *Flake's Bulletin*, May 27, June 1, 1871.
13. *The Reformer*, June 17, July 1, 15, 22, 1871; *Flake's Bulletin*, June 23, July 19, 1871; *Galveston News*, July 20, 1871.
14. J. G. Tracy to J. P. Newcomb, June 1, 1871, G. T. Ruby to J. P. Newcomb, July 6, 1871, H. C. Hunt to J. P. Newcomb, July 15, 1871, James Walker to J. P. Newcomb, August 2, 1871, Newcomb Papers, University of Texas Archives; *Flake's Bulletin*, June 29, 1871.
15. G. T. Ruby to J. P. Newcomb, June 29, 1871, Newcomb Papers, University of Texas Archives; *Galveston News*, April 23, 25, May 4, June 21, 1871.
16. *Galveston News*, May 27, 1871; *Flake's Bulletin*, May 27, 1871; T. G. Barker to J. P. Newcomb, June 1, 15, 26, July 22, 1871, G. T. Ruby to J. P. Newcomb, June 13, 1871, Newcomb Papers, University of Texas Archives.
17. *New York Tribune*, January 10, 1871; Charles H. Wesley, *Negro Labor in the United States, 1850–1925: A Study in Economic History* (New York: Macmillan Co., 1927), pp. 177–179, 182–184; Foster R. Dulles, *Labor in America: A History* (New York: T. Y. Crowell Co., 1949), pp. 105–106; *Flake's Bulletin*, June 18, 1871; *Galveston News*, June 6, 7, 9, 13, 1871; Maude Cuney Hare, *Norris Wright Cuney: A Tribune of the Black People* (Austin: Steck-Vaughn Co., 1968), p. 13; James V. Reese, "The Early History of Labor Organizations in Texas, 1838–1876," *Southwestern Historical Quarterly*, 72 (July 1968), pp. 9–11, 12–13.

18. *The Reformer*, July 8, 15, 1871; *Flake's Bulletin*, July 14, 1871; G. T. Ruby to J. P. Newcomb, July 13, 1871, Newcomb Papers, University of Texas Archives.
19. J. G. Tracy to J. P. Newcomb, July 6, 1871, Ed T. Randle to J. P. Newcomb, July 8, 1871, George Lawrence to J. P. Newcomb, July 11, 1871, T. G. Baker to J. P. Newcomb, July 22, 1871, Newcomb Papers, University of Texas Archives; *Galveston News*, July 11, 26, 1871; *Flake's Bulletin*, July 27, 1871.
20. *Galveston News*, August 2, 3, September 5, 1871; *Flake's Bulletin*, August 3, 4, 5, 26, 1871; Republican Party of Texas, *Proceedings of the Congressional Nominating Convention, Third District of Texas: Held in the City of Houston, Wednesday, August 2d, 1871* (Houston: Houston Union Book & Job Office, 1871), pp. 24, 16–18, 23.
21. Hans Teichmueller to E. M. Pease, August 28, 1871, Pease-Graham-Niles Papers, Austin Public Library; *The Reformer*, September 23, 1871. The interpretation of this convention by the Democrats and by other historians is that it was nonpartisan throughout. See Ramsdell, *Reconstruction in Texas*, pp. 308–309.
22. *Proceedings of the Tax Payer's Convention for the State of Texas* (Galveston: *Galveston News* Printing Office, 1871), pp. 73–75; *Galveston News*, August 15, 18, 19, 22, 1871.
23. *State Journal*, September 22, 1871; *Galveston News*, September 27, 1871; *Democratic Statesman*, September 23, 26, 1871.
24. *Galveston News*, August 2, 18, September 13, 1871; *Flake's Bulletin*, August 18, 1871; M. C. Hamilton to Ferdinand Flake, August 10, 1871, in *Flake's Bulletin*, August 16, 1871.
25. J. P. Newcomb, *Vindication of the Republican State Administration of Texas* (Austin: State Journal Printing, 1871); *Opening of the Campaign in the West: Speech of Hon. J. P. Newcomb at the San Antonio Mass Meeting, August 16, 1871* (n.p., 1871); *Galveston News*, August 17, 1871; *Flake's Bulletin*, August 17, 1871.
26. *Galveston News*, August 17, 1871; George W. Paschal, *A Digest of the Laws of Texas from 1864 to 1872* (Washington, D.C.: W. H. & O. H. Morrison, 1873), 2:1605–1609; U.S. Congress, *House Reports*, 42d Cong., 2d Sess., no. 22, pt. 1 (Serial 1529), pp. 208–212. In 1871 the administration proposed to raise about $3,000,000 in taxes. Based on the property valuation for the state that amount represented a rate of 1.5 percent on the dollar. The rate was higher than in seven other Confederate states but was comparable to the 1.7 in North Carolina, 1.9 in Alabama and Mississippi, 2,5 in Louisiana, and 3.0 in Arkansas. The Davis administration figured that their taxes were $3.50 per capita per annum. In the North at the same time the per

capita tax was $11.55 for New York, $14.35 for Massachusetts, $8.72 in Ohio, and $5.29 in Vermont. See New York Commissioners to Revise the Laws for Assessment and Collection of Taxes, *Local Taxation* (New York: Harper & Brothers, 1871), p. 10.

27. E. J. Davis to A. M. Hobby, September 5, 1871, in *Flake's Bulletin*, September 10, 1871; *Galveston News*, August 15, 8, 10, September 10, 1871.

28. W. C. Tomlinson to Editor, October 15, 1871, in *Galveston News*, October 18, 1871; Report of the Military Commission on the Limestone Riot, in *Galveston News*, November 26, 1871; *Galveston News*, October 4, 10, 11, 14, 18, December 10, 1871.

29. *Appleton's Annual Cyclopaedia*, 11 (1871), p. 736; U.S. Congress, *House Misc. Documents*, 42d Cong., 2d Sess., no. 182 (Serial 1526), pp. 10–11, no. 163 (Serial 1526), pp. 6–7; *Galveston News*, October 11, November 23, 1871.

30. L. D. Kelley to John H. Thomson, October 8, 1871, W. T. Clark to J. P. Newcomb, October 13, 1871, I. L. Wood to J. P. Newcomb, October 18, 1871, Newcomb Papers, University of Texas Archives; William Phillips to E. J. Davis, October 7, 1871, W. A. Ellet to James Davidson, October 8, 1871, Governor's Papers, Texas State Library Archives; U.S. Congress, *House Misc. Documents*, 42d Cong., 2d Sess., no. 163 (Serial 1526), pp. 26–88.

31. E. J. Davis to J. P. Newcomb, November 4, 14, 15, 1871, Newcomb Papers, University of Texas Archives; *Galveston News*, October 11, November 23, 1871.

32. *Galveston News*, January 18, 24, 28, 1872; *Congressional Globe*, 42d Cong., 2d Sess., pp. 3148, 3385, Appendix, pp. 484–490; U.S. Congress, *House Misc. Documents*, 42d Cong., 2d Sess., no. 163 (Serial 1526).

33. E. J. Davis to J. P. Newcomb, November 14, 15, 1871, Newcomb Papers, University of Texas Archives; Texas Legislature, *General Laws of the Twelfth Legislature of the State of Texas, Second Session, 1871* (Austin: J. G. Tracy, 1871), p. 16.

34. *Chicago Tribune*, October 3, 1871; *New York Tribune*, October 10, 24, 1871; "Rep." to E. J. Davis, October 4, 1871, Newcomb Papers, University of Texas Archives; Guy M. Bryan to Rutherford B. Hayes, December 15, 1871, typescript in Bryan Papers, University of Texas Archives.

Chapter 9. "We Have Met the Enemy and We Are Theirs"

1. E. J. Davis to C. Delano, January 29, 1872, Appointment Files (J. L. Haynes), Treasury Department, R.G. 56, National Ar-

chives; *Galveston News*, March 5, 1872; *Flake's Bulletin*, March 12, 1872.

2. J. G. Tracy to William E. Chandler, March 14, 1872, Chandler Papers, Library of Congress; J. G. Tracy to J. P. Newcomb, April 8, June 18, 1872, Newcomb Papers, University of Texas Archives.

3. *United States Statutes at Large*, 16:140–146, 433–440, 17: 13–15; Hyman, *A More Perfect Union*, pp. 525–529.

4. *Galveston News*, January 18, 24, 28, February 2, 10, 27, 29, March 1, 8,June 13, 1872.

5. E. J. Davis to W. T. Clark, March 13, 1872, W. T. Clark to Col. Chas. Worthington, March 21, 1872, Thomas P. Ochiltree to J. W. Flanagan, November 24, 1872, all in Appointment Files (Thomas P. Ochiltree), Justice Department, R.G. 90, National Archives; *Galveston News*, March 1, June 13, 14, July 7, December 6, 1872.

6. W. T. Clark to William Chandler, February 28, 1872, Chandler Papers, Library of Congress; *Flake's Bulletin*, February 1, 25, 1872; *Galveston News*, March 1, 1872.

7. W. T. Clark to J. P. Newcomb, February 19, 1872, A. R. Parsons to J. P. Newcomb, March 17, 1872, W. R. Bonner to J. P. Newcomb, July 22, 1872, Newcomb Papers, University of Texas Archives.

8. J. G. Tracy to William Chandler, March 14, 1872, Chandler Papers, Library of Congress; J. R. Runs to J. P. Newcomb, April 17, 1872, Newcomb Papers, University of Texas Archives; *San Antonio Express* in *Galveston News*, March 27, 1872; *Galveston News*, April 24, 1872.

9. James N. Fisk to James P. Newcomb, April 28, 1872, Newcomb Papers, San Antonio Public Library; *San Antonio Express*, April 14, 16, 17, 20, 23, 1872; *Galveston News*, April 25, 1872.

10. *Houston Union* in *Galveston News*, May 24, 1872; *Galveston News*, May 15, 16, 1872; *San Antonio Express*, May 16, 21, 1872; *Norton's Union Intelligencer*, May 25, 1872.

11. Winkler, *Platforms of Political Parties in Texas*, pp. 141– 143.

12. *Flake's Bulletin*, March 26, 1872; for a discussion of the national Liberal Republican movement see Keller, *Affairs of State*, pp. 276–279; John G. Sproat, *"The Best Men": Liberal Reformers in the Gilded Age* (New York: Oxford University Press, 1968), pp. 71–83; Patrick W. Riddleberger, "The Break in the Radical Ranks: Liberals vs. Stalwarts in the Election of 1872," *Journal of Negro History*, 44 (1959), pp. 136–157.

13. Ferdinand Flake to E. M. Pease, March 29, 1872, Thomas H. Stribling to E. M. Pease, March 30, 1872, Pease-Graham-Niles Papers, Austin Public Library.

14. *Galveston News*, April 7, 1872; *New York Tribune*, May 1,

1872; C. B. Sabin to Col. S. A. Waldron in *Galveston News*, May 19, 1872; *Houston Times* in *Galveston News*, May 1, 1872; Paul Casdorph, *History of the Republican Party in Texas* (Austin: Pemberton Press, 1965) p. 20.

15. P. Newcomb to William Chandler, May 1, 1872, William Chandler Papers, Library of Congress.

16. A. S. Broaddus to Editor, May 23, 1872, in *Galveston News*, May 28, 1872; *Galveston News*, May 22, 1872.

17. *Galveston News*, May 23, 1872; John Hancock to William Walton, May 5, 1872, in *Galveston News*, May 22, 1872; John C. Conner to John D. Elliott, May 9, 1872, in *Galveston News*, May 23, 1872.

18. *Galveston News*, August 22, June 18, 19, 1872; *State Journal*, June 19, 1872; William H. Huston to J. P. Newcomb, August 5, 1872, Newcomb Papers, San Antonio Public Library.

19. E. Degener to J. G. Tracy, May 20, 30, 1872, in *San Antonio Express*, June 12, 1872.

20. J. R. Burns to J. P. Newcomb, September 18, 1872, Newcomb Papers, University of Texas Archives.

21. C. DeGress to Newcomb, September 13, 1872, J. R. Burns to Newcomb, September 14, 1872, F. G. Franks to Newcomb, October 25, 1872, in Newcomb Papers, University of Texas Archives; for a discussion of the dynamics of the black-white coalition in Louisiana see Keller, *Affairs of State*, p. 224.

22. J. G. Tracy to J. P. Newcomb, October 8, 1872, F. G. Franks to Newcomb, October 25, 1872, J. R. Burns to Newcomb, September 18, 1872, Newcomb Papers, University of Texas Archives; Fort Bend to Editor, October 31, 1872, in *Galveston News*, November 6, 1872; *Galveston News*, October 20, 22, 1872.

23. T. M. Paschal to J. P. Newcomb, September 11, 1872, Newcomb Papers, San Antonio Public Library; Simon B. Newcomb to J. P. Newcomb, November 12, 1872, A. J. Fountain to Newcomb, December 25, 1872, Newcomb Papers, University of Texas Archives; S. W. Wadsworth to E. D. Morgan, September 28, 1872, William Chandler Papers, Library of Congress.

24. *Galveston News*, August 25, 1872.

25. Ibid., October 24, 18, 19, 22, 23, 1872; William H. Houston to J. P. Newcomb, July 31, 1872, Newcomb Papers, San Antonio Public Library.

26. J. G. Tracy to William Chandler, March 14, 1872, G. E. Dodge to E. D. Morgan, July 27, 1872, William Chandler Papers, Library of Congress; J. G. Tracy to J. P. Newcomb, July 29, 1872, A. J. Fountain to Newcomb, September 28, 1872, J. K. McCreary to Newcomb, October 23, 1872, Newcomb Papers, University of Texas Archives.

27. O. H. Bounnelle to J. P. Newcomb, November 27, 1872, New-comb Papers, University of Texas Archives; *Galveston News*, August 12, 21, September 4, 14, 17, 21, October 1, 1872.
28. A. I. Lockwood to J. P. Newcomb, November 10, 1872, New-comb Papers, San Antonio Public Library; *New York Tribune Almanac for 1874*, p. 69; W. J. Barker, comp., *Directory of Members of the Thirteenth Legislature of the State of Texas* (Austin: State Journal Printing, 1873).
29. *New York Tribune Almanac for 1874*, p. 69.
30. J. P. Hogue to J. P. Newcomb, November 11, 1872, J. C. De-Gress to J. G. Tracy, November 12, 1873, Newcomb Papers, University of Texas Archives.
31. A. I. Lockwood to J. P. Newcomb, November 10, 1872, New-comb Papers, San Antonio Public Library.

Chapter 10. The Last Fight

1. *Galveston News*, December 31, 1872, February 25, 1873.
2. Texas Legislature, *Journal of the Senate of Texas: Being the Session of the Thirteenth Legislature* (Austin: John Cardwell, 1873), pp. 40, 36, 26–27, 46, 40–41, 30–32, 38; Ann Patton Baenziger, "The Texas State Police during Reconstruction: A Re-examination," *Southwestern Historical Quarterly*, 72 (April 1969):478.
3. *General Laws of the State of Texas, Session of the Thirteenth Legislature*, pp. 16–18, 41, 84–95, 100–101; *Special Laws of the State of Texas, Session of the Thirteenth Legislature*, pp. 686–689.
4. *Galveston News*, May 31, 1873; *San Antonio Express*, June 3, 1873.
5. A. J. Fountain, W. A. Saylor, Julius Schutze, E. H. Quick, W. T. Clark, N. H. Owings, J. H. Baker, C. B. Sabin, B. Rush Plumly, A. H. Longley, W. B. Foreman to U. S. Grant, June 18, 1873, in *Galveston News*, August 9, 1873.
6. *San Antonio Express*, June 24, 1873; *Houston Union*, in *Galveston News*, July 10, 1872; J. C. DeGress to J. G. Tracy, November 12, 1872, J. C. DeGress to J. P. Newcomb, November 16, 1872, Newcomb Papers, University of Texas Archives.
7. E. J. Davis to J. P. Newcomb, July 15, 1873, F. L. Britton to J. P. Newcomb, July 13, 1873, Newcomb Papers, University of Texas Archives; *Galveston News*, July 23, 1873.
8. *Galveston News*, July 5, 6, 1873; *Weekly State Journal*, July [n.p.], 1873; Winkler, *Platforms of Political Parties in Texas*, pp. 148–151.
9. *Galveston News*, August 8, 10, 13, 1873.

10. Ibid., August 13, 14, 19, 20, 21, 22, 1873; Edward T. Wallace to J. P. Newcomb, August 12, 1873, Newcomb Papers, University of Texas Archives; Casdorph, *Republican Party in Texas*, p. 28.

11. *Galveston News*, August 21, 22, 1873; Winkler, *Platforms of Political Parties in Texas*, pp. 155–157.

12. Granger to Editor, August 22, 1873, in *Galveston News*, August 28, 1873; *Galveston News*, July 23, 31, September 2, August 31, 1873; D. M. Short to O. M. Roberts, July 29, 1873, Roberts Papers, University of Texas Archives.

13. D. M. Short to O. M. Roberts, July 29, 1873, Roberts Papers, University of Texas Archives; J. W. Throckmorton to Editor, *Democratic Statesman*, September 2, 1873, in *Galveston News*, September 3, 1873; *Galveston News*, September 2–6, 1873; Winkler, *Platforms of Political Parties in Texas*, pp. 159–162.

14. *Texas Observer*, in *Galveston News*, September 16, 1873; *Galveston News*, October 21, 23, 31, November 13, 15, 1873.

15. *Galveston News*, September 17, 18, October 13, 21, 23, 24, November 12, 14, 16, 18, 1873; *Daily Ranchero and Republican*, October 19, 22, 25, 1873; *San Antonio Express*, November 15, 1873; G. T. Ruby to John Ireland, September 11, 1873, in *Galveston News*, September 14, 1873.

16. J. L. Haynes to J. P. Newcomb, November 26, 1873, Newcomb Papers, University of Texas Archives; *San Antonio Express*, November 13, 1873; Speech of Robert H. Taylor, in *Galveston News*, November 16, 1873; *Galveston News*, July 30, August 1, 12, September 11, October 16, 17, 19, 21, 31, 1873.

17. Election Returns, Records of the Secretary of State, Texas State Library Archives; W. P. Ballinger Diary, December 2, 1873, Ballinger Papers, University of Texas Archives; W. J. Clayton to E. J. Davis, December 29, 1873; J. W. Baughman to E. J. Davis, November 16, 1873, Governor's Papers, Texas State Library Archives; *San Antonio Express*, December 5, 1873; Casdorph, *Republican Party in Texas*, p. 29.

18. H. P. N. Gammel, comp., *Laws of Texas, 1822–1897* (Austin: Gammel Book Co., 1898), 7:399; *Galveston News*, December 9, 1873.

19. W. P. Ballinger Diary, December 18, 23, 28, 1873, January 7, 1874, Ballinger Papers, University of Texas Archives; Richard Coke to O. M. Roberts, December 29, 1873; A. W. Terrell to O. M. Roberts, January 5, 1874, Roberts Papers, University of Texas Archives; *Galveston News*, December 12, 9, 13, 1873; *San Antonio Express*, December 9, 1873.

20. *Ex parte* Rodriguez, 39 *Texas Reports*, pp. 705–776 (1873); *Galveston News*, December 19, 20, 22, 28, 1873, January 6, 7, 8, 10, 11, 1874; E. J. Davis to L. J. Gallant, December 22,

1873, Telegrams, Governor's Papers, Texas State Library Archives; E. J. Davis to U. S. Grant, January 11, 1874, in *Weekly State Journal*, January 22, 1874.

21. U. S. Grant to E. J. Davis, January 12, 1874, in *New York Times*, January 13, 1874; E. J. Davis to U. S. Grant, January 12, 1874, in *Weekly State Journal*, January 22, 1874; Keller, *Affairs of State*, p. 223; Everette Swinney, "Enforcing the Fifteenth Amendment, 1870–1877," *Journal of Southern History*, 28 (1962):202–218.

22. George H. Williams to E. J. Davis, January 17, 1874, E. J. Davis to John J. Stevens, January 19, 1874, in *Weekly State Journal*, January 22, 1874.

23. Rice, *The Negro in Texas*, pp. 113–139; Chester A. Barr, *Reconstruction to Reform: Texas Politics, 1876–1906* (Austin: University of Texas Press, 1971), pp. 36, 60, 194–198, 204.

24. Casdorph, *A History of the Republican Party*, pp. 34–45; Stanley P. Hirshson, *Farewell to the Bloody Shirt: Northern Republicans and the Southern Negro, 1877–1893* (Chicago: Quadrangle Books, 1962), Chapter 1.

25. Barr, *Reconstruction to Reform*, pp. 36, 48, 56–57, 65, 71; Casdorph, *A History of the Republican Party*, pp. 34–45; E. J. Davis to J. P. Newcomb, July 8, 1876, Newcomb Papers, University of Texas Archives.

Bibliographical Essay

A detailed bibliography of materials that deal with the problem of reconstruction in Texas is available in Edgar P. Sneed, "A Historiography of Reconstruction in Texas: Some Myths and Problems," *Southwestern Historical Quarterly*, 72 (1969):435–448. In addition, J. G. Randall and David Donald, *The Civil War and Reconstruction* (Lexington, Mass.: D. C. Heath and Company, 1969), provide an extensive bibliography of reconstruction literature. Rather than duplicate their efforts, this essay tries to provide information on the manuscript and other sources that were particularly useful in preparing this volume. Only the books and articles that proved especially valuable appear below.

Manuscripts

The Texas Republicans did not leave large numbers of personal papers to posterity. Those of James P. Newcomb at the University of Texas Archives are probably the most extensive. Newcomb received numerous letters in his capacities as secretary of state, secretary of the Union League, and secretary of the Republican party. A major problem with this collection is unfortunate gaps in the correspondence at critical times. Nonetheless, the Newcomb Papers contain the best letters written by George T. Ruby and Edmund J. Davis. The letters of Davis, however, are not always helpful since the governor tended to be both terse and cryptic in what he wrote. Because Newcomb did not return to Texas until 1867, these papers provide no information on the early years of reconstruction.

A small amount of material appears in the papers of James H. Bell, Reading W. Black, and Edwin M. Wheelock in the University of Texas Archives. The papers of various Democrats and Conservatives, however, were more useful. Among those consulted were the papers of O. M. Roberts, Richard Coke, Guy M. Bryan, and Ashbel Smith. The letters of James W. Throckmorton and Benjamin Epperson were particularly useful and remarkably candid concerning the situation immediately following the war.

A small collection of Newcomb Papers exists at the San Antonio Public Library. When Newcomb's papers were given to the University of Texas, the papers that dealt with local matters were kept in his hometown. This set of papers is a treasure of information on matters in San Antonio. I did not use them extensively in preparing this manuscript, but they appear to be a gold mine for anyone interested in developing a history of Republicanism at the county level.

The gaps in the Newcomb papers are filled in with the correspondence of Governor Pease in the Pease-Graham-Niles Collection at the Austin Public Library. Materials in the collection include everything from Pease's business dealings to his political correspondence. After his break with Davis, Morgan Hamilton turned to Pease, and the collection contains many letters from him. Although almost impossible to read, they are the best source on the changing thought of the U.S. Senator from Texas. The Pease Papers provide insights into the activities of the Conservative Republicans throughout reconstruction. As in the case of the Newcomb Papers, there are frustrating lapses in correspondence at times of critical decisions and actions.

In addition to these private collections, the course of Republicanism can be followed in the papers of the governors in the archives of the Texas State Library. They do not often provide insight into the internal workings of the party, but they are an excellent record of complaints about state affairs. These papers offer a full view of the extent of violence in the state, since most pleas for help were directed to the governor's office. I had hoped to find a great deal of patronage material in these collections, but this type of correspondence was minimal.

Various collections in the Manuscripts Division of the Library of Congress contained correspondence relating to Texas affairs. The number of letters, however, is not large. The best were the Andrew Johnson Papers and those of William E. Chandler. The Johnson letters contain A. J. Hamilton's reports on the course of reconstruction in 1865 and 1866. Chandler, as secretary of the national executive committee, received a large number of letters relating to patronage and printing matters. In addition to these, some Texas materials appear in the papers of Nathaniel P. Banks, George S. Boutwell, Benjamin F. Butler, Zachariah Chandler, Schuyler Colfax, Salmon Chase, Hamilton Fish, Ulysses S. Grant, Philip H. Sheridan, Carl Schurz, John Sherman, William T. Sherman, Thaddeus Stevens, and Elihu B. Washburne.

The papers in the National Archives are indispensable for this work. The appointment papers of the Justice and Treasury Departments are filled with useful information on local political factions and the lives of individual Republicans. The Department of Justice, Record Group 60, contains letters supporting candidates for federal judges, district attorneys, and U.S. marshals. Record Group 56 of the Treasury Department contains applications for major positions in the internal revenue and customs service. Record Group 393, Records of the Fifth Military District and the District of Texas, contains much information on civil-military operations and, consequently, on local political matters. The Fifth Military District received complaints and protests about local matters to forward to Washington. They are relatively easy to use since they were indexed as they were filed. Included in this collection are the manuscript returns for the 1869 election. A final set of papers in the National Archives that proved interesting despite the scarcity of material in them was Record Group 233, the Papers of the House Select Committee on Reconstruction. These dealt with House hearings on Texas matters in the spring of 1869 and provided some insights into Congressional views about the contending parties. When I used these papers the approval of the clerk of the House of Representatives was still necessary but not difficult to obtain with the approval of the congressman from my home district.

Newspapers

I used many newspapers for this study, but two proved to be the most helpful. In part this was because they had unbroken runs through the entire period of reconstruction. But they also tended to have the widest news coverage for the state. *Flake's Bulletin*, with daily, weekly, and triweekly variations, was a personal document of its editor, the Conservative Republican Ferdinand Flake. While he supported the policies of Jack Hamilton and Pease, Flake maintained a moderate editorial tone and tried to deal with all groups fairly. In addition, he printed a first-rate newspaper that filled its pages with news from throughout the state and nation. In part Flake's professionalism was a response to his major competitor, the *Galveston News*, edited by Willard Richardson. Richardson represented the moderate elements in the Democratic party and his paper generally gave the Republicans fair treatment, although in years of growing Democratic militancy preceding the overthrow of Davis, its moderation tended to break down. One of the best aspects of the *News* was its reprinting of items from other state newspapers and the broad range of local information that it consequently provided.

Several newspapers exist in broken runs which were important for a study of Republicanism. The *Austin Republican* had frequent changes of editors and editorial policy, but it provides much information on events in Austin between 1867 and 1873. The *San Antonio Express* also changed editors frequently and included among them A. Siemering, E. M. Wheelock, E. Quick, and James P. Newcomb. From 1867 to 1874, however, it generally was behind E. J. Davis, except for a short period of support for Liberal Republicanism, and provides much on the party line. The *State Journal* was the organ of the Davis administration and was useful for the same insights. James G. Tracy's *Houston Union* was one of the most articulate of the Republican newspapers, but unfortunately it exists only in scattered numbers.

The *New York Times* and the *New York Tribune* were useful in providing information on the national scene and how Texas events fit into it. The *Times* and *Tribune* both ran a large number of items on Texas affairs during reconstruction.

In addition to the above, the newspaper collection at the Barker Texas History Center at the University of Texas at Austin contained newspapers that were used. These include the Brownsville *Ranchero and Republican*, Dallas *Herald*, *Houston Telegraph*, *Norton's Union Intelligencer*, *Texas State Gazette*, and *The Reformer*.

Books, Articles, and Public Documents

While I do not agree with their conclusions concerning Texas Republicanism, Charles W. Ramsdell, *Reconstruction in Texas* (New York: Columbia University Press, 1910), and William C. Nunn, *Texas under the Carpetbaggers* (Austin: University of Texas Press, 1962), provide the groundwork from which every study of reconstruction in the state must proceed. Throughout my work I was impressed with the solid scholarship and insights of Ramsdell, and I have engaged in a personal dialogue with him as I wrote.

Among the works that have helped provide the framework within which this study developed are John Hope Franklin, *Reconstruction: After the Civil War* (Chicago: University of Chicago Press, 1961), and Allen W. Trelease, *Reconstruction, the Great Experiment* (New York: Harper & Row, 1971). Both impressed me with the influence on Southern Republicanism of their constituencies—Franklin indicating the role of blacks and Trelease the importance of political outsiders. In addition there is a large body of literature on Republicanism in other Southern states. Among the most useful and important are David Donald, "The Scalawag in Mississippi Reconstruction," *Journal of Southern History*, 10 (1944):447–460; Thomas Alexander, "Whiggery and Reconstruction in Tennessee," *Journal of Southern History*, 16 (1950):291–305; idem, "Persistent Whiggery in Alabama and the Lower South, 1860–1867," *Alabama Review*, 12 (1959): 35–52; and Allen W. Trelease, "Who Were the Scalawags?" *Journal of Southern History*, 29 (1963):445–468.

Probably the best recent study providing a national context for this work is Morton Keller, *Affairs of State: Public Life in Late Nineteenth Century America* (Cambridge: Belknap Press of Harvard University Press, 1977). The idea of constitutional restraints upon national reconstruction policy presented by Keller, by Michael Les Benedict, *A Compromise of Principle; Congressional Republicans and Reconstruction, 1863–1869* (New York: W. W. Norton, 1974), by Harold M. Hyman, *A More Perfect Union: The Impact of the Civil War and Reconstruction on the Constitution* (New York: Alfred A. Knopf, 1973), and by Phillip S. Paludan, *A Covenant with Death: The Constitution, Law, and Equality in the Civil War Era* (Urbana: University of Illinois Press, 1975), offers an important key to understanding the relationship between Republicans in national offices and those in Texas. It provided both the independence for development and the lack of support that led to failure.

The antebellum origins of local Republicanism may be seen in Llerena B. Friend's *Sam Houston: The Great Designer* (Austin: University of Texas Press, 1954); Claude Elliott, "Union Sentiment in Texas," *Southwestern Historical Quarterly*, 50 (1947):449–477; and Floyd F. Ewing, Jr., "Origins of Unionist Sentiment on the West Texas Frontier," *West Texas Historical Association Year Book*, 32 (1956): 3–29. Ralph A. Wooster, "An Analysis of the Texas Know-Nothings," *Southwestern Historical Quarterly*, 70 (1967):414–423, shows the backgrounds of another source of Republican strength.

Several published sources increase our understanding of the early shift of Unionists to Republicanism and the relationship between Texans and national events in 1865 and 1866. Conditions in Texas are reported in *House Executive Documents*, No. 1, "Report of the Secretary of War, 1865," *House Reports*, No. 30, "Report of the Joint Committee on Reconstruction," *Senate Executive Documents*, No. 2, "Conditions in the Southern States," and *Senate Executive Documents*, No. 43, "Report of Benjamin C. Truman to the President," among the reports of the 2nd Session, including *House Executive Documents*, No. 1, "Report of the Secretary of War, 1866," *House Reports*, No. 61, "Condition of Affairs in the State of Texas," and *House Miscellaneous Documents*, No. 35, "Petition of Citizens of Western Texas." *Journal of the State Convention, Assembled at Austin, February 7, 1865*, Austin: Southern Intelligencer Office, 1866, indicates the views of many Texans on efforts at reconstruction and on the role of blacks in society. Andrew J. Hamilton's *An Address on "Suffrage and Reconstruction": The Duty of the People, the President, and Congress, Delivered December 3, 1866*, Boston: Impartial Suffrage League, 1866, is an important document for understanding the change in Hamilton's political position.

In addition to Benedict's *Compromise of Principle*; LaWanda Cox, *Politics, Principle, and Prejudice, 1865–1866* (New York: Atheneum, 1969); Eric L. McKitrick, *Andrew Johnson and Reconstruction* (Chicago: University of Chicago Press, 1960); and Michael Perman, *Reunion Without Compromise: The South and Reconstruction, 1865–1868* (Cambridge: Cambridge University Press, 1973) demonstrate the various forces at work between president and Congress, and both and the South. The course of those Texans who sided with the president is shown in Richard Moore, "Radical Reconstruction: The Texas Choice," *East Texas Historical Association*, 16 (1978): 15–23.

The relationship of the federal army with Texas affairs has been explored at great length by William L. Richter. Most useful for this study were "The Army in Texas during Reconstruction," Ph.D. dissertation, Louisiana State University, 1970, and "'We Must Rubb Out and Begin Anew': The Army and the Republican Party in Texas Reconstruction, 1867–1870," *Civil War History*, 19 (1973): 334–352. Useful information also appeared in "Spread-Eagle Eccentricities: Military-Civilian Relations in Reconstruction Texas," *Texana*, 8 (1970): 311–327, and "Outside . . . My Profession: The Army and Civil Affairs in Texas Reconstruction," *Military History of Texas and the Southwest*, 9 (1971): 5–21.

Various materials show the emergence of policies for the two major Texas Republican factions. *The Journal of the Reconstruction Convention Which Met at Austin, Texas, June 1, A.D., 1868*, 2 vols., Austin: Tracy, Siemering & Co., Printers, 1870, the *Journal of the House of Representatives*, the *Journal of the Senate*, plus the *Session Laws* for the Twelfth and Thirteenth Legislatures provide basic information on what Republicans did rather than what they tried to do or said they wanted to do. *The Letter of Resignation of Attorney General William Alexander*, October 28, 1867, n.p., n.d., in the Barker Texas History Center at the University of Texas, a *Proposed Constitution of the State of West Texas*, n.p., n.d., at the same place, the state comptroller's *Biennial Report of the Comptroller of Public Accounts, State of Texas, From September 1, 1867, to August 31, 1869*, Austin: Tracy, Siemering & Co., 1870, *Memorial to the Senators and Representatives of the Forty-first Congress from the Commissioners Elected by the Reconstruction Convention of the State of Texas to Represent the Condition of the State and the Wants of the Loyal People*, Washington, D.C.: J. L. Pearson, Printing, 1869, and *Statement and Memorial in Relation to Political Affairs in Texas by Members of the State Convention and Other Citizens of the State Addressed to Hon. B. F. Butler*, Washington, D.C.: McGill & Wetherow Printers, 1869, indicate problems that separated Republicans. Betty J. Sandlin, "The Texas Reconstruction Constitutional Convention of 1868–1869," Ph.D. dissertation, Texas Tech, 1970, is the only full length study of that assembly. James A. Baggett, "Beginnings of Radical Rule in Texas: The Special Legislative Session of 1870," *Southwestern Journal of Social Education*, 2 (1972): 28–39, is an examination of the first stages in the development of the Republican legislative program.

Something of the internal operations of the Republican party is apparent in the proceedings of several conventions. Recording the split of Republicanism into Radical and Conservative factions is *Proceedings of the Republican State Convention Assembled at Austin, August 12, 1868*, Austin: Daily Republican Book & Job Office, 1868, located in the Barker Texas History Center. *Proceedings of the Congressional Nominating Convention, Third District of Texas: Held in the City of Houston, Wednesday, August 2d, 1871*, Houston: Houston Union Book & Job Office, 1871, chronicles the efforts of W. T. Clark to obtain renomination prior to his election disaster that year. Paul Casdorph, *A History of the Republican Party in Texas*, Austin: Pemberton Press, 1965, provides other useful information in these matters.

Several aspects of the Republican era have received special attention. The operations of the Texas Congressional delegation are somewhat mysterious, especially Morgan C. Hamilton and J. W. Flanagan's. Philip Avillo, Jr. has provided new insights into these gentlemen in "Phantom Radicals: Texas Republicans in Congress, 1870–1873," *Southwestern Historical Quarterly*, 77 (1974): 431–444.

Violence and Governor Davis's efforts to curtail it have received extensive investigation. Federal observations on the question are presented in *House Miscellaneous Documents*, No. 127, "Report and Statistics on Violence in Texas," 40th Congress, 2nd Session; *House Executive Documents*, No. 145, "Burning of Brenham, Texas, 1866," 41st Congress, 3rd Session; *House Miscellaneous Documents*, No. 163, "Disputed Congressional Election in Texas," and *House Miscellaneous Documents*, No. 182, "Disputed Congressional Election in Texas," 42nd Congress, 2nd Session. The best study of the entire problem in its national context is Allen W. Trelease, *White Terror: The Ku Klux Klan Conspiracy and Southern Reconstruction* (New York: Harper & Row, 1971). Thomas L. Wilson, *Sufferings Endured for a Free Government; or, A History of the Cruelties and Atrocities of the Rebellion*, Washington: Thomas L. Wilson, 1864, and Sam Acheson and Julia A. H. O'Connell, eds., *George Washington Diamond's Account of the Great Hanging at Gainesville, 1862*, Austin: Texas State Historical Association, 1963, I found useful in providing the background for feelings between Confederates and Unionists after the war. Ann Patton Baenziger, "The Texas State Police during Reconstruction: A Reexamination," *Southwestern Historical Quarterly*, 72 (1969): 470–491; William T. Field, Jr., "The Texas State Police, 1870–1873," *Texas Military History*, 5 (1965): 139–141; and Otis A. Singletary, "Texas Militia during Reconstruction," *Southwestern Historical Quarterly*, 60 (1956): 23–35, deal with the Davis administration's efforts to suppress violence. Another factor that contributed to violence, race relations, has been examined by Barry A. Crouch and L. J. Schultz, "Crisis in Color: Racial Separation in Texas during Reconstruction," *Civil War History*, 16 (1870): 37–49.

Financial problems were a major weakness of Republicans

throughout the Davis years. A full treatment remains to be done, but Edmund T. Miller, "State Finances during Reconstruction," *Quarterly of the Texas State Historical Association*, 14 (1910–1911):87–109, and *Financial History of Texas* (Austin: Texas Historical Association, 1916), provide a basis for understanding the issues. The best rebuttals to Democratic charges of corruption and misuse of public funds appear in James P. Newcomb, *Opening of the Campaign in the West: Speech of Hon. J. P. Newcomb at the San Antonio Mass Meeting, August 16, 1871*, n.p., 1871, and *Vindication of the Republican Administration of Texas* (Austin: State Journal Printing, 1871) in the Barker Texas History Center.

Another area that needs more detailed attention is the political role not only of Republican courts but the entire judiciary in the state during reconstruction. Basic details are in James R. Norvell, "The Reconstruction Courts of Texas: 1867–1873," *Southwestern Historical Quarterly*, 62 (1958):141–163, and J. H. Davenport, *The History of the Supreme Court of Texas with Biographies of the Chief and Associate Justices* (Austin: Southern Law Book Publishers, 1917). An analysis of the supreme court at the time of Davis's overthrow appears in George E. Shelley, "The Semicolon Court of Texas," *Southwestern Historical Quarterly*, 48 (1945):451–468.

Keller's *Affairs of State* provides the best recent synthesis on the declining interest among national Republicans in Southern affairs, but see John G. Sproat, *"The Best Men": Liberal Reforms in the Gilded Age* (New York: Oxford University Press, 1968); Everette Swinney, "Enforcing the Fifteenth Amendment, 1870–1877," *Journal of Southern History*, 28 (1962):202–218; Patrick W. Riddleberger, "The Break in the Radical Ranks: Liberal vs. Stalwarts in the Election of 1872," *Journal of Negro History*, 44 (1959):136–157; and "The Radicals' Abandonment of the Negro During Reconstruction," *Journal of Negro History*, 45 (1960):88–102. Although Whigs did not "redeem" Texas from Republican rule, I think that C. Vann Woodward's analysis of the forces behind redemption presented in *Origins of the New South, 1877–1913* (Baton Rouge: Louisiana State University Press, 1951), is valid in the case of Texas.

There is an unfortunate lack of published material on the lives of individual Republican leaders—memoirs, autobiography, or biography. The only full length study of any of them is John L. Waller, *Colossal Hamilton of Texas* (El Paso: Texas Western Press, 1968). N. Wright Cuney's daughter wrote a biography of that important party leader, *Norris Wright Cuney: A Tribune of the Black People* (Austin: Steck-Vaughn Company, 1968), but it contains little information on Cuney prior to Davis's death. Further material on Cuney is presented in Paul D. Casdorph, "Norris Wright Cuney and Texas Republican Politics, 1883–1896," *Southwestern Historical Quarterly*, 68 (1965):455–466, and Virginia Neal Hinze, "Norris Wright

Cuney," M.A. thesis, Rice University, 1965. The only work on New-comb is Dale A. Somers, "James P. Newcomb: The Making of a Radical," *Southwestern Historical Quarterly*, 72 (1969):449–469. Claude H. Hall, "The Fabulous Tom Ochiltree," *Southwestern Historical Quarterly*, 71 (1969):347–376, provides information on a party candidate for Congress and U.S. marshal, although not on his political career. Although it does not give much information on his political activities, W. W. Mills, *Forty Years at El Paso* (El Paso: Carl Hertzog, 1962), is useful on Republicanism in the Far West.

Democratic leaders have been dealt with more extensively. Among the biographical studies necessary for this work are Claude Elliott, *Leathercoat: The Life History of a Texas Patriot* (San Antonio: Standard Printing Company, 1938), and Ben H. Proctor, *Not Without Honor: The Life of John H. Reagan* (Austin: University of Texas Press, 1962). The Democrats also left more memoirs, including Francis R. Lubbock, *Six Decades in Texas* (Austin: Ben C. Jones and Company, Printers, 1900); Stephen B. Oates, ed., *R.I.P. Ford's Texas* (Austin: University of Texas Press, 1963); and T. B. Wheeler, "Reminiscences of Reconstruction in Texas," *Quarterly of the Texas State Historical Association*, 11 (1907):56–65. Louise Horton, ed., "Samuel Bell Maxey in the Coke-Davis Controversy," *Southwestern Historical Quarterly*, 72 (1969):499–525, provides that politician's insights into the collapse of Texas Republicanism. Buck Walton, *An Epitome of My Life: Civil War Reminiscence* (Austin: Waterloo Press, 1965), presents only an occasional glimpse into operations of this important politician.

Numerous sources provided information on the social and economic background of Texas politics. The *Eighth Census of the United States* (Washington, D.C.: Government Printing Office, 1861), provided an indispensable guide to the population and economy of the state. In addition the *Texas Almanac*, published by Willard Richardson of Galveston through the reconstruction era, furnishes a rich source of information on a variety of problems ranging from planting to railroad construction. Particularly useful for their analysis of the latter are Charles S. Potts, *Railroad Transportation in Texas* (Austin: University of Texas Press, 1909), and St. Clair Griffin Reed, *A History of the Texas Railroads and of Transportation Conditions under Spain and Mexico and the Republic and the State* (Houston: St. Clair Publishing Co., 1941). More impressionistic, but still useful, are the observations of travelers and immigrant guides such as Viktor Bracht, *Texas in 1848* (San Antonio: Naylor Printing Co., 1931), John H. Beadle, *The Undeveloped West* (Philadelphia: National Printing Company, 1873), Captain Flack, *The Texas Rifle Hunter or Field Sports on the Prairies* (London: John Maxwell and Company, 1866), and Frederick Law Olmsted, *A Journey through Texas; or, a Saddle-Trip in the Southwestern Frontier: With a Statistical Appendix* (New York:

Dix, Edwards & Co., 1857). Providing a general view over much of the latter portion of reconstruction is Seth S. McKay, "Economic Conditions in Texas in the 1870s," *West Texas Historical Association Year Book*, 15 (October 1939):84–127.

Olmsted provides the best insights into the cultural divisions of Texas and has been backed up by modern scholarship. The sections that he thought existed are similar to those used by Weston J. McConnell, *Social Cleavages in Texas* (New York: Columbia University Press, 1925), and D. W. Meinig, *Imperial Texas: An Interpretive Essay in Cultural Geography* (Austin: University of Texas Press, 1969). An excellent article showing how sectionalism played a role in Texas politics is Roger A. Griffin, "Intrastate Sectionalism in the Texas Governor's Race of 1853," *Southwestern Historical Quarterly*, 76 (1972):142–160. Useful for its insights into the place of cities in this social milieu is Kenneth W. Wheeler, *To Wear A City's Crown: The Beginnings of Urban Growth in Texas, 1836–1865* (Cambridge: Harvard University Press, 1968).

The most recent examination of wealth and class in Texas is Randolph B. Campbell and Richard G. Lowe, *Wealth and Power in Antebellum Texas* (College Station: Texas A & M University Press, 1977), which expands their "Wealthholding and Political Power in Antebellum Texas," *Southwestern Historical Quarterly*, 79 (1975): 21–30. Ralph A. Wooster, "Wealthy Texans, 1860," *Southwestern Historical Quarterly*, 71 (1967):163–180, and Llerena B. Friend, "The Texan of 1860," *Southwestern Historical Quarterly*, 62 (1958): 1–17, add to this area.

The role of various racial and ethnic groups in Texas in reconstruction has not been extensively investigated. The best work on blacks is Lawrence D. Rice, *The Negro in Texas, 1874–1900* (Baton Rouge: Louisiana State University Press, 1971). It may be supplemented by J. Mason Brewer, *Negro Legislators of Texas and Their Descendents: A History of the Negro in Texas Politics from Reconstruction to Disfranchisement* (Dallas: Mathis Publishing Co., 1935); Walter F. Colton, *History of Negroes in Limestone County from 1860 to 1939* (Mexia: J. A. Chatman & S. M. Merriwether News Print Co., 1939); Monroe N. Work, "Some Negro Members of Reconstruction Legislatures: Texas," *Journal of Negro History*, 5 (1929):111–113, and two M.A. theses, John R. Gordon, "The Negro in McLennan County, Texas," Baylor University, 1932, and Bettie Hayman, "A Short History of the Negro of Walker County, 1860–1942," Sam Houston State College, 1942. The Germans are dealt with in Rudolph L. Beisele, *The History of the German Settlements in Texas, 1831–1861* (Austin: Press of Von Boeckmann-Jones Co., 1930), and Terry Jordan, *German Seed in Texas Soil: Immigrant Farmers in Nineteenth Century Texas* (Austin: University of Texas Press, 1966). The story of Mexican-Americans has not been told.

Although of differing value, several county and city histories were useful for the information that they provided. The best are Earl W. Fornell, *The Galveston Era, The Texas Crescent on the Eve of Secession* (Austin: University of Texas Press, 1961), and David G. McComb, *Houston: The Bayou City* (Austin: University of Texas Press, 1969). I also used Lelia M. Batte, *History of Milam County, Texas* (San Antonio: Naylor Company, 1956), Ernest Berglund, *A History of Marshall* (Austin: The Steck Co., 1948), E. L. Blair, *An Early History of Grimes County* (Austin: n.p., 1930), John H. Cochran, *Dallas County: A Record of its Pioneers and Progress* (Dallas: Arthur S. Mathis, Service Publishing Co., 1928), R. Farmer Garland, *The Realm of Rusk County* (Henderson: The Henderson Times, 1951), Hobart Huson, *Refugio: A Comprehensive History of Refugio County from Aboriginal Times to 1953*, 2 vols. (Woodsboro, Tx.: n.p., 1953), A. W. Neville, *A History of Lamar County* (Paris: The North Texas Publishing Company, 1937), C. F. Schmidt, *Washington County* (San Antonio: The Naylor Company, 1949), A. N. Sowell, *History of Fort Bend County* (Waco: W. M. Morrison, 1964), and Amie Lee Williams, *A History of Wharton County, 1846–1961* (Austin: n.p., 1964).

Index

ab initio: origins of (1866), 8–39; in Pease administration, 72–74; supported by Union League, 74; supporters of, in 1868, 83; West Texans and, 85; in constitutional convention (1868), 86–90; blacks and, 90; in state Republican convention (1868), 97; used by A. J. Hamilton (1869), 105; as campaign issue (1869), 117

administration bloc: in constitutional convention (1868), 83

agrarian interests: in Twelfth Legislature, 133; on railroad vetoes, 142

agriculture: dominated antebellum state economy, 4–5; soil exhaustion as a problem in, 5–6, 14; as a political factor, 8–9, 12; increased production in, 9

Alexander, William: views of, on black civil rights, 26–27; helped organize state Republican party, 62; in Austin Union League, 63; on state Republican central committee (1867), 67; views of, on *ab initio*, 72; indicted for election fraud, 165; involved in *ex parte* Rodriguez, 193; mentioned, 25, 41

Alford, E. L.: and agrarian interests, 133; on government costs,

139; on administration policies, 139

amnesty: President Johnson's pardon policy, 3; A. J. Hamilton's views on, 23–24, 25; efforts to exclude large property owners from, 30

Anderson, M. G., 63

Anderson County: election condition in (1871), 165

Arkansas: emigration to Texas from, 17

arms control: proposed, 140, 149

Armstrong, James, 33

Armstrong, M. L., 102

Arthur, Chester A., 195

Austin: as urban center, 4

Austin County: Negro vote in, 191

Austin Republican, 67, 88, 145

Austin Unionist meeting, 62

Baker, J. M.: on Negro education, 20; on Andrew Johnson, 31

Baker, Thomas G., 159

Baker, Thomas H.: in Austin Unionist meeting, 62; in state Senate, 133; on militia bill, 141

Baldwin, D. J., 64

banks: lack of, in antebellum Texas, 6

Banks, Nathaniel P., 22

Bastrop: violence in, 79, 95

Bastrop Advertiser, 145

Bates, John, 19
Beaman, Fernando C., 91
Bell, James H.: named secretary of state, 24; views of, on Negroes, 27; appealed to Andrew Johnson, 30; candidate for constitutional convention (1866), 32; helped form Union League, 63; in state Republican convention (1867), 66; observer at Conservative Reconstructionist convention (1868), 76; candidate for president of state Union League (1868), 95; chairman of state Republican convention (1868), 96; attempted to break up state Union League, 98
Bell, John G.: in state Senate, 133; on militia bill, 141
Bell County: election returns from, invalidated (1869), 122
Benedict, Michael L., 4
Bexar County: county Republican convention (1872), 173
Binkley, C. C., 43
blacks: racial stereotypes of, 9; percentage of, in antebellum population, 9; reactions of, to emancipation, 19; desired education, 19–20; impact of Military Bill on, 59; organized into Republican party, 63; in election of 1868, 78–80; in constitutional convention (1868), 85, 87; attempted to take over Union League, 96; in election of 1869, 123; in state Senate, 134; and efforts to cut back on police measures, 170; conflict of, with Germans, 178; sought political offices, 179; Davis's unwillingness to abandon, 185; decline in voting by, 194; mentioned, passim
Bledsoe, A., 122
Borajo, Father, 179–180

Bosque County: election returns from, rejected, 165
Boston Impartial Suffrage League, 56
Bounnelle, O. H., 181
Bourland, James G., 18
Boutwell, George, 114, 116
Boys in Blue, 180
Brackenridge, George W., 91
Braman, D. E. E., 6
Brazos County: election returns from, partially rejected, 165; Negro vote declined in, 191
Brazos Santiago: occupied by federal troops, 22
Brenham newspaper editors convention (1869), 119–120
Britton, Forbes, 130
Brooks, George E., 95
Brown, Leander, 62
Brown, Miles, 95
Bryan, Guy M., 64
Bryant, Anthony M., 164
Bryant, Charles W., 79
Bureau of Immigration: proposed, 137
Burns, J. R., 178
Burton, Walter, 179
Butler, Benjamin, 106

Caldwell, Colbert: attempted assassination of, 78; nominated for president of constitutional convention (1868), 86; resolution of, on *ab initio*, 89–90; as commissioner to Washington, 93; and Union League, 99; on suffrage for former Confederates, 100
Caldwell County: Republican rally held in, 63
Campbell, Donald: elected president of state Senate, 133; arrested Senate bolters, 141
Canby, E. R. S., 101, 102–103
carpetbaggers: helped organize state Republican party, 62; in

state Republican convention (1867), 65; W. T. Clark as an example of, 120; in state Senate, 131; L. W. Stevenson as an example of, 156

Carter, George W., 64

Central Texas. *See* Third Congressional District

Chandler, William, 172, 181

Chicago Tribune, 166

civil rights: Unionist views on, 26–28; provisions for, in Constitution of 1866, 37–38; restricted by Eleventh Legislature, 51; called for by Austin Unionist meeting, 62; varied views on, in constitutional convention (1868), 83–85; debated in constitutional convention (1868), 90; in election campaign (1869), 118; in Twelfth Legislature, 166; Congressional provisions for, 170

Civil War: impact of, on Texas economy, 17

Clark, William T.: as Congressional candidate, 120–121; elected to Congress, 122; and effort to sell frontier bonds, 150; opposed for reelection, 153; and Matthew Gaines, 156; and G. T. Ruby, 158; renominated for Congress, 160; and disputed election results, 164–166; on party reorganization, 172; removal of, attempted by E. J. Davis, 186

Coke, Richard: as candidate for governor, 188; elected, 191; efforts of, to unseat E. J. Davis, 192–193

Colorado County: and violence in election (1873), 191

Colored National Labor Convention, 134

Compromise of 1850, 8

Confederates: viewed by Unionists, 19; in Republican party, 82

Congress: and restoration of Union, 4; opposed to President Johnson, 30–31; and Texas Unionists, 52–53; appealed to (1869), 105; considered readmission of Texas to the Union, 126–128; heard Clark-Giddings election case, 165–166; passed Force Bills, 170

Conner, John C., 122, 153, 165

Conservative coalition (in 1866 convention), 34–35

Conservative party: opposition of, to Republican efforts among Negroes, 64; in election of delegates to constitutional convention (1868), 75; state convention of (1868), 76; and Conservative Reconstructionist party, 76–77; claimed to control Twelfth Legislature, 123; response of, to administration program, 137

Conservative Reconstructionist party, 76–77

Conservative Republican clubs, 119

Conservative Republican party: origins of, 98; changed attitudes of, toward former Confederates, 99–100; in state election (1869), 105–128; and charges against Governor Davis, 145. *See also* fusion movement; Republican party

Conservative Union party, 44–45. *See also* Conservative party

constitutional convention (1866): call for election of delegates to, 32; factions in, 33; chairman of, elected, 34; problem of loyalty considered by, 34–35; Governor Hamilton's program introduced in, 35–36; struggle of, over the right of secession, 37; debate in, over status of freedmen, 37–38; repudiated state debt, 39; indicated failure of Governor Hamilton's political efforts, 41

constitutional convention (1868): order for election of delegates to, 75; results of election for, 79; composition of delegates to, 82–83; blocs in, 83–86; exhausted funds and adjourned, 93; reassembled, 100; adjourned, 102–103. *See also ab initio*; civil rights; division; violence

Constitution of 1866, 37–40

Constitution of 1868, 91, 101–102

Convention of the Colored People of Texas: mobilized black voters (1873), 186–187

Cooke, Jay, & Co., 150

corn: importance of, as crop, 5

corruption: charged by Ferdinand Flake, 145

cotton: production of, in 1860, 5; regional importance of, 15

courts, federal: hostility of, to Governor Davis, 165; record of, on civil rights, 170

courts, state: charged with political persecution, 50–51; reorganization of, proposed, 135; reorganized, 144

Cox, Jacob D., 114

Creswell, John A. J., 54, 116

Crudup, R. P., 96

Cuney, Norris Wright: named to Galveston school board, 158; chaired National Labor Convention of the Working Men of Texas, 159; as president of Galveston Union League, 160; chaired Convention of the Color People of Texas, 186; rise to power of, 195

Curtis, Stephen, 66

Cutler, R. King, 57

Dalrymple, W. C., 32

Davidson, James G.: in election campaign (1870), 148; in Congressional election (1871), 162; appointed special police, 163; misappropriated state funds, 184

Davis, Edmund J.: on election failure (1866), 47; on white election participation (1868), 80, headed West Texas bloc, 84; supported universal manhood suffrage, 85; elected chairman of constitutional convention (1868), 86; proposed *ab initio* compromise, 88; supported Ruby's revolt (1868), 96; and state Republican convention (1868), 97; and constitutional convention (1868), 101, 102; letter of, to House Select Committee on Reconstruction, 105–106; views of, on middle party movement (1869), 108; effort of, to compromise with A. J. Hamilton, 111; nominated by middle party movement for governor, 112; attacked J. L. Haynes, 115; position of, in election (1869), 117; opened campaign (1869), 117; biography of, 129–131; message of, to Twelfth Legislature, 135; inaugurated as governor, 134–135; first legislative package of, 135–137; interest of, in presidency of state Senate, 138; use of patronage by, 140; attempted to obtain state police and militia legislation, 140: hired private detective, 141; railroad vetoes of, 142; efforts of, to compromise with

Twelfth Legislature, 143; opposed to M. C. Hamilton, 148; second legislative package of, 149; vetoed Southern Pacific bill, 149; attempted to sell frontier bonds, 150; attempted to reconcile candidates in Third Congressional District, 160; responded to taxpayers' convention, 162; in congressional campaign (1871), 162; on M. C. Hamilton, 163; controlled local police, 163; declared martial law in Limestone County, 164; views of, on Clark-Giddings election appeal, 165; indicted for election fraud, 165; attempted to stop legislature's panic, 166; rewarded J. L. Haynes, 169; and failure to secure Klan indictments, 171; and renomination of President Grant, 171; in election (1872), 180; retained ability to exercise veto, 182; efforts of, to appease Democrats, 183; message of, to Thirteenth Legislature, 183; met with President Grant, 186; supported in state Republican convention (1873), 187; responded to Richard Coke, 189; defeated in election (1873), 191; position of, on expiration of term of office, 192; appealed for military aid, 193; resigned as governor, 193–194; continued control of state Republican party, 195; death of, 195

Declaration of Wrongs Suffered by the People of Texas, 144–145

Degener, Edward: in West Texas bloc of constitutional convention (1868), 84; signed petition for division, 91; elected to Congress, 122; opposed for reelection, 153; defeated, 164;

refused to serve as presidential elector (1872), 178

DeGress, Jacob: used public schools for patronage, 158; in election campaign (1871), 162; worked for renomination of President Grant (1872), 173; tried to prevent all-Negro slate in Sixteenth Legislative District, 179; supported Republican ticket (1873), 185; supported fusion (1878), 195

Democratic party: charges against, (1859), 16; record of, during Civil War, 21; used split among Unionists, 29; efforts to link with President Johnson, 30; efforts by secessionist faction to recapture, 30; reorganization of (1867), 77; role of, in selection of president of constitutional convention (1868), 86; local organization of (1868), 94; propaganda of, 94; reaction of, to G. T. Ruby's takeover of Union League, 96; response of, to A. J. Hamilton's compromise efforts, 107; reluctance of, to support A. J. Hamilton (1869), 119–120; opposed to state police bill, 139; supported fusion movement (1870), 145; conservative secessionists in, 152; moderates in, 152; and "straight out" movement, 152–153; state convention of (1871), 153; and taxpayers' convention, 161; organizational efforts of, 163; on violence in Limestone County, 163; state convention of (1872), 173; fusion with, sought by Liberal Republicans, 176; moderate faction in, 176; increased power of "straight outs" in, 176; moderate control of state convention of,

177; supported black Republicans against white, 179; in 1872 canvass, 182; confidence of, in 1873, 183; "agrarian" and "railroad" factions of, 188; distrust of Governor Davis by, 192; demand of, for resignation of Governor Davis, 192
Dickinson, Henry, 67
Dillard, J. E., 140
disfranchisement, 100–102
division: supported by L. D. Evans, 14; Governor Pease on, 83; variety of Republican views on, 83–86; report of Committee on Division, 91; in second session of constitutional convention (1868), 100–102
Dodge, Grenville M., 181
Duval, Thomas H., 30, 170

East Texas: *See* First Congressional District
Education: in antebellum Texas, 8; for blacks, 19–20; in constitutional convention (1866), 38; in Eleventh Legislature, 52; and views of Austin Unionist meeting (1867), 62; and views of black bloc in constitutional convention, 86; connection of, with railroad issues, 87; in constitutional convention (1868), 91; *See also* public schools
elections: gubernatorial (1859), 16; secession (1861), 16; for constitutional convention (1866), 32–33; general (1866), 42–49; U.S. Senate (1866), 49–50; for constitutional convention (1868), 75–80; general (1869), 104–128; U.S. Senate (1870), 123, 126; special legislative (1870), 146–149; Congressional (1871), 152–167; general (1872), 168–182;

gubernatorial (1873), 185–194; general (1876), 195; general (1878), 195; general (1880), 195
Eliot, Jacob, 121–122
Eliot, Thomas A., 57
El Paso: bribery charged in election in, 182
El Paso County: election returns from, invalidated, 122
Engerman, Stanley L., 6
Epperson, Benjamin: and J. W. Throckmorton, 29; as candidate for lieutenant governor (1866), 43, 47; co-chaired fusion committee, 145
Evans, Andrew J.: as Republican organizer, 63; in state Republican convention (1867), 66; introduced *ab initio* resolution, 86; as district attorney in federal Western District, 171; defeated for Congress (1872), 181
Evans, Lemmuel D., 14
ex parte Rodriguez, 192–193

Farmers Loan & Trust Company, 150
federal relations: relationship of, to local politics, 4; problems with, 128
Fifth Military District: officer of, involved in state politics, 63
Fifty-fifth Legislative District: election in (1866), 33
Fifty-sixth Legislative District: election in (1866), 32
First Congressional District: interests of, identified, 12, 14; election results in (1866), 49; election results in (1869), 122; election results in (1871), 164; election results in (1871), 191
First National Bank of New York: suit against, 150
First Texas Cavalry Union Volunteers, 19, 130, 134

Flake, Ferdinand: warned Democrats, 30; on election of O. M. Roberts, 50; on black suffrage, 65; on efforts to sell railroads, 89; on breaking up Union League, 98; on middle party movement, 112; on race in Third Congressional District, 121; sought Conservative Republican–Democratic fusion, 145; met with Horace Greeley, 155; urged against third party movement, 175

Flake's Bulletin, on Negro education, 20; on Conservative Union party, 35; on 1866 election, 46

Flanagan, James W.: as leader in constitutional convention (1868), 84; on *ab initio*, 88; on division, 101; position of, in 1868, 103; nominated for lieutenant governor, 112; elected lieutenant governor, 123; elected U.S. Senator, 126; broke with Governor Davis, 143; and use of Union League, 172; district of, supported Davis, 187

Flanagan, Webster: in state Senate, 133; on election of Senate president, 138; on militia bill, 141; supported Conservative Republican–Democratic fusion (1870), 145

Fogel, Robert W., 6

Force Bills, 170

Fort Bend County: violence during election in, 194

Foster, A. R., 149

Fountain, A. J.: in state Senate, 131; represented frontier interests, 133; bribery of, attempted, 141; indicted for forgery, 171; supported Independent movement (1873), 185; opposed Governor Davis, 185

Fourth Congressional District: identified with West Texas, 12; interests of, identified, 14; election results in (1866), 49; election results in (1869), 124; election results in (1871), 164; election in (1872), 179–180; election results in (1872), 182; election results in (1873), 191

Fowler, Joseph S., 52

Freedmen's Bureau: started operations, 19; started schools for freedmen, 20; officer of, in Republican party, 63; recorded violence in 1866, 78; violence directed against, 95

freed slaves: laws directed against, 51; needs and interests of, 61

Freestone County: election returns from, rejected, 165

frontier protection, 8, 136, 138–139

fusion movement, 145–146, 154

Gaines, Matthew: in state Senate, 131; as spokesman for agrarian interests, 134; on Democratic opposition to Governor Davis, 139; Congressional ambitions of, 155–156; supported Slaughter Union League movement, 157; complained about immigration policies, 157; demanded all-Negro slate, 178; supported Governor Davis, 187

Gainesville: hanging at, 8

Gallagher, ——, 163

Galveston: as urban center, 4; and Third Congressional District, 12; hostility of West Texans to, 15; as center of support for L. W. Stevenson, 160; poor turnout of black voters in, 171; as source of Republican funds, 180

Galveston customs house: importance of, to local politics, 115

Galveston National Republican Association, 62, 64

Galveston News: on black education, 20; on George T. Ruby as Union League president, 96; endorsed Conservative Republican club, 119; supported fusion movement, 145; supported "straight out" movement, 154; supported Horace Greeley, 176; encouraged racial tension, 179; attempted to halt Northern aid for Governor Davis, 181; cautioned patience in election of 1873, 183

Galveston Union Association, 23

Garfield, James A., 195

Garland, C. T., 170–171

Gaston, R. K., 50

Geological Bureau: requested by Governor Davis, 149

Geological Survey: proposed, 137

Georgia: attempt to expel black legislators in, 105

Germans: in antebellum politics, 10; in 1869 election, 122, 124; in state Senate, 133; attracted to Liberal Republicanism, 171; abandoned Governor Davis, 178; conflicts of, with blacks, 178; in election of 1872, 182; supported Governor Davis in 1873, 187; returned to Republican party, 189

Giddings, Dewitt C.: as candidate for Congress, 153; on limits of central government, 154; election victory of, 164; refused election certificate by Governor Davis, 165; seated in Congress, 166

Grand Army of the Republic: organized, 155

Grand Masonic Lodge of Texas: approached by A. J. Hamilton for support, 119

Grangers, 188

Grant, Ulysses S.: blocked initial effort to remove Governor Throckmorton, 68; campaign promises of, 104–105; ambiguity of stand of, on Texas politics, 106; concern of, for factional cooperation, 112–113; and delay of Texas election, 114; supported "regular party candidates," 114; turned against A. J. Hamilton, 116; signed bill to readmit Texas to Union, 128; reelection of, important to Texas Republicans, 168; strength of, greater than local ticket, 182; failed to support Governor Davis, 186; refused to send troops to Texas, 193; politics of, aided Democrats, 194

Grant and Wilson clubs, 180

Gray, Peter W., 62

Greeley, Horace: encouraged third party movement, 154–155; nomination of, supported by Democrats, 176; nominated by state Democratic convention, 177; received majority in Texas, 181

Green, Frank, 63

Greenbackers, 195

Griffin, Charles, 67–69

Griffin, William H., 158

Groesbeck: election violence in, 163–164

Gunter, N. J., 78

Hamilton, Andrew J. (Jack): selected provisional governor, 21; early career of, 21–22; views of, on reconstruction, 23–24; broke with President

Johnson on voter registration, 25; views of, on Negroes' rights, 27, 56–57; and President Johnson, 31, 52; called constitutional convention (1866), 32; program of, submitted to constitutional convention (1866), 35–36; on rights of freedmen, 36–37; condemned constitutional convention (1866), 40; in Southern Loyalist Convention, 52; campaigned in North, 55; helped prepare "Louisiana Bill," 57; and Conservative Reconstructionists, 76; dominated state Republican party, 82; in constitutional convention (1868), 83; motives of, on *ab initio*, 88; on division, 101; opposition to Union League, 98; defended record in constitutional convention (1868), 99, 105; candidacy of, for governor (1869), 107–108, 110, 111, 116–118; contested election results (1869), 126; and fusion movement (1870), 145; advocated third party, 154; met with Horace Greeley, 155; in Congressional election (1871), 160; on M. C. Hamilton, 162; aided prosecution of Governor Davis, 171; and Liberal Republican movement, 175; characterized by J. P Newcomb, 176; in Rodriguez case, 193

Hamilton, Morgan C.: and *ab initio*, 72; land holdings of, 73; opposition of, to tax laws, 73–74; role of, in Republican party's organization, 82; in constitutional convention (1868), 84, 86, 87; on internal improvements, 85; sought federal intervention in Texas

(1868), 93; supported G. T. Ruby (1868), 96; supported division, 105, 106; and middle party movement, 110–112; on General Reynolds' endorsement of E. J. Davis, 117; elected to U.S. Senate, 126; as spokesman for agrarian interests, 133; and opposition to Southern Pacific bill, 142, 150; on J. W. Flanagan, 143; abandoned Governor Davis, 147–148; supported Slaughter Union League movement, 157; reconciled with A. J. Hamilton, 161; in Congressional election (1871), 162; on J. L. Haynes, 169; on efforts to remove officers of federal court, 171

Hancock, George, 76

Hancock, John: support of, sought by Democrats, 29; as candidate for constitutional convention (1866), 33; and President Johnson, 45; denied seat in U.S. Senate, 50; and Negro voters, 64; and analysis of Twelfth Legislature, 123; attempted bribery, 141; as candidate for Congress, 153; elected to Congress, 164–165; opposed fusion, 176–177

Hancock, Winfield S., 69

Harris, Sam, 43

Harrison County: growth of, prior to war, 14

Harrison Telegraph, 20

Hayes, Rutherford B., 194

Haynes, John L.: on state courts, 51; and organization of state Republican party, 62; chaired state Republican central committee (1867), 67; in state Republican convention (1868), 98; on disfranchisement, 100; and middle party movement,

111; on party convention (1869), 114; removed from Galveston customs house, 115–116; in Third Congressional District, 121; as candidate for Congress, 122; and fusion movement, 145–146; broke with third party movement, 154; appointed to Brownsville customs house, 169

Herndon, W. S., 153, 164–165

Hertzberg, Theodore, 63, 133–134

Hill County: Negro vote declined in, 191

Hogan, Harry, 19

Holliday, William, 95

Honey, George W., 66, 122

Horne, William, 90

House, T. W., 143

House Select Committee on Reconstruction, 106

Houston, Sam, 16

Houston: as urban center, 4, 12; efforts to divert commerce from, 14, 15

Houston Telegraph, 107

Houston Union, 147, 174

Hunsacker, Oscar F., 62, 64

Hyman, Harold, 170

immigration: Austin Unionist meeting on, 62

Immigration Bureau: requested by governor, 149

Indianola: as trade center, 15

indictment of Governor Davis: 165

internal improvements: and policies of Davis administration, 36; J. G. Tracy sought support for, 170

Jefferson: violence in, 95

Jefferson Radical, 153

Johnson, Andrew: program of, in Texas, 3–4; relationship of, with Governor Hamilton, 31–32; provided inadequate guidelines to Governor Hamilton, 35

Johnson, Jack, 191

Jones, George W., 79, 195

Julian, George W., 58

Keuchler, Jacob, 122, 195

King, Richard, 143

Know-Nothing Party, 181

Ku Klux Klan: organized, 94; in Millican riot, 95; in Leon County, 148; federal courts failed to indict, 171

labor: employed in manufacturing (1860), 4; implications of Governor Hamilton's policies for, 37; regulated by Eleventh Legislature, 51; and organizations of blacks, 159

Latimer, Albert H.: named state comptroller, 24; in constitutional convention (1866), 34; on ordinance of secession, 37

law and order: Davis proposals to insure, 135

legislature, antebellum: provisions of, for railroads, 12

Legislature, Eleventh: met, 49; elected U.S. Senators, 49–50; reorganized courts, 50; passed black codes, 51; private acts of, 51; railroad measures of, 52; expanded state government, 52; provided for collection of back taxes, 73

Legislature, Thirteenth: seats at stake in election for, 168; losses by Republicans in election for, 181–182; enacted measures against Governor Davis, 184–185; Republican program undermined in, 194

Legislature, Twelfth: composition of membership of, 123, 131; special session of, 129; and problems for Governor Davis, 131; railroad measures of, 142, 143; and arrest of members of state Senate, 142–143; first regular session of, 152; impact of Congressional elections on (1871), 166

Leon County: Ku Klux Klan in, 148

Liberal Republican party: basis of, in Texas, 155; as national movement, 171; strength of, in San Antonio, 173; opinions of Texans on, 175; state convention of, 176; and fusion effort with Democrats, 177; and opposition to Governor Davis, 185

Liberty County: election intimidation in, 191

Limestone County: election violence in, 163–164; election results from, rejected, 165

Lincoln, Abraham: election of, viewed by Texans, 17; relationship of, with A. J. Hamilton, 22

Lindsay, Livingston, 47

Longley, Alfred H.: as leader of Union League, 47; as Republican organizer, 63; as editor of *Austin Republican,* 67

Longworth, William, 69

Louisiana: emigration from, to Texas, 17

Louisiana Bill, 57

loyalty: problems with definition of, 23 ff.; as an issue in constitutional convention (1866), 34–35; in constitutional convention (1869), 123

Luter v. *Hunter,* 83

McClellan, George, 29

McCreary, J. K., 180–181

McKee, Scipio: as Republican speaker, 63; in state Republican convention (1867), 66; supported A. J. Hamilton, 119

McKinney: as home of J. W. Throckmorton, 28

McLennan County: Republican meeting held in, 63; black vote declined in, 191

McMahan, T. H., 76

manufacturing: extent of in 1860, 4

Marshall: riot in, 78

martial law: declared in Limestone County, 164

Maryland: opposition to Negro suffrage in, 54

Matamoros, Mexico: as center of wartime trade, 17

Merry, Thomas, 63

Mexicans: in antebellum politics, 10; in election of 1869, 122, 124

Mexico: impact of, on wartime economy, 17

middle party movement: origins of, 108; view of E. J. Davis on, 108; backed by J. G. Tracy and E. M. Wheelock, 109; view of J. J. Reynolds on, 109–110; and call for convention, 110; convention and nominations, 111–112; supported by President Grant, 112–113; recognized as regular Republican party, 114

Milam County: riot in, 123–124

Military Bill, 58–59

militia: bill to establish, 135; considered by Senate and House, 138; bill passed, 141–142; used in Limestone County, 164; Tracy attempted to reduce, 170; Governor Davis

agreed to change, 183; executive control over, reduced, 184
Millican riot, 95
Mills, J. S., 140
Mills, Roger Q., 181
Mills, William W., 92, 133
money: inadequate supply of, in antebellum Texas, 6–7; impact of war on supply of, 17
Moore, William B.: in state Republican convention (1867), 66; replaced as editor of *San Antonio Express*, 109; as lobbyist for middle party movement in North, 113; hired to edit antiadministration newspaper, 157
Morton, Oliver P., 126
Mosebach, F. C., 158
Moss, Charles E., 54

Nacogdoches: in First Congressional District, 14
National Guards: as alternative to Union League, 172
National Labor Convention of the Working Men of Texas, 159
National Labor Reform party, 159
National Labor Union, 159
National Republican Committee: recognized middle party movement, 114
National Union League: aided middle party movement, 114
Navarro County: polls closed in, 123–124; black vote declined in, 191
Negroes. *See* blacks
Negro Longshoremen's Benevolent Association, 159
Newcomb, James P.: in constitutional convention (1868), 84–85, 102; supported G. T. Ruby, 96; defended Union

League, 99; as secretary of Union League, 118; opposed railroads, 142; elected president of Union League, 146; in election of 1870, 148; attempted to sell frontier bonds, 150; attacked Union League, 155; used patronage in election of 1871, 158; issued new Union League charters, 160; in election campaign of 1871, 162; indicted for election fraud, 165; in Bexar County convention, 173; differences of, with J. G. Tracy, 174; characterized by Liberal Republicans, 176; connections of, with Know-Nothing party, 181; in election crisis of 1873, 193
"New Departure" movement, 154
New Orleans, La.: threatened power of Galveston and Houston, 14
newspapers: patronage of, sought in constitutional convention (1868), 88
New York Tribune, 166
Norton, Anthony B., 174, 181
Nueces River massacre, 18

Ochiltree, Tom, 121
Ogden, Wesley, 193
Olmsted, Frederick Law, 6–7, 9–10

Paludan, Phillip S., 3
Pana Maria: election of 1872 in, 179
Panola County: antebellum growth of, 14
Paris Press, 47
Parsons, William H.: in state Senate, 133; as candidate for president of Senate, 138; on frontier protection, 139

Paschal, George W.: on middle party movement, 113; in *Texas v. White*, 100; in state Republican convention (1868), 96

Paschal, Isaiah A.: in constitutional convention (1866), 34; as Republican organizer, 63; petitioned for division, 91

patronage: used by A. J. Hamilton, 24–25; under military government, 67–69; federal policies on, in 1869, 113, 115–117; state offices used for, by Governor Davis, 140; schools used for, 158, 172–173; and federal offices at stake in 1872, 168; changes sought, 186

Patten, Nathan, 116, 158

Pease, Elisha M.: as former governor, 24; views of, on blacks, 27–28; appealed to President Johnson, 30; as candidate for constitutional convention (1866), 33; gubernatorial campaign of (1866), 43, 46; attempted to change President Johnson's policies, 53; in North, 55; as president of state Republican convention (1867), 65–66; appointed provisional governor, 68; relationship of, with Fifth Military District, 68–70; views of, on *ab initio*, 72–75; role of, in Republican party, 82; on division, 83; and Union League, 96, 98; charged with party treason, 105; in gubernatorial campaign (1869), 108–109, 111, 114, 116; resignation of, as governor, 116; planned campaign against Governor Davis, 144; met with Horace Greeley, 155; supported fusion movement (1871), 160, 162; in election of

1872, 175; characterized J. P. Newcomb, 176; appointed collector of customs at Galveston, 194; death of, 195

Perry, R. H., 75

Petit, E., 133

Philadelphia: Southern Loyalist convention in, 53

planters: and production problems, 5; in antebellum politics, 9

police law: considered, 135, 138, 141; defended, 162; changed, 183; repealed, 184

Polish community: Democrats appealed to, 179

population growth after Civil War, 168

Prairie Lea: Republican meeting held in, 63

Price, William D., 112

Pridgen, B. J.: agrarian interests of, 133; expelled from Senate, 139; supported fusion movement (1870), 145

Priest, Mijamin: in state Senate, 140, 141; nominated to district judgeship, 142; importance of vacated Senate seat of, 146

public schools: blacks interested in, 134; proposed by Governor Davis, 136; superintendent named for, 138; initial bill for, passed, 144; proposed changes in law establishing, 149; used for patronage, 158, 172–173; supported by J. P. Newcomb, 174; modification of, proposed by Governor Davis, 183–184; system of, changed by Thirteenth Legislature, 184

Purnell, Thomas J., 170

race: in antebellum politics, 9; in election of 1866, 32; view of Conservative Unionists on, 45;

as an issue within the Republican party, 72; white views on, 90; as an issue in the election of 1868, 94; view of Conservative Republicans on, 98, 118–119; as an education issue, 138; as a problem in the Twenty-sixth Legislative District, 148; as a problem for the Republican party, 168; used by Coke in the election of 1873, 189

radicalism: as a campaign issue in 1866, 44–46; among Texas Unionists, 59–60

Radical Republican party: organized, 97; platform of, 97; on constitution of 1868, 102; nature of coalition in, 103; members of, before House Select Committee on Reconstruction, 105–106; relationship of, with middle party movement, 110–111; won support in Washington, 114–115; election victory of, 122–123; problems of, 129; controlled legislature, 131; state Senators of, compared to Democrats, 131; attempted to attract white support, 155–156. *See also* Conservative Republican party; middle party movement; Republican party

railroads: and shipping costs, 7; state policies toward, 12; favored by Civil War legislation, 17, 87; in constitutional convention (1866), 36; and state debt, 39; in Eleventh Legislature, 51–52; in constitutional convention (1868), 88; in state Senate, 131; viewed by Governor Davis, 137; opposed by J. P. Newcomb, 142, 174; in Twelfth Legislature, 142; supported by J. G. Tracy, 174; in

Thirteenth Legislature, 184–185; controlled state Democratic convention, 188
—Buffalo Bayou, Brazos and Colorado, 7
—Houston and Great Northern, 87
—Houston and Texas Central, 140, 142
—International, 143
—Memphis and El Paso, 140
—Southern Pacific, 140, 141, 142, 158
—Southern Transcontinental, 150

Raney, Jacob, 63–64

Reagan, John H., 107, 188

Red River: opened to steamboat traffic, 15

Reed, Johnson, 160

Reformer, The, 157–158, 161

refugees: racial views of, 26

Refugees, Freedmen, and Abandoned Lands, Bureau of. *See* Freedmen's Bureau

Republican caucus: bolted by Senators, 138; expelled bolting members, 139

Republican party
—national: opposed President Johnson, 4; influenced Texans, 26; intervened in 1869 election, 114–116; failed to intervene in 1872 election, 181; failed to help in 1873 election, 193–194
—in Texas: local origins of, 59–60; limits of racial cooperation in, 61–62; organized, 62; relationship of, with federal military officers, 63; participation of blacks in, 63; appeal of, to blacks, 64–65; state convention of (1867), 65–67; and the Fifth Military District, 67; internal racial problems in,

74–75; voting strength of (1868), 79–80; in constitutional convention (1868), 82–83, 86, violence against, 95, 163; state convention of (1868), 96–100; development of Conservative and Radical factions in, 98; relationship of, to national politics, 104; factionalism within, 128; state executive committee of, 146, 185; solidarity of, in Twelfth Legislature, 149; in congressional election (1871), 155–161, 164; used federal patronage, 168–169; needed to attract white voters, 168–169; in national convention (1872), 168; reorganized in 1872, 172; state convention of (1872), 173–174; lack of funds of, 180–181; state convention of (1873), 185, 187–188; district conventions of, 187; unified in 1873, 189; attempted to build white support, 194. *See also* Conservative Republican party; Liberal Republican party; middle party movement

Reynolds, Joseph J.: political role of, 69; on *ab initio*, 74; and constitutional convention (1868), 93; used by A. J. Hamilton, 105; friendship of, with President Grant, 106; opposed E. J. Davis and M. C. Hamilton, 106; and middle party movement, 109; questioned loyalty of A. J. Hamilton, 115–116; M. C. Hamilton on, 117; refused to call new elections, 126; ordered officials to take office, 126; involved in corrupt bargain charge, 126; turned over civil government to elected officials, 128

Richardson, Willard, 71

Rives, George C., 62

Roberts, Marshall O., 150

Roberts, Oran M.: on Unionist dilemma, 16–17; in constitutional convention (1866), 35; racial views of, 38; led secessionists, 44; elected U.S. Senator, 50

Rodriguez, Joseph, 192–193

Roman Catholic Church: opposed to Republican candidates, 179

Ruby, George T.: in state Republican convention (1867), 65, 66; as candidate for constitutional convention (1868), 75; in constitutional convention (1868), 85, 102; challenged white control of Union League, 96; supported formation of Radical Republican party, 97; bribery of, charged, 99; opposed A. J. Hamilton, 110; prevented nomination of black candidate, 118; in state Senate, 131; and black labor, 134; replaced as president of Union League, 146; nominated to Galveston school board, 158; reconciled with W. T. Clark, 158; and Negro Longshoremen's Benevolent Association, 159; in district convention, 160; called convention of blacks, 186; groomed N. W. Cuney, 195

Runnels, Hardin R., 34

Rusk County: antebellum growth of, 14

Sabin, Chauncey B.: opposed Southern Pacific, 142; defended Governor Davis, 147; supported Slaughter Union League movement, 157; supported Liberal Republican party, 175

San Antonio: as urban center, 4; potential of, for ethnic politics, 10; Republican rivalries in, 173
San Antonio Express: on corrupt bargain charge, 126; opposed to J. P. Newcomb's use of schools, 173; supported Governor Davis, 186, 187
Saylor, William A., 141
scalawags: in constitutional convention (1868), 82, 84; in Twelfth Legislature, 131
Schenck, R. C., 105
school fund: used for railroad construction, 8; impact of Civil War on, 17; in constitutional convention (1866), 36; implications for, of debt repudiation, 39; payments to, in 1864, 87; bill to relieve indebtedness to, by Houston and Texas Central, 140; as a campaign issue (1869), 117
Scroggins, Anderson, 64
secession: split Unionists, 16
secessionists: in election of 1866, 44
Second Congressional District: identified with Northeastern Texas, 12; interests of, 15–16; in election of 1866, 49; in election of 1869, 121; in election of 1871, 153, 164; in election of 1873, 191
sectionalism: economic and cultural subdivisions, 12; eastern interests prior to the war, 14; frontier interests, 133
semicolon case. *See ex parte* Rodriguez
Shaw, James H., 43
Shelby, J. O., 18
Sheridan, Philip: supported efforts to remove Governor Throckmorton, 68; authorized removal of county officials, 69;

used by A. J. Hamilton, 105
Sheriff, Thomas, 148
Sherman, Sidney, 7
Sherwood, Lorenzo, 26, 55
Shields, Benjamin G., 121
Shreveport: involved in trade with Northeastern Texas, 14
Siemering, A.: supported middle party movement, 109; attracted to Liberal Republicanism, 173; promoted German meeting in support of governor Davis, 187
Sixteenth Legislative District: effort to secure all-Negro slate in, 179
Slaughter, George H., 157
Slaughter Union League movement, 157–160
slavery: growth of, in First District prior to Civil War, 15
Sloanaker, A. B., 76, 99
Smith, Ashbel, 31, 108
Smith, Robert K., 99
Smith County: antebellum growth of, 14; election violence in, 191
Sons of Liberty, 172
Southern Banner, 145
Southern Intelligencer: supported Elisha M. Pease, 43; editor of, associated with Union League, 47; lost patronage, 51
Southern Loyalist convention, 52–55
Southern Republican Association, 57
Stancel, Jesse, 55, 66
state finances: indebtedness, 36, 39, 188; government costs, 137, 144; credit, 150; Republican defense of, 163; frontier bonds, 166, 184–185
State Gazette, 153
State Journal, 161
state police: cut in, attempted,

169–170. *See also* police law
state printing: used in legislature,
    140
Statistical Bureau: proposed, 137
Stevens, Thaddeus: supported
    Military Bill, 58; supported di-
    vision, 91–92; mentioned, 45,
    106
Stevenson, Louis W., 156–157,
    159–160
Stewart, Harris, 191
Stockbridge, C. J., 142
Stokes, William B., 52
"straight out" Democrats, 152–
    154, 176
Stuart, Hamilton, 76, 120
suffrage, Negro: as issue in elec-
    tion of 1866, 32; in Southern
    Loyalist convention, 54–55;
    acceptance of, by Texas Union-
    ists, 56–57; opposed by
    moderate Unionists, 65; view
    of Governor Davis on, 130
sugar: produced in Fourth Con-
    gressional District, 15
Sumner, Charles, 45
Sydnor, Charles, 5

Talbot, Joseph W., 138
Tanner's Clubs, 180
taxation: antebellum, 7–8;
    blacks and, 134; viewed by
    Governor Davis, 137; unfair-
    ness in, charged, 146; Davis
    policies on, defended, 147,
    163; and taxpayers' conven-
    tion, 161; changes in, recom-
    mended, 184; as issue in 1873
    election, 187–188
taxpayers' convention, 160–162
taxpayers' revolt, 166
tax relief: problems connected
    with, 169–170
Taylor, Robert H., 24, 174
Taylor, William M., 34
Teichmueller, Hans, 161

Tendick, R. P., 149
Texas Observer, 189
Texas Rangers, 135
Texas State Gazette: on cotton
    production, 5; received state
    printing, 51; praised A. J.
    Hamilton, 107
Texas v. *White,* 100
Third Congressional District:
    identified with Central Texas,
    12; described, 12–14; chal-
    lenged by A. J. Hamilton, 21;
    in election of 1866, 49; in elec-
    tion of 1869, 120–122; in elec-
    tion of 1871, 153, 156–160,
    165–166; in election of 1872,
    193
Third Legislative District:
    violence in, 148
third party movement:
    encouraged in Texas, 154–155
Thomas, J. W., 47
Thompson, Wells, 149
Throckmorton, James W.: views
    of, on Negroes' rights, 28;
    early career of, 28; in constitu-
    tional convention (1866), 34;
    views of, on reconstruction op-
    tions, 44; as candidate for gov-
    ernor, 44; secured Benjamin
    Epperson's removal from
    Unionist ticket, 48; encouraged
    Unionists, 49; used patronage
    against A. J. Hamilton, 51;
    conferred with black leaders,
    64; removed from office, 68;
    and effort to bribe legislator,
    141; opposed repudiation of
    state debt, 188
Tracy, James G.: and middle
    party movement, 109–110;
    and reorganization of Republi-
    can party, 146; charged with
    political treason, 147; policies
    of, 147–148; attempted to
    create a biracial party, 155–

156; responded to reform movements (1871), 158; aided in reconciliation of G. T. Ruby and W. T. Clark, 158; chaired district convention, 160; attempted to change party policies, 169; appointed delegates to national Republican convention (1872), 171–172; differed with J. P. Newcomb, 174; appealed to national Republican party for aid, 181; proposed no Republican ticket in 1873, 185; proposed recall of Thirteenth Legislature, 193; supported fusion with greenbackers, 195

Transportation: antebellum, 7; and shipping costs, 7; favored by prewar policies, 8; political climate toward, 12; unique problems of, in Texas, 14–15; policies of constitutional convention (1866) on, 39–40; in constitutional convention (1868), 84–85

Travis County: intervention in county convention of, 173

Truman, Benjamin C.: on Texas Unionists, 18; on constitutional convention (1866), 33; characterized constitutional provisions concerning blacks, 37

Twenty-fifth Legislative District: inactivity of Republicans in (1871), 148; racial problems in (1872), 178

Twenty-fourth Legislative District: election of 1871 in, 149

Twenty-sixth Legislative District: racial problems in, 148

Union Association, 23, 95
Union Caucus, 42
Union Club, 98

Union Intelligencer, 95

Unionists in Texas prior to the Civil War, 16; in postwar politics, 17, 21, 25–29; among Germans, 18; attempted use of, by Governor Hamilton, 24; factions within, 26–29; racial views of, 26–29; appealed to, by Democrats, 29; opposition to Governor Hamilton among, 32–33; in constitutional convention (1866), 33–34, 35, 37, 38, 39; failed to restore coalition, 40–41; Union party among, 42–44; Conservative Unionists emerged from, 44–45; in election of 1866, 46–49; persecution of, 53; accepted Negro suffrage, 55–57; Republicanism emerged from, 59–60, 62–63; in constitutional convention (1868), 83, 84–85; and vote for Governor Davis (1869), 124; in Congressional election of 1872, 174; in election of 1873, 189

Union League: in election of 1866, 47; addressed by Governor Hamilton, 53, 55; officially organized in 1867, 63; views of leaders of, on Negro office holding, 63; and *ab initio,* 74; supported M. C. Hamilton, 74–75; supported G. T. Ruby, 75; violence against, 95; state convention of (1868), 95–96; support of, sought, 97; attacked by Conservative Republicans, 98–99; tied to Radical Republicans, 99; in election of 1869, 107, 110, 113, 115, 118, 120; reorganized, 146; attacked by J. G. Tracy, 155; and Slaughter Union League movement, 157–160; unreliability of, 172; undermined, 180

Union party: in election of 1866,
42–49; charged with radicalism, 44–46; purged from state
judiciary, 50; clerks belonging
to, removed, 51. *See also*
Unionists
Union Republican coalition, 175
United States Army: members of,
in state Republican party, 82;
in Millican riot, 95. *See also*
Fifth Military District
Upshur County: antebellum
growth of, 14
urbanization: extent of, in 1860,
4

Vallandigham, Clement L., 154
violence: in wartime Texas,
18–19; in election of 1868,
77–79; as an issue in constitutional convention (1868),
92–95; related to reorganization of Democratic party, 93;
in election of 1869, 123; in
election of 1870, 148; feared
by Governor Davis, 163; in
election of 1871, 164; in Wharton County, 181; in election of
1873, 191. *See also* state
police; police law
Virginia: importance of gubernatorial election in, 113
voter registration: in 1865, 25; in
1867, 70–71; provided for,
144

Waco: blacks organized in, 63
Wade, Benjamin, 105
Walker, Gilbert, 113

Walker, Richard, 193
Walton, William: postwar plight
of, 18; and Conservative
Republican–Democratic fu-
sion, 145–146; chaired Demo-
cratic party, 152–153; and
prosecution of Governor
Davis, 171
Washington County: blacks or-
ganized in, 63; supported L. W.
Stevenson, 160; white boxes
from, rejected, 165
Webb, Frank, 157
Welles, Gideon, 23, 53
Western Union Telegraph Co.,
184
West Texas. *See* Fourth Congres-
sional District
West Virginia: opposed Negro
suffrage, 54
Wharton County: election in-
timidation in, 181
wheat: importance of, in antebel-
lum economy, 5; in Second
Congressional District, 15
Wheelock, Edwin M.: 62, 108–
110
Whigs, 81
White, Francis M., 43
Whitemore, Benjamin F., 106
Whitmore, George W.: elected to
Congress in First Congres-
sional District, 122; in election
of 1872, 153, 156, 157,
164
Wilkinson, Ed., 67
Williams, George H., 193
Willie, Asa H., 181
Wilson, A. R., 95